W9-AJS-303

enVisionMATH 2.0

Scott Foresman • Addison Wesley

Volume 2 Topics 9-16

Authors

Randall I. Charles
Professor Emeritus
Department of Mathematics
San Jose State University
San Jose, California

Janet H. Caldwell
Professor of Mathematics
Rowan University
Glassboro, New Jersey

Juanita Copley
Professor Emerita, College of
Education
University of Houston
Houston, Texas

Warren Crown
Professor Emeritus of Mathematics
Education
Graduate School of Education
Rutgers University
New Brunswick, New Jersey

Francis (Skip) Fennell
L. Stanley Bowlsbey Professor
of Education and Graduate and
Professional Studies
McDaniel College
Westminster, Maryland

Stuart J. Murphy
Visual Learning Specialist
Boston, Massachusetts

Kay B. Sammons
Coordinator of Elementary
Mathematics
Howard County Public Schools
Ellicott City, Maryland

Jane F. Schielack
Professor of Mathematics
Associate Dean for Assessment
and Pre K-12 Education,
College of Science
Texas A&M University
College Station, Texas

Mathematicians

Roger Howe
Professor of Mathematics
Yale University
New Haven, Connecticut

Gary Lippman
Professor of Mathematics and
Computer Science
California State University East Bay
Hayward, California

Glenview, Illinois   Boston, Massachusetts   Chandler, Arizona   Upper Saddle River, New Jersey

Contributing Authors

Zachary Champagne
District Facilitator, Duval County
Public Schools
Florida Center for Research in
Science, Technology, Engineering,
and Mathematics (FCR-STEM)
Jacksonville, Florida

Jonathan A. Wray
Mathematics Instructional
Facilitator
Howard County Public Schools
Ellicott City, Maryland

ELL Consultants

Janice Corona
Retired Administrator
Dallas ISD, Multi-Lingual
Department
Dallas, Texas

Jim Cummins
Professor
The University of Toronto
Toronto, Canada

Texas Reviewers

Theresa Bathe
Teacher
Fort Bend ISD

Chrissy Beltran
School Wide Project Coordinator
Ysleta ISD

Renee Cutright
Teacher
Amarillo ISD

Sharon Grimm
Teacher
Houston ISD

Esmeralda Herrera
Teacher
San Antonio ISD

Sherry Johnson
Teacher
Round Rock ISD

Elvia Lopez
Teacher
Denton ISD

Antoinese Pride
Instructional Coach
Dallas ISD

Joanna Ratliff
Teacher
Keller ISD

Courtney Jo Ridehuber
Teacher
Mansfield ISD

Nannie D. Scurlock-McKnight
Mathematics Specialist
A.W. Brown Fellowship-Leadership
Academy
Dallas, TX

Brian Sinclair
Math Instructional Specialist
Fort Worth ISD

Copyright © 2015 by Pearson Education, Inc., or its affiliates. All Rights Reserved. Printed in the United States of America. This publication is protected by copyright, and permission should be obtained from the publisher prior to any prohibited reproduction, storage in a retrieval system, or transmission in any form or by any means, electronic, mechanical, photocopying, recording, or likewise. For information regarding permissions, write to Rights Management & Contracts, Pearson Education, Inc., One Lake Street, Upper Saddle River, New Jersey 07458.

Pearson, Scott Foresman, Pearson Scott Foresman, and enVisionMATH are trademarks, in the U.S. and/or in other countries, of Pearson Education Inc., or its affiliates.

ISBN-13: 978-0-328-76729-8
ISBN-10: 0-328-76729-8

11 V011 17 16

Digital Resources

Look for these digital resources in every lesson!

 Go to PearsonTexas.com

 **Solve**

Solve & Share problems plus math tools

 Learn

Visual Learning Animation Plus with animation, interaction, and math tools

A-Z **Glossary**

Animated Glossary in English and Spanish

 Tools

Math Tools to help you understand

 Check

Quick Check for each lesson

 **Games**

Math Games to help you learn

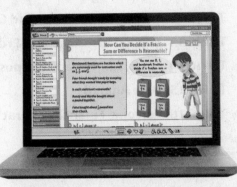

eText
The pages in your book online

PearsonTexas.com
Everything you need for math anytime, anywhere

Key

Number and Operations
Algebraic Reasoning
Geometry and Measurement
Data Analysis
Personal Financial Literacy

Mathematical Process Standards are found in all lessons.

Digital Resources at PearsonTexas.com

Solve

Learn

Glossary

Check

Tools

Games

And remember, the pages in your book are also online!

Contents

★ Topics

Volume 1

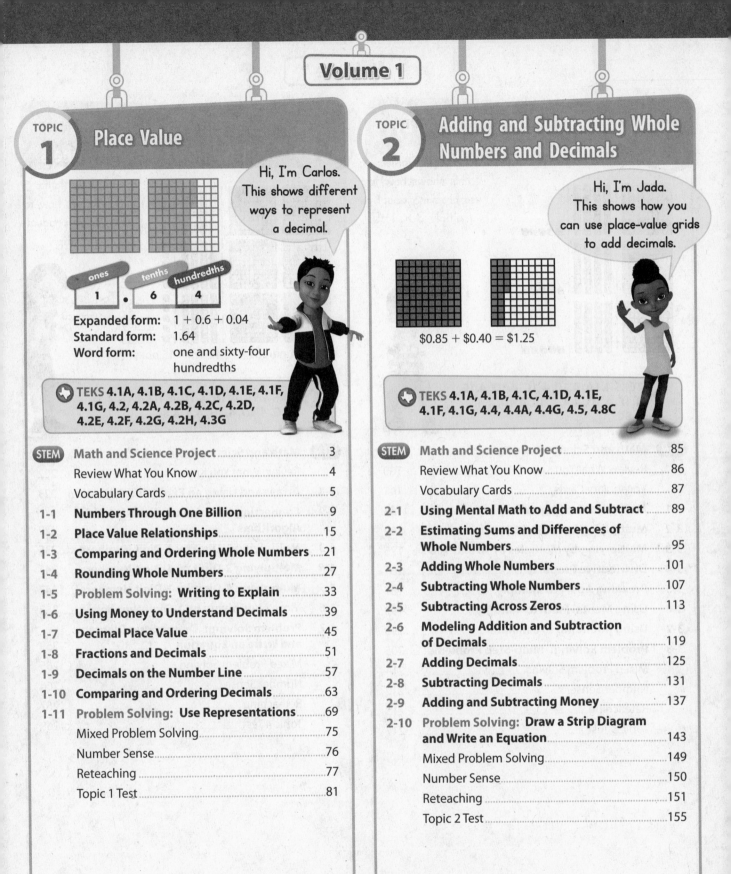

TOPIC 1 — Place Value

Hi, I'm Carlos. This shows different ways to represent a decimal.

ones	tenths	hundredths
1	6	4

Expanded form: $1 + 0.6 + 0.04$
Standard form: 1.64
Word form: one and sixty-four hundredths

TEKS 4.1A, 4.1B, 4.1C, 4.1D, 4.1E, 4.1F, 4.1G, 4.2, 4.2A, 4.2B, 4.2C, 4.2D, 4.2E, 4.2F, 4.2G, 4.2H, 4.3G

TOPIC 2 — Adding and Subtracting Whole Numbers and Decimals

Hi, I'm Jada. This shows how you can use place-value grids to add decimals.

$\$0.85 + \$0.40 = \$1.25$

TEKS 4.1A, 4.1B, 4.1C, 4.1D, 4.1E, 4.1F, 4.1G, 4.4, 4.4A, 4.4G, 4.5, 4.8C

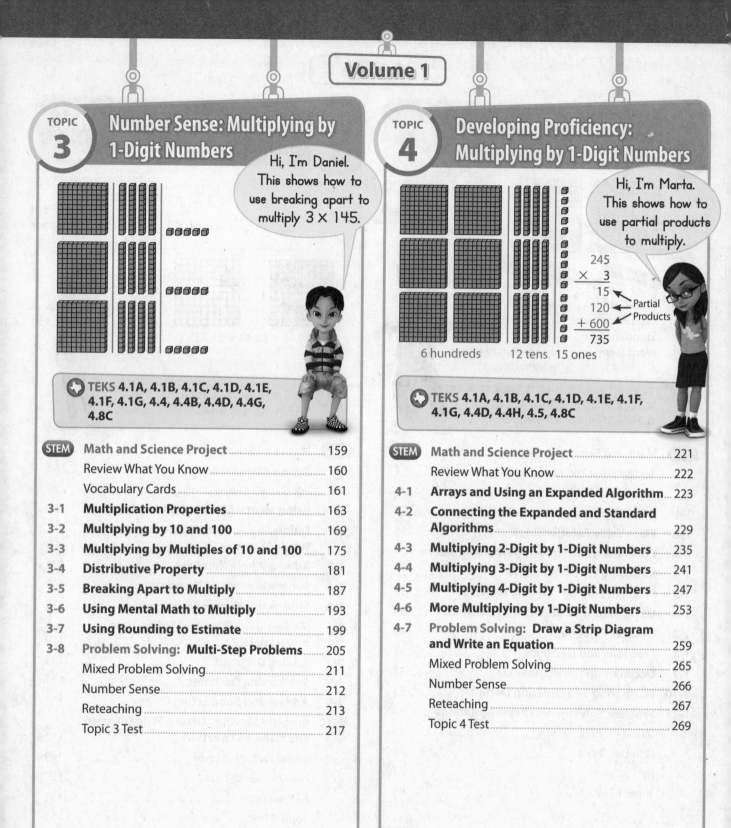

Volume 1

TOPIC 3 — Number Sense: Multiplying by 1-Digit Numbers

Hi, I'm Daniel. This shows how to use breaking apart to multiply 3 × 145.

TEKS 4.1A, 4.1B, 4.1C, 4.1D, 4.1E, 4.1F, 4.1G, 4.4, 4.4B, 4.4D, 4.4G, 4.8C

TOPIC 4 — Developing Proficiency: Multiplying by 1-Digit Numbers

Hi, I'm Marta. This shows how to use partial products to multiply.

$$\begin{array}{r} 245 \\ \times\ \ \ 3 \\ \hline 15 \\ 120 \\ +\ 600 \\ \hline 735 \end{array}$$

Partial Products

6 hundreds   12 tens   15 ones

TEKS 4.1A, 4.1B, 4.1C, 4.1D, 4.1E, 4.1F, 4.1G, 4.4D, 4.4H, 4.5, 4.8C

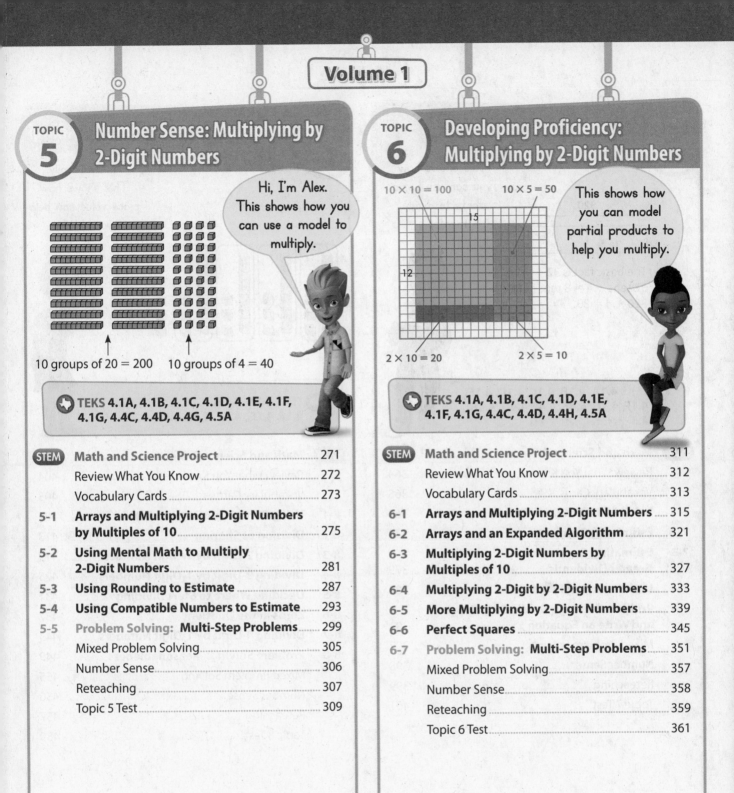

Volume 1

TOPIC 5 — Number Sense: Multiplying by 2-Digit Numbers

Hi, I'm Alex. This shows how you can use a model to multiply.

10 groups of 20 = 200   10 groups of 4 = 40

TEKS 4.1A, 4.1B, 4.1C, 4.1D, 4.1E, 4.1F, 4.1G, 4.4C, 4.4D, 4.4G, 4.5A

TOPIC 6 — Developing Proficiency: Multiplying by 2-Digit Numbers

10 × 10 = 100   10 × 5 = 50

15

12

2 × 10 = 20   2 × 5 = 10

This shows how you can model partial products to help you multiply.

TEKS 4.1A, 4.1B, 4.1C, 4.1D, 4.1E, 4.1F, 4.1G, 4.4C, 4.4D, 4.4H, 4.5A

Volume 1

TOPIC 7

Number Sense: Dividing by 1-Digit Divisors

320

| ? | ? | ? | ? |

This shows how you can use basic facts to divide mentally.

The basic fact is $32 \div 4 = 8$.
32 tens $\div 4 = 8$ tens or 80.
$320 \div 4 = 80$

TEKS 4.1A, 4.1B, 4.1C, 4.1D, 4.1E, 4.1F, 4.1G, 4.4E, 4.4F, 4.4G, 4.4H, 4.5

TOPIC 8

Developing Proficiency: Dividing by 1-Digit Divisors

Hi, I'm Emily. This shows how place value can help you divide.

$$\begin{array}{r} 13 \text{ R3} \\ 4\overline{)55} \\ -4 \\ \hline 15 \\ -12 \\ \hline 3 \end{array}$$

TEKS 4.1A, 4.1B, 4.1C, 4.1D, 4.1E, 4.1F, 4.1G, 4.4E, 4.4F, 4.4G, 4.4H

Volume 2

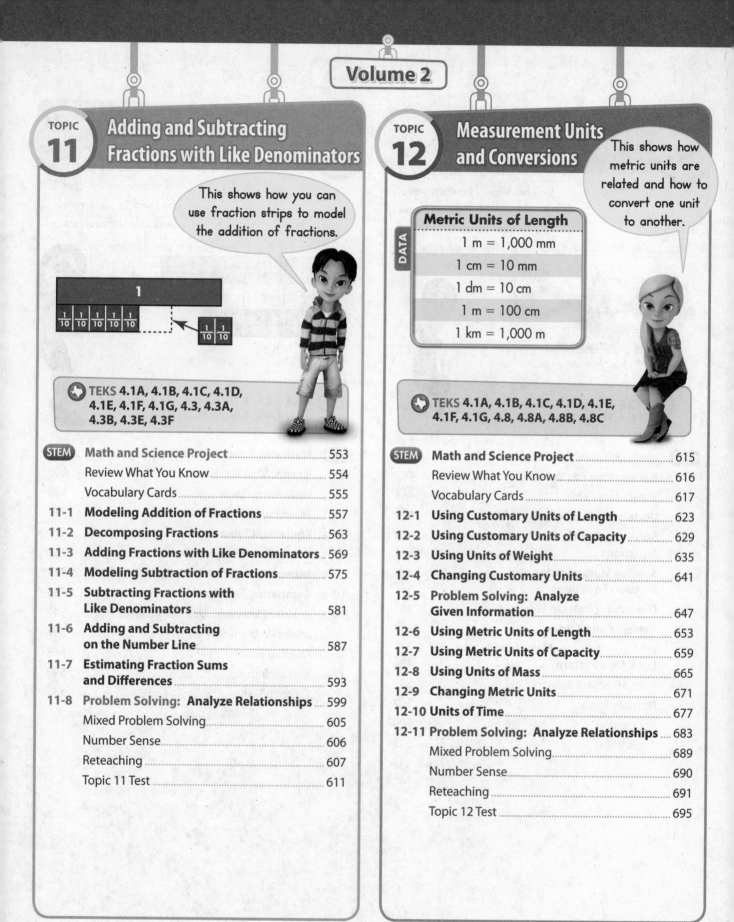

Volume 2

TOPIC 11 Adding and Subtracting Fractions with Like Denominators

This shows how you can use fraction strips to model the addition of fractions.

TEKS 4.1A, 4.1B, 4.1C, 4.1D, 4.1E, 4.1F, 4.1G, 4.3, 4.3A, 4.3B, 4.3E, 4.3F

TOPIC 12 Measurement Units and Conversions

This shows how metric units are related and how to convert one unit to another.

DATA

Metric Units of Length
1 m = 1,000 mm
1 cm = 10 mm
1 dm = 10 cm
1 m = 100 cm
1 km = 1,000 m

TEKS 4.1A, 4.1B, 4.1C, 4.1D, 4.1E, 4.1F, 4.1G, 4.8, 4.8A, 4.8B, 4.8C

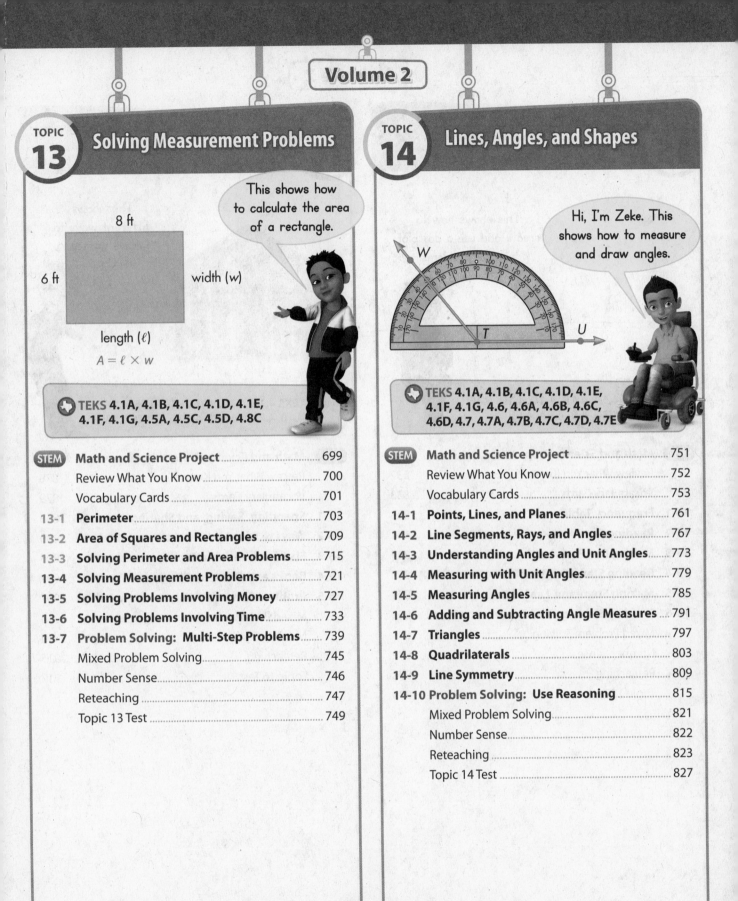

Volume 2

TOPIC 13 — Solving Measurement Problems

This shows how to calculate the area of a rectangle.

8 ft

6 ft   width (w)

length (ℓ)

$A = \ell \times w$

TEKS 4.1A, 4.1B, 4.1C, 4.1D, 4.1E, 4.1F, 4.1G, 4.5A, 4.5C, 4.5D, 4.8C

TOPIC 14 — Lines, Angles, and Shapes

Hi, I'm Zeke. This shows how to measure and draw angles.

W   U
T

TEKS 4.1A, 4.1B, 4.1C, 4.1D, 4.1E, 4.1F, 4.1G, 4.6, 4.6A, 4.6B, 4.6C, 4.6D, 4.7, 4.7A, 4.7B, 4.7C, 4.7D, 4.7E

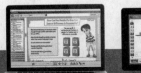

TOPIC 15 — Data Analysis

This shows how to create and use a dot plot to solve problems.

5 10 15 20

TEKS 4.1A, 4.1B, 4.1C, 4.1D, 4.1E, 4.1F, 4.1G, 4.9, 4.9A, 4.9B

TOPIC 16 — Personal Financial Literacy

This shows different ways to save money.

BANK

TEKS 4.1A, 4.1B, 4.1C, 4.1D, 4.1E, 4.1F, 4.1G, 4.10, 4.10A, 4.10B, 4.10C, 4.10D, 4.10E

Volume 2

Step Up to Grade 5

These lessons help prepare you for Grade 5.

TEKS 5.1A, 5.1B, 5.1C, 5.1D, 5.1E, 5.1F, 5.1G, 5.3A, 5.3H, 5.3I, 5.3J, 5.4, 5.4H, 5.6A, 5.6B

Have a great year!

Problem-Solving Handbook

Applying Math Processes

Analyze
- How does this problem connect to previous ones?
- What am I asked to find?
- What information do I know?

Plan
- What is my plan?
- What strategies can I use? (See the list of some helpful strategies.)
- How can I use tools?
- How can I organize and record information?

Solve
- How can I use number sense?
- How can I estimate?
- How can I communicate and represent my thinking?

Justify
- How can I explain my work?
- How can I justify my answer?

Evaluate
- Have I checked my work?
- Is my answer reasonable?

Use this Problem-Solving Handbook throughout the year to help you solve problems.

Some Helpful Strategies
- Represent the Problem
  - Draw a Picture or Strip Diagram
  - Write an Equation
  - Make a Table or List
- Look for a Pattern
- Use Reasoning
- Analyze Given Information
- Analyze Relationships

Problem-Solving Tools	Problem-Solving Techniques

Problem-Solving Tools

Real Objects

$$\frac{1}{4} \qquad \frac{2}{4} \qquad \frac{3}{4}$$

Manipulatives

Distance Run

Ann	$\frac{3}{4}$ mile
Tom	$\frac{1}{3}$ mile
Maria	$\frac{5}{8}$ mile

$\frac{1}{4}$	$\frac{1}{4}$	$\frac{1}{4}$

$\frac{1}{3}$

$\frac{1}{8}$	$\frac{1}{8}$	$\frac{1}{8}$	$\frac{1}{8}$	$\frac{1}{8}$

Paper and Pencil

$$\begin{array}{r} \overset{1}{34} \\ \times\ 3 \\ \hline 102 \end{array} \qquad \begin{array}{r} 102 \\ +260 \\ \hline 362 \end{array}$$

Technology

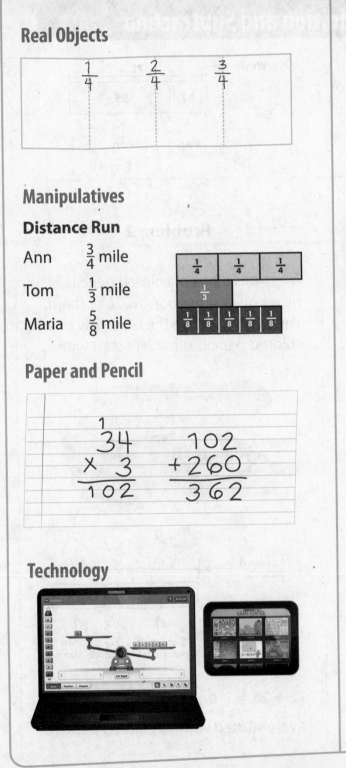

Problem-Solving Techniques

Mental Math

Sale!

Table......$129
Chair.........$69
Desk.......$229

$129 + 69 + 229 = ?$
$130 + 70 + 230 = 430$
$430 - 3 = 427$

Estimation

There are 192 seats in a local concert hall. A jazz band plays there 3 nights each week.

$192 \times 3 = ?$
About $200 \times 3 = $ 600 people can see the band each week.

Number Sense

Students per Grade

DATA		
	Kindergarten	50
	Grade 1	56
	Grade 2	58
	Grade 3	57
	Grade 4	54
	Grade 5	55

Each grade has between 50 and 60 students.
There are 6 grades.
The total number of students will be between 300 and 360.

Strip Diagrams

You can draw a **strip diagram** to show how the quantities in a problem are related. Then you can write an equation to solve the problem.

Part-Part-Whole: Addition and Subtraction

Draw this **strip diagram** for situations that involve joining parts of a whole or separating a whole into parts.

Whole → | 72 |
| 17 | 55 |
↑ Part   ↑ Part

Problem 1

Monica had $153. She spent some of it on a table. How much did she have left over?

$42

$153 → | 153 |
| 42 | ? |
↑ $42 spent   ↑ ? dollars left

$153 - 42 = ?$ or $153 - ? = 42$

Monica had $111 left over.

Problem 2

Avery has a box of colored pencils. He let his brother borrow 26 of them. There are 72 left in the box. How many colored pencils did Avery start with?

? colored pencils → | ? |
| 72 | 26 |
↑ 72 colored pencils left   ↑ 26 colored pencils shared

$72 + 26 = ?$ or $? - 26 = 72$

Avery started with 98 colored pencils.

Pictures help you understand.
Don't trust key words in a problem.

Comparison: Addition and Subtraction

Draw this **strip diagram** for comparison situations involving how much more one quantity is than another quantity.

Larger quantity → | 126 |
| 78 | 48 |

Smaller quantity ↑   How much more is needed ↑

Problem 1

Perri has read the entire book shown below. Jae has read 221 facts in the book. How many more facts has Perri read than Jae?

999 FACTS ABOUT REPTILES

999 facts Perri read → | 999 |
| 221 | ? |

221 facts Jae read ↑   ? more facts ↑

999 − 221 = ?

Perri has read 778 more facts than Jae.

Problem 2

Stanley has 128 classical songs on his computer. He has 234 more pop songs than classical songs. How many pop songs does Stanley have?

? pop songs → | ? |
| 128 | 234 |

128 classical songs ↑   234 more songs ↑

128 + 234 = ?

Stanley has 362 pop songs.

More Strip Diagrams

The **strip diagrams** on these pages can help you solve problems involving multiplication and division.

Equal Parts: Multiplication and Division

Draw this **strip diagram** for situations that involve joining equal parts of a whole or separating a whole into equal parts.

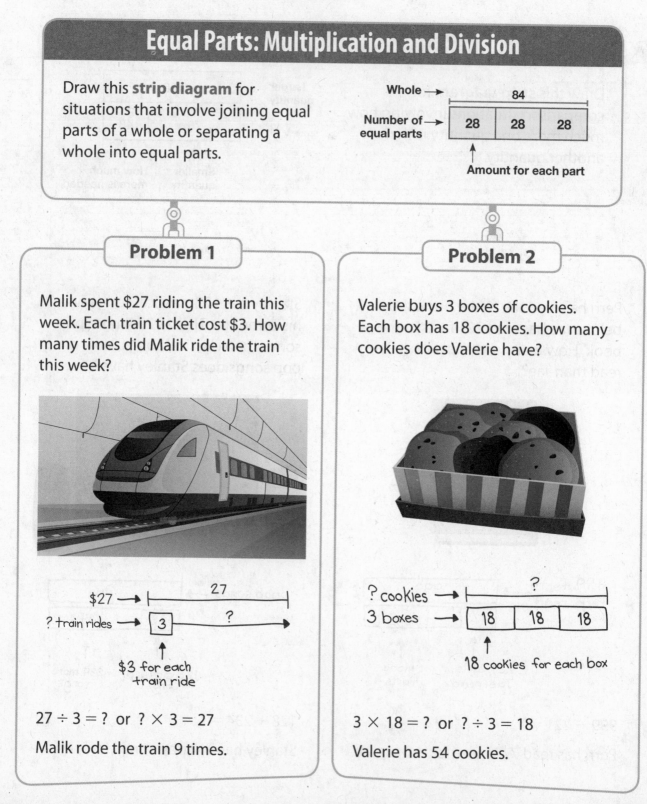

Whole → | 84 |
Number of → equal parts | 28 | 28 | 28 |
↑
Amount for each part

Problem 1

Malik spent $27 riding the train this week. Each train ticket cost $3. How many times did Malik ride the train this week?

$27 → | 27 |
? train rides → | 3 | ? →
↑
$3 for each train ride

$27 \div 3 = ?$ or $? \times 3 = 27$

Malik rode the train 9 times.

Problem 2

Valerie buys 3 boxes of cookies. Each box has 18 cookies. How many cookies does Valerie have?

? cookies → | ? |
3 boxes → | 18 | 18 | 18 |
↑
18 cookies for each box

$3 \times 18 = ?$ or $? \div 3 = 18$

Valerie has 54 cookies.

Multiplication and division are similar to addition and subtraction.

Comparison: Multiplication and Division

Draw this **strip diagram** for comparison situations involving how many times one quantity is of another quantity.

	78	

Larger quantity → | 26 | 26 | 26 | 3 times as many

Smaller quantity → | 26 |

Problem 1

Cal's jacket costs 4 times as much as his hat cost. Cal spent $40 on his coat. How much did Cal spend on his hat?

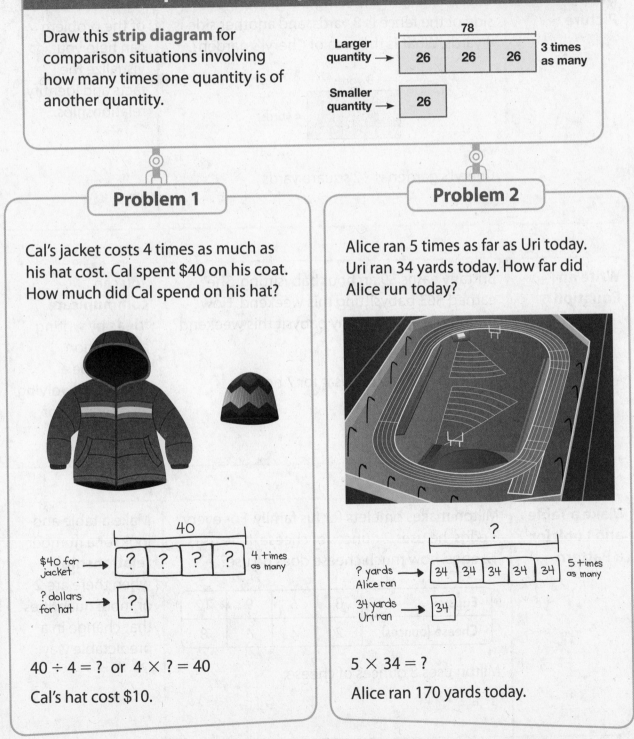

40

$40 for jacket → | ? | ? | ? | ? | 4 times as many

? dollars for hat → | ? |

$40 \div 4 = ?$ or $4 \times ? = 40$

Cal's hat cost $10.

Problem 2

Alice ran 5 times as far as Uri today. Uri ran 34 yards today. How far did Alice run today?

?

? yards Alice ran → | 34 | 34 | 34 | 34 | 34 | 5 times as many

34 yards Uri ran → | 34 |

$5 \times 34 = ?$

Alice ran 170 yards today.

More Problem-Solving Strategies

Creating a solution plan involves choosing and trying a strategy and then sometimes trying a different strategy.

Strategy	Example	When I Use It
Draw a Picture	Cheryl fences in a rectangular garden. One side of the fence is 8 yards, and another side is 4 yards. What is the area of Cheryl's garden? 8 yards 4 yards Cheryl's garden is 32 square yards.	A **representation** of the problem can help you visualize the facts and identify relationships.
Write an Equation	Brittany earns $9 an hour babysitting. She earned $63 babysitting this weekend. How many hours did Brittany babysit this weekend? Find $63 \div 9 = h$. $h = 7$, so Brittany babysat for 7 hours.	You can **communicate ideas** by writing an equation to describe a situation involving an operation or operations.
Make a Table and Look for a Pattern	Milton makes omelets for his family. For every 3 eggs, he uses 2 ounces of cheese. If he uses 12 eggs, how much cheese does he use? <table><tr><td>Eggs</td><td>3</td><td>6</td><td>9</td><td>12</td></tr><tr><td>Cheese (ounces)</td><td>2</td><td>4</td><td>6</td><td>8</td></tr></table> Milton uses 8 ounces of cheese.	Make a table and look for a number **relationship** when there are 2 or more quantities that change in a predictable way.

There's almost always more than one way to solve a problem.

Strategy	Example	When I Use It
Use Reasoning	Max has a flight at 7:30 P.M. It takes him 50 minutes to get from his home to the airport. He wants to arrive at the airport $1\frac{1}{2}$ hours before his flight. When is the latest he should leave his home? Time Max leaves home ← 50 minutes ← Time Max gets to airport ← $1\frac{1}{2}$ hours ← Time of Max's flight 7:30 Max should leave his home at 5:10 P.M.	**Reason** with the facts you know to find what actions cause the end result.
Analyze Given Information	Leon bought twelve of the same kind of flower. He spent $48. What type of flower did he buy? $12 \times \$2 = \$24$ $12 \times \$3 = \$36$ $12 \times \$4 = \$48$ $12 \times \$5 = \$60$ **Flower Prices** Tulip — $2 Rose — $3 Iris — $4 Lily — $5 Leon bought irises.	**Analyze given information** to help find a solution.
Analyze Relationships	A newspaper has 58 articles. Twelve are sports, five are editorials, ten are business, and the rest are news. How many of the articles are news? $12 + 5 + 10 = 27$ There are 27 articles that are sports, editorial, or business. $58 - 27 = 31$ So, 31 articles are news.	You can **analyze relationships** in information you are given to find unknown information.

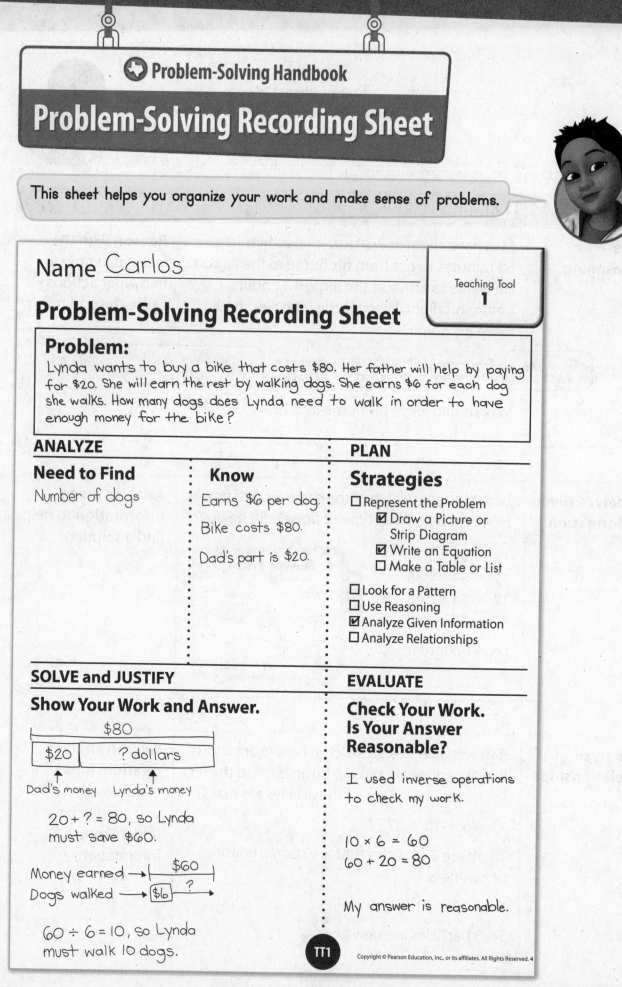

Problem-Solving Handbook

Problem-Solving Recording Sheet

This sheet helps you organize your work and make sense of problems.

Name **Carlos**

Teaching Tool
1

Problem-Solving Recording Sheet

Problem:

Lynda wants to buy a bike that costs $80. Her father will help by paying for $20. She will earn the rest by walking dogs. She earns $6 for each dog she walks. How many dogs does Lynda need to walk in order to have enough money for the bike?

ANALYZE

Need to Find

Number of dogs

Know

Earns $6 per dog.

Bike costs $80.

Dad's part is $20.

PLAN

Strategies

☐ Represent the Problem
☑ Draw a Picture or Strip Diagram
☑ Write an Equation
☐ Make a Table or List

☐ Look for a Pattern
☐ Use Reasoning
☑ Analyze Given Information
☐ Analyze Relationships

SOLVE and JUSTIFY

Show Your Work and Answer.

$80

| $20 | ? dollars |

Dad's money   Lynda's money

20 + ? = 80, so Lynda must save $60.

Money earned → | $60 |
Dogs walked → |$6| ? →

60 ÷ 6 = 10, so Lynda must walk 10 dogs.

EVALUATE

Check Your Work. Is Your Answer Reasonable?

I used inverse operations to check my work.

10 × 6 = 60
60 + 20 = 80

My answer is reasonable.

TT1

Copyright © Pearson Education, Inc., or its affiliates. All Rights Reserved. 4

Patterns and Equations

Essential Questions:
How can equations be solved?
How can patterns be used to describe how two quantities are related?
How can a relationship between two quantities be shown on a table?

> Temperature can be measured in degrees Fahrenheit or degrees Celsius.

> Water boils at 212°F or 100°C. Water freezes at 32°F or 0°C.

> I should get my thermometer! Here's a project on temperature and using rules.

Math and Science Project: Temperature

Do Research Use the Internet or other sources to find information about the size, shape, temperature, and other properties of water in each of its three forms: a solid, a liquid, and a gas.

Journal: Write a Report Include what you found. Also in your report:

- Tell about the two main ways of measuring temperature, Fahrenheit and Celsius.

- Use the equation shown below to convert 20 degrees Celsius (°C) to degrees Fahrenheit (°F).
  $F = (C \times 9 \div 5) + 32$

Review What You Know

Vocabulary

Choose the best term from the box. Write it on the blank.

- inverse operations
- greater than symbol (>)
- less than symbol (<)
- variable

1. A symbol that points toward a lesser amount is called a

_____.

2. A symbol or letter that stands for a

number is called a _____.

3. Operations that undo each other are

called _____.

Number Patterns

Write the missing number in each pattern.

4. 3, 6, 9, 12, _____, 18

5. 4, 8, 12, _____, 20, 24

6. 8, 7, 6, _____, 4, 3

7. 30, 25, 20, 15, _____, 5

Multiplication Facts

Find each product.

8. 4×3 **9.** 3×5

10. 7×2 **11.** 5×6

12. 2×4 **13.** 3×7

Division Facts

14. $20 \div 4$ **15.** $10 \div 5$

16. $18 \div 6$ **17.** $28 \div 4$

18. $24 \div 6$ **19.** $56 \div 8$

20. Explain A sporting goods store has 423 cans of tennis balls. There are 3 tennis balls in each can. How many tennis balls does the store have? Explain how you solved the problem.

© Pearson Education, Inc. 4

My Word Cards

Use the examples for each word on the front of the card to help complete the definitions on the back.

A-Z

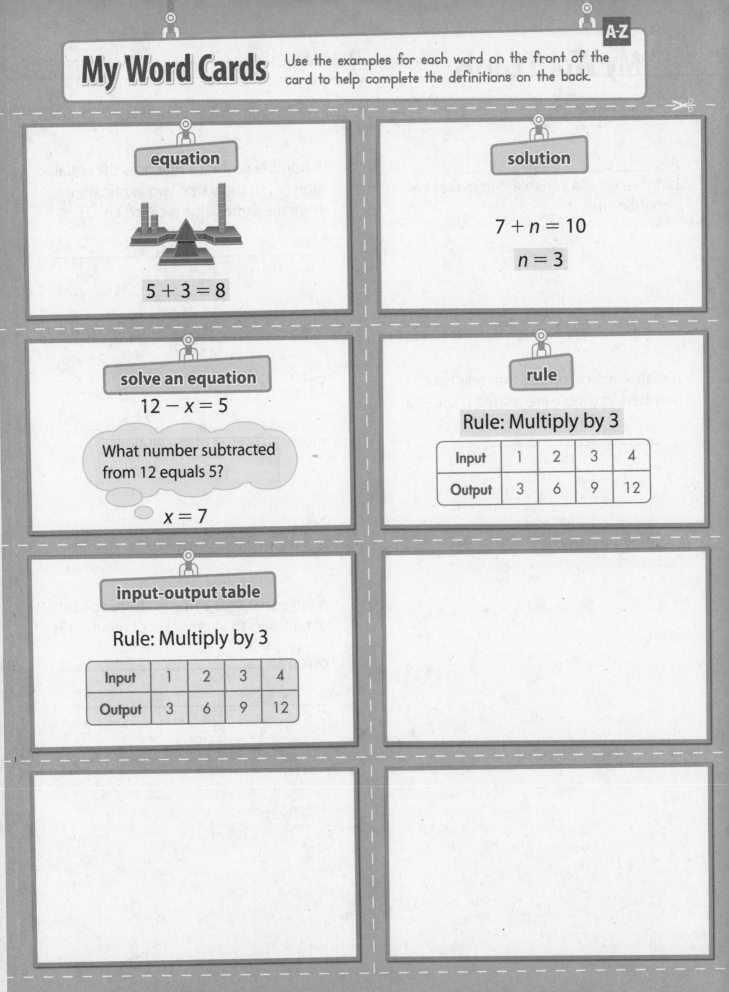

equation

$5 + 3 = 8$

solution

$7 + n = 10$

$n = 3$

solve an equation

$12 - x = 5$

What number subtracted from 12 equals 5?

$x = 7$

rule

Rule: Multiply by 3

Input	1	2	3	4
Output	3	6	9	12

input-output table

Rule: Multiply by 3

Input	1	2	3	4
Output	3	6	9	12

My Word Cards

A _____ is the value of a variable that makes an equation true.

A number sentence that uses the equal sign (=) to show that two expressions have the same value is called an

_____.

A mathematical phrase that tells how numbers in a table are related is called a

_____.

To _____

_____ means to find all of its solutions.

A table that uses a rule to relate one set of numbers to another set of numbers is

called an _____

_____.

© Pearson Education, Inc. 4

Name _____

Solve & Share

The two sides of a number sentence can be equal or not equal.

= means "is equal to"

≠ means "is not equal to"

Write = or ≠ in each ◯. Explain your answer for each. **Solve these problems any way you choose.**

⭐ TEKS 4.5 The student applies mathematical process standards to develop concepts of expressions and equations. Mathematical Process Standards 4.1B, 4.1C, 4.1D, 4.1E, 4.1G

Digital Resources at PearsonTexas.com

Solve Learn Glossary Check Tools Games

1. 3 hundreds + 2 tens + 8 ones ◯ 328

2. 356 ◯ 30 + 500 + 6

3. 200 × 50 × 4 ◯ 254

4. 56 × 76 × 0 × 25 ◯ 0

You can use **number sense.** Sometimes you can decide if the two sides of a number sentence are equal or not equal just by looking at the numbers.

5. 125 + 5,286 − 125 ◯ 5,286

6. 1 × 10 × 100 ◯ 1,000

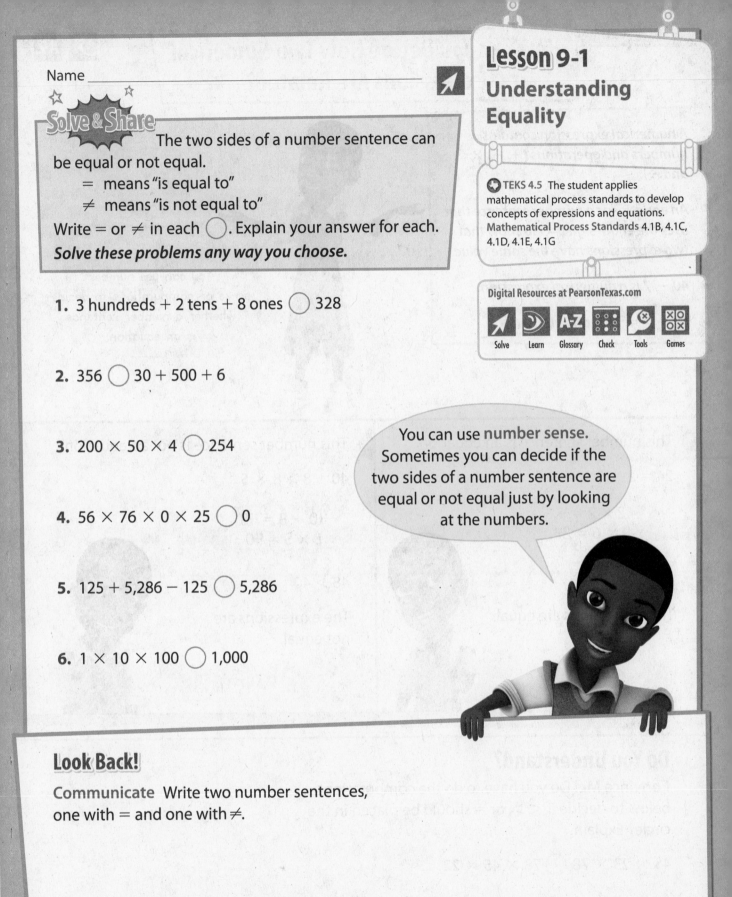

Look Back!

Communicate Write two number sentences, one with = and one with ≠.

How Can You Decide How Two Numerical Expressions Are Related?

A-Z

A numerical expression contains numbers and operations (+, −, ×, and ÷).

An equation is a number sentence that uses the equal sign (=) to show that two expressions have the same value.

40 − 7 is a numerical expression.

40 − 7 = 33 is an equation.

You can use number sense or computations to decide whether a number sentence is an equation.

B This number sentence is an equation.

$24 = 2 \times 2 \times 6$

$2 \times 2 = 4$
$4 \times 6 = 24$

$24 = 24$

The expressions are equal.

C This number sentence is not an equation.

$40 + 8 > 8 \times 5$

$40 + 8 = 48$
$8 \times 5 = 40$

$48 > 40$

The expressions are not equal.

Do You Understand?

Convince Me! Do you have to do the computations below to decide if <, >, or = should be placed in the circle? Explain.

$45 \times 23 \times 78 \bigcirc 78 \times 45 \times 22$

© Pearson Education, Inc. 4

☆ Guided Practice *

In **1** through **4**, use number sense or computations to decide whether each number sentence is an equation. Write $<$, $>$, or $=$ in each ◯.

1. $8 + 6 + 2$ ◯ $14 + 2$

2. $50 \div 10$ ◯ $8 \div 2$

3. 12×3 ◯ 24×3

4. $15 - 5$ ◯ $10 - 5$

Look for terms that are the same on both sides.

5. Connect Write a problem using the number sentence $9 + 2 > 4 + 5$.

6. Explain If 5 is subtracted from both sides of an equation, is the equation still true?

☆ Independent Practice ☆

Leveled Practice In **7** through **12**, write $=$ or $\neq$ in each ◯. Explain your answer for each.

7. 6 hundreds + 5 tens + 4 ones ◯ 654

8. 2 hundreds + 0 tens + 8 ones ◯ 280

9. $2,840$ ◯ $2,000 + 80 + 4$

10. $100 \times 30 \times 2$ ◯ 132

11. $39 + 244 - 39$ ◯ 244

12. 0 ◯ $42 \times 5 \times 11 \times 0$

In **13** through **18**, use number sense or computations to decide whether each number sentence is an equation. Write $<$, $>$, or $=$ in each ◯.

13. $15 - 8$ ◯ $12 - 8$

14. $3 \times 4 \times 5$ ◯ 3×20

15. $4 + 7 - 2$ ◯ $11 - 9$

16. $6 \times 3 + 10$ ◯ $18 + 10$

17. $2 \times 3 + 6$ ◯ $6 + 6$

18. $16 - 9$ ◯ $25 - 9$

Problem Solving

19. **Represent** The equation $8 + 4 = 7 + 5$ shows that Hope and Cole have the same number of bookmarks. What equation would show how many bookmarks each has after giving away 3 bookmarks?

20. **Number Sense** Frank made three 3-point baskets. Bob made five 2-point baskets. Write numbers and insert a symbol in the spaces below to complete a number sentence that compares the points scored by Frank and Bob.

21. Mr. Wilson has 16 boxes containing 12 test tubes each. He plans to divide the test tubes into 6 equal groups. How many test tubes will be in each group?

22. Which of the following keeps equal the equation $40 \times 8 = 320$?

  A $(40 \times 8) \times 2 = 320 \times 2$
  B $(40 \times 8) + 3 = 320 - 3$
  C $(40 \times 8) \div 8 = 320 - 8$
  D $(40 \times 8) + 12 = 320 + 18$

23. Carolyn baked 98 cupcakes for a fundraiser bake sale. She will put 4 cupcakes on each plate. How many plates will Carolyn need? Will there be any cupcakes left over?

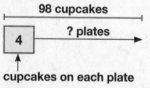

24. Write 2 different numbers in the first set of blanks to make 2 expressions that are equal. Then write 2 different numbers in the second set of blanks to make 2 expressions that are not equal.

$12 + \underline{\hspace{0.5cm}} = 35 - \underline{\hspace{0.5cm}}$

$12 + \underline{\hspace{0.5cm}} \neq 35 - \underline{\hspace{0.5cm}}$

25. Al and Jiro had some toy animals. Al had 8 lizards and 3 frogs. Jiro had 11 lizards and 2 frogs. Who had more toy animals?

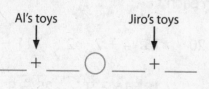

26. **Extend Your Thinking** If you know that $24 \times 6 = 144$, do you also know that $(24 \times 6) - 72 = 144 - 72$? Explain your reasoning.

© Pearson Education, Inc. 4

Name _____

Another Look!

Use an equal sign (=) to show that two expressions have the same value. Use a not equal to sign (≠), greater than sign (>), or less than sign (<) if two expressions do not have the same value.

These number sentences are equations.

12 + 12 = 24   Think: 12 + 12 = 24
24 = 24

The expressions are equal.

40 − 5 = 7 × 5   Think: 40 − 5 = 35
35 = 35   7 × 5 = 35

The expressions are equal.

These number sentences are not equations.

20 > 2 × 2 × 4   Think: 2 × 2 × 4 = 16
20 > 16

The expressions are not equal.

7 × 8 > 50 + 4   Think: 7 × 8 = 56
56 > 54   50 + 4 = 54

The expressions are not equal.

In **1** through **4**, write = or ≠ in each ◯. Explain your answer for each.

1. 7 hundreds + 2 tens + 3 ones ◯ 732

2. 9 hundreds + 0 tens + 5 ones ◯ 905

3. 4,000 + 500 + 60 + 7 ◯ 4,567

4. 10 × 3 + 5 ◯ 150

In **5** through **10**, use number sense or computations to decide whether each number sentence is an equation. Write <, >, or = in each ◯.

5. 18 + 19 ◯ 20

6. 9 − 1 ◯ 9 × 1

7. 24 ◯ 4 × 4 × 2

8. 3 × 3 + 1 ◯ 2 × 5

9. 5 + 8 − 1 ◯ 6 × 2

10. 7 × 2 + 5 ◯ 5 × 4 − 3

11. Which of the following shows the numbers 4.75, 5.74, 4.57, and 5.47 in order from least to greatest?

   A 4.57, 4.75, 5.74, 5.47
   B 5.74, 5.47, 4.75, 4.57
   C 4.75, 4.57, 5.47, 5.74
   D 4.57, 4.75, 5.47, 5.74

12. Reason Suppose Malcolm adds 2 to the left side of an equation and subtracts 5 from the right side. What number should he now subtract from the left side to make a true equation again?

13. The number below each block tells how many are in a set. Val used all of the small and large cylinders. Jen used all of the small and large cubes. Who used more blocks?

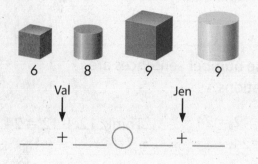

____ + ____ ◯ ____ + ____

14. Construct Arguments Salvadore wrote the following equation on his paper. If he writes the number 5 in the square, what symbol could he write in the circle? Explain.

$4 + 2 - 3 \bigcirc 6 - \square$

15. Formulate a Plan Claire and Karl both write expressions. Whose expression is greater than $28 - 19$?

Claire's Expression	Karl's Expression
3×4	$10 + 5$

   A Claire's
   B Karl's
   C Both Claire's and Karl's
   D Neither Claire's nor Karl's

16. Number Sense How can you decide if $<$, $>$, or $=$ should be placed in the circle without doing the calculations?

$52 \times 34 \times 63 \bigcirc 63 \times 52 \times 35$

17. Extend Your Thinking Which symbol, $\neq$ or $>$, gives you more information about two numerical expressions? Explain.

© Pearson Education, Inc. 4

Name_____

Solve & Share

A pan balance stays level if the total weight on the left side is the same as the total weight on the right side. Find the missing numbers so each pan balance stays level. *Solve these problems any way you choose.*

⭐ TEKS 4.5 The student applies mathematical process standards to develop concepts of expressions and equations.
Mathematical Process Standards 4.1C, 4.1D, 4.1G

You can use **mental math** to find the missing numbers. *Show your work in the space below!*

Digital Resources at PearsonTexas.com

Solve Learn Glossary Check Tools Games

1.
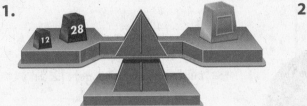

2.

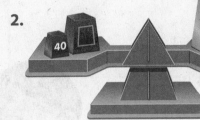

Look Back!

Communicate Explain how addition and subtraction can be used to find the missing number for the pan balance in Exercise 2.

A

A solution to an equation is a number for the variable that makes the value on the left side of the equal sign the same as the value on the right side of the equal sign.

To solve an equation means to find all of its solutions.

Solve each equation:

$20 + n = 45$

$120 = x - 20$

> When you find the correct value for n, the pan balance is level!

20 | n   45

B Solve $20 + n = 45$.

> To solve, think: What number can I add to 20 to get 45?

20 plus 20 equals 40.
5 more makes 45.

So, $20 + 25 = 45$

$n = 25$

C Solve $120 = x - 20$.

> To solve, think: What number can I start with, subtract 20, and get 120?

$140 - 20 = 120$

So, $120 = 140 - 20$

$x = 140$

Do You Understand?

Convince Me! Melissa said, "I cannot solve this equation." Explain what Melissa might have been thinking. Is she correct?

$320 + m = 320$

© Pearson Education, Inc. 4

☆ Guided Practice*

In **1** through **4**, solve each equation.

1. $n + 8 = 12$

2. $100 - x = 70$

3. $65 = 40 + c$

4. $120 = b - 80$

To check your answer, substitute it for the variable and check that the equation is still true.

5. **Explain** How could you use a pan balance to show that your answer to Exercise 1 is correct?

6. **Communicate** Explain how a pan balance can be used to model an equation.

Independent Practice ☆

In **7** through **21**, solve each equation.

7. $17 + b = 20$

8. $14 - d = 10$

9. $29 = 21 + x$

10. $13 + q = 24$

11. $32 = g - 7$

12. $52 = 40 + x$

13. $a - 10 = 11$

14. $x + 7 = 19$

15. $87 = 100 - x$

16. $105 = 140 - m$

17. $230 + x = 250$

18. $140 - v = 115$

19. $89 = x + 12$

20. $30 + 20 = x + 10$

21. $50 - w = 20$

Problem Solving

22. What is the missing number that will keep the pan balance level?

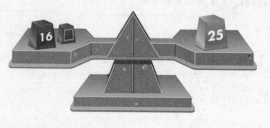

23. Monica has 89 DVDs in her collection. She wants to put the same number of DVDs on each of 3 shelves. To find how many DVDs go on each shelf, Monica finds the quotient 89 ÷ 3. Interpret the remainder.

24. Explain If you add or subtract weight from one side of a pan balance, what must you do to the other side in order to keep the pans level?

25. To solve the equation $53 - n = 39$, Melanie used the guess and check method with the numbers shown below until she found one that resulted in a true equation. What is the solution to the equation?

53	
n	39

A 12
B 13
C 14
D 15

26. Number Sense Decide if the solution to each equation below is greater than 100 or less than 100. Explain how you decided.

a. $345 + n = 410$
b. $604 = 835 - m$
c. $p - 34 = 110$

27. Extend Your Thinking Write an equation for the pan balance shown at the right. Then solve the equation.

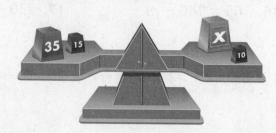

© Pearson Education, Inc. 4

Another Look!

Solve $60 + x = 90$.

To solve, think: What number can I add to 60 to get 90?

$60 + 30 = 90$

$x = 30$

To check, think: If I replace the variable with my solution, are both sides of the equation the same?

$60 + 30 = 90$

$90 = 90$

Both sides of the equation are 90. The solution $x = 30$ is correct!

What value of x keeps the pan balance level? That value is the solution of the equation.

In **1** through **18**, solve each equation.

1. $v + 6 = 20$

2. $37 - k = 33$

3. $8 = 15 - z$

4. $21 = 15 + m$

5. $u - 14 = 3$

6. $66 = x + 16$

7. $98 - r = 28$

8. $p + 15 = 15$

9. $70 - t = 50$

10. $40 = 10 + z$

11. $24 = n - 2$

12. $s + 4 = 100$

13. $44 = m + 14$

14. $33 - n = 23$

15. $50 = 65 - p$

16. $16 + q = 17$

17. $100 = s + 85$

18. $125 - t = 25$

19. Personal Financial Literacy Reese spent $4.95 buying supplies to make cookies. He sold 24 cookies for $2 each. His profit is how much more he got from selling the cookies than he spent. What was Reese's profit?

20. Mrs. Rivas wants to install carpet in her basement and family room. Her basement is 62 square yards, and her family room is 18 square yards. If carpet costs $13 per square yard, how much will it cost to carpet these two rooms?

21. Which equation is shown in the pan balance to the right?

A $n - 15 = 32$
B $n + 15 = 32$
C $n + 32 = 15$
D $n - 32 = 15$

22. Math and Science This morning, the thermometer outside Anthony's window showed that it was 57°F. When he got home from school, the thermometer read 74°F. Use the strip diagram to write and solve an equation. How much did the temperature increase?

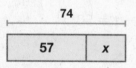

74	
57	x

23. Extend Your Thinking There are 20 more girls than boys in 4th grade. In total there are 100 students in this grade. Use the strip diagram and equation to help you find the number of boys, b. How many boys are in 4th grade? How many girls are in 4th grade?

100	
b	b + 20

$$b + (b + 20) = 100$$

24. Tools Write an equation for the pan balance shown to the right and solve for x.

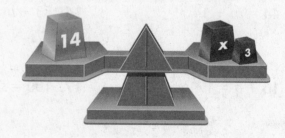

© Pearson Education, Inc. 4

Name _____

☆ **Solve & Share** ☆

The pan balance stays level if the total weight on the left side is the same as the total weight on the right side. Find the value of the variable so each pan balance stays level. *Solve these problems any way you choose.*

You can **use representations**. All boxes showing the same variable are the same weight. *Show your work here and use digital tools to solve the problem.*

⊕ TEKS 4.5 The student applies mathematical process standards to develop concepts of expressions and equations. Mathematical Process Standards 4.1C, 4.1D, 4.1E, 4.1F, 4.1G

Digital Resources at PearsonTexas.com

Solve   Learn   Glossary   Check   Tools   Games

1. *n* = _____

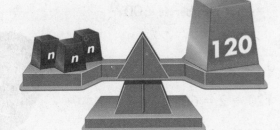

2. *m* = _____

Look Back!

Communicate Explain how you found the value of the variable *n*.

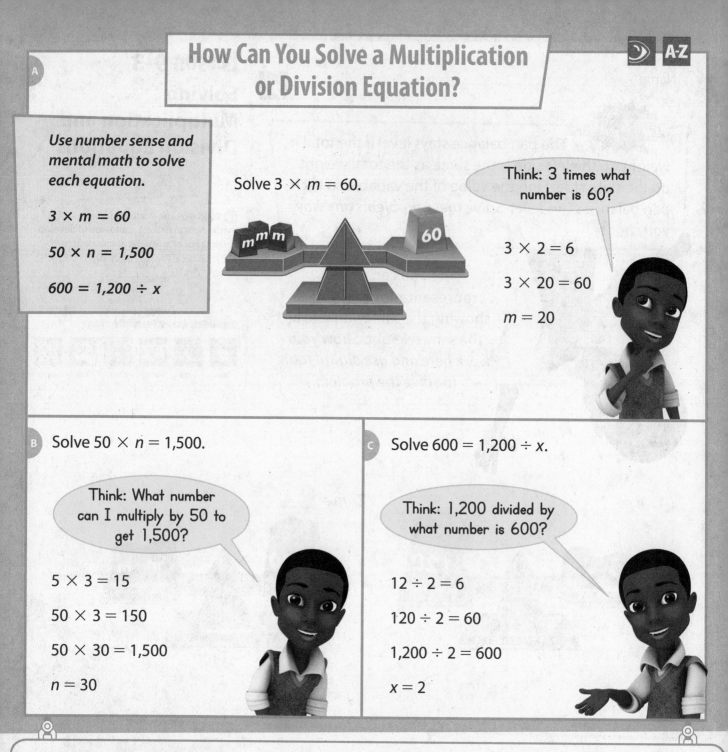

A

Use number sense and mental math to solve each equation.

$3 \times m = 60$

$50 \times n = 1,500$

$600 = 1,200 \div x$

Solve $3 \times m = 60$.

m m m   60

Think: 3 times what number is 60?

$3 \times 2 = 6$

$3 \times 20 = 60$

$m = 20$

B Solve $50 \times n = 1,500$.

Think: What number can I multiply by 50 to get 1,500?

$5 \times 3 = 15$

$50 \times 3 = 150$

$50 \times 30 = 1,500$

$n = 30$

C Solve $600 = 1,200 \div x$.

Think: 1,200 divided by what number is 600?

$12 \div 2 = 6$

$120 \div 2 = 60$

$1,200 \div 2 = 600$

$x = 2$

Do You Understand?

Convince Me! Devon said that the solution to the equation is 0. Is he correct? Explain.

$3,200 \div p = 3,200$

© Pearson Education, Inc. 4

☆ **Guided Practice** *

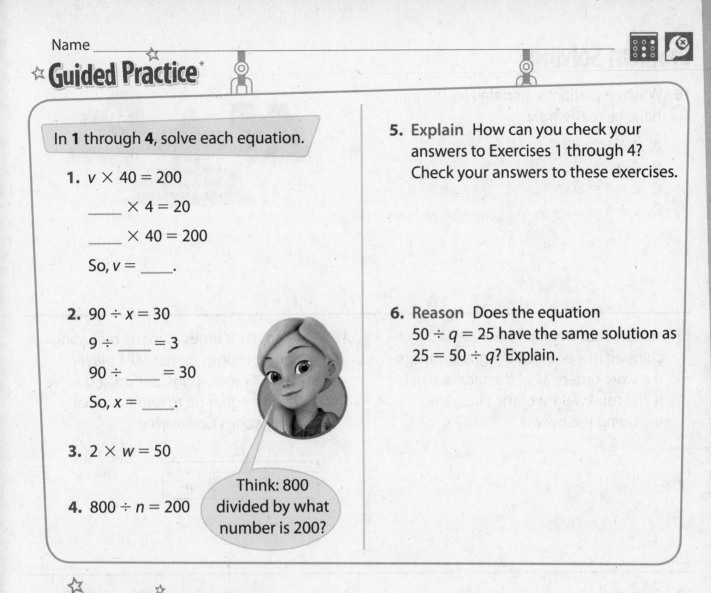

In **1** through **4**, solve each equation.

1. $v \times 40 = 200$

_____ $\times 4 = 20$

_____ $\times 40 = 200$

So, $v =$ _____.

2. $90 \div x = 30$

$9 \div$ _____ $= 3$

$90 \div$ _____ $= 30$

So, $x =$ _____.

3. $2 \times w = 50$

Think: 800 divided by what number is 200?

4. $800 \div n = 200$

5. **Explain** How can you check your answers to Exercises 1 through 4? Check your answers to these exercises.

6. **Reason** Does the equation $50 \div q = 25$ have the same solution as $25 = 50 \div q$? Explain.

☆ **Independent Practice** ☆

Leveled Practice In **7** through **15**, solve each equation.

7. $120 = t \times 4$

$12 =$ _____ $\times 4$

$120 =$ _____ $\times 4$

So, $t =$ _____.

8. $2,100 \div x = 700$

$21 \div$ _____ $= 7$

$210 \div$ _____ $= 70$

$2,100 \div$ _____ $= 700$

So, $x =$ _____.

9. $300 = 900 \div k$

$3 = 9 \div$ _____

$30 = 90 \div$ _____

$300 = 900 \div$ _____

So, $k =$ _____.

10. $7 \times z = 70$

11. $p \div 5 = 7$

12. $50 = 10 \times u$

13. $64 = 8 \times w$

14. $500 \div c = 250$

15. $a \times 60 = 720$

Problem Solving

16. Which equation is modeled by the pan balance to the right?

   A $4 \times c = 80$
   B $4 \times c = 20$
   C $c \div 4 = 80$
   D $c \div 4 = 20$

17. A radio that weighs 18 ounces is shipped in a box that weighs 3 ounces. If a store orders 24 of the radios, what is the total weight of the shipment, including the boxes?

18. Colleen has 3 times as many rock songs as country songs on her MP3 player. She has 75 rock songs. Set up and solve a division equation to find how many country songs Colleen has.

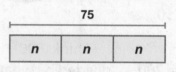

19. **Connect** There are 90 students on the playground during recess. This is 3 times the number of students playing in the gym. Set up and solve a multiplication equation to find how many students are playing in the gym.

20. **Extend Your Thinking** What number does t represent in the pan balance below? Explain.

You can use a variable to represent the number of students in the gym.

© Pearson Education, Inc. 4

Name _____

Another Look!

Use number sense and mental math to solve each equation.

$3 \times d = 120$

$500 = 2{,}500 \div z$

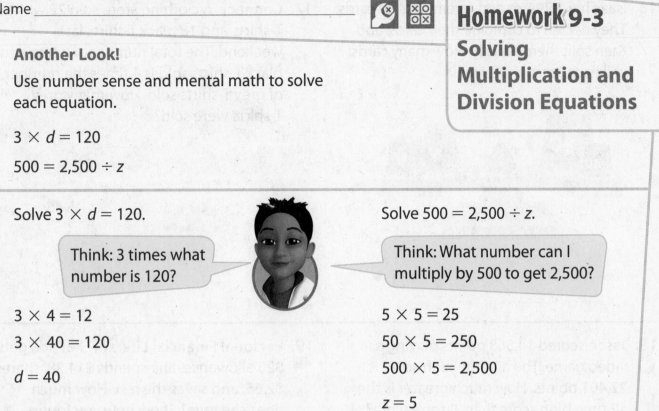

Solve $3 \times d = 120$.

Think: 3 times what number is 120?

$3 \times 4 = 12$

$3 \times 40 = 120$

$d = 40$

Solve $500 = 2{,}500 \div z$.

Think: What number can I multiply by 500 to get 2,500?

$5 \times 5 = 25$

$50 \times 5 = 250$

$500 \times 5 = 2{,}500$

$z = 5$

In **1** through **15**, solve each equation.

1. $300 = 1{,}500 \div c$

$3 = 15 \div$ _____

$30 = 150 \div$ _____

$300 = 1{,}500 \div$ _____

So, $c =$ _____.

2. $400 = 10 \times h$

$40 = 10 \times$ _____

$400 = 10 \times$ _____

So, $h =$ _____.

3. $1{,}200 \div d = 300$

$12 \div$ _____ $= 3$

$120 \div$ _____ $= 30$

$1{,}200 \div$ _____ $= 300$

So, $d =$ _____.

4. $m \times 8 = 80$

5. $60 \div x = 10$

6. $280 = 2 \times m$

7. $32 = h \times 4$

8. $400 \div k = 400$

9. $750 \div r = 250$

10. $2 \times g = 100$

11. $8 = h \div 2$

12. $400 - 100 = 30 \times v$

13. $810 \div m = 90$

14. $560 = n \times 80$

15. $70 = 490 \div s$

16. Isaac has 80 cards and Jeremy has 40 cards. They decide to combine their cards, and then split them equally. How many cards will each person receive?

17. Connect A clothing store sold 22 white T-shirts and 18 black T-shirts last weekend. The total number of white and black T-shirts sold is 4 times the number of grey T-shirts sold. How many grey T-shirts were sold?

18. Jason scored 14,568 points playing a video game. The all-time high score is 22,401 points. How much greater is the all-time high score than Jason's score?

   A 7,733 points

   B 7,833 points

   C 14,568 points

   D 36,969 points

19. Personal Financial Literacy Kalinda gets $25 allowance. She spends $14.28, shares $2.65, and saves the rest. How much does she save? Show how you found the answer.

20. Extend Your Thinking Patrick set up the three pan balances shown below. Write the equation represented by each pan balance. Solve each equation. Explain how the equations are alike and how they are different.

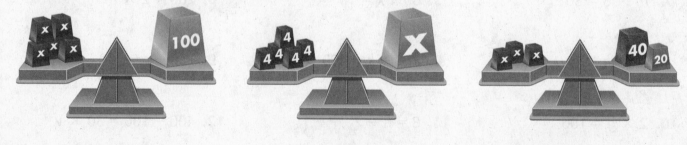

© Pearson Education, Inc. 4

Name _____

Solve & Share

What is a rule for relating the numbers in the table below? *Solve this problem any way you choose.*

Bob's Age	4	10	8		
Ali's Age	2	8	6		

⭐ TEKS 4.5B Represent problems using an input-output table and numerical expressions to generate a number pattern that follows a given rule....
Mathematical Process Standards 4.1B, 4.1C, 4.1D, 4.1F, 4.1G

Digital Resources at PearsonTexas.com

| Solve | Learn | Glossary | Check | Tools | Games |

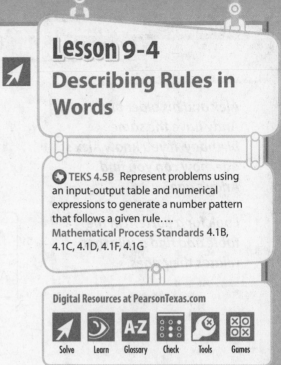

You can analyze relationships. How do these pairs of number relate to each other? *Show your work in the space above!*

Look Back!

Reason Give two other sets of numbers that fit the rule for the table.

What Is a Math Rule for the Situation?

Alex and his older brother Andy have the same birthday. If you know Alex's age, how can you find Andy's age?

Look for a pattern in the table and find a rule that relates their ages.

Patterns can be used to identify some relationships.

Alex's Age	2	4	6	7	9
Andy's Age	8	10	12	13	15

Look for a pattern.

Step 1

Find a rule for the table.

Compare each pair of numbers. Look for a pattern.

Alex's Age	2	4	6	7	9
Andy's Age	8	10	12	13	15

In each pair, Andy's age is 6 more than Alex's age. A rule for the table is "add 6."

Step 2

Check that your rule works for all pairs.

Rule: Add 6.

$$2 + 6 = 8$$
$$4 + 6 = 10$$
$$6 + 6 = 12$$
$$7 + 6 = 13$$
$$9 + 6 = 15$$

Your rule works for each pair.

Do You Understand?

Convince Me! If you know Andy's age, what is the rule to find Alex's age? Explain.

© Pearson Education, Inc. 4

☆Guided Practice☆

In **1** and **2**, use the table below.

Hours Worked	4	8	7	2	6
Amount Earned	$24	$48		$12	

1. Write a rule for the table.

2. What are the missing numbers?

3. In the previous example about Alex's and Andy's ages, what does the rule "add 6" mean in the problem?

4. Marty uses the rule "subtract 9" for his table. If the first number in Marty's table is 11, what is the second number in that pair?

Independent Practice ☆

In **5** through **9**, find a rule for each table. Use your rules to complete the tables.

Remember to look for a pattern.

5.

Earned	$15	$12	$17	$9	$11
Spent	$7		$9		$3

6.

Earned	$14	$18	$12	$16	$8
Saved	$7	$9			$4

7.

Price	Discount
$36	$24
$28	$16
$33	
$40	$28
$25	

8.

Number of Chairs	Number of Legs
3	12
2	8
5	20
7	
	36

9.

Number of Teams	Number of Players
4	20
3	15
5	
6	30
8	

Problem Solving

In **10** and **11**, use the table at the right.

10. The table shows the ages of a velvet mesquite tree and a saguaro cactus plant at a garden. When the velvet mesquite tree was 48 years old, how old was the saguaro cactus?

11. Check for Reasonableness Phil says the saguaro cactus is about 100 years older than the velvet mesquite tree. Is his estimate reasonable? Explain.

Plant's Age in Years	
Velvet Mesquite Tree	Saguaro Cactus
1	36
15	50
67	102
48	

12. An art museum has 48 paintings in one room and 31 paintings in another room. What is a reasonable estimate for the total number of paintings in these two rooms? Explain.

13. ⭐ Esther is 8 years older than Manuel. Which of these shows the ages that Esther and Manuel could be?

A Esther 15, Manuel 23
B Esther 16, Manuel 15
C Esther 15, Manuel 7
D Esther 7, Manuel 15

14. Use the table below. How many eggs can 4 ostrich hens lay in one year? How many can 5 ostrich hens lay?

Eggs Laid in a Year					
Number of Ostrich Hens	1	2	3	4	5
Number of Eggs	50	100	150		

15. Extend Your Thinking Refer to the table and information given in Exercise 14. Suppose a group of ostrich hens at a zoo is expected to lay 350 eggs this year. How many ostrich hens are there? Explain.

16. ⭐ The table shows the number of baskets that Betty needs for different numbers of apples. She wants to put an equal number of apples in each basket. How many baskets does Betty need for 56 apples?

Betty's Apple Baskets					
Number of Apples	28	56	7	21	14
Number of Baskets	4		1	3	2

A 8 baskets
B 7 baskets
C 6 baskets
D 5 baskets

© Pearson Education, Inc. 4

Name _____

Another Look!

Old Price	New Price
$15	$10
$22	$17
$28	$23
$37	$32
$51	$46

Each pair of numbers in the table to the left follows a rule. If you can find a rule that works, you can extend the table.

It is important to check that the rule works for all values in the table.

Step 1

Find the pattern. Check the first pair of numbers to see how the first number changed to become the second number.

$15 - 5 = 10$

A rule for the first pair of numbers is "subtract 5."

Step 2

See if this rule works for all the values.

$22 - 5 = 17$ $\qquad$ $37 - 5 = 32$

$28 - 5 = 23$ $\qquad$ $51 - 5 = 46$

The rule "subtract 5" works for every pair of values.

In **1** through **5**, find the missing numbers in each table. Write a rule for the table.

1.

Earned	Spent
$21	$14
$30	$23
$42	
$48	$41
$59	

2.

Teams	Players
3	27
8	72
6	
9	
2	18

3.

Tickets	Cost
2	$1
6	$3
12	
10	$5
20	

4.

Days	1	2	3	4
Miles	14	28		56

5.

Carts	2	5	3	7
Plants	24	60		84

6. The table below shows Max's age and Carol's age. Write a rule for the table and fill in the missing numbers.

Max's Age	Carol's Age
7	13
10	
14	20
18	24
	31

7. Math and Science Ice begins melting at 32°F or at 0°C. Lead melts at 621.5°F. How many degrees Fahrenheit above the melting point of ice does lead melt?

8. The table shows shows the number of days Jim and Ken have been practicing. Which is a rule that works for this table?

Jim	8	12	20	30
Ken	16	20	28	38

A Add 8. **C** Subtract 10.

B Multiply by 2. **D** Divide by 2.

9. Formulate a Plan An elevator began on the 4th floor of a building. From there the elevator traveled 8 floors up, then 3 floors down, then 4 floors down, then 1 floor up. On what floor did the elevator stop?

10. Explain Explain how to find a rule for the table. Then explain how to use the rule to find the two missing numbers.

Earned	$21	$27	$12	$18	$33
Saved	$7	$9		$6	

11. Extend Your Thinking The table to the right shows the number of players on a volleyball team. If there are 12 teams, how many players will there be? Explain.

Teams	Players
4	24
8	48
6	36
5	30

© Pearson Education, Inc. 4

Name _____

Solve & Share

A restaurant manager uses a rule to decide how many tables are needed for a party.

Rule: To find the number of tables, divide the number of guests by 4.

Use the rule to complete the table. What patterns do you see in the table? *Solve this problem any way you choose.*

TEKS 4.5B Represent problems using an input-output table and numerical expressions to generate a number pattern that follows a given rule…. Also, 4.5. Mathematical Process Standards 4.1A, 4.1C, 4.1D, 4.1E, 4.1F

Digital Resources at PearsonTexas.com

Solve Learn Glossary Check Tools Games

You can **use a representation.** Recording numbers in a table can help you see number patterns.

Number of Guests	4	8	12	16	20
Number of Tables					

Look Back!

Communicate Complete this rule for the situation above:

To find the total number of people if all tables are full,

_____ the number of tables by _____.

How Can You Use a Table to Describe a Pattern?

Cammy is making bead strings for her bedroom. She uses a rule to make her strings.

Rule: Multiply the number of blue beads by 3 to get the number of yellow beads.

Make an input-output table to show the pattern. What patterns do you see in the table?

This string has 2 blue beads. You can use the numerical expression 2 × 3 to find the number of yellow beads.

B

Put numbers 1 to 5 in the top row. ⟶

Multiply each number in the top row by 3 ⟶

		1	2	3	4	5
●	Number of Blue Beads	1	2	3	4	5
●	Number of Yellow Beads	3	6	9	12	15

You can use the rule to complete the table and then look for a pattern in the sequence of numbers in a row.

The numbers in the bottom row are multiples of 3. 1 × 3 = 3, 2 × 3 = 6, 3 × 3 = 9, and so on.

Do You Understand?

Convince Me! In the example above, if you know the number of yellow beads, what is the rule to find the number of blue beads? Tell how you decided.

© Pearson Education, Inc. 4

Name _____

In **1** and **2**, use the rule to complete each input-output table.

1. Rule: Add 7 to the input.

Input	2	4	6	8	10
Output	9				

2. Rule: Divide the input by 5.

Input	50	40	30	20	10
Output	10				

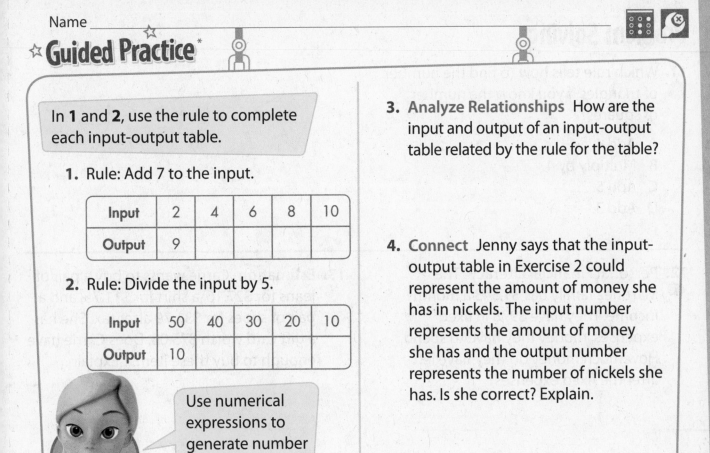

Use numerical expressions to generate number patterns.

3. Analyze Relationships How are the input and output of an input-output table related by the rule for the table?

4. Connect Jenny says that the input-output table in Exercise 2 could represent the amount of money she has in nickels. The input number represents the amount of money she has and the output number represents the number of nickels she has. Is she correct? Explain.

Independent Practice ☆

Leveled Practice In **5** through **10**, use the rule to complete each input-output table.

5. Rule: Multiply the input by 4.

Input	1	2	3	4	5
Output	4	8			

6. Rule: Add 6 to the input.

Input	2	5	8	12	18
Output	8	11			

7. Rule: Subtract 9 from the input.

Input	25	20	18	16	11
Output					

8. Rule: Divide the input by 4.

Input	108	96	64	44	20
Output					

9. Rule: Multiply the input by 12.

Input	2	5	6	8	9
Output					

10. Rule: Subtract 15 from the input.

Input	24	36	40	55	62
Output					

Problem Solving

11. Which rule tells how to find the number of triangles if you know the number of squares?

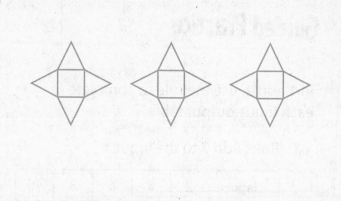

A Add 4.

B Multiply by 4.

C Add 5.

D Add 3.

---

12. Personal Financial Literacy The Martinez family has $1,543 a month income. They have $978 in fixed expenses, money they have to spend. How much money do they have left after the fixed expenses?

13. Estimation Carrie wants to buy a pair of jeans for $27.16, a shirt for $11.75, and a pair of shoes for $31.79 after tax. She has a gift card worth $75.00. Does Carrie have enough to buy these items? Explain.

---

14. It costs $6 per ticket to see a movie during the matinee showings. Use the rule below to complete the table. Write a numerical expression to find the cost of 8 tickets.

Rule: Multiply by 6.

Number of Tickets	1	2	3	4	5
Total Cost					

---

15. A company manufactures shoes and puts a pair of shoes in each shoebox. For every 2 shoes made, 1 shoebox is needed. Use the rule below to complete the table.

Rule: Divide by 2.

Number of Shoes	12	16	20	28	34
Number of Shoeboxes					

16. Extend Your Thinking There is a $6 charge per car to get into an amusement park and a $2 charge per person in the car. Use the rule below to complete the table. Describe the pattern in the total cost.

Rule: Multiply by $2 and then add $6.

Number of People per Car	1	2	3	4	5
Total Cost					

© Pearson Education, Inc. 4

Name _____

Another Look!

Alexandria is making TV trays to sell at a crafts market. She uses a rule to determine how many table legs she needs.

Rule: Multiply the number of TV trays being built by 4 to get the number of table legs needed.

Put numbers 1 to 5 in the top row.

Multiply each number in the top row by 4.

Make an input-output table to show the pattern.

Number of TV Trays	1	2	3	4	5
Number of Table Legs	4	8	12	16	20

In **1** through **8**, use the rule to complete each input-output table.

1. Rule: Add 12 to the input.

Input	1	5	11	14	20
Output	13	17			

2. Rule: Multiply the input by 8.

Input	2	3	6	7	9
Output	16	24			

3. Rule: Divide the input by 7.

Input	77	70	35	28	21
Output					

4. Rule: Subtract 5 from the input.

Input	8	12	19	30	32
Output					

5. Rule: Subtract 11 from the input.

Input	15	22	29	45	50
Output					

6. Rule: Multiply the input by 14.

Input	2	3	5	7	8
Output					

7. Rule: Add 19 to the input.

Input	1	6	15	21	32
Output					

8. Rule: Divide the input by 5.

Input	0	15	50	100	500
Output					

9. Carmen is setting tables and chairs as shown at the right. Which rule tells how to find the number of chairs needed if you know how many tables there are?

Tables and Chairs

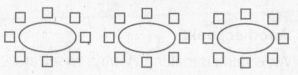

  A Add 8.
  B Divide by 8.
  C Subtract 8.
  D Multiply by 8.

10. Math and Science A science class measured the mass of a balloon to be 4 grams. After the balloon was inflated, the mass was 8 grams. What was the mass of the air inside the inflated balloon?

11. Number Sense Write the numbers 14.61, 16.4, 14.6, and 146.1 in order from least to greatest.

12. It takes 3 cups of flour to make a batch of oatmeal raisin cookies. Use the rule below to complete the table.

Rule: Divide by 3.

Cups of Flour	3	6	9	12	15
Batches of Cookies					

13. Frannie has a coupon good for $10 off her total purchase at a store. Use the rule below to complete the table.

Rule: Subtract $10.

Purchase Price	$19	$28	$34	$40	$55
Price After Coupon					

14. Extend Your Thinking Tommy has saved $65. He plans to save an additional $10 per week from his allowance. Use the rule below to complete the table. Rule: To find the total amount saved, multiply the number of weeks by $10 and then add $65.

Number of Weeks	1	2	3	4	5
Total Savings					

© Pearson Education, Inc. 4

Name _____

Look at the towers of cubes shown below. Do you see a pattern in the number of cubes in each tower? What would the next two towers look like? *Solve this problem any way you choose.*

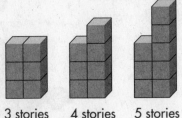

3 stories   4 stories   5 stories

⭐ TEKS 4.1C Select tools, including real objects, manipulatives, paper and pencil, and technology as appropriate … to solve problems.
TEKS 4.1E Create and use representations to organize, record, and communicate mathematical ideas. Also, 4.5B.
Mathematical Process Standards 4.1B, 4.1F, 4.1G

Digital Resources at PearsonTexas.com

Solve   Learn   Glossary   Check   Tools   Games

You can **use tools,** such as cubes, to model a tower. *Show your work in the space above!*

Look Back!

Connect Ideas How can you determine the number of cubes in a tower with 10 stories without using a model?

How Can You Find a Pattern to Solve a Problem?

A Analyze

Talisa made three block towers. She recorded her pattern. If she continued the pattern, how many blocks would be in a 10-story tower? How many would be in a 100-story tower?

Some sequences of objects change in predictable ways.

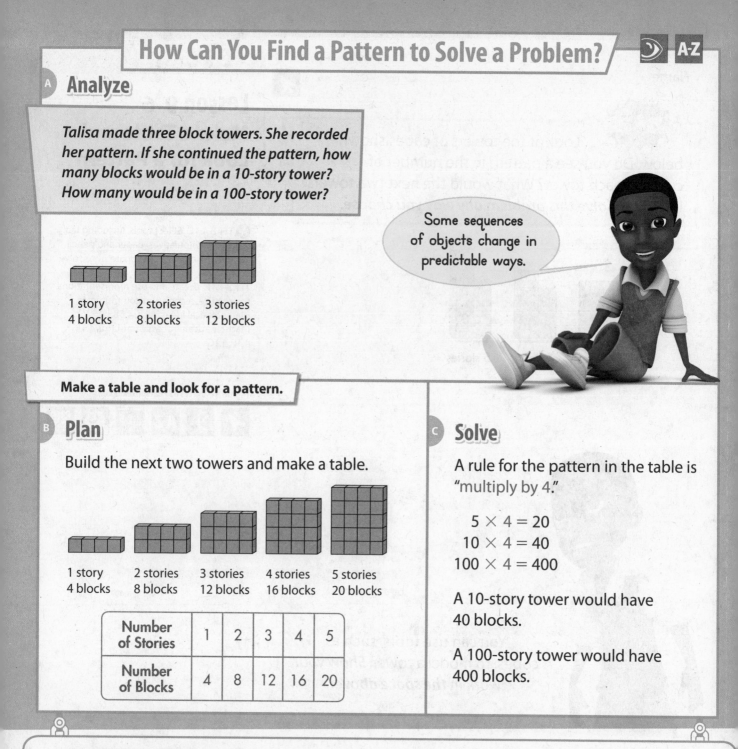

1 story
4 blocks

2 stories
8 blocks

3 stories
12 blocks

Make a table and look for a pattern.

B Plan

Build the next two towers and make a table.

1 story
4 blocks

2 stories
8 blocks

3 stories
12 blocks

4 stories
16 blocks

5 stories
20 blocks

Number of Stories	1	2	3	4	5
Number of Blocks	4	8	12	16	20

C Solve

A rule for the pattern in the table is "multiply by 4."

$$5 \times 4 = 20$$
$$10 \times 4 = 40$$
$$100 \times 4 = 400$$

A 10-story tower would have 40 blocks.

A 100-story tower would have 400 blocks.

Do You Understand?

Convince Me! Clarence said, "Another rule for the block towers above is *add 4*. Look: 4, 8, 12."

Is Clarence correct? Explain.

© Pearson Education, Inc. 4

Name _____

Draw the next two towers in the pattern. You may use grid paper to help. Find the missing numbers in the table.

1.

Number of Stories	1	2	3	4	5
Number of Blocks	2	4	6		

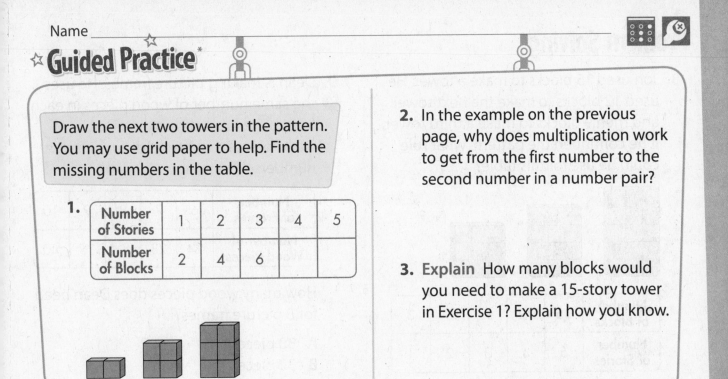

2. In the example on the previous page, why does multiplication work to get from the first number to the second number in a number pair?

3. Explain How many blocks would you need to make a 15-story tower in Exercise 1? Explain how you know.

☆ Independent Practice ☆

In **4** through **7**, use patterns to find the missing numbers in each table. You may draw the next two figures on grid paper to help.

4.

Number of Stories	7	6	5	4	3
Number of Blocks	21	18	15		

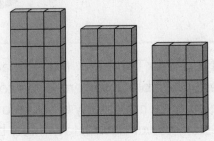

5.

Number of Stories	1	2	3	4	5
Number of Blocks	4	8	12		

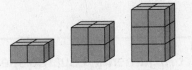

6.

Number of Rows	2	3	4	5	6
Number of Squares	3	5	7		

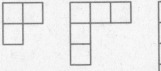

7.

Number of Rows	1	2	3	4	5
Number of Small Triangles	1	4	9		

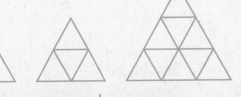

Problem Solving

8. Jon used 15 blocks to make a tower. He used 12 blocks to make the next tower, and then 9 blocks to make a third tower. If he continued the pattern, what rule could he use for this table?

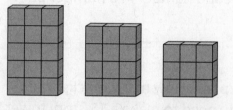

Number of Blocks	15	12	9	6	3
Number of Stories	5	4	3	2	1

9. Dean is making picture frames. He uses the same number of wood pieces in each frame. The table shows the number of wood pieces that he needs for different numbers of frames.

Number of Frames	6	7	8	9	10
Number of Wood Pieces	24	28		36	40

How many wood pieces does Dean need for 8 picture frames?

A 30 pieces

B 32 pieces

C 34 pieces

D 36 pieces

10. Tools During the first week of summer vacation, Phil made 1 new friend. The second week he made 3 new friends. The third week he made 5 new friends. If the pattern continued, how many new friends would Phil make during the eighth week of summer vacation?

You can use objects to model problems. Each cube can represent 1 friend. Each tower can represent 1 week.

11. Construct Arguments Eduardo spent $3.78 on groceries. He paid with a $5 bill. How do you know that his change included at least two pennies?

12. Extend Your Thinking Maura made these three block towers. If she continued the pattern, how many blocks would a 10-story tower have? How many blocks would a 100-story tower have?

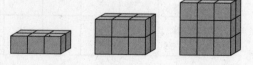

© Pearson Education, Inc. 4

Name _____

Another Look!

Number of Figure	1	2	3	4	5
Number of Squares	2	4	6		

Find a pattern to complete the table.

Step 1	**Step 2**	**Step 3**
Look at the pattern. See how the figure has changed.\n\nEach figure grows by 1 square in height and 1 square in width.	Make the next two figures.	The rule is "multiply the figure number by 2." Fill in the table.

Number of Figure	1	2	3	4	5
Number of Squares	2	4	6	8	10

In **1** through **3**, use patterns to find the missing numbers in each table.

1.

Number of Stories	1	2	3	4	5	
Number of Blocks		3	4	5		7

2.

Length of 1 Side	1	2	3	4	5
Sum of All Sides	5	10	15		

3.

Number of Stories	1	2	3	4	5
Number of Blocks	2	6	12		

4. Lindy made three block towers which are shown below. The table shows her pattern. If she continued the pattern, how many blocks would the next tower have?

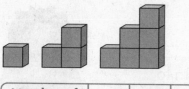

Number of Stories	1	2	3	4
Number of Blocks	1	3	6	

5. Formulate a Plan Jessica had 129 comic books. She sold her entire comic book collection to a store. One of her books was rare and worth $43. All the rest were worth $3. How much did Jessica receive for all of her comic books?

Look for a hidden question.

6. Use the pattern shown below to complete the table.

Number of Stories	1	2	3	4	5	
Number of Blocks	3	6	9			30

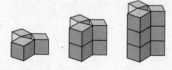

7. Tools Wes made three block towers which are shown below. He recorded his pattern. If he continued the pattern, how many blocks would a 100-story tower have?

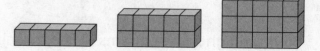

8. Which is the rule for the table below?

Input	3	9	4	7
Output	7	13	8	11

A Add 4.
B Multiply by 2.
C Multiply by 4.
D Add 5.

9. Extend Your Thinking Look at the towers in Exercise 7 above. If you only saw the first two towers, would you be able to find the pattern? Explain.

© Pearson Education, Inc. 4

Name _____

1. **Connect** An office supply store is having a sale. For every 4 packs of paper you buy, you get 1 pack free. If you know the number of packs of paper purchased, what rule can you use to find the number of free packs of paper?

every 4 packs get 1 extra free

Applying Math Processes
- How does this problem connect to previous ones?
- What is my plan?
- How can I use tools?
- How can I use number sense?
- How can I communicate and represent my thinking?
- How can I organize and record information?
- How can I explain my work?
- How can I justify my answer?

2. **Number Sense** For the sale in Exercise 1, if you buy 16 packs of paper, how many packs will you get free?

4

3. **Represent** A tour bus runs 9 times a day, 6 days a week. The bus can carry 30 passengers. Write and solve an equation to find the greatest number of people who can ride the tour bus each day.

(9×6) 54 270

4. **Analyze Information** Emily buys a sandwich, salad, and drink. If she pays with a $20 bill, how much change will she receive?

	Item	Price
DATA	Sandwich	$5.75
	Salad	$3.25
	Drink	$1.45

A $10.55
B $9.65
C $9.55
D $9.45

5. **Extend Your Thinking** A community center has adopted 2 miles, or 3,520 yards, of a highway to pick up trash along the side of the road. Volunteers are divided into 7 groups. Each group is assigned an equal length of highway to clean up. How many yards will each group clean up? Explain.

050 2r6
7⟌3520

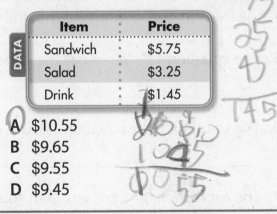

Be sure to interpret any remainder you find.

TOPIC 9 Number Sense

Error Search

Find each solution that is not correct. Circle what is wrong and give the correct solution for the equation.

1. $54 \div b = 6; b = 9$

2. $275 + h = 600; h = 425$

3. $18 = 50 - m; m = 32$

4. $32 = 4 \times k; k = 6$

Reasoning

Write whether each statement is true or false. If you write false, change the numbers or words so that the statement is true.

5. The equation $17 - q = 8$ has the same solution as the equation $36 = 4 \times q$.

_____

6. The solution to the equation $1{,}800 \div a = 1{,}800$ is $a = 0$.

_____

7. The expression $60 \div p$ is less than $40 \div p$ for all values of p that are greater than 1.

_____

8. If 3 is added to both sides of the equation $16 = 10 + 6$, the equation will still be true.

_____

9. The solution to the equation $8 \times w = 64$ is $w = 9$.

_____

10. To solve $150 = x - 70$, you should ask yourself, "What number can I add to 70 to get 150?"

_____

© Pearson Education, Inc. 4

Name _____

Reteaching

Set A | pages 465–470

Write = or ≠ in the ◯.

872 ◯ 8 hundreds + 7 tens + 2 ones

Write the expression on the right as a number.

8 hundreds + 7 tens + 2 ones =
800 + 70 + 2 = 872

So, 872 = 8 hundreds + 7 tens + 2 ones.

Remember that when two numerical expressions are not equal (≠), you can use the symbols < or > to compare the expressions.

Write <, >, or = in each ◯.

1. $12 + 18$ ◯ 34

2. $30 - 8$ ◯ 11×2

3. 651 ◯ 6 hundreds + 1 ten + 5 ones

4. $21 \div 3$ ◯ $12 - 5$

Set B | pages 471–476

Solve $c + 7 = 13$.

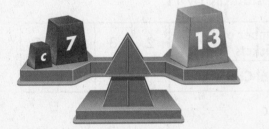

Think: What number can I add to 7 to get 13?

$6 + 7 = 13$

So, $c = 6$.

Remember that you can use mental math to solve addition and subtraction equations.

Solve each equation.

1. $n - 4 = 13$ 2. $120 - y = 80$

3. $19 = z + 4$ 4. $40 + b = 52$

5. $28 = v + 8$ 6. $800 = 1,000 - h$

Set C | pages 477–482

Solve $a \times 3 = 33$.

Use digital tools to solve these and other Reteaching problems.

Think: What number can I multiply by 3 to get 33?

$11 \times 3 = 33$

So, $a = 11$.

Remember that you can check your solutions by using inverse operations.

Solve each equation.

1. $4 \times k = 24$ 2. $100 = 5 \times g$

3. $60 \div b = 6$ 4. $81 = 9 \times h$

5. $4 = v \div 5$ 6. $600 \div w = 200$

Set D pages 483–488

Write a rule for the table.

Item Cost	$4	$11	$15	$12	$9
Selling Price	$8	$22	$30	$24	$18

Compare each pair of numbers. Look for a pattern.

In each pair, the selling price is twice the item cost. A rule for the table is "multiply the item cost by 2."

Remember that once you find a rule for a table, you must check that your rule works for all pairs of numbers in the table.

Find a rule for each table. Use your rule to complete the table.

1.

Tammy's Age	4	8	10	13	18
Kendall's Age	2	6		11	

Set E pages 489–494

Maria earns $8 per hour babysitting. She uses a rule to find how much she will earn.

Rule: Multiply by 8.

Make a table to show the pattern.

Number of Hours	1	2	3	4	5
Maria's Earnings	$8	$16	$24	$32	$40

Remember that a pattern is a set of numbers or shapes that repeats according to a rule.

Use the rule to complete each table.

1. Rule: Multiply by 11.

Number of Tickets	1	2	3	4	5
Total Cost					

Set F pages 495–500

Craig made three block towers. Draw the next two towers. Complete the table.

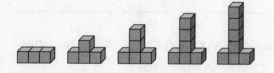

Each tower has 3 blocks as a base. With each additional tower, 1 more block is stacked in the middle.

Figure Number	1	2	3	4	5
Number of Blocks	3	4	5	6	7

Remember to look for a rule that describes how to use the figure number to find the number of blocks.

Draw the next two towers in the pattern. Find the missing numbers in the table.

1.

Figure Number	1	2	3	4	5
Number of Blocks	4	5	6		

© Pearson Education, Inc. 4

1. Nicole puts the same number of flowers in each vase. How many vases does she need for 32 flowers?

Number of Flowers	16	56	32	48	24
Number of Vases	2	7		6	3

A 8 vases

B 7 vases

C 5 vases

D 4 vases

2. What is the missing number that will keep the pan balance level?

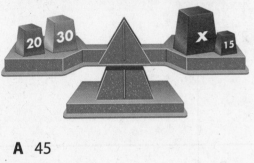

A 45

B 35

C 30

D 25

3. Write <, >, or = in the circle to make the number sentence true.

19 − 4 ◯ 5 × 3

4. Donna read 34 books last year, and Arlene read 26 books. The total number of books read by both students is 3 times the number of books Diego read last year. How many books did Diego read last year?

A 57 books

B 30 books

C 20 books

D 15 books

5. Which rule tells how to find the number of triangles if you know the number of circles?

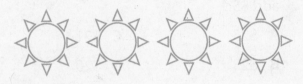

A Add 1.

B Multiply by 8.

C Add 8.

D Divide by 8.

6. Ben used blocks to make the first 3 towers of a pattern. If he continues the pattern, how many blocks will he need to make the 6th tower?

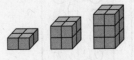

7. The table shows the cost of adult tickets to the zoo. What is the rule for the table?

Number of Tickets	3	2	6	8	5
Total Cost	$27	$18	$54	$72	$45

A Multiply by 9.

B Divide by 7.

C Add 16.

D None of the above

---

8. A drive-in movie theater charges $5 per car plus $3 for each passenger in the car. Use the rule below to find the cost for a car with 6 passengers.

Rule: To find the total cost, multiply the number of passengers by $3 and then add $5.

A $25

C $21

B $23

D $20

---

9. Vince has scored 3 times as many points as Paul so far this season. Vince has scored 120 points. Solve the equation $3 \times p = 120$ to find the number of points Paul has scored.

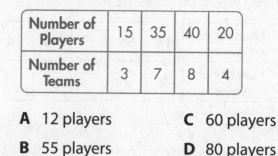

---

10. The table shows the number of players on a basketball team. If there are 12 teams in a tournament, how many players will there be?

Number of Players	15	35	40	20
Number of Teams	3	7	8	4

A 12 players

C 60 players

B 55 players

D 80 players

---

11. Which number can you **NOT** put in both blanks to make the inequality true?

$15 + \underline{\quad} < 20 - \underline{\quad}$

A 0

B 1

C 2

D 3

---

12. When Regina went to bed last night, the outside temperature was 68°F. By morning, the temperature had dropped to 52°F. Solve the equation $68 - x = 52$ to find how many degrees the temperature dropped overnight.

© Pearson Education, Inc. 4

Fraction Meanings and Equivalence

Essential Questions:
What are different meanings of fractions?
How can fractions be compared?

The change in seasons is a pattern caused by the placement of the Earth in relation to the Sun.

The seasons have a huge impact on how we lead our daily lives.

I better prepare for the upcoming season! Here's a project on seasons and fractions.

Math and Science Project: Seasons

Do Research Use the Internet or other sources to find information about patterns of change in the different seasons where you live. Include information about where the Sun's light directly strikes the Earth during each season.

Journal: Write a Report Include what you found. Also in your report:

- Include the dates this year that spring, summer, fall, and winter officially begin.

- Officially, each season is about 3 months long. Write the number of months for each season as a fraction of the year. Then write the fraction in simplest form.

Name _____

Review What You Know

Vocabulary

Choose the best term from the box. Write it on the blank.

- =
- ≠
- equation
- numerical expression

1. The symbol _____ is used to indicate two expressions are equal.

2. A _____ contains numbers and at least one operation.

3. A number sentence that uses the equal sign (=) to show that two expressions have the same value is

called a(n) _____.

Division

Divide.

4. 454 ÷ 5   **5.** 600 ÷ 3

6. 336 ÷ 4   **7.** 625 ÷ 5

8. 387 ÷ 3   **9.** 878 ÷ 7

Fraction Concepts

Name the number of equal parts in each figure.

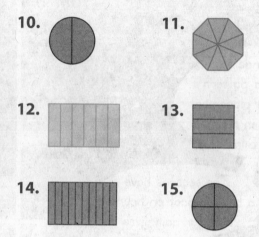

10.   **11.**

12.   **13.**

14.   **15.**

16. Explain Is $\frac{1}{4}$ of the figure below red? Why or why not?

Numerical Expressions

17. Janet gets $25 a week to buy lunch at school. She spends $4 each day and saves the rest. Which expression can be used to find how much money Janet will save at the end of the 5 days?

A $(4 \times 5) + 25$
B $25 + (5 - 4)$
C $(25 - 5) + 4$
D $25 - (5 \times 4)$

© Pearson Education, Inc. 4

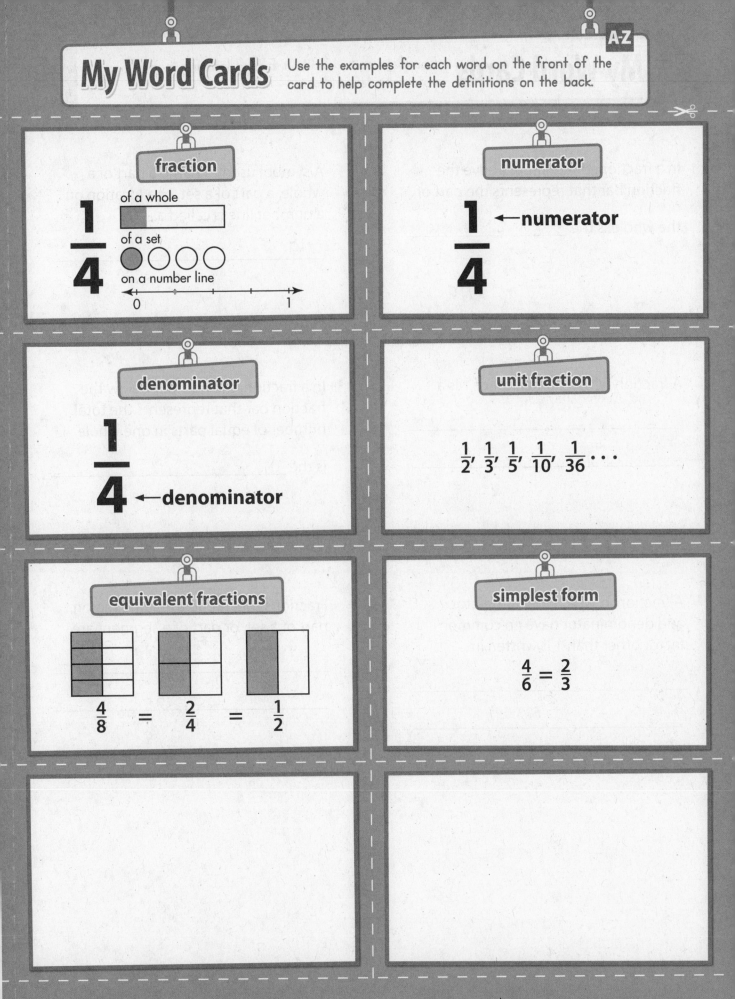

A-Z

My Word Cards

Use the examples for each word on the front of the card to help complete the definitions on the back.

fraction

$\dfrac{1}{4}$

of a whole

of a set

on a number line

0   1

numerator

$\dfrac{1}{4}$ ← numerator

denominator

$\dfrac{1}{4}$ ← denominator

unit fraction

$\dfrac{1}{2}, \dfrac{1}{3}, \dfrac{1}{5}, \dfrac{1}{10}, \dfrac{1}{36} \cdots$

equivalent fractions

$\dfrac{4}{8}$ = $\dfrac{2}{4}$ = $\dfrac{1}{2}$

simplest form

$\dfrac{4}{6} = \dfrac{2}{3}$

My Word Cards

Complete each definition. Extend learning by writing your own definitions.

In a fraction, the number above the fraction bar that represents the part of the whole is the _____.

A symbol used to name a part of a whole, a part of a set, or a location on a number line is called a

_____.

A fraction with a numerator of 1 is a

_____

_____.

In a fraction, the number below the fraction bar that represents the total number of equal parts in one whole

is the _____.

A fraction in which the numerator and denominator have no common factor other than 1 is written in

_____

_____.

Fractions that name the same region, part of a set, or part of a segment are

_____

_____.

510

© Pearson Education, Inc. 4

Name _____

Solve & Share

Complete each number line to show about where the given fraction is located. Tell how you decided.

⊙ **TEKS 4.3A** Represent a fraction $\frac{a}{b}$ as a sum of fractions $\frac{1}{b}$, where a and b are whole numbers and $b > 0$, including when $a > b$.
Mathematical Process Standards 4.1A, 4.1C, 4.1D, 4.1E

1. $\frac{2}{3}$

$\longleftarrow$|————|——————————————$\longrightarrow$
   0        $\frac{1}{3}$

Digital Resources at PearsonTexas.com

Solve   Learn   Glossary   Check   Tools   Games

2. $\frac{4}{5}$

$\longleftarrow$|————|——————————————$\longrightarrow$
   0      $\frac{1}{5}$

You can use number sense to think about the whole and equal parts.

3. $\frac{8}{8}$

$\longleftarrow$|————|——————————————$\longrightarrow$
   0   $\frac{1}{8}$

4. $\frac{6}{4}$

$\longleftarrow$|————|——————————————$\longrightarrow$
   0   $\frac{1}{4}$

Look Back!

Create and Use Representations If you know where $\frac{1}{3}$ is on the number line, what would you do to find 1 whole unit?

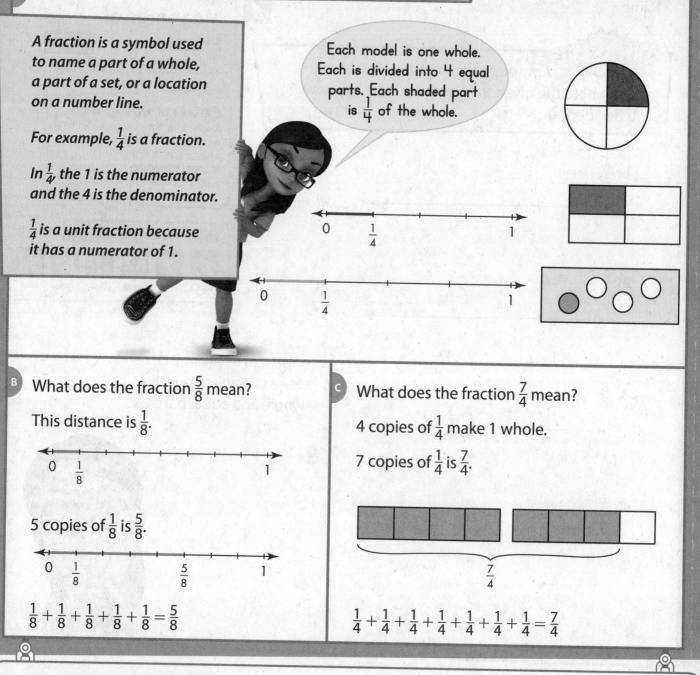

A

A fraction is a symbol used to name a part of a whole, a part of a set, or a location on a number line.

For example, $\frac{1}{4}$ is a fraction.

In $\frac{1}{4}$, the 1 is the numerator and the 4 is the denominator.

$\frac{1}{4}$ is a unit fraction because it has a numerator of 1.

Each model is one whole. Each is divided into 4 equal parts. Each shaded part is $\frac{1}{4}$ of the whole.

B What does the fraction $\frac{5}{8}$ mean?

This distance is $\frac{1}{8}$.

5 copies of $\frac{1}{8}$ is $\frac{5}{8}$.

$$\frac{1}{8} + \frac{1}{8} + \frac{1}{8} + \frac{1}{8} + \frac{1}{8} = \frac{5}{8}$$

C What does the fraction $\frac{7}{4}$ mean?

4 copies of $\frac{1}{4}$ make 1 whole.

7 copies of $\frac{1}{4}$ is $\frac{7}{4}$.

$$\frac{1}{4} + \frac{1}{4} + \frac{1}{4} + \frac{1}{4} + \frac{1}{4} + \frac{1}{4} + \frac{1}{4} = \frac{7}{4}$$

Do You Understand?

Convince Me! Park Su said, "The distance from 0 to A is greater than the distance from 0 to B." Karina said, "Yes, but both point A and point B show $\frac{1}{10} + \frac{1}{10} + \frac{1}{10} + \frac{1}{10} + \frac{1}{10} = \frac{5}{10}$." Is Karina correct? Explain.

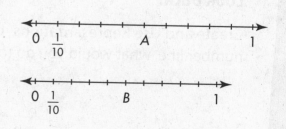

© Pearson Education, Inc. 4

☆ Guided Practice *

1. What fraction does the model show?

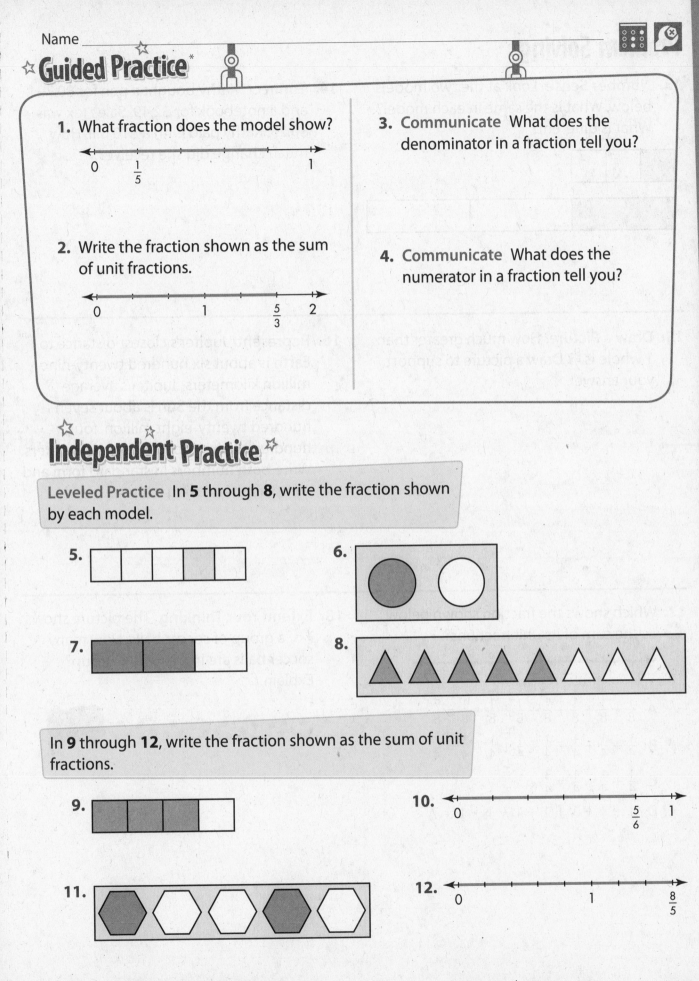

   0    $\frac{1}{5}$ 1

2. Write the fraction shown as the sum of unit fractions.

   0   1 $\frac{5}{3}$ 2

3. **Communicate** What does the denominator in a fraction tell you?

4. **Communicate** What does the numerator in a fraction tell you?

Independent Practice ☆

Leveled Practice In **5** through **8**, write the fraction shown by each model.

5.

6.

7.

8.

In **9** through **12**, write the fraction shown as the sum of unit fractions.

9.

10.   0 $\frac{5}{6}$ 1

11.

12.   0   1 $\frac{8}{5}$

Problem Solving

13. Number Sense Look at the two models below. What is the same in each model? What is different?

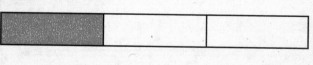

14. Connect Kathy bought a pen for $0.79 and a notebook for $2.49. Sales tax was $0.25. Kathy paid with a $10 bill. How much change did she receive?

15. Draw a Picture How much greater than 1 whole is $\frac{9}{7}$? Draw a picture to support your answer.

16. Represent Jupiter's closest distance to Earth is about six hundred twenty-nine million kilometers. Jupiter's average distance from the Sun is about seven hundred twenty-eight million, four hundred twelve thousand, ten kilometers. Write both numbers in standard form and compare them using $<$ or $>$.

17. ★ Which shows the fraction shown below as the sum of its unit fractions?

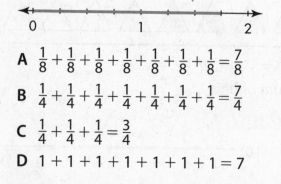

A $\frac{1}{8}+\frac{1}{8}+\frac{1}{8}+\frac{1}{8}+\frac{1}{8}+\frac{1}{8}+\frac{1}{8}=\frac{7}{8}$

B $\frac{1}{4}+\frac{1}{4}+\frac{1}{4}+\frac{1}{4}+\frac{1}{4}+\frac{1}{4}+\frac{1}{4}=\frac{7}{4}$

C $\frac{1}{4}+\frac{1}{4}+\frac{1}{4}=\frac{3}{4}$

D $1+1+1+1+1+1+1=7$

18. Extend Your Thinking The picture shows $\frac{4}{5}$ of a group of soccer balls. How many soccer balls are in the whole group? Explain.

© Pearson Education, Inc. 4

Homework 10-1
Meanings of Fractions

Another Look!

What fractions are modeled below?

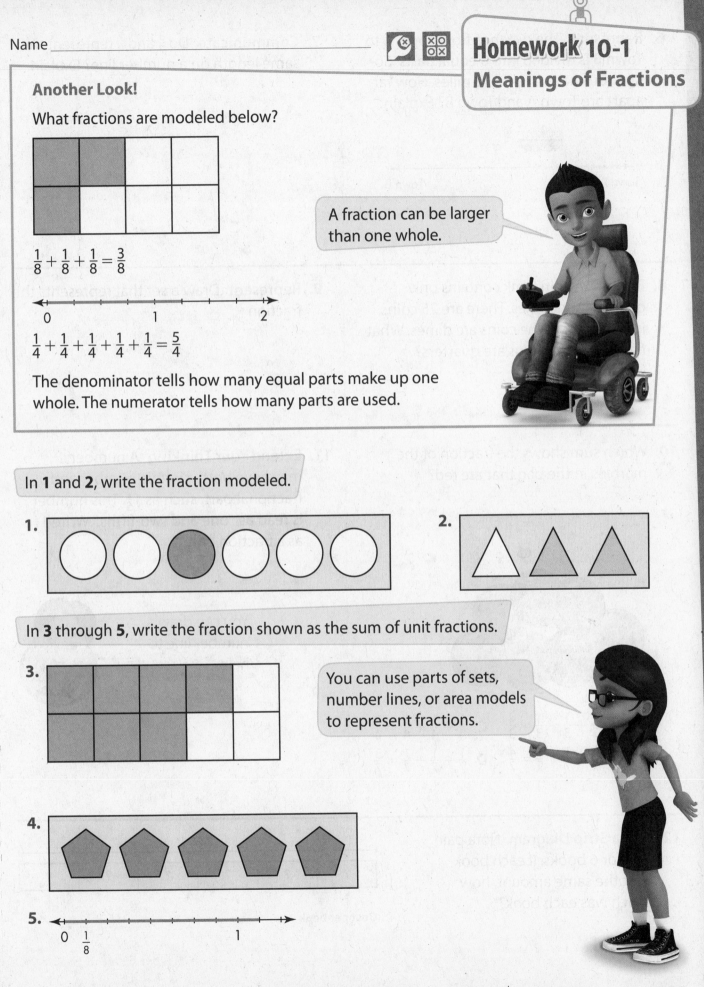

$\frac{1}{8} + \frac{1}{8} + \frac{1}{8} = \frac{3}{8}$

$\frac{1}{4} + \frac{1}{4} + \frac{1}{4} + \frac{1}{4} + \frac{1}{4} = \frac{5}{4}$

The denominator tells how many equal parts make up one whole. The numerator tells how many parts are used.

A fraction can be larger than one whole.

In **1** and **2**, write the fraction modeled.

1.

2.

In **3** through **5**, write the fraction shown as the sum of unit fractions.

3.

You can use parts of sets, number lines, or area models to represent fractions.

4.

5.

6. Represent The distance from Town A to Town B is divided into 8 equal parts. So far, a bus has traveled 12 miles. How far apart are Town A and Town B? Explain.

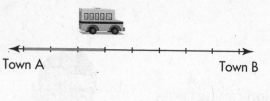

Town A   Town B

7. Communicate Do $\frac{3}{7}$ and $\frac{7}{3}$ represent the same length on a number line? Explain.

8. Reason A coin bank contains only quarters and dimes. There are 25 coins in all. Seven of the coins are dimes. What fraction of the coins are quarters?

9. Represent Draw a set that represents the fraction $\frac{3}{5}$.

10. ⭐ Which sum shows the fraction of the marbles in the bag that are red?

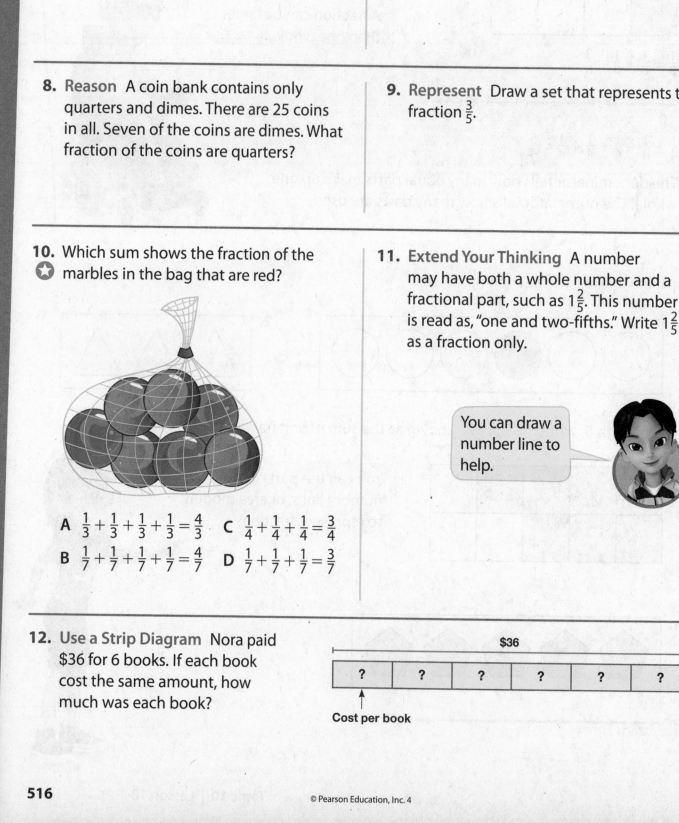

A $\frac{1}{3} + \frac{1}{3} + \frac{1}{3} + \frac{1}{3} = \frac{4}{3}$ C $\frac{1}{4} + \frac{1}{4} + \frac{1}{4} = \frac{3}{4}$

B $\frac{1}{7} + \frac{1}{7} + \frac{1}{7} + \frac{1}{7} = \frac{4}{7}$ D $\frac{1}{7} + \frac{1}{7} + \frac{1}{7} = \frac{3}{7}$

11. Extend Your Thinking A number may have both a whole number and a fractional part, such as $1\frac{2}{5}$. This number is read as, "one and two-fifths." Write $1\frac{2}{5}$ as a fraction only.

You can draw a number line to help.

12. Use a Strip Diagram Nora paid $36 for 6 books. If each book cost the same amount, how much was each book?

$36

| ? | ? | ? | ? | ? | ? |

↑
Cost per book

516

© Pearson Education, Inc. 4

Name _____

Solve & Share

Find as many fractions as you can that are equal to $\frac{1}{3}$. Write each fraction and use drawings or words to explain your work. *Solve this problem any way you choose.*

TEKS 4.3C Determine if two given fractions are equivalent using a variety of methods.
Mathematical Process Standards 4.1A, 4.1C, 4.1D, 4.1E, 4.1G

Digital Resources at PearsonTexas.com

| Solve | Learn | Glossary | Check | Tools | Games |

You can use tools. Fraction strips can help you solve this problem. *Show your work in the space above!*

Look Back!

Justify Explain how two different fractions can both be equivalent to $\frac{1}{3}$.

What Are Some Ways to Name the Same Part of a Whole?

Equivalent fractions name the same part of a whole. Someone ate part of the pizza shown in the picture.

James says that $\frac{3}{4}$ of the pizza is left.

Cardell says that $\frac{6}{8}$ of the pizza is left.

How can you determine if $\frac{3}{4}$ and $\frac{6}{8}$ are equivalent fractions?

There is more than one way to determine if two fractions are equivalent.

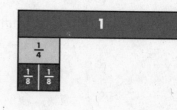

Find equivalent fractions.

B You can use fraction strips to find or determine equivalent fractions.

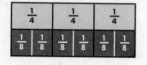

Both $\frac{3}{4}$ and $\frac{6}{8}$ name the same part of a whole. So, $\frac{3}{4}$ and $\frac{6}{8}$ are equivalent fractions.

C You can multiply the numerator and denominator by the same number to find an equivalent fraction.

$$\frac{3}{4} = \frac{6}{8}$$
$\times 2$

So, $\frac{3}{4}$ and $\frac{6}{8}$ are equivalent fractions.

D You can divide the numerator and denominator by the same number to find an equivalent fraction.

$$\frac{6}{8} = \frac{3}{4}$$
$\div 2$

So, $\frac{3}{4}$ and $\frac{6}{8}$ are equivalent fractions.

Do You Understand?

Convince Me! The model shows that $\frac{1}{4}$ and $\frac{2}{8}$ are equivalent fractions. Name another fraction that is equivalent to $\frac{1}{4}$. Use the drawing to show that your fraction is equivalent to $\frac{1}{4}$.

© Pearson Education, Inc. 4

☆ Guided Practice *

In **1** through **6**, multiply or divide to find an equivalent fraction.

1. $\times\,3$

$$\frac{2}{3} = \frac{\square}{\square}$$

$\times\,3$

2. $\div\,5$

$$\frac{5}{10} = \frac{\square}{\square}$$

$\div\,5$

3. $\frac{5}{6} = \frac{\square}{12}$

4. $\frac{10}{12} = \frac{5}{\square}$

5. $\frac{3}{12} = \frac{\square}{4}$

6. $\frac{3}{4} = \frac{9}{\square}$

7. Suppose a pizza was cut into 12 equal-sized slices. $\frac{3}{4}$ of the pizza is left. How many slices are left? Explain.

8. Construct Arguments Josh, Lisa, and Vicki each ate $\frac{1}{2}$ of a pizza. Their pizzas were the same size, but Josh ate 1 slice, Lisa ate 3 slices, and Vicki ate 4 slices. How is this possible?

Independent Practice ☆

Leveled Practice In **9** through **16**, multiply or divide to find equivalent fractions.

You can check your answers using fraction strips.

9. $\times\,5$

$$\frac{1}{2} = \frac{\square}{\square}$$

$\times\,5$

10. $\div\,3$

$$\frac{9}{12} = \frac{\square}{\square}$$

$\div\,3$

11. $\times\,2$

$$\frac{5}{6} = \frac{\square}{\square}$$

$\times\,2$

12. $\div\,2$

$$\frac{2}{4} = \frac{\square}{\square}$$

$\div\,2$

13. $\frac{10}{10} = \frac{1}{\square}$

14. $\frac{3}{4} = \frac{6}{\square}$

15. $\frac{1}{2} = \frac{\square}{6}$

16. $\frac{3}{5} = \frac{6}{\square}$

In **17** through **20**, find an equivalent fraction for each.

17. $\frac{4}{6}$

18. $\frac{2}{10}$

19. $\frac{1}{3}$

20. $\frac{3}{5}$

*For another example, see Set B on page 549.

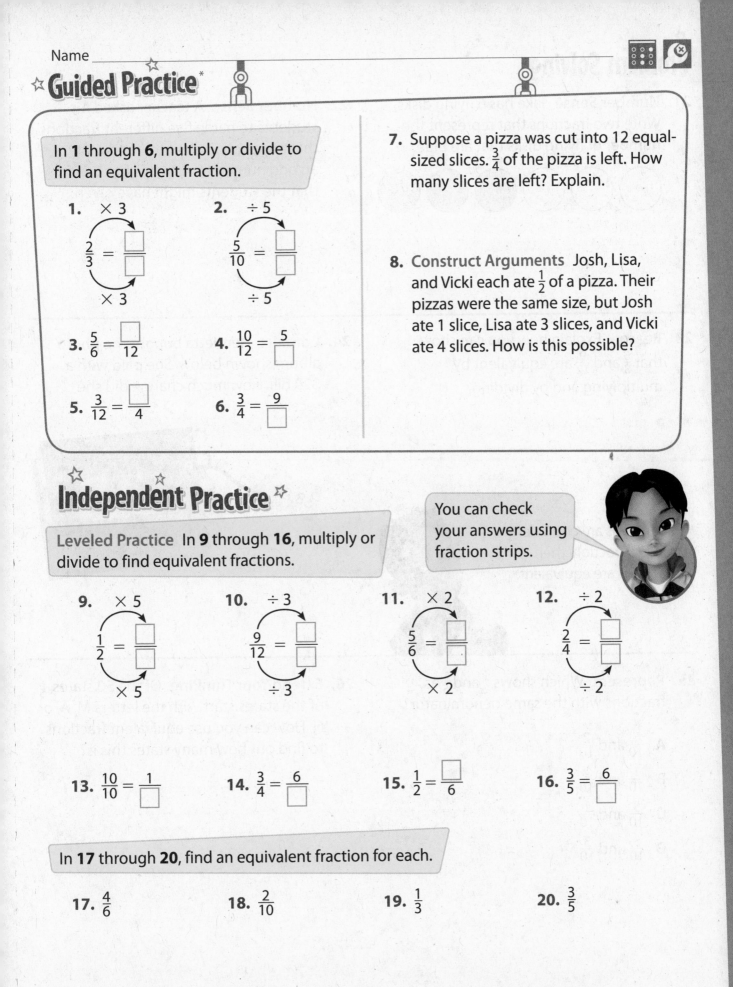

Problem Solving

21. Number Sense Jake has 6 flying disks. Write two fractions that represent the number of flying disks that are blue.

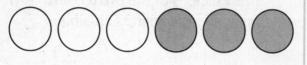

22. Number Sense A teacher asked his students to name five different fractions that are all equivalent to $\frac{1}{2}$ and that have an odd numerator. List five fractions that the students might have given.

23. Reason Explain how you can show that $\frac{6}{8}$ and $\frac{9}{12}$ are equivalent by multiplying and by dividing.

If 2 fractions are equivalent to a third fraction, then all 3 fractions are equivalent.

24. Connect Henrietta bought the photo album shown below. She paid with a $20 bill. How much change did she receive?

$8.29

25. Represent Which shows $\frac{1}{2}$ and $\frac{1}{5}$ as fractions with the same denominator?

A $\frac{5}{10}$ and $\frac{2}{10}$

B $\frac{1}{10}$ and $\frac{2}{10}$

C $\frac{5}{10}$ and $\frac{1}{10}$

D $\frac{5}{10}$ and $\frac{3}{10}$

26. Extend Your Thinking Of the 50 states, $\frac{2}{5}$ of the states start with the letters M, A, or N. How can you use equivalent fractions to find out how many states this is?

© Pearson Education, Inc. 4

Another Look!

Write a fraction equivalent to $\frac{1}{2}$ and another fraction equivalent to $\frac{10}{12}$.

Use multiplication to write a fraction equivalent to $\frac{1}{2}$.

Multiply the numerator and denominator by the same number.

$$\frac{1}{2} = \frac{3}{6}$$ ×3, ×3

three times as many shaded parts

three times as many parts in all

$\frac{1}{2}$ and $\frac{3}{6}$ are equivalent fractions.

$$\frac{10}{12} = \frac{5}{6}$$ ÷2, ÷2

You could instead use division.

$\frac{10}{12}$ and $\frac{5}{6}$ are equivalent fractions.

In **1** through **4**, find the missing number.

1. $\frac{1}{4} = \frac{\square}{8}$

2. $\frac{9}{12} = \frac{\square}{4}$

3. $\frac{2}{3} = \frac{\square}{6}$

4. $\frac{4}{5} = \frac{\square}{10}$

In **5** through **8**, multiply to find an equivalent fraction.

5. $\frac{1}{3} =$

6. $\frac{1}{2} =$

7. $\frac{1}{6} =$

8. $\frac{3}{4} =$

In **9** through **16**, divide to find an equivalent fraction.

9. $\frac{8}{12} =$

10. $\frac{12}{16} =$

11. $\frac{2}{4} =$

12. $\frac{2}{6} =$

13. $\frac{4}{10} =$

14. $\frac{5}{10} =$

15. $\frac{6}{10} =$

16. $\frac{6}{8} =$

17. Number Sense Write two fractions that represent the part of the rectangle that is shaded.

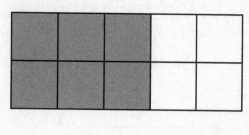

18. Number Sense A teacher asked her class to name three different fractions that are all equivalent to $\frac{2}{3}$ and that have an odd denominator. List three fractions that the students might have given.

19. Reason Ned walks $\frac{6}{10}$ of a mile to school. Fred walks $\frac{9}{15}$ of a mile to school. Who walks farther? Explain.

20. Communicate When asked to write a fraction equivalent to $\frac{3}{4}$, Josie wrote $\frac{9}{16}$. Was she correct? Explain.

21. Connect Ted ate 4 pieces of pizza from the pizza below. What unit fraction describes the amount of pizza Ted ate?

22. Extend Your Thinking In Missy's sports-card collection, $\frac{3}{4}$ of the cards are baseball cards. In Frank's collection, $\frac{8}{12}$ are baseball cards. Frank says they have the same fraction of baseball cards. Is he correct? Explain.

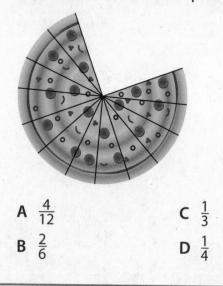

A $\frac{4}{12}$ **C** $\frac{1}{3}$

B $\frac{2}{6}$ **D** $\frac{1}{4}$

23. The fourth-grade students are running a food drive. They want to collect 1,000 cans of food. They need to collect 8 times as many cans as they already have in order to reach their goal. How many cans do they already have?

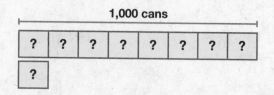

© Pearson Education, Inc. 4

Name _____

Solve & Share

Find fractions equivalent to $\frac{8}{12}$. Which of those fractions seems the simplest to you? Explain why. **Solve this problem any way you choose.**

⊙ TEKS 4.3C Determine if two given fractions are equivalent using a variety of methods.
Mathematical Process Standards 4.1C, 4.1E, 4.1G

You can **construct arguments.** In math, what does it mean to be simplest? *Show your work in the space below!*

Digital Resources at PearsonTexas.com

Solve Learn Glossary Check Tools Games

Look Back!

Number Sense What is the only number you can divide evenly into both the numerator and denominator of the simplest fraction you found?

How Do You Write a Fraction in Simplest Form?

A

A fraction is in simplest form when the numerator and denominator have no common factor other than 1.

Jason has run part way around the track. Write the part of the track that Jason has run in simplest form.

$\frac{4}{12}$ of the way

If the numerator and denominator are even numbers, they have 2 as a common factor.

Divide the numerator and denominator by a common factor.

B ## One Way

Write $\frac{4}{12}$ in simplest form by dividing twice.

$$\frac{4}{12} = \frac{2}{6} = \frac{1}{3}$$

÷ 2   ÷ 2

Since 4 and 12 are even numbers, 2 is a common factor.

Since 2 and 6 are even numbers, 2 is a common factor.

C ## Another Way

Since 4 is a common factor of 4 and 12, write $\frac{4}{12}$ in simplest form by dividing by 4.

$$\frac{4}{12} = \frac{1}{3}$$

÷ 4

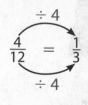

Either way, the simplest form of $\frac{4}{12}$ equals $\frac{1}{3}$. Jason has run $\frac{1}{3}$ of the way around the track.

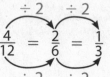

Do You Understand?

Convince Me! Carrie said, "The numerator has to be 1 or the fraction cannot be in simplest form." Is Carrie correct? Use the fraction at the right to explain.

$\frac{3}{4}$

© Pearson Education, Inc. 4

☆ Guided Practice *

In **1** through **6**, write each fraction in simplest form.

1. $\frac{6}{8}$　　　2. $\frac{15}{45}$

3. $\frac{10}{100}$　　　4. $\frac{16}{80}$

5. $\frac{21}{33}$　　　6. $\frac{12}{14}$

7. **Explain** How can you tell $\frac{4}{9}$ is in simplest form?

8. Jamal ran $\frac{8}{12}$ of the way around a track. Write this fraction in simplest form.

☆ Independent Practice ☆

In **9** through **33**, write each fraction in simplest form. If it is in simplest form, then write *simplest form*.

9. $\frac{3}{12}$　　10. $\frac{2}{10}$　　11. $\frac{4}{8}$　　12. $\frac{12}{16}$　　13. $\frac{4}{6}$

14. $\frac{2}{5}$　　15. $\frac{2}{6}$　　16. $\frac{3}{16}$　　17. $\frac{8}{10}$　　18. $\frac{5}{12}$

19. $\frac{3}{7}$　　20. $\frac{8}{20}$　　21. $\frac{9}{10}$　　22. $\frac{9}{15}$　　23. $\frac{12}{20}$

24. $\frac{5}{6}$　　25. $\frac{3}{9}$　　26. $\frac{15}{18}$　　27. $\frac{30}{40}$　　28. $\frac{30}{35}$

29. $\frac{2}{3}$　　30. $\frac{7}{14}$　　31. $\frac{9}{16}$　　32. $\frac{4}{12}$　　33. $\frac{5}{15}$

Problem Solving

In **34** and **35**, use the table at the right.

34. What fraction of the band members practice for more than 2 hours a week? Write your answer in simplest form.

35. What fraction of the band members spend more time on lessons than on practice? Write your answer in simplest form.

Weekly Band Log		
Band Member	**Lessons (Hours)**	**Practice (Hours)**
Will	1.5	1
Kaitlyn	1	3.5
Madison	0.75	1.75
Ryan	1.5	1.25
Kirk	1.25	4
Gina	1	0.75

36. Number Sense At the theater complex, 23 movies were shown one day. The ticket sales showed that 78 people attended each show. How many people saw a movie that day at the theater complex?

37. Number Sense Which fraction is **NOT** in simplest form?

A $\frac{3}{7}$

B $\frac{3}{8}$

C $\frac{3}{9}$

D $\frac{3}{10}$

38. Personal Financial Literacy Quincy uses the rule "multiply by 24" to describe how much he has saved after *n* months. Complete the table to show how much Quincy has saved after each number of months.

Months	1	2	3	4	5
Money Saved	$24	$48			

39. Extend Your Thinking Is a unit fraction always in simplest form? Explain.

Math definitions can help you write a precise explanation.

© Pearson Education, Inc. 4

Another Look!

There are 24 students in Jenna's class. Today, 6 students are wearing blue shirts. In simplest form, what fraction of the students are wearing blue shirts?

Use division to write a fraction that is equivalent to $\frac{6}{24}$.

> Continue to divide the numerator and denominator by the same number until the only number you can divide by is 1.

$$\overset{\div 3}{\underset{\div 3}{\frac{6}{24}}} = \overset{\div 2}{\underset{\div 2}{\frac{2}{8}}} = \frac{1}{4}$$

$\frac{2}{8}$ and $\frac{1}{4}$ are both equivalent to $\frac{6}{24}$.

Only $\frac{1}{4}$ is in simplest form.

In Jenna's class, $\frac{1}{4}$ of the students are wearing blue shirts.

In **1** through **4**, find the missing number.

1. $\frac{2}{8} = \frac{\square}{4}$

2. $\frac{15}{20} = \frac{\square}{4}$

3. $\frac{7}{21} = \frac{\square}{3}$

4. $\frac{9}{27} = \frac{\square}{3}$

In **5** through **20**, write each fraction in simplest form.

5. $\frac{6}{10}$

6. $\frac{4}{10}$

7. $\frac{25}{30}$

8. $\frac{24}{32}$

9. $\frac{10}{15}$

10. $\frac{9}{24}$

11. $\frac{21}{28}$

12. $\frac{25}{35}$

13. $\frac{8}{20}$

14. $\frac{9}{18}$

15. $\frac{8}{18}$

16. $\frac{15}{40}$

17. $\frac{2}{18}$

18. $\frac{4}{16}$

19. $\frac{32}{34}$

20. $\frac{12}{26}$

21. Represent What fraction of the shapes are circles? Write your answer in simplest form.

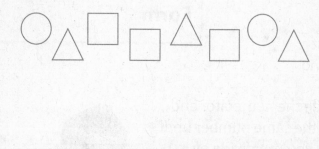

22. From a plate of 18 apple slices, Nancy ate 3. Then Meg came along and ate 4 slices. Jim then ate 3 slices. Bruce took 6 slices for himself and a friend. In simplest form, what fraction of the apple slices are still on the plate?

23. Math and Science The amount of daylight each day changes because of the tilt of the Earth's axis. In Seattle, on the first day of summer, there are 16 hours of daylight. In simplest form, what fraction of the day has daylight?

There are 24 hours in 1 day.

24. Number Sense In simplest form, what fraction of the marbles in the bag are red?

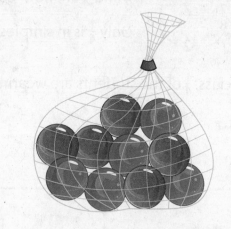

25. Extend Your Thinking Peter knows that when both the numerator and denominator are even numbers, the fraction cannot be in simplest form since each number could be divided by 2. What about when both numbers are odd? Give an example.

26. Which of the following steps can you do to find the simplest form of $\frac{4}{8}$?

A Add 4 to 8 and add 8 to 4.

B Subtract 3 from 4 and subtract 3 from 8.

C Multiply 4 by 4 and multiply 8 by 4.

D Divide 4 by 4 and divide 8 by 4.

© Pearson Education, Inc. 4

Name _____

Solve & Share

How can a point on the number line have more than one fraction name? *Solve this problem any way you choose.*

You can **use tools.** Number lines can help you show equivalent fractions. *Show your work in the space below!*

⊕ **TEKS 4.3G** Represent fractions and decimals to the tenths or hundredths as distances from zero on a number line. Also, 4.3C.
Mathematical Process Standards 4.1C, 4.1D, 4.1F, 4.1G

Digital Resources at PearsonTexas.com

Solve Learn Glossary Check Tools Games

Look Back!

Construct Arguments Why can you always find another fraction name for any fraction point on the number line?

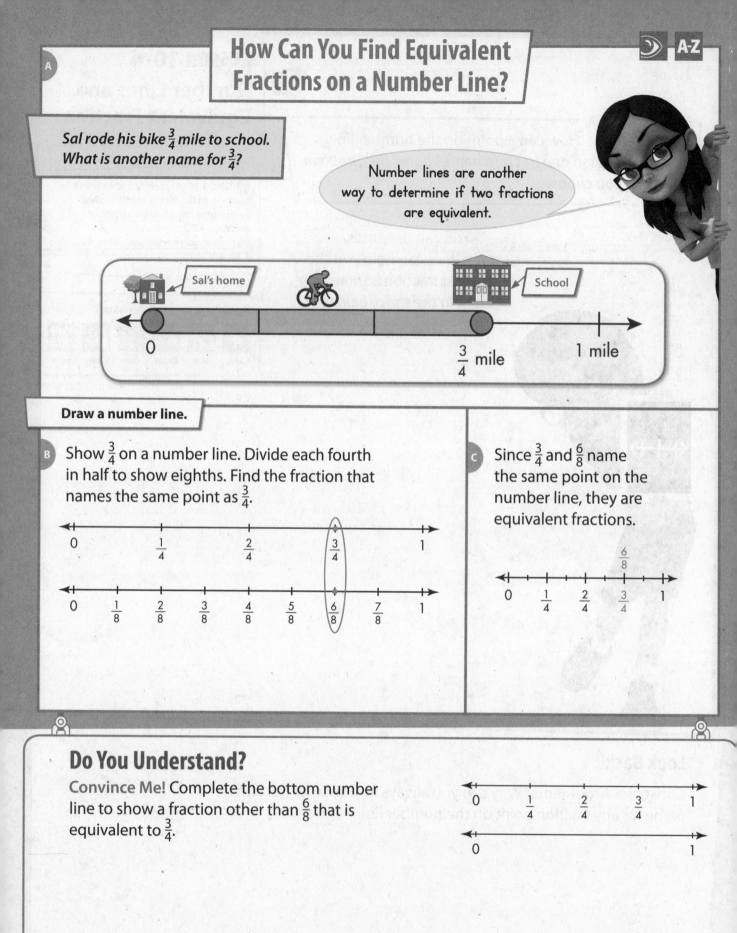

How Can You Find Equivalent Fractions on a Number Line?

A

Sal rode his bike $\frac{3}{4}$ mile to school. What is another name for $\frac{3}{4}$?

Number lines are another way to determine if two fractions are equivalent.

Sal's home   School

0                $\frac{3}{4}$ mile   1 mile

Draw a number line.

B Show $\frac{3}{4}$ on a number line. Divide each fourth in half to show eighths. Find the fraction that names the same point as $\frac{3}{4}$.

0        $\frac{1}{4}$ $\frac{2}{4}$ $\frac{3}{4}$ 1

0    $\frac{1}{8}$ $\frac{2}{8}$ $\frac{3}{8}$ $\frac{4}{8}$ $\frac{5}{8}$ $\frac{6}{8}$ $\frac{7}{8}$ 1

C Since $\frac{3}{4}$ and $\frac{6}{8}$ name the same point on the number line, they are equivalent fractions.

$\frac{6}{8}$

0    $\frac{1}{4}$ $\frac{2}{4}$ $\frac{3}{4}$ 1

Do You Understand?

Convince Me! Complete the bottom number line to show a fraction other than $\frac{6}{8}$ that is equivalent to $\frac{3}{4}$.

0    $\frac{1}{4}$ $\frac{2}{4}$ $\frac{3}{4}$ 1

0   1

© Pearson Education, Inc. 4

Name _____

In **1** through **3**, find an equivalent fraction on the number line.

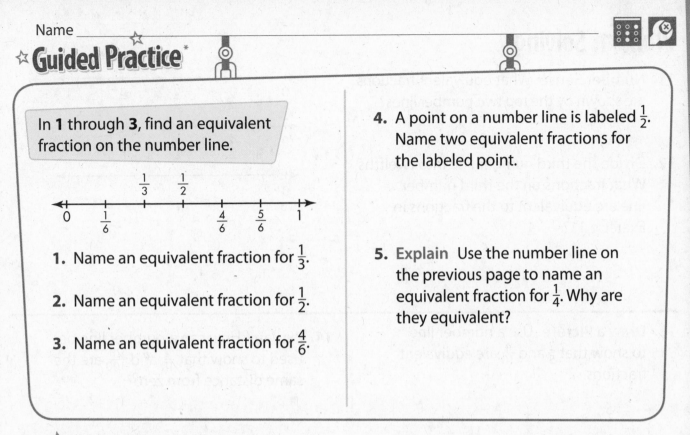

1. Name an equivalent fraction for $\frac{1}{3}$.

2. Name an equivalent fraction for $\frac{1}{2}$.

3. Name an equivalent fraction for $\frac{4}{6}$.

4. A point on a number line is labeled $\frac{1}{2}$. Name two equivalent fractions for the labeled point.

5. **Explain** Use the number line on the previous page to name an equivalent fraction for $\frac{1}{4}$. Why are they equivalent?

☆ Independent Practice ☆

In **6** through **10**, use the number line to find equivalent fractions. Choose the correct answer.

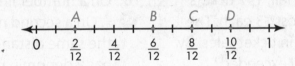

6. Which of the following fractions name an equivalent fraction for point *A*?

   $\frac{3}{4}$ $\frac{2}{3}$ $\frac{1}{6}$ $\frac{1}{4}$

7. **Number Sense** Which of the following fractions does **NOT** name an equivalent fraction for point *B*?

   $\frac{2}{4}$ $\frac{3}{6}$ $\frac{4}{10}$ $\frac{12}{24}$

8. Which of the following fractions name an equivalent fraction for point *C*?

   $\frac{2}{6}$ $\frac{2}{3}$ $\frac{1}{2}$ $\frac{3}{4}$

9. Which of the following fractions name an equivalent fraction for point *D*?

   $\frac{4}{6}$ $\frac{1}{2}$ $\frac{1}{10}$ $\frac{5}{6}$

10. Name two fractions that are equivalent to $\frac{4}{12}$.

There are many names for the same point on a number line.

Problem Solving

11. Number Sense What equivalent fractions are shown by the top two number lines?

12. Divide the third number line into twelfths. What fractions on the third number line are equivalent to the fractions in Exercise 11?

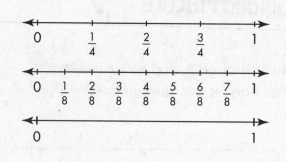

13. Draw a Picture Use a number line to show that $\frac{2}{5}$ and $\frac{4}{10}$ are equivalent fractions.

14. Explain How can a number line be used to show that $\frac{2}{10}$ and $\frac{20}{100}$ are the same distance from zero?

15. Connect At the school fair, 147 tickets were sold. The tickets cost $3 each. The goal was to make $300 in ticket sales. By how much was the goal exceeded?

16. On a number line, point A is located at $\frac{3}{5}$. On a second number line, point B is the same distance from 0 as point A, but has a denominator of 15. What is the numerator of point B?

   A 9
   B 12
   C 15
   D 25

17. Extend Your Thinking Make a number line showing thirds and another number line showing fifths. How does $\frac{2}{3}$ compare to $\frac{4}{5}$? Explain.

© Pearson Education, Inc. 4

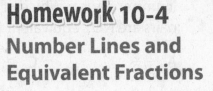

Homework 10-4
Number Lines and Equivalent Fractions

Another Look!

Write two equivalent fractions that name the point shown on the number line.

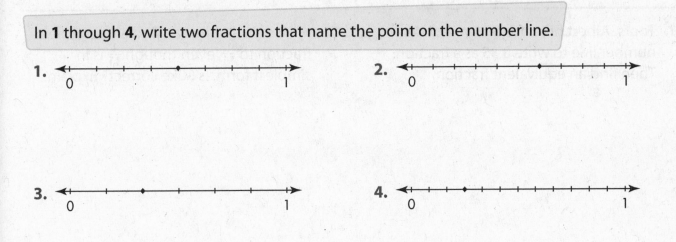

0   1

Label the same number line in two different ways.

0.01 0.02 0.03 0.04 0.05 0.06 0.07 0.08 0.09
0.1 0.2 0.3 0.4 0.5 0.6 0.7 0.8 0.9

0   $\frac{1}{10}$ $\frac{2}{10}$ $\frac{3}{10}$ $\frac{4}{10}$ $\frac{5}{10}$ $\frac{6}{10}$ $\frac{7}{10}$ $\frac{8}{10}$ $\frac{9}{10}$ 1

$\frac{10}{100}$ $\frac{20}{100}$ $\frac{30}{100}$ $\frac{40}{100}$ $\frac{50}{100}$ $\frac{60}{100}$ $\frac{70}{100}$ $\frac{80}{100}$ $\frac{90}{100}$

Equivalent fractions are the same distance from 0 on a number line and represent the same fractional amounts.

The point is at $\frac{3}{10}$ and $\frac{30}{100}$.

$\frac{3}{10} = \frac{30}{100}$

$\frac{3}{10}$ and $\frac{30}{100}$ are equivalent fractions.

In **1** through **4**, write two fractions that name the point on the number line.

1.
0   1

2.
0   1

3.
0   1

4.
0   1

5. Are $\frac{3}{8}$ and $\frac{3}{4}$ equivalent fractions? Use a number line to decide.

6. Draw a number line to show that $\frac{1}{4}$ and $\frac{4}{16}$ are equivalent.

7. **Number Sense** Which of the following pairs are **NOT** equivalent fractions?

A $\frac{1}{3}, \frac{5}{8}$ C $\frac{3}{5}, \frac{6}{10}$

B $\frac{2}{4}, \frac{4}{8}$ D $\frac{3}{4}, \frac{9}{12}$

8. **Connect** There are 267 students and 21 adults going on a school trip. An equal number of people will ride on each bus. If there are 9 buses, how many people will ride on each bus?

9. On a number line, point X is located at $\frac{2}{3}$. On a second number line, point Y is the same distance from 0 as point X, but has a numerator of 8. What is the denominator of point Y?

You can draw a picture to show this problem.

10. **Extend Your Thinking** A recipe calls for $\frac{1}{4}$ cup of flour. Carter does not have a quarter-cup measuring cup, though he has a measuring cup that holds an eighth of a cup. How can Carter measure the flour he needs for his recipe?

11. **Tools** Albert hikes for 0.35 mile. Use a number line to write 0.35 as a fraction. Then find an equivalent fraction.

12. Mike says that he can find an equivalent fraction to $\frac{1}{11}$, even though $\frac{1}{11}$ is in simplest form. Is Mike correct? Explain.

13. **Math and Science** Ocean high tides occur twice each day. The pull of gravity from both the Sun and the Moon affect ocean tides. Because the Sun is much farther away, its effect on tides is only about $\frac{4}{10}$ that of the Moon. Write $\frac{4}{10}$ in simplest form.

© Pearson Education, Inc. 4

Name _____

Solve & Share

Juan read for $\frac{5}{6}$ of an hour. Larissa read for $\frac{1}{3}$ of an hour. Who read for a longer period of time? Explain. **Solve this problem any way you choose.**

★ TEKS 4.3D Compare two fractions with different numerators and different denominators and represent the comparison using the symbols >, =, or <. Mathematical Process Standards 4.1C, 4.1D, 4.1E, 4.1F, 4.1G

Digital Resources at PearsonTexas.com

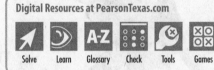

Solve Learn Glossary Check Tools Games

You can **connect ideas.** What fractions do you know how to compare? *Show your work in the space above!*

Look Back!

Communicate Write your answer with a number sentence using >, <, or =.

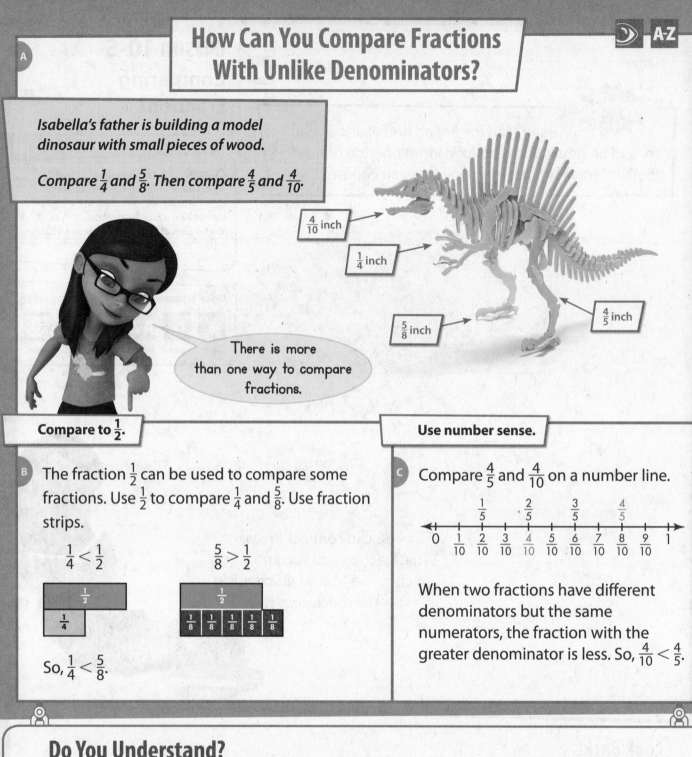

How Can You Compare Fractions With Unlike Denominators?

A-Z

Isabella's father is building a model dinosaur with small pieces of wood.

Compare $\frac{1}{4}$ and $\frac{5}{8}$. Then compare $\frac{4}{5}$ and $\frac{4}{10}$.

$\frac{4}{10}$ inch

$\frac{1}{4}$ inch

$\frac{5}{8}$ inch

$\frac{4}{5}$ inch

There is more than one way to compare fractions.

Compare to $\frac{1}{2}$.

B The fraction $\frac{1}{2}$ can be used to compare some fractions. Use $\frac{1}{2}$ to compare $\frac{1}{4}$ and $\frac{5}{8}$. Use fraction strips.

$$\frac{1}{4} < \frac{1}{2} \qquad\qquad \frac{5}{8} > \frac{1}{2}$$

$\frac{1}{2}$
$\frac{1}{4}$

$\frac{1}{2}$				
$\frac{1}{8}$	$\frac{1}{8}$	$\frac{1}{8}$	$\frac{1}{8}$	$\frac{1}{8}$

So, $\frac{1}{4} < \frac{5}{8}$.

Use number sense.

C Compare $\frac{4}{5}$ and $\frac{4}{10}$ on a number line.

When two fractions have different denominators but the same numerators, the fraction with the greater denominator is less. So, $\frac{4}{10} < \frac{4}{5}$.

Do You Understand?

Convince Me! Kelly looked at the fractions on the right and said, "These are easy to compare. I just think about $\frac{1}{8}$ and $\frac{1}{6}$." Explain what Kelly was thinking.

Circle the greater fraction.

$\frac{5}{8}$ $\frac{5}{6}$

© Pearson Education, Inc. 4

Name _____

Another Example

Compare $\frac{2}{3}$ and $\frac{3}{5}$.

Step 1 Rename the fractions to have the same denominator.

$$\frac{2}{3} = \frac{2 \times 5}{3 \times 5} = \frac{10}{15} \qquad \frac{3}{5} = \frac{3 \times 3}{5 \times 3} = \frac{9}{15}$$

Step 2 Use the numerators of the renamed fractions to compare.

$$\frac{10}{15} > \frac{9}{15} \quad \text{So,} \frac{2}{3} > \frac{3}{5}.$$

☆ Guided Practice *

In **1** through **4**, write $>$, $<$, or $=$. Use fraction strips or drawings to help.

1. $\frac{3}{4} \bigcirc \frac{6}{8}$ 2. $\frac{1}{4} \bigcirc \frac{1}{10}$

3. $\frac{3}{5} \bigcirc \frac{5}{10}$ 4. $\frac{2}{5} \bigcirc \frac{4}{5}$

When two fractions have different numerators but the same denominator, the fraction with the lesser numerator is less.

5. **Explain** Mary says that $\frac{1}{8}$ is greater than $\frac{1}{4}$ because 8 is greater than 4. Is she correct? Explain your answer.

6. Mr. Arnold uses wood measuring $\frac{1}{2}$ foot, $\frac{1}{3}$ foot, and $\frac{3}{8}$ foot to build a birdhouse. Compare these lengths of wood.

☆ Independent Practice ☆

In **7** through **22**, compare, then write $>$, $<$, or $=$.

7. $\frac{5}{6} \bigcirc \frac{10}{12}$ 8. $\frac{3}{10} \bigcirc \frac{7}{10}$ 9. $\frac{5}{12} \bigcirc \frac{1}{2}$ 10. $\frac{7}{8} \bigcirc \frac{3}{4}$

11. $\frac{7}{10} \bigcirc \frac{11}{12}$ 12. $\frac{7}{12} \bigcirc \frac{4}{12}$ 13. $\frac{5}{12} \bigcirc \frac{4}{5}$ 14. $\frac{2}{6} \bigcirc \frac{3}{12}$

15. $\frac{6}{8} \bigcirc \frac{8}{10}$ 16. $\frac{3}{5} \bigcirc \frac{3}{6}$ 17. $\frac{2}{10} \bigcirc \frac{2}{12}$ 18. $\frac{5}{6} \bigcirc \frac{4}{5}$

19. $\frac{4}{4} \bigcirc \frac{1}{1}$ 20. $\frac{2}{4} \bigcirc \frac{8}{10}$ 21. $\frac{7}{8} \bigcirc \frac{3}{5}$ 22. $\frac{3}{9} \bigcirc \frac{1}{3}$

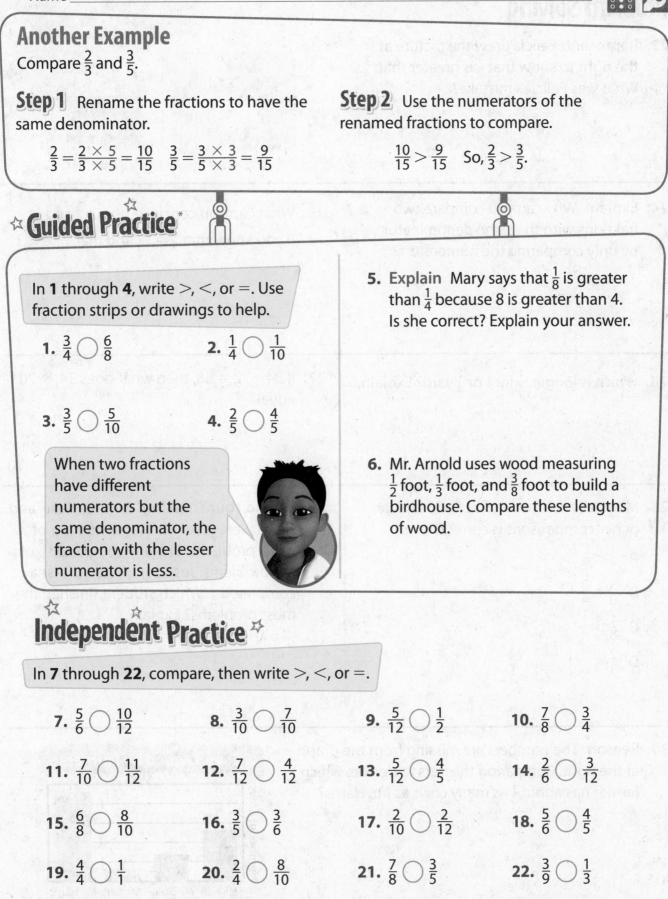

Problem Solving

23. Represent Felicia drew the picture at the right to show that $\frac{3}{8}$ is greater than $\frac{3}{4}$. What was Felicia's mistake?

24. Explain Why can you compare two fractions with the same denominator by only comparing the numerators?

25. What can you conclude about $\frac{3}{5}$ and $\frac{12}{20}$ if you know that $\frac{3}{5} = \frac{6}{10}$ and that $\frac{6}{10} = \frac{12}{20}$?

26. Which is longer, $\frac{1}{4}$ foot or $\frac{1}{4}$ yard? Explain.

27. If $34 \times 2 = 68$, then what does 34×20 equal?

28. Maggie is comparing fractions. Which ⭐ of her comparisons is correct?

A $\frac{1}{3} < \frac{1}{6}$

B $\frac{3}{8} < \frac{3}{4}$

C $\frac{1}{8} > \frac{1}{4}$

D $\frac{2}{3} < \frac{4}{6}$

29. Extend Your Thinking Brittany, José, and Tasha were given the same number of math problems. Brittany completed $\frac{5}{6}$ of the problems. José completed $\frac{7}{8}$. Tasha completed $\frac{2}{3}$. Which student finished the most problems? Explain.

30. Reason The numbers are missing from the graph at the right. Comparing the bars to decide, which farmer has about $\frac{1}{3}$ as many cows as Mr. Harris?

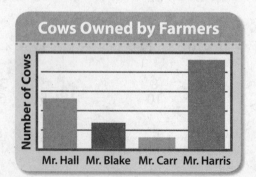

Cows Owned by Farmers

Number of Cows

Mr. Hall   Mr. Blake   Mr. Carr   Mr. Harris

© Pearson Education, Inc. 4

Name _____

Another Look!

Leanne wanted to compare $\frac{4}{6}$ and $\frac{3}{4}$.

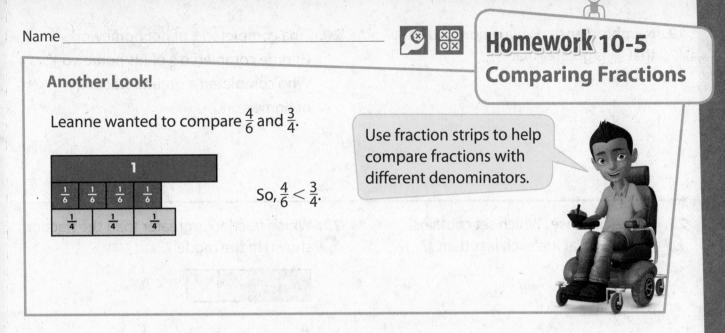

So, $\frac{4}{6} < \frac{3}{4}$.

Use fraction strips to help compare fractions with different denominators.

In **1** through **16**, write $>$, $<$, or $=$. Use fraction strips or equivalent fractions to help.

1. $\frac{5}{6} \bigcirc \frac{2}{3}$

2. $\frac{1}{5} \bigcirc \frac{2}{8}$

3. $\frac{9}{10} \bigcirc \frac{6}{8}$

4. $\frac{3}{4} \bigcirc \frac{1}{4}$

5. $\frac{7}{8} \bigcirc \frac{5}{10}$

6. $\frac{2}{5} \bigcirc \frac{2}{6}$

7. $\frac{1}{3} \bigcirc \frac{3}{8}$

8. $\frac{2}{10} \bigcirc \frac{3}{5}$

9. $\frac{8}{10} \bigcirc \frac{3}{4}$

10. $\frac{3}{8} \bigcirc \frac{11}{12}$

11. $\frac{2}{3} \bigcirc \frac{10}{12}$

12. $\frac{7}{8} \bigcirc \frac{1}{6}$

13. $\frac{3}{8} \bigcirc \frac{7}{8}$

14. $\frac{2}{4} \bigcirc \frac{4}{8}$

15. $\frac{6}{8} \bigcirc \frac{8}{12}$

16. $\frac{1}{3} \bigcirc \frac{4}{9}$

In **17** and **18**, the same number of students attended school each day.

17. Did more students buy lunch on Tuesday or on Wednesday?

18. Did more students buy lunch on Thursday or on Friday?

DATA	Day	Fraction of students buying lunch
	Monday	$\frac{1}{2}$
	Tuesday	$\frac{2}{5}$
	Wednesday	$\frac{3}{4}$
	Thursday	$\frac{5}{8}$
	Friday	$\frac{4}{6}$

19. Number Sense Explain how you know that $\frac{21}{30}$ is greater than $\frac{2}{3}$.

20. Tina completed $\frac{2}{3}$ of her homework. George completed $\frac{7}{8}$ of his homework. Who completed a greater fraction of homework?

21. Number Sense Which set contains fractions that are each less than $\frac{5}{8}$?

A $\frac{6}{8}, \frac{7}{8}$

B $\frac{5}{6}, \frac{5}{7}$

C $\frac{1}{8}, \frac{2}{8}, \frac{3}{8}, \frac{4}{8}$

D $\frac{1}{2}, \frac{2}{3}, \frac{3}{4}$

22. Which fraction is greater than the fraction shown in the model?

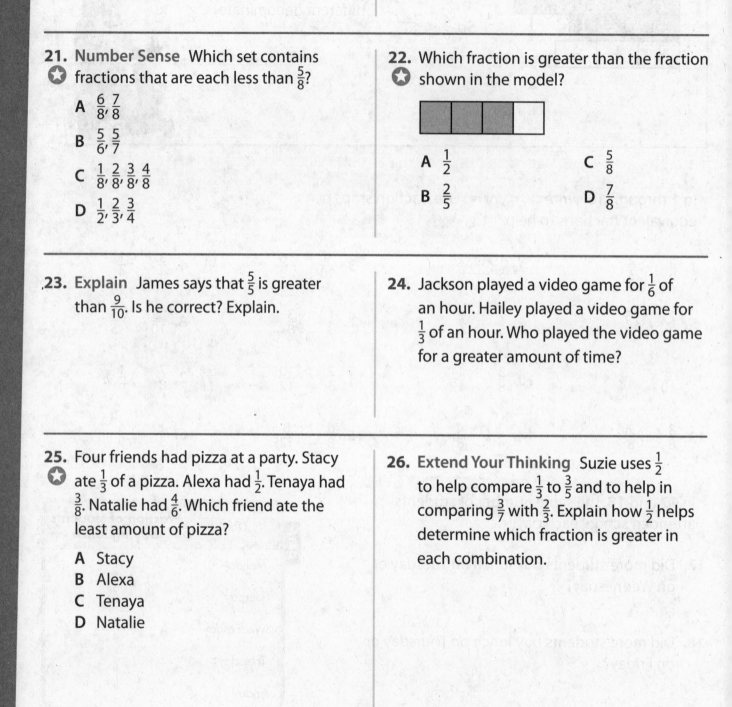

A $\frac{1}{2}$ C $\frac{5}{8}$

B $\frac{2}{5}$ D $\frac{7}{8}$

23. Explain James says that $\frac{5}{5}$ is greater than $\frac{9}{10}$. Is he correct? Explain.

24. Jackson played a video game for $\frac{1}{6}$ of an hour. Hailey played a video game for $\frac{1}{3}$ of an hour. Who played the video game for a greater amount of time?

25. Four friends had pizza at a party. Stacy ate $\frac{1}{3}$ of a pizza. Alexa had $\frac{1}{2}$. Tenaya had $\frac{3}{8}$. Natalie had $\frac{4}{6}$. Which friend ate the least amount of pizza?

A Stacy

B Alexa

C Tenaya

D Natalie

26. Extend Your Thinking Suzie uses $\frac{1}{2}$ to help compare $\frac{1}{3}$ to $\frac{3}{5}$ and to help in comparing $\frac{3}{7}$ with $\frac{2}{3}$. Explain how $\frac{1}{2}$ helps determine which fraction is greater in each combination.

© Pearson Education, Inc. 4

Name _____

☆ ☆
Solve & Share

Sort the fractions listed below into three groups: fractions less than $\frac{1}{2}$, fractions equal to $\frac{1}{2}$, and fractions greater than $\frac{1}{2}$.

$$\frac{5}{9}, \frac{5}{8}, \frac{5}{12}, \frac{25}{50}, \frac{9}{20}, \frac{6}{11}$$

Solve this problem any way you choose.

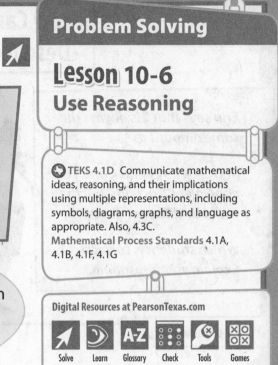

You can use reasoning. Look at the relationships between numerators and denominators. *Show your work in the space below!*

⬢ TEKS 4.1D Communicate mathematical ideas, reasoning, and their implications using multiple representations, including symbols, diagrams, graphs, and language as appropriate. Also, 4.3C.
Mathematical Process Standards 4.1A, 4.1B, 4.1F, 4.1G

Digital Resources at PearsonTexas.com

Solve   Learn   Glossary   Check   Tools   Games

Look Back!

Analyze Relationships Write a rule to use to determine whether a fraction is greater than $\frac{1}{2}$.

How Can Equivalent Fractions Describe Different Amounts?

Erin says that $\frac{1}{2}$ is always the same amount as $\frac{2}{4}$.

Matthew says that $\frac{1}{2}$ and $\frac{2}{4}$ are equivalent fractions, but they could be different amounts.

Which student is correct? Explain your reasoning.

Think about what you know about fraction models and ways to show $\frac{1}{2}$ and $\frac{2}{4}$.

Use reasoning.

B Plan

Equivalent fractions that have the same size whole describe the same amount.

The circles are the same size.

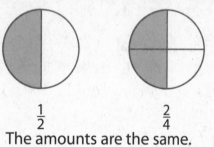

$\frac{1}{2}$ $\frac{2}{4}$

The amounts are the same.

C Solve

Equivalent fractions that have different size wholes do not describe the same amount.

The circles are not the same size.

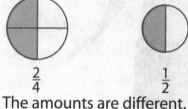

$\frac{2}{4}$ $\frac{1}{2}$

The amounts are different.

Matthew is correct. $\frac{1}{2}$ and $\frac{2}{4}$ are equivalent fractions, but they could be different amounts.

Do You Understand?

Convince Me! Do each of the shaded parts of the square below show $\frac{1}{4}$? Explain.

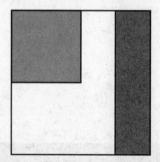

© Pearson Education, Inc. 4

☆ Guided Practice *

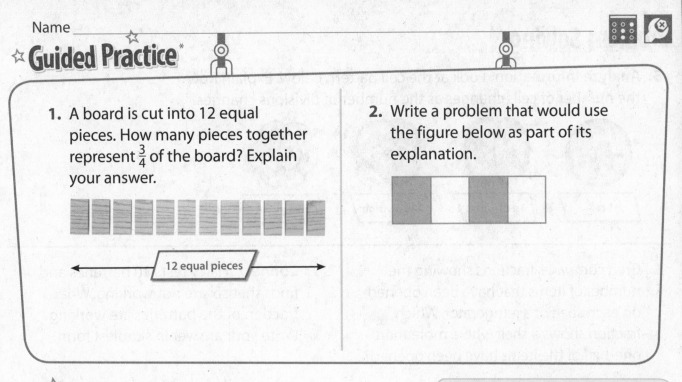

1. A board is cut into 12 equal pieces. How many pieces together represent $\frac{3}{4}$ of the board? Explain your answer.

12 equal pieces

2. Write a problem that would use the figure below as part of its explanation.

Independent Practice ☆

3. **Draw a Picture** Devon and Amanda knit the same size scarf. Devon's scarf is $\frac{3}{5}$ yellow. Amanda's scarf is $\frac{3}{4}$ yellow. How can you use a picture to show whose scarf is more yellow?

You can use a different method of finding equivalent fractions to check your work.

4. **Reason** The school newspaper has a total of 18 articles and ads. There are 6 more articles than ads. How many articles are there? How many ads are there? Explain.

Problem Solving

5. Analyze Information Look at the cell pattern below. Explain how the number of cells changes as the number of divisions changes.

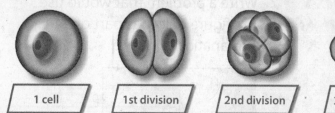

| 1 cell | 1st division | 2nd division | 3rd division |

6. ⭐ Greg compares fractions showing the number of items that have been opened on each shelf of a refrigerator. Which fraction shows a shelf where more than one-half of the items have been opened?

A $\frac{3}{7}$ C $\frac{5}{8}$

B $\frac{4}{9}$ D $\frac{1}{3}$

7. Connect Harry tests 10 batteries and finds that six are not working. What fraction of the batteries are working? Write your answer in simplest form.

8. Personal Financial Literacy Hasan got $12 allowance and saved $4. What fraction of his allowance did he save? Write your answer in simplest form.

9. Extend Your Thinking George has 20 quarters. Use equivalent fractions to explain how many dollars he has.

10. Justify Bella, Gerard, and Ming played 36 holes of miniature golf. Bella made par 12 times during the game. Gerard made par on $\frac{12}{16}$ of the holes. Ming made par on half of the holes. Gerard said he and Bella made par the same number of times, and Ming made par the greatest number of times. Is Gerard correct? Explain.

11. Use a Strip Diagram Timmy weighs 85 pounds. This is 5 times as much as his bicycle. How much does Timmy's bicycle weigh?

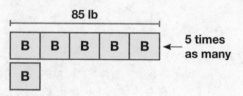

85 lb

B B B B B ← 5 times as many

B

© Pearson Education, Inc. 4

Homework 10-6
Use Reasoning

Another Look!

Gina and her brother Don made homemade pasta with their mother. Gina made $\frac{1}{4}$ of a pan of pasta. Don made $\frac{3}{8}$ of a pan. Which person made more pasta?

> Equivalent fractions with the same denominator can help solve problems comparing fractions.

Writing to Explain

- Write your explanation in steps to make it clear.

- Tell what the numbers mean in your explanation.

- Tell why you took certain steps.

Example

Because $\frac{1}{4}$ and $\frac{3}{8}$ have different denominators, I multiplied the numerator and denominator of $\frac{1}{4}$ by 2 to get $\frac{2}{8}$.

Then I could compare the numerators of $\frac{2}{8}$ and $\frac{3}{8}$. Because $\frac{3}{8}$ is greater than $\frac{2}{8}$, I knew that Don made more pasta.

1. **Explain** Humans usually have 20 baby teeth, which are replaced by 32 adult teeth. Raul said he has lost 6 of his baby teeth. Write two fractions equivalent to this number. Explain your answer.

> Remember, a good explanation is correct, simple, complete, and easy to understand.

2. An actor is rehearsing his lines in two scenes. He has 12 lines in Scene 1, and 16 lines in Scene 2. There are 24 lines total in Scene 1, and 30 lines total in Scene 2. In which scene does the actor have a greater share of the lines? Explain.

3. Reason Find the area of the entire figure. What fraction of the total area is rectangle *A*? Find an equivalent fraction.

4. Reason Do rectangle *B* and square *C* have the same area? Explain.

5. Communicate Mary has 23 marbles. $\frac{7}{23}$ of the marbles are yellow, and $\frac{13}{23}$ of the marbles are blue. The rest of the marbles are green. How many marbles are green? Explain.

6. Construct Arguments Adam wants to compare the fractions $\frac{2}{5}$, $\frac{1}{6}$, and $\frac{1}{3}$. He wants to order them from least to greatest and rewrite them so they all have the same denominator. Explain how Adam can rewrite the fractions.

7. Maria recorded how many water bottles from each table in the cafeteria were placed in the recycling bin. She wrote the number of recycled bottles from each table as a fraction. Which fraction shows that less than $\frac{1}{2}$ of the bottles were recycled?

  A $\frac{3}{7}$ **C** $\frac{5}{7}$

  B $\frac{3}{5}$ **D** $\frac{6}{9}$

8. Extend Your Thinking Traci has four blue pens and three red pens. She has twice as many black pens as blue pens. What fraction represents the number of blue pens out of the total number of pens? Explain.

9. Write 1.2 as a fraction in simplest form. Explain your reasoning.

Use a representation such as decimal grids or a number line.

© Pearson Education, Inc. 4

Name _____

1. **Number Sense** Barb drew a number line and divided it into twelfths. She then marked a point at $\frac{9}{12}$. Bill divided the same number line into fourths. He marked a point the same distance from 0 as did Barb. What fraction represents the point Bill marked?

Applying Math Processes

- How does this problem connect to previous ones?
- What is my plan?
- How can I use tools?
- How can I use number sense?
- How can I communicate and represent my thinking?
- How can I organize and record information?
- How can I explain my work?
- How can I justify my answer?

2. From a plate of 16 apple slices, Val ate 3 of the slices. Then Victor came along and ate 4 slices. Judy and a friend ate 7 more slices. What fraction of the apple slices, in simplest form, were eaten?

   A $\frac{14}{16}$ of the slices   **C** $\frac{7}{8}$ of the slices

   B $\frac{7}{16}$ of the slices   **D** $\frac{3}{4}$ of the slices

3. **Justify** When is a fraction in simplest form? Give an example of a fraction that is in simplest form and one that is not.

4. **Construct Arguments** Tom walks $\frac{3}{5}$ mile to school. Ted walks $\frac{5}{8}$ mile to school. Who walks farther? How do you know?

5. **Extend Your Thinking** Cliff drew a number line and marked a point at $\frac{3}{4}$. Carla drew a number line and divided it into sixths. She marked a point the same distance from 0 as Cliff. How many sixths was the point Carla marked?

You can use a number line to show your thinking.

TOPIC 10 — Number Sense

Error Search

Decide whether the second fraction is equivalent to the first fraction and in simplest form. If not, give the correct equivalent fraction in simplest form.

1. $\frac{9}{12}$ and $\frac{3}{4}$

2. $\frac{8}{12}$ and $\frac{4}{6}$

3. $\frac{6}{10}$ and $\frac{2}{3}$

4. $\frac{2}{8}$ and $\frac{4}{16}$

Over or Under

Decide whether the given fraction is greater than (over) $\frac{1}{2}$ or less than (under) $\frac{1}{2}$. Circle your choice.

5. $\frac{3}{4}$

Over $\frac{1}{2}$

Under $\frac{1}{2}$

6. $\frac{1}{6}$

Over $\frac{1}{2}$

Under $\frac{1}{2}$

7. $\frac{7}{10}$

Over $\frac{1}{2}$

Under $\frac{1}{2}$

8. $\frac{3}{5}$

Over $\frac{1}{2}$

Under $\frac{1}{2}$

9. $\frac{5}{12}$

Over $\frac{1}{2}$

Under $\frac{1}{2}$

10. $\frac{3}{8}$

Over $\frac{1}{2}$

Under $\frac{1}{2}$

11. $\frac{1}{4}$

Over $\frac{1}{2}$

Under $\frac{1}{2}$

12. $\frac{3}{10}$

Over $\frac{1}{2}$

Under $\frac{1}{2}$

13. $\frac{7}{8}$

Over $\frac{1}{2}$

Under $\frac{1}{2}$

14. $\frac{7}{12}$

Over $\frac{1}{2}$

Under $\frac{1}{2}$

15. $\frac{1}{3}$

Over $\frac{1}{2}$

Under $\frac{1}{2}$

16. $\frac{4}{6}$

Over $\frac{1}{2}$

Under $\frac{1}{2}$

© Pearson Education, Inc. 4

Set A pages 511–516

What fraction represents the shaded part of each diagram?

Reteaching

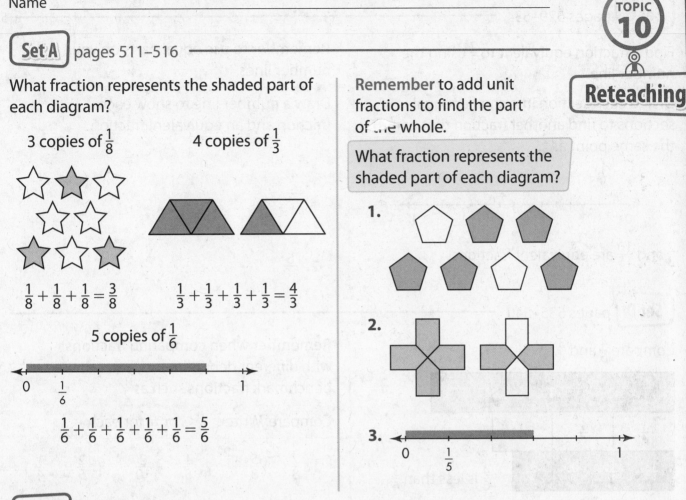

3 copies of $\frac{1}{8}$

$\frac{1}{8} + \frac{1}{8} + \frac{1}{8} = \frac{3}{8}$

4 copies of $\frac{1}{3}$

$\frac{1}{3} + \frac{1}{3} + \frac{1}{3} + \frac{1}{3} = \frac{4}{3}$

5 copies of $\frac{1}{6}$

0    $\frac{1}{6}$ 1

$\frac{1}{6} + \frac{1}{6} + \frac{1}{6} + \frac{1}{6} + \frac{1}{6} = \frac{5}{6}$

Remember to add unit fractions to find the part of the whole.

What fraction represents the shaded part of each diagram?

1.

2.

3. 0 $\frac{1}{5}$ 1

Set B pages 517–528

Find an equivalent fraction for $\frac{2}{6}$.

Multiply or divide the numerator and the denominator by the same number to find an equivalent fraction.

$$\frac{2}{6} \overset{\times 2}{=} \frac{4}{12} \quad \text{and} \quad \frac{2}{6} \overset{\div 2}{=} \frac{1}{3}$$

$$\frac{1}{3} = \frac{2}{6} = \frac{4}{12}$$

Write $\frac{4}{10}$ in simplest form.

Divide by a common factor.

$$\frac{4}{10} \overset{\div 2}{=} \frac{2}{5} \quad \text{In simplest form, } \frac{4}{10} = \frac{2}{5}.$$

Remember that a fraction is in simplest form if the numerator and the denominator have no common factor other than 1.

Find two equivalent forms for each fraction using multiplication and division.

1. $\frac{8}{12}$ **2.** $\frac{6}{8}$

3. $\frac{9}{15}$ **4.** $\frac{2}{16}$

Write each fraction in simplest form.

5. $\frac{10}{12}$ **6.** $\frac{28}{32}$

7. $\frac{12}{15}$ **8.** $\frac{9}{36}$

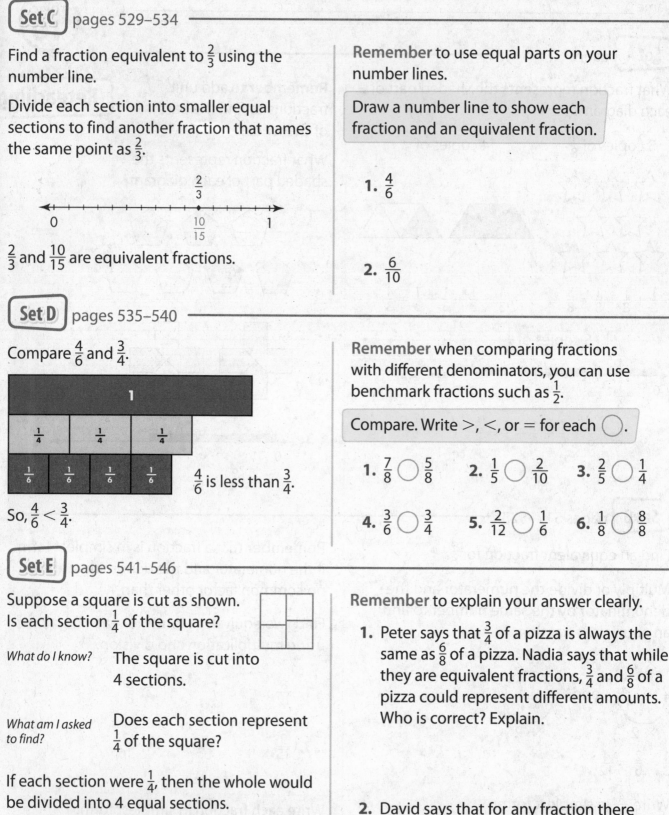

Set C pages 529–534

Find a fraction equivalent to $\frac{2}{3}$ using the number line.

Divide each section into smaller equal sections to find another fraction that names the same point as $\frac{2}{3}$.

$\frac{2}{3}$ and $\frac{10}{15}$ are equivalent fractions.

Remember to use equal parts on your number lines.

Draw a number line to show each fraction and an equivalent fraction.

1. $\frac{4}{6}$

2. $\frac{6}{10}$

Set D pages 535–540

Compare $\frac{4}{6}$ and $\frac{3}{4}$.

$\frac{4}{6}$ is less than $\frac{3}{4}$.

So, $\frac{4}{6} < \frac{3}{4}$.

Remember when comparing fractions with different denominators, you can use benchmark fractions such as $\frac{1}{2}$.

Compare. Write $>$, $<$, or $=$ for each $\bigcirc$.

1. $\frac{7}{8} \bigcirc \frac{5}{8}$ 2. $\frac{1}{5} \bigcirc \frac{2}{10}$ 3. $\frac{2}{5} \bigcirc \frac{1}{4}$

4. $\frac{3}{6} \bigcirc \frac{3}{4}$ 5. $\frac{2}{12} \bigcirc \frac{1}{6}$ 6. $\frac{1}{8} \bigcirc \frac{8}{8}$

Set E pages 541–546

Suppose a square is cut as shown. Is each section $\frac{1}{4}$ of the square?

What do I know? The square is cut into 4 sections.

What am I asked to find? Does each section represent $\frac{1}{4}$ of the square?

If each section were $\frac{1}{4}$, then the whole would be divided into 4 equal sections.

The sections are not the same size. So, each section is not $\frac{1}{4}$ of the square.

Remember to explain your answer clearly.

1. Peter says that $\frac{3}{4}$ of a pizza is always the same as $\frac{6}{8}$ of a pizza. Nadia says that while they are equivalent fractions, $\frac{3}{4}$ and $\frac{6}{8}$ of a pizza could represent different amounts. Who is correct? Explain.

2. David says that for any fraction there are an unlimited number of equivalent fractions. Is he correct? Explain.

© Pearson Education, Inc. 4

Name _____

1. Marci's glass of milk is about $\frac{2}{3}$ full. What does the fraction $\frac{2}{3}$ represent?

   A There are two parts with milk for each three parts without.

   B If the glass is separated into three equal parts, two of them are full.

   C Marci has two glasses of milk.

   D Two out of three parts of the glass are empty.

4. Leslie used more than $\frac{1}{2}$ cup of flour in a recipe. Which might be the amount Leslie used?

   A $\frac{5}{8}$ cup of flour

   B $\frac{4}{8}$ cup of flour

   C $\frac{3}{8}$ cup of flour

   D $\frac{1}{3}$ cup of flour

2. Johnny found a fraction equivalent to the one shown by the point on the number line. Which fraction could he have found?

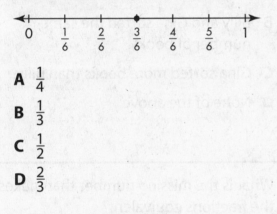

   A $\frac{1}{4}$

   B $\frac{1}{3}$

   C $\frac{1}{2}$

   D $\frac{2}{3}$

5. Only one of the comparisons below is correct. Which is a correct statement?

   A $\frac{2}{3} < \frac{1}{2}$

   B $\frac{1}{2} = \frac{3}{5}$

   C $\frac{3}{4} < \frac{4}{5}$

   D $\frac{3}{4} < \frac{2}{3}$

3. Tony made 8 goals in 12 penalty kicks. Which fraction shows $\frac{8}{12}$ in simplest form?

   A $\frac{4}{6}$

   B $\frac{2}{3}$

   C $\frac{1}{3}$

   D $\frac{6}{9}$

6. Which pair of fractions is **NOT** equivalent?

   A $\frac{3}{4}, \frac{6}{8}$

   B $\frac{2}{5}, \frac{4}{10}$

   C $\frac{1}{4}, \frac{2}{8}$

   D $\frac{1}{3}, \frac{2}{7}$

7. Jacob has 21 marbles in a bag. Of those marbles, 7 are blue. Which shows the fraction of his marbles that are blue in simplest form?

A $\frac{1}{7}$ of the marbles

B $\frac{1}{3}$ of the marbles

C $\frac{2}{3}$ of the marbles

D $\frac{7}{14}$ of the marbles

---

8. Which fraction is equivalent to $\frac{3}{5}$?

A $\frac{3}{10}$

B $\frac{6}{15}$

C $\frac{9}{15}$

D $\frac{15}{20}$

---

9. Antonio read $\frac{1}{2}$ of the pages in a chapter in his book. If he read 9 pages, how many pages are in the chapter?

			•		
⓪	⓪	⓪		⓪	⓪
①	①	①		①	①
②	②	②		②	②
③	③	③		③	③
④	④	④		④	④
⑤	⑤	⑤		⑤	⑤
⑥	⑥	⑥		⑥	⑥
⑦	⑦	⑦		⑦	⑦
⑧	⑧	⑧		⑧	⑧
⑨	⑨	⑨		⑨	⑨

---

10. Mario ate less than $\frac{1}{3}$ of a pizza. Which fraction could show the amount he ate?

A $\frac{2}{8}$ of a pizza

B $\frac{3}{8}$ of a pizza

C $\frac{2}{6}$ of a pizza

D $\frac{3}{6}$ of a pizza

---

11. Billy and Gina each sorted half of the books in different sections of the library. If there were more books in Billy's section, what do we know about the amount of books each sorted?

A Billy sorted more books than Gina.

B Billy and Gina sorted the same number of books.

C Gina sorted more books than Billy.

D None of the above

---

12. What is the missing number that makes the fractions equivalent?

$$\frac{5}{6} = \frac{10}{?}$$

			•		
⓪	⓪	⓪		⓪	⓪
①	①	①		①	①
②	②	②		②	②
③	③	③		③	③
④	④	④		④	④
⑤	⑤	⑤		⑤	⑤
⑥	⑥	⑥		⑥	⑥
⑦	⑦	⑦		⑦	⑦
⑧	⑧	⑧		⑧	⑧
⑨	⑨	⑨		⑨	⑨

© Pearson Education, Inc. 4

Adding and Subtracting Fractions with Like Denominators

Essential Questions:
What is a standard procedure for adding and subtracting fractions with like denominators?
How can fractions be added and subtracted on a number line?

Fractions can be used to communicate results supported by data.

In the United States, an average of $2\frac{3}{5}$ people live in each household.

My family is above average! There are 5 of us. Here's a project on surveys and fractions.

Math and Science Project: Surveys

Do Research Conduct a survey asking your classmates how many people live in their household.

Journal: Write a Report Include what you found. Also in your report:

- What is the greatest number of people living in a household?

- Which size household is the most common?

- Use fractions to represent the portion of your class that have each size household.

Review What You Know

Vocabulary

Choose the best term from the box.
Write it on the blank.

> • denominator
>
> • simplest form
>
> • unit fraction
>
> • numerator

1. In the fraction $\frac{2}{3}$, the number 2 is

the _____ of the fraction

and 3 is the _____ of the
fraction.

2. A fraction in which the numerator
and denominator have no common
factor other than 1 is written in

_____ .

Equivalent Fractions

Write the missing values to show pairs of
equivalent fractions.

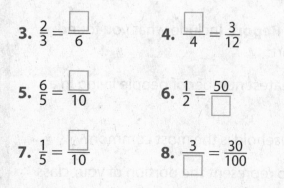

3. $\frac{2}{3} = \frac{\square}{6}$ **4.** $\frac{\square}{4} = \frac{3}{12}$

5. $\frac{6}{5} = \frac{\square}{10}$ **6.** $\frac{1}{2} = \frac{50}{\square}$

7. $\frac{1}{5} = \frac{\square}{10}$ **8.** $\frac{3}{\square} = \frac{30}{100}$

Models for Fractions

Tell what fraction is represented by the
shaded portion of each model or
number line.

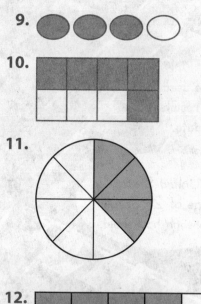

9.

10.

11.

12.

13.

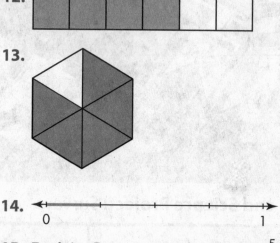

14.

15. Explain Draw two ways to model $\frac{5}{6}$.
Explain why there can be more than
one way to model a fraction.

© Pearson Education, Inc. 4

My Word Cards

Use the examples for each word on the front of the card to help complete the definitions on the back.

A-Z

decomposing

$$\frac{4}{5} = \frac{1}{5} + \frac{2}{5} + \frac{1}{5}$$

mixed number

$$1\frac{1}{3}, \; 4\frac{1}{2}, \; 6\frac{5}{8}$$

benchmark fraction

$$\frac{1}{4}, \; \frac{1}{2}, \; \frac{3}{4}$$

My Word Cards

Complete each definition. Extend learning by writing your own definitions.

A number that has a whole number part and a fraction part is a

_____.

Breaking into parts is called

_____.

A known fraction that is commonly used for estimating is called a

_____.

© Pearson Education, Inc. 4

Name _____

Solve & Share

Kyle and Jillian are working on a sports banner. They painted $\frac{3}{8}$ of the banner green and $\frac{4}{8}$ purple. How much of the banner have they painted so far? *Solve this problem any way you choose.*

You can use tools. Use fraction strips to model this problem. *Show your work in the space below!*

⭐ TEKS 4.3E Represent and solve addition and subtraction of fractions with equal denominators using objects and pictorial models that build to the number line and properties of operations. Also, 4.3. Mathematical Process Standards 4.1C, 4.1D, 4.1E, 4.1F, 4.1G

Digital Resources at PearsonTexas.com

Solve   Learn   Glossary   Check   Tools   Games

Look Back!

Connect Ideas Is your answer in simplest form? Explain why or why not.

How Can You Use Fraction Strips To Add Fractions?

Ten canoeing teams are racing downriver. Five teams have silver canoes and two teams have brown canoes. What fraction of the canoes are either silver or brown?

Objects such as fraction strips can be used to add two or more fractions.

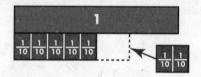

Use objects.

B $\frac{5}{10}$ of the canoes are silver and $\frac{2}{10}$ of the canoes are brown. Use five $\frac{1}{10}$ strips to show $\frac{5}{10}$ and two $\frac{1}{10}$ strips to show $\frac{2}{10}$.

1
$\frac{1}{10}$ $\frac{1}{10}$ $\frac{1}{10}$ $\frac{1}{10}$ $\frac{1}{10}$

$\frac{1}{10}$ $\frac{1}{10}$

Seven $\frac{1}{10}$ strips are needed.

C Add the numerators. Write the sum over the like denominator.

$$\frac{5}{10} + \frac{2}{10} = \frac{7}{10}$$

Seven out of ten, or $\frac{7}{10}$, of the total canoes are either silver or brown.

Do You Understand?

Convince Me! What two fractions would you add to find the fraction of all the canoes that are either green or brown? What is the sum?

© Pearson Education, Inc. 4

☆ **Guided Practice** *

In **1–6**, use objects such as fraction strips to add fractions. Simplify, if possible.

1. $\frac{1}{3} + \frac{1}{3}$

2. $\frac{2}{5} + \frac{1}{5}$

3. $\frac{1}{4} + \frac{2}{4}$ 4. $\frac{2}{6} + \frac{2}{6}$

5. $\frac{1}{6} + \frac{1}{6}$ 6. $\frac{1}{5} + \frac{3}{5}$

7. **Reason** In the problem on the previous page, what does the red fraction strip labeled 1 represent? Why aren't the purple $\frac{1}{10}$ strips shown the same length as the red strip?

8. **Draw a Picture** What two fractions are being added below? What is the sum?

☆ **Independent Practice** ☆

Leveled Practice In **9–23**, use object such as fraction strips to find each sum.

Remember to simplify if possible.

9. $\frac{3}{12} + \frac{4}{12}$

10. $\frac{4}{10} + \frac{1}{10}$

11. $\frac{2}{12} + \frac{4}{12}$

12. $\frac{1}{6} + \frac{2}{6} + \frac{3}{6}$

13. $\frac{4}{10} + \frac{3}{10}$

14. $\frac{4}{8} + \frac{2}{8}$

15. $\frac{5}{8} + \frac{1}{8}$

16. $\frac{3}{4} + \frac{1}{4}$

17. $\frac{7}{12} + \frac{2}{12}$

18. $\frac{1}{4} + \frac{1}{4}$

19. $\frac{2}{10} + \frac{3}{10}$

20. $\frac{1}{10} + \frac{2}{10} + \frac{1}{10}$

21. $\frac{4}{6} + \frac{1}{6}$

22. $\frac{2}{3} + \frac{1}{3}$

23. $\frac{1}{8} + \frac{5}{8} + \frac{1}{8}$

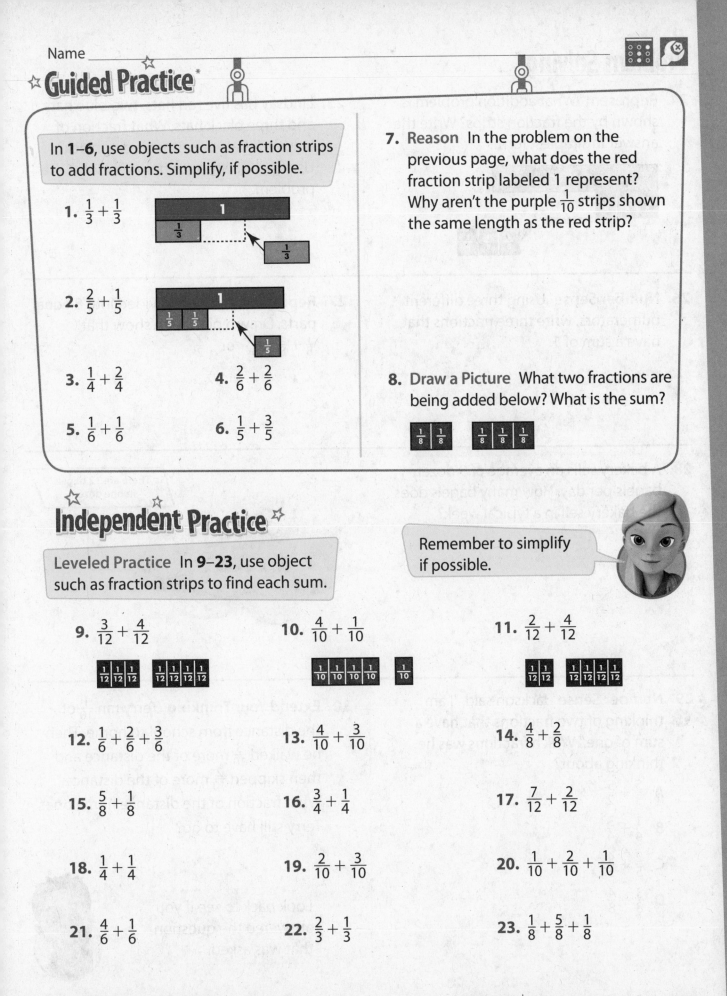

Problem Solving

24. Represent What addition problem is shown by the fraction strips? Write the answer in simplest form.

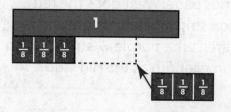

25. Lindsay has five red hats, two blue hats, and three black hats. What fraction of Lindsay's hats are either red or black? Use fraction strips to help you solve the problem.

26. Number Sense Using three different numerators, write three fractions that have a sum of 1.

27. Represent A rope is divided into 8 equal parts. Draw a picture to show that $\frac{1}{8} + \frac{3}{8} = \frac{4}{8}$ or $\frac{1}{2}$.

28. A bakery sells an average of 9 dozen bagels per day. How many bagels does the bakery sell in a typical week?

There are 12 bagels in one dozen.

29. Number Sense Jackson said, "I am thinking of two fractions that have a sum of one." Which fractions was he thinking about?

A $\frac{5}{3} + \frac{5}{2}$

B $\frac{1}{4} + \frac{3}{4}$

C $\frac{2}{5} + \frac{4}{5}$

D $\frac{3}{8} + \frac{4}{8}$

30. Extend Your Thinking Terry ran $\frac{1}{10}$ of the distance from school to home. Then he walked $\frac{3}{10}$ more of the distance and then skipped $\frac{2}{10}$ more of the distance. What fraction of the distance home does Terry still have to go?

Look back to see if you answered the question that was asked.

© Pearson Education, Inc. 4

Name _____

Another Look!

Eight friends went out to eat lunch. Four of them had pizza. Two had hamburgers and two had soup. What fraction of the group had either pizza or soup?

> You can use a circle model to add fractions.

Divide a circle into eighths to represent each of the eight people in the group. 	Four people had pizza. Shade four of the sections to represent $\frac{4}{8}$. Two people had soup. Shade two more sections to represent $\frac{2}{8}$.	Count the number of shaded sections. There are six shaded sections. So, $\frac{6}{8}$ of the group had either pizza or soup. $\frac{4}{8} + \frac{2}{8} = \frac{6}{8}$ Write the sum in simplest form. $\frac{6 \div 2}{8 \div 2} = \frac{3}{4}$

In **1** through **12**, find each sum. You may use fraction strips or models to help. Simplify, if possible.

1. $\frac{2}{5} + \frac{1}{5}$

2. $\frac{4}{6} + \frac{1}{6}$

3. $\frac{3}{8} + \frac{3}{8}$

4. $\frac{1}{6} + \frac{1}{6}$

5. $\frac{2}{5} + \frac{3}{5}$

6. $\frac{2}{10} + \frac{3}{10}$

7. $\frac{5}{8} + \frac{3}{8}$

8. $\frac{3}{10} + \frac{1}{10}$

9. $\frac{3}{4} + \frac{1}{4}$

10. $\frac{5}{10} + \frac{4}{10}$

11. $\frac{1}{6} + \frac{1}{6} + \frac{1}{6}$

12. $\frac{1}{12} + \frac{5}{12} + \frac{2}{12}$

13. Represent Sandy made 9 friendship bracelets. She gave 1 bracelet to her best friend and 5 bracelets to her friends on the tennis team. Use the drawing to find the fraction that represents the number of bracelets Sandy gave away.

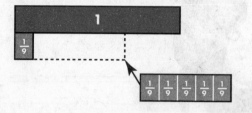

14. Extend Your Thinking Billy did some of his homework on Friday. He did $\frac{1}{6}$ of his homework on Saturday. Billy still had $\frac{4}{6}$ of his homework to finish. How much of his homework did Billy do on Friday?

15. Explain To find $\frac{1}{5} + \frac{2}{5}$, Jared wrote the answer $\frac{3}{10}$. Is Jared correct? Explain.

16. Number Sense Leah wrote two different fractions with the same denominator. Both fractions were less than 1. Can their sum equal 1? Can their sum be greater than 1? Explain why or why not.

17. Sasha has a box of postcards. She wants to give an equal number to each of her 5 friends. How many postcards will each friend receive?

There are 130 postcards in the box.

18. Roberto shares a bag of almonds with 2 friends. He shares $\frac{1}{8}$ of the bag with Jeremy and $\frac{2}{8}$ of the bag with Emily. He eats $\frac{3}{8}$ of the bag of almonds himself. What fraction of the almonds do Roberto and his friends eat?

A $\frac{1}{24}$ of the bag

B $\frac{3}{8}$ of the bag

C $\frac{6}{8}$ of the bag

D $\frac{6}{24}$ of the bag

19. Extend Your Thinking Julia writes two fractions with the same denominator that have numerators 5 and 7. What could the denominator be if the sum is less than 1? Equal to 1? Greater than 1?

© Pearson Education, Inc. 4

Lesson 11-2
Decomposing Fractions

⭐ TEKS 4.3B Decompose a fraction in more than one way into a sum of fractions with the same denominator using concrete and pictorial models and recording results with symbolic representations. Also, 4.3A. Mathematical Process Standards 4.1A, 4.1C, 4.1D, 4.1E, 4.1F, 4.1G

Solve & Share

Karyn has $\frac{11}{8}$ pounds of chili to put into three bowls. The amount of chili in each bowl does not have to be the same. How much could she put into each bowl? **Solve this problem any way you choose.**

You can **use representations.** How can you represent the total amount of chili? **Show your work in the space below!**

Digital Resources at PearsonTexas.com

Solve   Learn   Glossary   Check   Tools   Games

Look Back!

Connect Ideas Which of the fractions that you found are in simplest form?

How Can You Represent a Fraction in a Variety of Ways?

Decomposing means to break into parts.

Charlene wants to leave $\frac{1}{6}$ of her garden empty. What are some different ways she can plant the rest of her garden?

The fraction of the garden that Charlene will plant can be broken apart in more than one way.

$\frac{5}{6}$ planted

$\frac{1}{6}$ empty

Decompose the fraction into parts.

B ## One Way

She could plant 4 sections of blue flowers and 1 section of red peppers.

$\frac{5}{6}$ is $\frac{4}{6}$ and $\frac{1}{6}$.

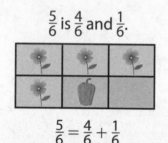

$$\frac{5}{6} = \frac{4}{6} + \frac{1}{6}$$

C ## Another Way

She could plant 1 section of green beans, 1 section of yellow squash, 1 section of red peppers, and 2 sections of blue flowers.

$\frac{5}{6}$ is $\frac{1}{6}$ and $\frac{1}{6}$ and $\frac{1}{6}$ and $\frac{2}{6}$.

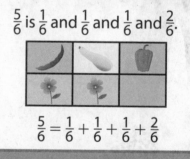

$$\frac{5}{6} = \frac{1}{6} + \frac{1}{6} + \frac{1}{6} + \frac{2}{6}$$

Do You Understand?

Convince Me! Draw pictures like the ones above to show why both of these equations are true.

$$\frac{5}{6} = \frac{3}{6} + \frac{2}{6} \qquad \frac{5}{6} = \frac{1}{6} + \frac{2}{6} + \frac{2}{6}$$

 © Pearson Education, Inc. 4

Another Example

A mixed number has a whole number part and a fraction part. The model below shows the mixed number $3\frac{1}{8}$. How can you decompose $3\frac{1}{8}$?

Each whole can be shown as eight equal parts. So $3\frac{1}{8}$ is $\frac{8}{8}$ and $\frac{8}{8}$ and $\frac{8}{8}$ and $\frac{1}{8}$.

$$3\frac{1}{8} = \frac{8}{8} + \frac{8}{8} + \frac{8}{8} + \frac{1}{8}$$

☆ Guided Practice *

In **1** and **2**, write each fraction or mixed number as a sum of fractions in two different ways.

1. $\frac{3}{5} = \frac{\square}{\square} + \frac{\square}{\square}$ $\frac{3}{5} = \frac{\square}{\square} + \frac{\square}{\square} + \frac{\square}{\square}$

2. $1\frac{3}{4} = \frac{\square}{\square} + \frac{\square}{\square}$ $1\frac{3}{4} = \frac{\square}{\square} + \frac{\square}{\square}$

3. Complete the following statement. Then draw a model to show that the statement is true.

   $\frac{7}{8}$ equals _____ plus _____.

4. **Justify** Paul said that the sum of $\frac{1}{10} + \frac{7}{10} + \frac{4}{10}$ is the same as the sum of $\frac{5}{10} + \frac{5}{10} + \frac{2}{10}$. Is he correct? Explain.

You can use fraction strips or draw a model to help you decompose fractions.

☆ Independent Practice ☆

Leveled Practice In **5** through **8**, write each fraction or mixed number as the sum of fractions in two different ways.

5. $\frac{4}{6} = \frac{\square}{\square} + \frac{\square}{\square}$ $\frac{4}{6} = \frac{\square}{\square} + \frac{\square}{\square} + \frac{\square}{\square}$

6. $\frac{8}{9} = \frac{\square}{\square} + \frac{\square}{\square}$ $\frac{8}{9} = \frac{\square}{\square} + \frac{\square}{\square} + \frac{\square}{\square}$

7. $1\frac{3}{5} = \frac{\square}{\square} + \frac{\square}{\square}$ $1\frac{3}{5} = \frac{\square}{\square} + \frac{\square}{\square} + \frac{\square}{\square}$

8. $2\frac{1}{2} = \frac{\square}{\square} + \frac{\square}{\square}$ $2\frac{1}{2} = \frac{\square}{\square} + \frac{\square}{\square} + \frac{\square}{\square}$

Problem Solving

9. Number Sense A teacher wants to distribute a stack of notebook paper to three groups of students, A, B, and C. Each group does not have to get the same amount of paper. List three ways the teacher can distribute all of the paper to the three groups.

$1\frac{2}{3}$ inches

10. Reason Jacqueline ate $\frac{1}{5}$ of a bag of popcorn. She then shared the rest with Enrique. The two of them finished eating the bag of popcorn. List three different ways they could have shared the remaining popcorn.

11. Number Sense Mrs. Anderson showed her class how to write $1\frac{3}{8}$ in several different ways. Which of the following shows one way Mrs. Anderson could have decomposed $1\frac{3}{8}$?

A $\frac{1}{8} + \frac{3}{8}$

B $\frac{3}{8} + \frac{4}{8} + \frac{6}{8}$

C $\frac{3}{8} + \frac{3}{8} + \frac{3}{8} + \frac{2}{8}$

D $\frac{10}{8} + \frac{3}{8}$

12. Mental Math Decompose the fraction $\frac{7}{10}$ into three fractions that all have a different numerator.

13. Extend Your Thinking Jason wrote the mixed number $1\frac{1}{3}$ as the sum of three fractions. None of the fractions had a denominator of 3. How is this possible? What fractions might Jason have used?

14. Connect In a class of 16 students, 8 students are boys. Write four equivalent fractions that tell which part of the class is boys. Then write the fraction in simplest form.

© Pearson Education, Inc. 4

Another Look!

Shannon wants to use $\frac{5}{8}$ of her garden space for flowers. She wants to plant petunias and marigolds. How can she use the available space?

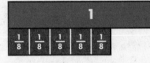

There are more than two solutions to this problem.

Write $\frac{5}{8}$ as the sum of two fractions in two different ways.

$$\frac{5}{8} = \frac{1}{8} + \frac{4}{8} \qquad \frac{5}{8} = \frac{2}{8} + \frac{3}{8}$$

Shannon could use $\frac{1}{8}$ of the space for petunias and $\frac{4}{8}$ for marigolds, or she could use $\frac{2}{8}$ of the space for petunias and $\frac{3}{8}$ for marigolds.

In **1** through **8**, write each fraction or mixed number as the sum of fractions in two different ways.

1. $\frac{4}{7} = \dfrac{\square}{\square} + \dfrac{\square}{\square}$ $\frac{4}{7} = \dfrac{\square}{\square} + \dfrac{\square}{\square} + \dfrac{\square}{\square}$

2. $\frac{7}{10} = \dfrac{\square}{\square} + \dfrac{\square}{\square}$ $\frac{7}{10} = \dfrac{\square}{\square} + \dfrac{\square}{\square} + \dfrac{\square}{\square}$

3. $\frac{4}{5} =$

   $\frac{4}{5} =$

4. $\frac{3}{10} =$

   $\frac{3}{10} =$

5. $1\frac{1}{4} =$

   $1\frac{1}{4} =$

6. $2\frac{2}{3} =$

   $2\frac{2}{3} =$

7. $1\frac{3}{5} =$

   $1\frac{3}{5} =$

8. $1\frac{1}{2} =$

   $1\frac{1}{2} =$

Challenge yourself! Include ways that break a fraction or mixed number into more than two parts.

9. **Number Sense** Yvonne ran $\frac{3}{8}$ of the race before stopping for water. She wants to stop for water one more time before finishing the race. List two ways she can do this.

10. **Connect** In a class of 24 students, 8 students did **NOT** check out a book from the library. What fraction of the students did check out a book? Write the fraction again in simplest form.

11. **Reason** A teacher noticed that $\frac{5}{9}$ of the students were wearing either blue shirts or white shirts. Write two different ways this could be done.

12. **Number Sense** Mrs. Evans asked the class to decompose $1\frac{3}{4}$. Which of the following is **NOT** a way to decompose $1\frac{3}{4}$?

A $\frac{4}{4} + \frac{3}{4}$

B $\frac{5}{4} + \frac{1}{4} + \frac{1}{4}$

C $\frac{2}{4} + \frac{5}{4}$

D $\frac{1}{4} + \frac{3}{4}$

13. **Extend Your Thinking** Mark said he can decompose the fraction $\frac{5}{6}$ into three fractions with three different numerators. Is this possible? Explain.

14. Connie made $1\frac{1}{3}$ pounds of trail mix for a hike. Is there a way Connie can break up the trail mix into four equal bags without having any left over? Explain.

Start by finding an equivalent fraction.

15. **Justify** Marcus walked $\frac{1}{8}$ mile to the park, then $\frac{4}{8}$ mile to the store, and finally $\frac{2}{8}$ mile home. To walk a mile, how much farther does Marcus need to walk? Explain how you know.

© Pearson Education, Inc. 4

Name _____

Solve & Share

Jonas is making nachos and tacos for a family party. He uses $\frac{2}{5}$ bag of shredded cheese for the nachos and $\frac{1}{5}$ bag for the tacos. How much of the bag of shredded cheese does Jonas use in all? *Solve this problem any way you choose.*

TEKS 4.3E Represent and solve addition and subtraction of fractions with equal denominators using objects and pictorial models that build to the number line and properties of operations. Also, 4.3. Mathematical Process Standards 4.1A, 4.1C, 4.1D, 4.1G

You can **reason**. What expression can you write to represent this problem? *Show your work in the space below!*

Digital Resources at PearsonTexas.com

Solve Learn Glossary Check Tools Games

Look Back!

Construct Arguments What do you notice about the denominators?

How Can You Add Fractions with Like Denominators?

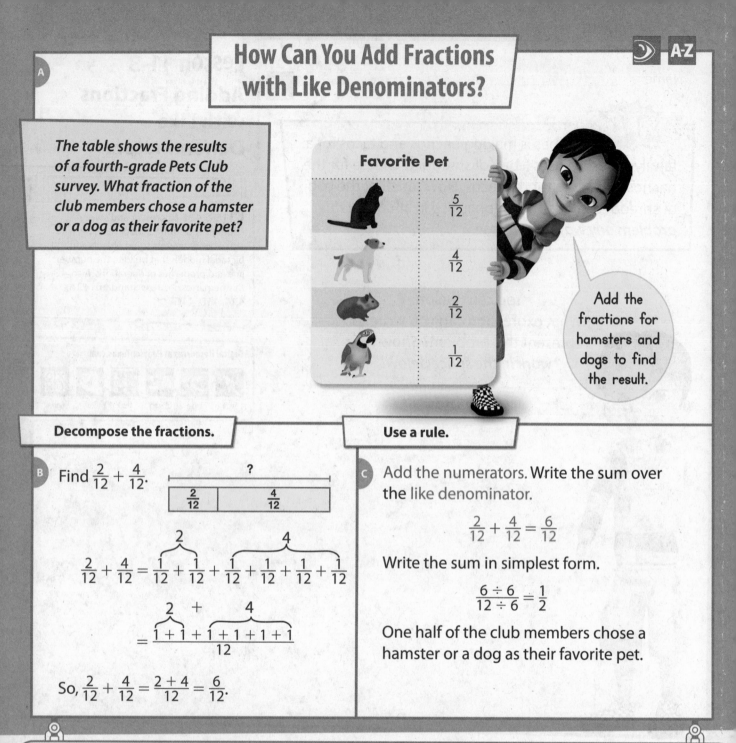

The table shows the results of a fourth-grade Pets Club survey. What fraction of the club members chose a hamster or a dog as their favorite pet?

Favorite Pet

(cat)	$\frac{5}{12}$
(dog)	$\frac{4}{12}$
(hamster)	$\frac{2}{12}$
(parrot)	$\frac{1}{12}$

Add the fractions for hamsters and dogs to find the result.

Decompose the fractions.

B Find $\frac{2}{12} + \frac{4}{12}$.

$$\frac{2}{12} + \frac{4}{12} = \frac{\overbrace{1}^{2} + \frac{1}{12} + \frac{1}{12}}{12} + \overbrace{\frac{1}{12} + \frac{1}{12} + \frac{1}{12} + \frac{1}{12}}^{4}$$

$$= \frac{\overbrace{1 + 1}^{2} + \overbrace{1 + 1 + 1 + 1}^{4}}{12}$$

So, $\frac{2}{12} + \frac{4}{12} = \frac{2+4}{12} = \frac{6}{12}$.

Use a rule.

C Add the numerators. Write the sum over the like denominator.

$$\frac{2}{12} + \frac{4}{12} = \frac{6}{12}$$

Write the sum in simplest form.

$$\frac{6 \div 6}{12 \div 6} = \frac{1}{2}$$

One half of the club members chose a hamster or a dog as their favorite pet.

Do You Understand?

Convince Me! Frank solved the problem above and found $\frac{2}{12} + \frac{4}{12} = \frac{6}{24} = \frac{1}{4}$.

What error did Frank make? Explain why his work is not correct.

© Pearson Education, Inc. 4

Name _____

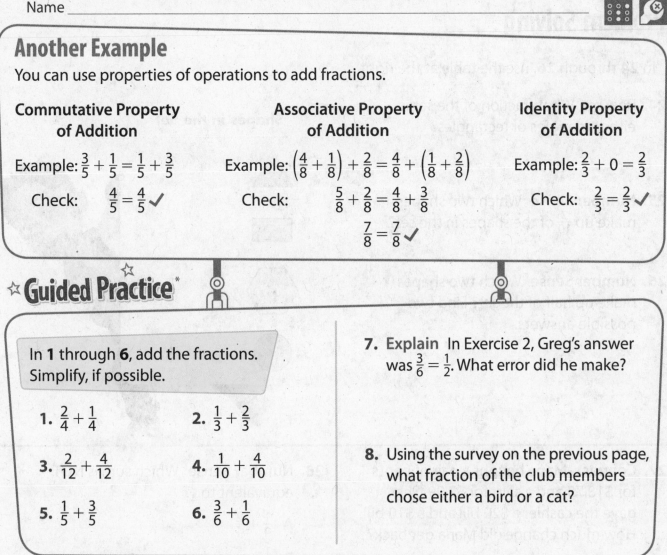

Another Example

You can use properties of operations to add fractions.

Commutative Property of Addition

Example: $\frac{3}{5} + \frac{1}{5} = \frac{1}{5} + \frac{3}{5}$

Check: $\frac{4}{5} = \frac{4}{5}$ ✓

Associative Property of Addition

Example: $\left(\frac{4}{8} + \frac{1}{8}\right) + \frac{2}{8} = \frac{4}{8} + \left(\frac{1}{8} + \frac{2}{8}\right)$

Check: $\frac{5}{8} + \frac{2}{8} = \frac{4}{8} + \frac{3}{8}$

$\frac{7}{8} = \frac{7}{8}$ ✓

Identity Property of Addition

Example: $\frac{2}{3} + 0 = \frac{2}{3}$

Check: $\frac{2}{3} = \frac{2}{3}$ ✓

☆ Guided Practice *

In **1** through **6**, add the fractions. Simplify, if possible.

1. $\frac{2}{4} + \frac{1}{4}$

2. $\frac{1}{3} + \frac{2}{3}$

3. $\frac{2}{12} + \frac{4}{12}$

4. $\frac{1}{10} + \frac{4}{10}$

5. $\frac{1}{5} + \frac{3}{5}$

6. $\frac{3}{6} + \frac{1}{6}$

7. **Explain** In Exercise 2, Greg's answer was $\frac{3}{6} = \frac{1}{2}$. What error did he make?

8. Using the survey on the previous page, what fraction of the club members chose either a bird or a cat?

☆ Independent Practice ☆

In **9** through **23**, add the fractions. Simplify, if possible. You may use models and properties of operations to help.

9. $\frac{2}{6} + \frac{2}{6}$

10. $\frac{3}{5} + \frac{2}{5}$

11. $\frac{2}{7} + \frac{1}{7}$

12. $\frac{3}{8} + \frac{5}{8}$

13. $\frac{5}{10} + \frac{3}{10}$

14. $\frac{5}{12} + \frac{4}{12}$

15. $\frac{3}{10} + \frac{2}{10}$

16. $\frac{1}{12} + \frac{3}{12}$

17. $\frac{2}{8} + \frac{4}{8}$

18. $\frac{2}{6} + \frac{1}{6}$

19. $\frac{2}{12} + \frac{6}{12}$

20. $\frac{3}{10} + \frac{2}{10} + \frac{4}{10}$

21. $\frac{4}{5} + \frac{3}{5} + \frac{2}{5}$

22. $\frac{30}{100} + \frac{40}{100}$

23. $\frac{3}{6} + \frac{9}{6}$

Problem Solving

In **24** through **26**, use the table at the right.

24. Reason What fraction of the set is either triangles or rectangles?

25. Number Sense Which two shapes make up $\frac{7}{10}$ of the shapes in the set?

26. Number Sense Which two shapes make up half of the set? Find two possible answers.

Shapes in the Set	
▲	$\frac{2}{10}$
▭	$\frac{4}{10}$
⬡	$\frac{1}{10}$
●	$\frac{3}{10}$

27. Connect Maria bought a pair of pants for $18.75 and a shirt for $7.99. She gave the cashier a $20 bill and a $10 bill. How much change did Maria get back?

28. Number Sense Which sum is **NOT** equivalent to $\frac{3}{4}$?

A $\frac{1}{4} + \frac{2}{4}$

B $\frac{1}{8} + \frac{5}{8}$

C $\frac{3}{8} + \frac{3}{8}$

D $\frac{3}{12} + \frac{5}{12}$

29. Connect There are 64 crayons in one box. A school bought 25 boxes of crayons for the art program. How many crayons did the school buy?

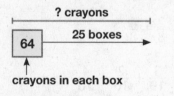

30. Extend Your Thinking Ken thinks that the sum of $\frac{3}{10}$ and $\frac{4}{10}$ is $\frac{7}{20}$. Explain how you would help Ken understand why his answer is incorrect.

© Pearson Education, Inc. 4

Name _____

Another Look!

Find the sum of $\frac{3}{8} + \frac{1}{8}$.

When you add fractions with like denominators, add the numerators and keep the denominator the same.

$$\frac{3}{8} + \frac{1}{8} = \frac{4}{8}$$

Then write the fraction in simplest form.

$$\frac{4 \div 4}{8 \div 4} = \frac{1}{2}$$

Remember, a fraction is in simplest form when the numerator and denominator have no common factor other than 1.

In **1** through **18**, find each sum. Simplify, if possible. You may use models and properties of operations to help.

1. $\frac{1}{3} + \frac{1}{3}$

2. $\frac{3}{10} + \frac{6}{10}$

3. $\frac{5}{12} + \frac{2}{12}$

4. $\frac{3}{12} + \frac{7}{12}$

5. $\frac{5}{10} + \frac{3}{10}$

6. $\frac{2}{8} + \frac{4}{8}$

7. $\frac{7}{10} + \frac{3}{10}$

8. $\frac{1}{8} + \frac{6}{8}$

9. $\frac{1}{10} + \frac{5}{10}$

10. $\frac{4}{5} + \frac{1}{5}$

11. $\left(\frac{2}{9} + \frac{6}{9}\right) + \frac{1}{9}$

12. $\frac{6}{10} + 0$

13. $\frac{1}{5} + \frac{2}{5} + \frac{2}{5}$

14. $\frac{2}{8} + \frac{1}{8} + \frac{4}{8}$

15. $\frac{2}{6} + \frac{1}{6}$

16. $\left(\frac{20}{100} + \frac{25}{100}\right) + \frac{25}{100}$

17. $\frac{2}{10} + \left(\frac{6}{10} + \frac{1}{10}\right)$

18. $\frac{20}{20} + \frac{20}{20} + \frac{20}{20}$

In **19** through **21**, use the table at the right.

19. **Reason** What fraction of the students voted for fruit juice or soda?

20. **Number Sense** Which two beverages have a sum of $\frac{5}{8}$ of the student votes?

21. **Number Sense** What combination of beverages makes up $\frac{3}{4}$ of the student votes?

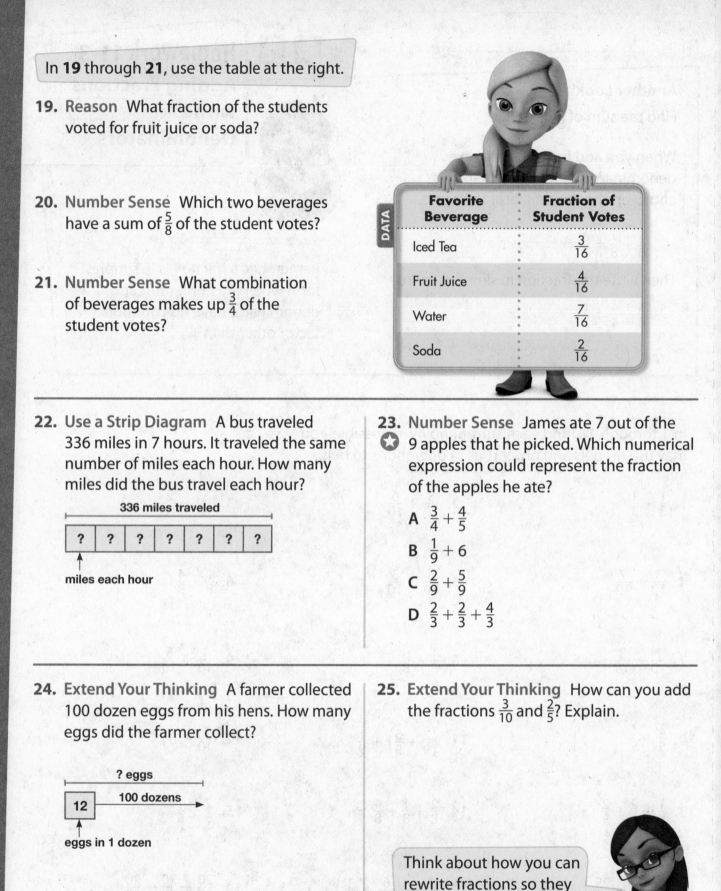

DATA

Favorite Beverage	Fraction of Student Votes
Iced Tea	$\frac{3}{16}$
Fruit Juice	$\frac{4}{16}$
Water	$\frac{7}{16}$
Soda	$\frac{2}{16}$

22. **Use a Strip Diagram** A bus traveled 336 miles in 7 hours. It traveled the same number of miles each hour. How many miles did the bus travel each hour?

336 miles traveled

?	?	?	?	?	?	?

miles each hour

23. **Number Sense** James ate 7 out of the 9 apples that he picked. Which numerical expression could represent the fraction of the apples he ate?

A $\frac{3}{4} + \frac{4}{5}$

B $\frac{1}{9} + 6$

C $\frac{2}{9} + \frac{5}{9}$

D $\frac{2}{3} + \frac{2}{3} + \frac{4}{3}$

24. **Extend Your Thinking** A farmer collected 100 dozen eggs from his hens. How many eggs did the farmer collect?

? eggs

12	100 dozens →

eggs in 1 dozen

25. **Extend Your Thinking** How can you add the fractions $\frac{3}{10}$ and $\frac{2}{5}$? Explain.

Think about how you can rewrite fractions so they have like denominators.

574

© Pearson Education, Inc. 4

Name _____

Solve & Share

Mr. Yetkin uses $\frac{4}{6}$ of a sheet of plywood to board up a window. How much of the plywood is left? *Solve this problem any way you choose.*

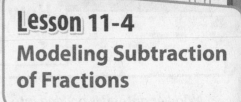

TEKS 4.3E Represent and solve addition and subtraction of fractions with equal denominators using objects and pictorial models that build to the number line and properties of operations. Also, 4.3. Mathematical Process Standards 4.1A, 4.1C, 4.1D, 4.1E

You can use tools. Fraction strips can help you model this problem. *Show your work in the space below!*

Digital Resources at PearsonTexas.com

Solve Learn Glossary Check Tools Games

Look Back!

Create and Use Representations What expression can you use to solve this problem?

How Can You Use Fraction Strips to Subtract Fractions?

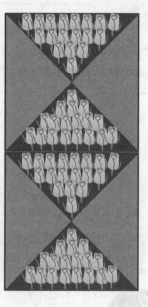

A flower garden is divided into eight equal sections.

If four sections are used to grow yellow roses, what fraction is left to grow other flowers?

Take away a part from the whole to find the difference.

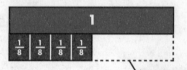
Use objects.

B Use eight $\frac{1}{8}$ fraction strips to represent the whole flower garden. Take four strips away.

1

$\frac{1}{8}$	$\frac{1}{8}$	$\frac{1}{8}$	$\frac{1}{8}$

Four strips are left.

$\frac{1}{8}$	$\frac{1}{8}$	$\frac{1}{8}$	$\frac{1}{8}$

So, $\frac{4}{8}$ of the garden is left to grow other flowers.

C Subtract the numerators. Write the part taken away over the like denominator.

$$\frac{8}{8} - \frac{4}{8} = \frac{4}{8}$$

Write the difference in simplest form.

$$\frac{4 \div 4}{8 \div 4} = \frac{1}{2}$$

So, $\frac{1}{2}$ of the garden is left to grow other flowers.

Do You Understand?

Convince Me! In the problem above, suppose four sections of the garden grow yellow roses and two other sections grow petunias. How much more of the garden is used for yellow roses than is used for petunias? Write your answer as a fraction.

© Pearson Education, Inc. 4

Name _____

In **1** through **4**, use fraction strips to subtract. Simplify, if possible.

1. $\frac{2}{3} - \frac{1}{3}$

| 1 |
| $\frac{1}{3}$ |
| $\frac{1}{3}$ |

2. $\frac{3}{5} - \frac{2}{5}$

| 1 |
| $\frac{1}{5}$ |
| $\frac{1}{5}$ $\frac{1}{5}$ |

3. $\frac{7}{12} - \frac{3}{12}$

4. $\frac{7}{8} - \frac{1}{8}$

5. **Reason** In the problem at the top of the previous page, suppose two other sections were used to grow peonies. What fraction of the garden is now available for other flowers? Show your work.

6. **Communicate** In Exercise 3, explain how you simplified your answer.

Leveled Practice In **7** through **20**, use objects, such as fraction strips, to subtract. Simplify, if possible.

7. $\frac{11}{12} - \frac{5}{12}$

| 1 |
| $\frac{1}{12}$ $\frac{1}{12}$ $\frac{1}{12}$ $\frac{1}{12}$ $\frac{1}{12}$ $\frac{1}{12}$ |
| $\frac{1}{12}$ $\frac{1}{12}$ $\frac{1}{12}$ $\frac{1}{12}$ $\frac{1}{12}$ |

8. $\frac{2}{2} - \frac{1}{2}$

| 1 |
| $\frac{1}{2}$ |
| $\frac{1}{2}$ |

9. $\frac{4}{5} - \frac{2}{5}$

10. $\frac{7}{8} - \frac{5}{8}$

11. $\frac{9}{10} - \frac{3}{10}$

12. $\frac{4}{6} - \frac{1}{6}$

13. $\frac{5}{8} - \frac{2}{8}$

14. $\frac{7}{10} - \frac{4}{10}$

15. $\frac{8}{10} - \frac{2}{10}$

16. $\frac{3}{5} - \frac{1}{5}$

17. $\frac{5}{6} - \frac{4}{6}$

18. $\frac{4}{5} - \frac{4}{5}$

19. $\frac{8}{10} - \frac{4}{10}$

20. $\frac{1}{3} - \frac{1}{3}$

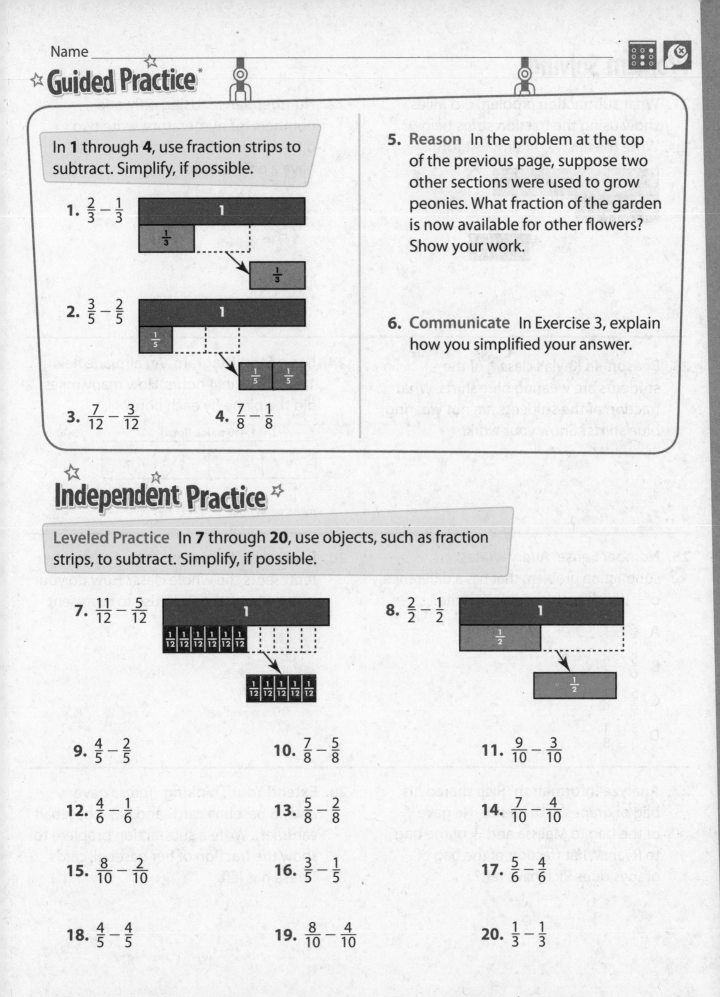

Problem Solving

21. What subtraction problem did Miles show using the fraction strips below? Write the answer in simplest form.

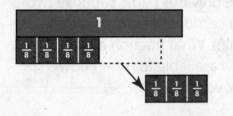

22. Number Sense Using only odd numbers for numerators, write two different subtraction problems that have a difference of $\frac{1}{2}$.

23. Reason In Kayla's class, $\frac{2}{9}$ of the students are wearing blue shirts. What fraction of the students are not wearing blue shirts? Show your work.

24. Use a Strip Diagram An airplane flew 1,440 miles in 4 hours. How many miles did the plane fly each hour?

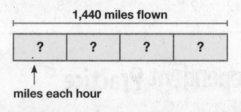

miles each hour

25. Number Sense Audry wrote a subtraction problem that has a difference of $\frac{1}{3}$. Which problem did she write?

A $\frac{2}{5} - \frac{1}{5}$

B $\frac{5}{6} - \frac{4}{6}$

C $\frac{5}{9} - \frac{2}{9}$

D $\frac{3}{8} - \frac{1}{8}$

26. Represent In Problem 23, what number represents the whole class? How do you know what fraction to use to represent this number?

27. Analyze Information Rich shared his bag of grapes with friends. He gave $\frac{2}{10}$ of the bag to Melissa and $\frac{4}{10}$ of the bag to Ryan. What fraction of the bag of grapes does Rich have left?

28. Extend Your Thinking Teresa gave away 8 baseball cards and has 4 baseball cards left. Write a subtraction problem to show the fraction of her baseball cards Teresa has left.

© Pearson Education, Inc. 4

Name _____

Another Look!

Kimberly made a pizza and cut it into 10 equal slices. She ate two of the slices. What fraction of the pizza is left?

Remember that $\frac{10}{10}$ = 1 whole pizza.

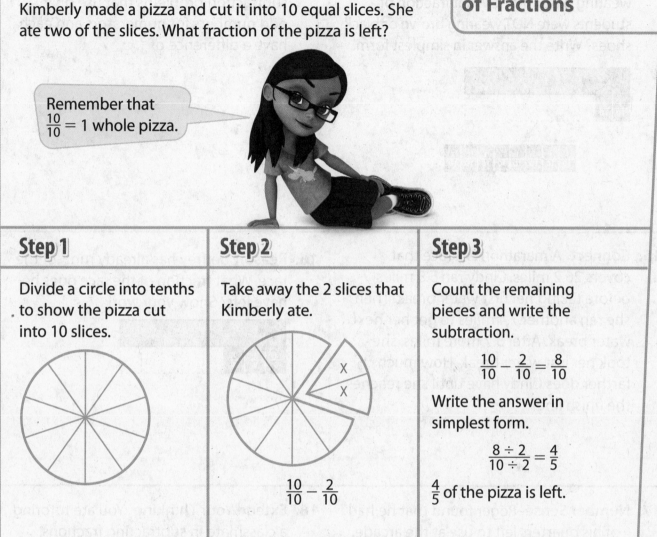

Step 1

Divide a circle into tenths to show the pizza cut into 10 slices.

Step 2

Take away the 2 slices that Kimberly ate.

$\frac{10}{10} - \frac{2}{10}$

Step 3

Count the remaining pieces and write the subtraction.

$\frac{10}{10} - \frac{2}{10} = \frac{8}{10}$

Write the answer in simplest form.

$\frac{8 \div 2}{10 \div 2} = \frac{4}{5}$

$\frac{4}{5}$ of the pizza is left.

In **1** through **12**, use fraction strips or models to subtract. Simplify, if possible.

1. $\frac{5}{5} - \frac{2}{5}$

2. $\frac{7}{10} - \frac{3}{10}$

3. $\frac{3}{4} - \frac{2}{4}$

4. $\frac{8}{10} - \frac{5}{10}$

5. $\frac{6}{6} - \frac{3}{6}$

6. $\frac{11}{12} - \frac{7}{12}$

7. $\frac{5}{6} - \frac{2}{6}$

8. $\frac{4}{8} - \frac{2}{8}$

9. $\frac{11}{12} - \frac{8}{12}$

10. $\frac{7}{12} - \frac{5}{12}$

11. $\frac{6}{10} - \frac{4}{10}$

12. $\frac{9}{12} - \frac{6}{12}$

13. Represent Eddie noticed that out of 10 students, one student was wearing brown shoes, and seven students were wearing black shoes. What fraction of students were **NOT** wearing brown or black shoes? Write the answer in simplest form.

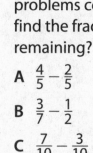

14. Number Sense Mrs. Granger is writing problems for a test about subtracting fractions. Help her write two different subtraction problems that use only odd numbers for numerators and each have a difference of $\frac{3}{4}$.

15. Connect A marathon is a race that covers 26.2 miles. Cindy ran 5.3 miles before taking her first water break. Then she ran another 7.4 miles to get her next water break. After 5.7 more miles, she took her last water break. How much farther does Cindy have until she reaches the finish line?

16. Reason Jeffrey has already run $\frac{3}{8}$ of the race. What fraction of the race does he have left? Show your work.

17. Number Sense Roger found that he had $\frac{2}{5}$ of his quarters left to use at the arcade. Which of the following subtraction problems could he have **NOT** used to find the fraction of quarters he had remaining?

A $\frac{4}{5} - \frac{2}{5}$

B $\frac{3}{7} - \frac{1}{2}$

C $\frac{7}{10} - \frac{3}{10}$

D $\frac{5}{5} - \frac{3}{5}$

18. Extend Your Thinking You are tutoring a classmate in subtracting fractions. How might you summarize the rules for subtracting fractions with like denominators?

You can number the rules to help make them clear.

© Pearson Education, Inc. 4

Name _____

☆ ☆
Solve & Share

Leah and Josh live in the same direction from school and on the same side of Forest Road. Leah's house is $\frac{8}{10}$ mile from school. Josh's house is $\frac{5}{10}$ mile from school. How much farther does Leah have to walk home when she reaches Josh's house? *Solve this problem any way you choose.*

🚩 **TEKS 4.3E** Represent and solve addition and subtraction of fractions with equal denominators using objects and pictorial models that build to the number line and properties of operations. Also, 4.3. Mathematical Process Standards 4.1C, 4.1D, 4.1E, 4.1F, 4.1G

Digital Resources at PearsonTexas.com

Solve   Learn   Glossary   Check   Tools   Games

You can **create and use representations.** What expression can you use to represent this problem? *Show your work in the space above!*

Look Back!

Connect Write your answer as a decimal.

How Can You Subtract Fractions with Like Denominators?

Tania is squeezing lemons to make lemonade. The recipe calls for $\frac{5}{8}$ cup of lemon juice. The amount she has squeezed is shown below. How much more lemon juice does she need to squeeze?

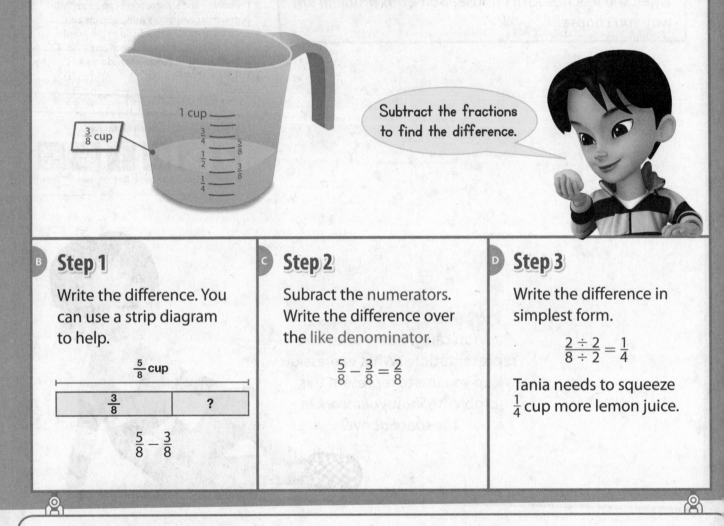

$\frac{3}{8}$ cup

1 cup
$\frac{3}{4}$
$\frac{5}{8}$
$\frac{1}{2}$
$\frac{3}{8}$
$\frac{1}{4}$

Subtract the fractions to find the difference.

Step 1

Write the difference. You can use a strip diagram to help.

$\frac{5}{8}$ cup

$\frac{3}{8}$	?

$\frac{5}{8} - \frac{3}{8}$

Step 2

Subract the numerators. Write the difference over the like denominator.

$$\frac{5}{8} - \frac{3}{8} = \frac{2}{8}$$

Step 3

Write the difference in simplest form.

$$\frac{2 \div 2}{8 \div 2} = \frac{1}{4}$$

Tania needs to squeeze $\frac{1}{4}$ cup more lemon juice.

Do You Understand?

Convince Me! In the problem above, suppose Tania decided to double the amount of lemonade she wants to make. Then how much more lemon juice would she need to squeeze?

 © Pearson Education, Inc. 4

Another Example

Use properties of operations to find $\frac{3}{5} - \frac{1}{5}$.

$$\frac{3}{5} - \frac{1}{5} = \left(\frac{1}{5} + \frac{1}{5} + \frac{1}{5}\right) - \frac{1}{5}$$

$$\frac{3}{5} - \frac{1}{5} = \left(\frac{1}{5} + \frac{1}{5}\right) + \left(\frac{1}{5} - \frac{1}{5}\right)$$

$$\frac{3}{5} - \frac{1}{5} = \frac{2}{5} + 0 = \frac{2}{5}$$

☆ Guided Practice ☆

In **1** through **6**, subtract the fractions. Simplify, if possible.

1. $\frac{2}{3} - \frac{1}{3}$　　　2. $\frac{3}{4} - \frac{2}{4}$

3. $\frac{5}{6} - \frac{2}{6}$　　　4. $\frac{9}{12} - \frac{3}{12}$

5. $\frac{7}{8} - \frac{3}{8}$　　　6. $\frac{7}{10} - \frac{1}{10}$

7. **Explain** Jesse has a bottle that contains $\frac{13}{20}$ liter of water. He drinks $\frac{3}{20}$ liter. Jesse says that he has $\frac{1}{2}$ liter left. Is he correct? Explain.

8. **Connect** Subtract $\frac{4}{16}$ from $\frac{9}{16}$. What addition sentence can you use to check your answer?

Independent Practice ☆

Leveled Practice In **9** through **16**, subtract the fractions.

Remember to simplify, if possible.

9.

$\frac{5}{6}$	
$\frac{1}{6}$	?

$\frac{5}{6} - \frac{1}{6}$

10.

$\frac{8}{100}$	
$\frac{3}{100}$	?

$\frac{8}{100} - \frac{3}{100}$

11. $\frac{3}{4} - \frac{1}{4}$　　　12. $\frac{6}{8} - \frac{4}{8}$　　　13. $\frac{5}{6} - \frac{4}{6}$

14. $\frac{3}{8} - \frac{1}{8}$　　　15. $\frac{80}{100} - \frac{40}{100}$　　　16. $\frac{9}{10} - \frac{8}{10}$

Problem Solving

17. A passenger train is $\frac{4}{6}$ full. What fraction of the train is empty?

  A $\frac{4}{6}$

  B $\frac{3}{6}$

  C $\frac{2}{3}$

  D $\frac{1}{3}$

18. **Number Sense** Joey ran $\frac{1}{4}$ mile in the morning and $\frac{2}{4}$ mile in the afternoon. If he wants to run a full mile, how much more does Joey have to run? Explain how you found your answer.

19. **Use a Strip Diagram** A piece of chalk is $\frac{13}{16}$ inch long. Brian breaks off a piece that is $\frac{6}{16}$ inch long. How long is the piece of chalk that is left?

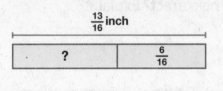

20. **Number Sense** Which of the following fractions is greater than the difference $\frac{8}{9} - \frac{2}{9}$?

  A $\frac{3}{4}$

  B $\frac{2}{3}$

  C $\frac{1}{2}$

  D $\frac{1}{3}$

21. The flags of all 5 Scandinavian countries are displayed at the right. What fraction describes how much more of the display is 2-color flags than is 3-color flags?

First find how many flags in all.

Denmark

Finland

Iceland

Norway

Sweden

22. **Extend Your Thinking** How is subtracting $\frac{4}{5} - \frac{3}{5}$ similar to subtracting $4 - 3$?

© Pearson Education, Inc. 4

Name _____

Another Look!

Flora needs an additional $\frac{2}{8}$ cup flour to make her dough. The dough recipe calls for $\frac{6}{8}$ cup flour. How many cups of flour does Flora have?

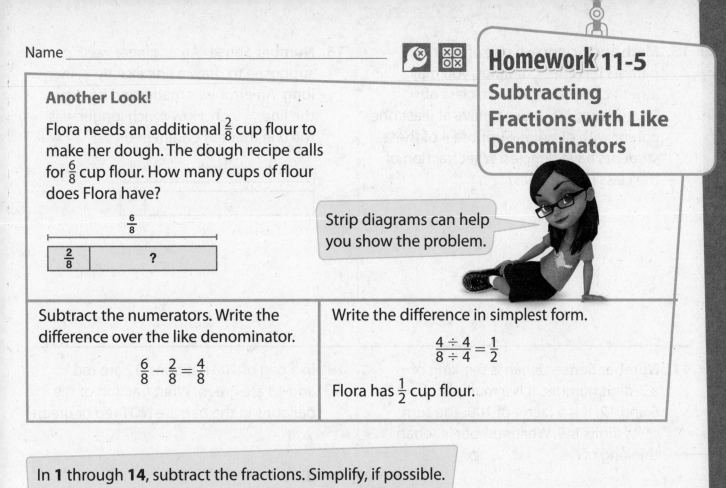

Strip diagrams can help you show the problem.

Subtract the numerators. Write the difference over the like denominator.	Write the difference in simplest form.
$\frac{6}{8} - \frac{2}{8} = \frac{4}{8}$	$\frac{4 \div 4}{8 \div 4} = \frac{1}{2}$ Flora has $\frac{1}{2}$ cup flour.

In **1** through **14**, subtract the fractions. Simplify, if possible.

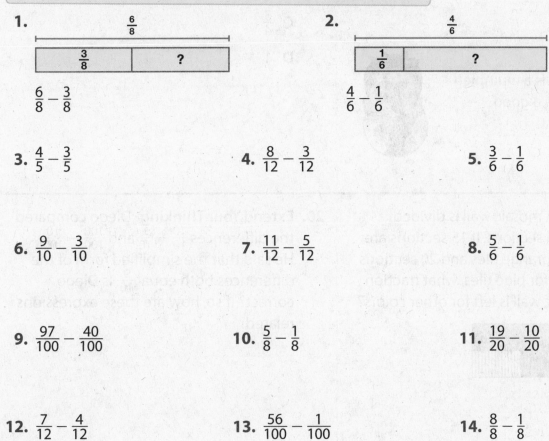

1.

$\frac{6}{8} - \frac{3}{8}$

2.

$\frac{4}{6} - \frac{1}{6}$

3. $\frac{4}{5} - \frac{3}{5}$

4. $\frac{8}{12} - \frac{3}{12}$

5. $\frac{3}{6} - \frac{1}{6}$

6. $\frac{9}{10} - \frac{3}{10}$

7. $\frac{11}{12} - \frac{5}{12}$

8. $\frac{5}{6} - \frac{1}{6}$

9. $\frac{97}{100} - \frac{40}{100}$

10. $\frac{5}{8} - \frac{1}{8}$

11. $\frac{19}{20} - \frac{10}{20}$

12. $\frac{7}{12} - \frac{4}{12}$

13. $\frac{56}{100} - \frac{1}{100}$

14. $\frac{8}{8} - \frac{1}{8}$

15. Math and Science If one of your parents has cheek dimples, you may inherit cheek dimples. In a class of 24 students, 10 students have at least one parent with dimples. Suppose 4 of these students have dimples. What fraction of the class has dimples?

16. Number Sense An engineer was supposed to draw a line exactly $\frac{27}{32}$ inch long. An error was made, and he drew the line $\frac{31}{32}$ inch. How much longer was the line that the engineer drew?

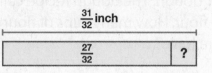

17. Number Sense Jonah is thinking of a 2-digit number. It is a multiple of 6 and 12. It is a factor of 108. The sum of its digits is 9. What number is Jonah thinking of?

You know it is a multiple of 12. That is a good place to start.

18. In a bag of 100 balloons, 12 are red and 13 are green. What fraction of the balloons in the bag are **NOT** red or green?

A $\frac{1}{4}$

B $\frac{1}{2}$

C $\frac{3}{4}$

D 1

19. Represent A mosaic wall is divided into 50 equal sections. If 15 sections are reserved for orange tiles and 20 sections are reserved for blue tiles, what fraction of the mosaic wall is left for other colors?

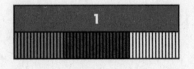

20. Extend Your Thinking Diego compared the differences $\frac{10}{10} - \frac{1}{10}$ and $\frac{100}{100} - \frac{10}{100}$. He said that the simplified form of the differences both equal $\frac{9}{10}$. Is Diego correct? If so, how are these expressions related?

© Pearson Education, Inc. 4

Name _____

Solve & Share

Sebastian has $\frac{6}{8}$ of the charge left on his phone. He uses $\frac{2}{8}$ of the charge playing a game. What fraction of the charge does he have left? *Solve this problem any way you choose.*

TEKS 4.3E Represent and solve addition and subtraction of fractions with equal denominators using objects and pictorial models that build to the number line and properties of operations. Mathematical Process Standards 4.1B, 4.1C, 4.1D, 4.1E, 4.1G

You can **use tools,** such as a number line, to model this problem. *Show your work in the space below!*

Digital Resources at PearsonTexas.com

Solve   Learn   Glossary   Check   Tools   Games

Look Back!

Number Sense What fraction is equivalent to the amount of charge that Sebastian used when playing the game?

A

Mary rides her bike $\frac{2}{10}$ mile to pick up her friend Marcy for soccer practice. Together, they ride $\frac{5}{10}$ mile to the soccer field. What is the distance from Mary's house to the soccer field?

Add to find the total distance.

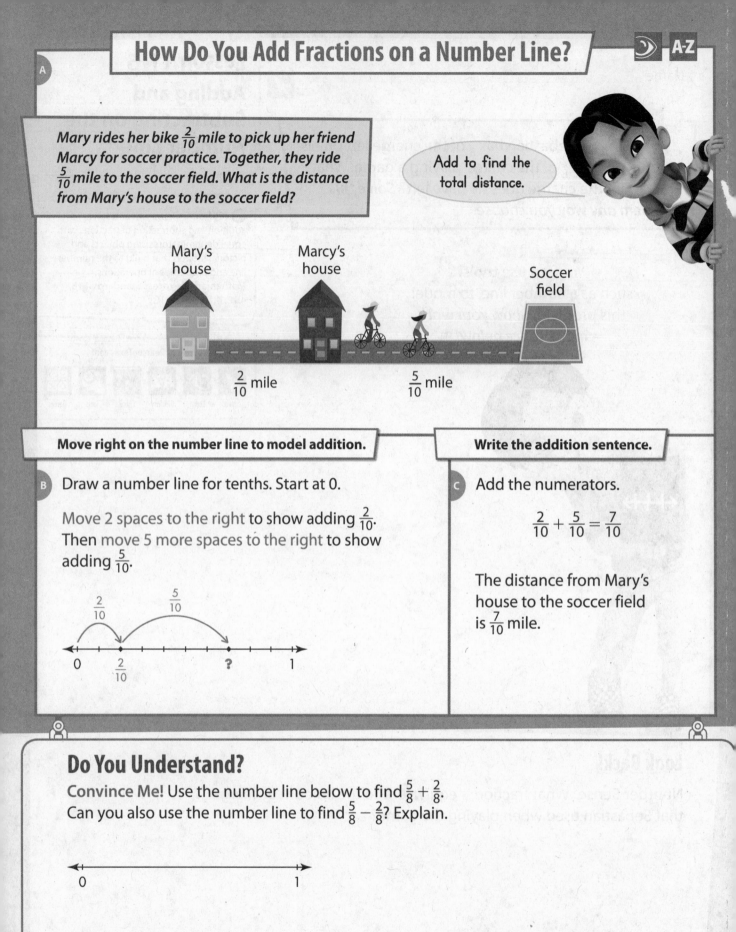

Mary's house   Marcy's house   Soccer field

$\frac{2}{10}$ mile $\frac{5}{10}$ mile

Move right on the number line to model addition.

B Draw a number line for tenths. Start at 0.

Move 2 spaces to the right to show adding $\frac{2}{10}$. Then move 5 more spaces to the right to show adding $\frac{5}{10}$.

$\frac{2}{10}$ $\frac{5}{10}$

0    $\frac{2}{10}$?   1

Write the addition sentence.

C Add the numerators.

$$\frac{2}{10} + \frac{5}{10} = \frac{7}{10}$$

The distance from Mary's house to the soccer field is $\frac{7}{10}$ mile.

Do You Understand?

Convince Me! Use the number line below to find $\frac{5}{8} + \frac{2}{8}$. Can you also use the number line to find $\frac{5}{8} - \frac{2}{8}$? Explain.

0   1

© Pearson Education, Inc. 4

Another Example

Find $\frac{6}{7} - \frac{4}{7}$.

- Start at $\frac{6}{7}$.

- Move 4 spaces to the left to subtract $\frac{4}{7}$.

- The ending point is $\frac{2}{7}$.

So, $\frac{6}{7} - \frac{4}{7} = \frac{2}{7}$.

Move left on the number line to model subtraction.

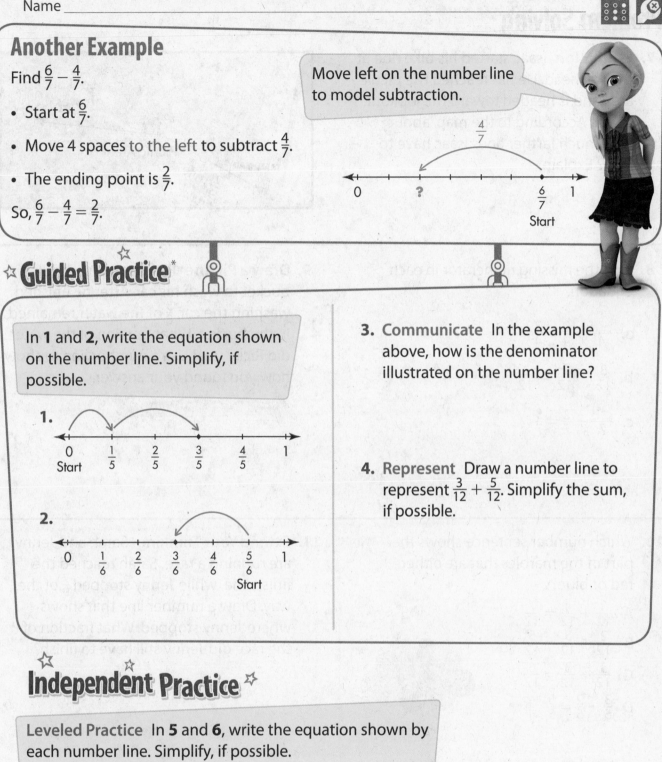

☆ Guided Practice ☆

In **1** and **2**, write the equation shown on the number line. Simplify, if possible.

1.

2.

3. Communicate In the example above, how is the denominator illustrated on the number line?

4. Represent Draw a number line to represent $\frac{3}{12} + \frac{5}{12}$. Simplify the sum, if possible.

Independent Practice ☆

Leveled Practice In **5** and **6**, write the equation shown by each number line. Simplify, if possible.

5.

6.

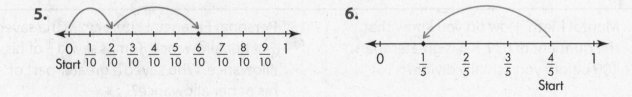

Problem Solving

7. Estimation Isaac started his bike ride at the trailhead. He has reached the picnic area and is headed toward the lookout tower. According to the map, about how much farther does Isaac have to bike? Explain.

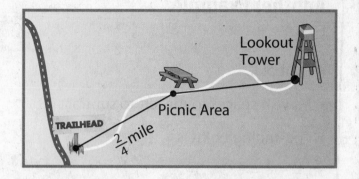

Lookout Tower

Picnic Area

TRAILHEAD

$\frac{2}{4}$ mile

---

8. Find the missing numerator in each equation.

a. $\dfrac{\square}{4} + \dfrac{2}{4} = \dfrac{3}{4}$

b. $\dfrac{8}{12} - \dfrac{\square}{12} = \dfrac{2}{12}$

c. $\dfrac{\square}{7} + \dfrac{2}{7} = \dfrac{5}{7}$

9. Draw a Picture Ricky completely filled a bucket to wash his car. After he finished washing the car, $\frac{5}{8}$ of the water remained in the bucket. What fraction of the water did Ricky use? Use a number line to show how you found your answer.

---

10. Which number sentence shows the part of the marbles that are either red or blue?

A $\dfrac{3}{12} + \dfrac{4}{12} = \dfrac{7}{12}$

B $\dfrac{2}{12} + \dfrac{3}{12} = \dfrac{5}{12}$

C $\dfrac{3}{12} + \dfrac{3}{12} = \dfrac{6}{12}$

D $\dfrac{3}{5} + \dfrac{2}{5} = \dfrac{5}{5}$

11. Extend Your Thinking Sarah and Jenny are running a race. Sarah reached the finish line, while Jenny stopped $\frac{7}{9}$ of the way. Draw a number line that shows where Jenny stopped. What fraction of the race did Jenny still have to finish?

---

12. Mental Math How do you know that the quotient of $639 \div 6$ is greater than 100 before you actually divide?

13. Personal Financial Literacy Maria saved $\frac{1}{4}$ of her allowance. Tomas saved $\frac{1}{6}$ of his allowance. Who saved a greater part of his or her allowance?

© Pearson Education, Inc. 4

Another Look!

Katie and Raul ran in a relay race. Katie ran $\frac{3}{8}$ mile, and Raul ran $\frac{7}{8}$ mile. How much farther did Raul run?

Subtract to find the difference. Always remember to simplify your answer.

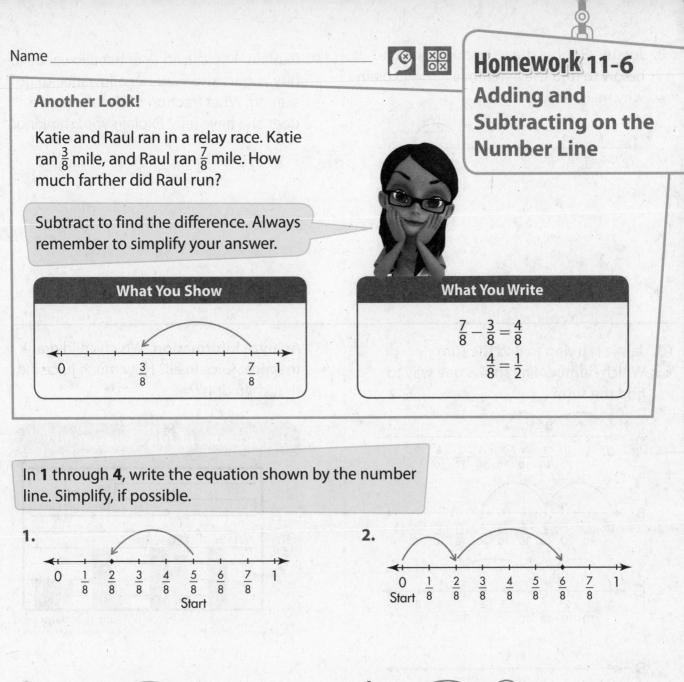

What You Show	What You Write
(number line from 0 to 1 with $\frac{3}{8}$ and $\frac{7}{8}$ marked, arc from $\frac{7}{8}$ to $\frac{3}{8}$)	$\frac{7}{8} - \frac{3}{8} = \frac{4}{8}$ $\frac{4}{8} = \frac{1}{2}$

In **1** through **4**, write the equation shown by the number line. Simplify, if possible.

1.
(number line 0 to 1 in eighths, arc from $\frac{5}{8}$ (Start) to $\frac{2}{8}$)

2.
(number line 0 to 1 in eighths, Start at 0, two arcs to $\frac{6}{8}$)

3.
(number line 0 to 1 in sixths, arc from $\frac{4}{6}$ (Start) to $\frac{1}{6}$)

4.
(number line 0 to 2 in fifths, Start at 0, two arcs to $\frac{6}{5}$)

In **5** through **7**, add or subtract the fractions. You may use a number line. Simplify your answer, if possible.

5. $\frac{2}{6} + \frac{1}{6}$

6. $\frac{7}{12} - \frac{2}{12}$

7. $\frac{1}{8} + \frac{5}{8}$

8. Justify Robbie drew the number line below to find the difference $\frac{4}{5} - \frac{1}{5}$. Explain why he is incorrect.

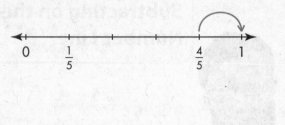

9. Explain Kayla used $\frac{4}{14}$ of her allowance to buy yogurt and $\frac{8}{14}$ of her allowance to go skating. What fraction of her allowance does she have left? Explain your thinking.

10. Jamie is trying to find the sum $\frac{3}{10} + \frac{5}{10}$. Which number line shows one way to find the sum?

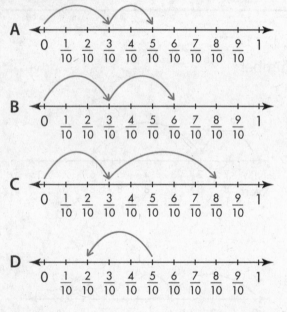

11. Analyze Information Which child drank the most juice in all? How much juice did that child drink?

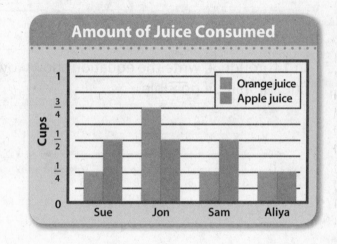

12. Use a Strip Diagram Val's construction team was supposed to build a frame $\frac{7}{10}$ meter long. They ended up building the frame $\frac{2}{10}$ meter too long. How long was the frame Val's team built?

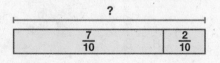

13. Extend Your Thinking Sofia bought bananas, cereal, and milk at the store. She spent all of her money. She spent $\frac{3}{10}$ of her money on bananas and $\frac{4}{10}$ of her money on cereal. What fraction of her money did she spend on milk?

© Pearson Education, Inc. 4

Name _____

☆ ☆
Solve & Share

In **1** and **2**, use the number lines below to help decide if each sum is greater than 1 or less than 1. Tell how you decided.

In **3** and **4**, use the number lines below to help decide if each difference is less than $\frac{1}{2}$ or greater than $\frac{1}{2}$. Tell how you decided. *Solve these problems any way you choose.*

⭐ TEKS 4.3F Evaluate the reasonableness of sums and differences of fractions using benchmark fractions 0, $\frac{1}{4}$, $\frac{1}{2}$, $\frac{3}{4}$, and 1, referring to the same whole. Mathematical Process Standards 4.1A, 4.1C, 4.1D

Digital Resources at PearsonTexas.com

Solve   Learn   Glossary   Check   Tools   Games

1. $\dfrac{5}{8} + \dfrac{8}{10}$

2. $\dfrac{1}{8} + \dfrac{1}{5} + \dfrac{1}{10}$

3. $\dfrac{7}{8} - \dfrac{1}{10}$

4. $\dfrac{9}{10} - \dfrac{5}{8}$

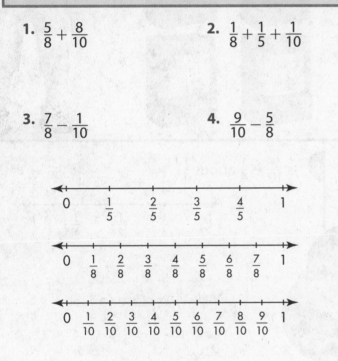

You can use **number sense** to think about how given fractions relate to 0, $\frac{1}{2}$, and 1.

Look Back!

Number Sense Which fractions above are close to 0? Close to 1? How did you decide?

How Can You Decide if a Fraction Sum or Difference Is Reasonable?

Benchmark fractions are fractions such as $\frac{1}{4}$, $\frac{1}{2}$, and $\frac{3}{4}$ that are commonly used for estimation.

Four friends bought candy by scooping what they wanted into paper bags.

Is each statement reasonable?

Together, Randy and Martha bought about 1 pound.

Fana bought about $\frac{1}{4}$ pound less than Chuck.

You can use 0, 1, and benchmark fractions to decide if a fraction sum or difference is reasonable.

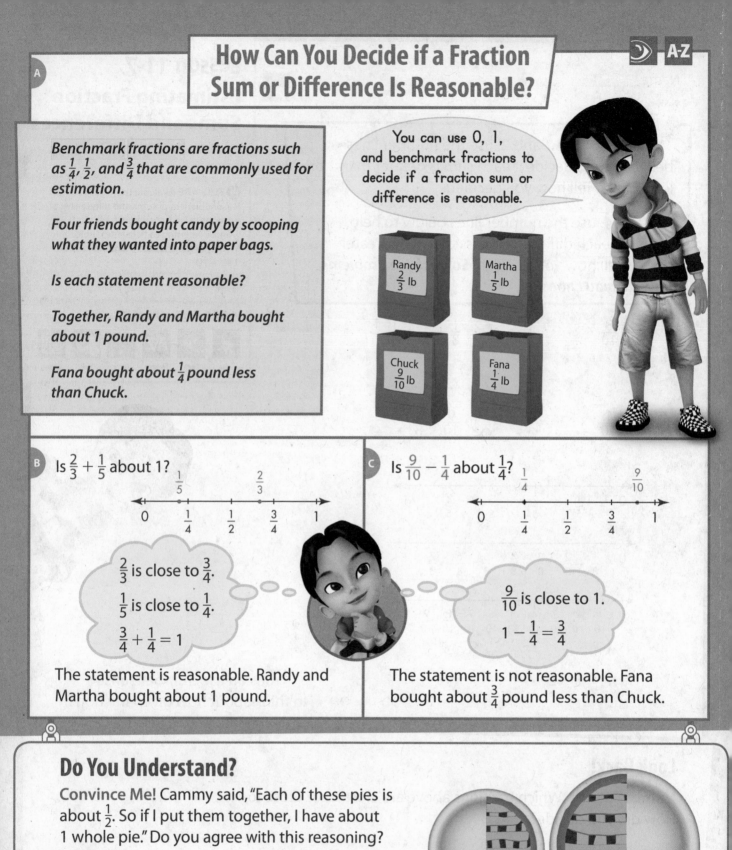

Randy $\frac{2}{3}$ lb   Martha $\frac{1}{5}$ lb

Chuck $\frac{9}{10}$ lb   Fana $\frac{1}{4}$ lb

B Is $\frac{2}{3} + \frac{1}{5}$ about 1?

$\frac{2}{3}$ is close to $\frac{3}{4}$.

$\frac{1}{5}$ is close to $\frac{1}{4}$.

$\frac{3}{4} + \frac{1}{4} = 1$

The statement is reasonable. Randy and Martha bought about 1 pound.

C Is $\frac{9}{10} - \frac{1}{4}$ about $\frac{1}{4}$?

$\frac{9}{10}$ is close to 1.

$1 - \frac{1}{4} = \frac{3}{4}$

The statement is not reasonable. Fana bought about $\frac{3}{4}$ pound less than Chuck.

Do You Understand?

Convince Me! Cammy said, "Each of these pies is about $\frac{1}{2}$. So if I put them together, I have about 1 whole pie." Do you agree with this reasoning? Explain.

© Pearson Education, Inc. 4

☆ Guided Practice ☆

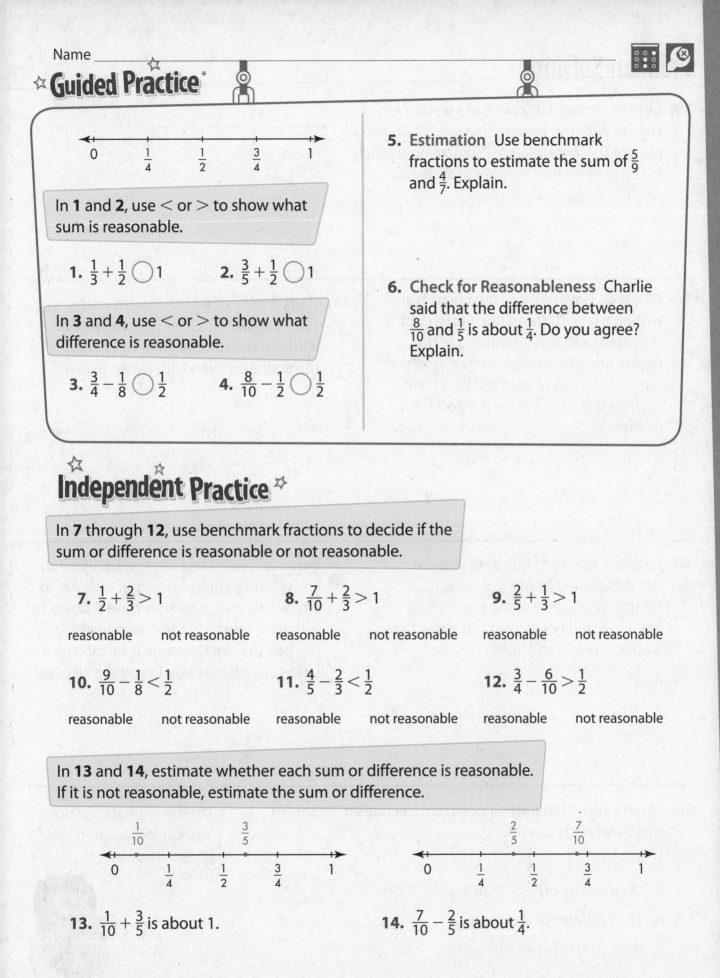

0    $\frac{1}{4}$ $\frac{1}{2}$ $\frac{3}{4}$ 1

In **1** and **2**, use < or > to show what sum is reasonable.

1. $\frac{1}{3} + \frac{1}{2} \bigcirc 1$ **2.** $\frac{3}{5} + \frac{1}{2} \bigcirc 1$

In **3** and **4**, use < or > to show what difference is reasonable.

3. $\frac{3}{4} - \frac{1}{8} \bigcirc \frac{1}{2}$ **4.** $\frac{8}{10} - \frac{1}{2} \bigcirc \frac{1}{2}$

5. Estimation Use benchmark fractions to estimate the sum of $\frac{5}{9}$ and $\frac{4}{7}$. Explain.

6. Check for Reasonableness Charlie said that the difference between $\frac{8}{10}$ and $\frac{1}{5}$ is about $\frac{1}{4}$. Do you agree? Explain.

☆ Independent Practice ☆

In **7** through **12**, use benchmark fractions to decide if the sum or difference is reasonable or not reasonable.

7. $\frac{1}{2} + \frac{2}{3} > 1$

reasonable   not reasonable

8. $\frac{7}{10} + \frac{2}{3} > 1$

reasonable   not reasonable

9. $\frac{2}{5} + \frac{1}{3} > 1$

reasonable   not reasonable

10. $\frac{9}{10} - \frac{1}{8} < \frac{1}{2}$

reasonable   not reasonable

11. $\frac{4}{5} - \frac{2}{3} < \frac{1}{2}$

reasonable   not reasonable

12. $\frac{3}{4} - \frac{6}{10} > \frac{1}{2}$

reasonable   not reasonable

In **13** and **14**, estimate whether each sum or difference is reasonable. If it is not reasonable, estimate the sum or difference.

$\frac{1}{10}$ $\frac{3}{5}$

0    $\frac{1}{4}$ $\frac{1}{2}$ $\frac{3}{4}$ 1

$\frac{2}{5}$ $\frac{7}{10}$

0    $\frac{1}{4}$ $\frac{1}{2}$ $\frac{3}{4}$ 1

13. $\frac{1}{10} + \frac{3}{5}$ is about 1.

14. $\frac{7}{10} - \frac{2}{5}$ is about $\frac{1}{4}$.

Problem Solving

15. Communicate Lucy ate $\frac{2}{8}$ of a watermelon, Lily ate $\frac{1}{10}$ of the watermelon, and Madelyn ate $\frac{1}{5}$ of the watermelon. Estimate how much of the watermelon they ate in all. Explain.

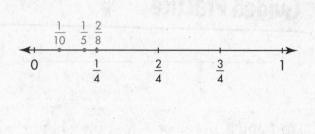

16. Connect Gavin, Olivia, and Michael are writing a report. Gavin has written $\frac{2}{5}$ of the report, Olivia has written $\frac{1}{8}$ of the report, and Michael has written $\frac{2}{10}$ of the report. Estimate to decide if they have more or less than $\frac{1}{2}$ of their report left to write.

17. Harry filled $\frac{1}{4}$ of a pitcher with water. Then he filled another $\frac{6}{10}$ of the pitcher with water. Estimate what fraction of the pitcher is filled with water. Explain.

18. Amelia is saving to buy a skateboard. Her dad agreed to pay $\frac{5}{8}$ of the cost. Amelia has saved $\frac{1}{5}$ of the cost. Which fraction listed below best estimates the amount Amelia still needs to save?

A $\frac{1}{4}$

B $\frac{1}{2}$

C $\frac{3}{4}$

D $\frac{4}{4}$

19. Personal Financial Literacy Last year the Levitz family sold 16 boxes of nuts for $6 a box. This year, they only have 8 boxes to sell. How much do they need to charge per box to have the same total income as last year? Tell how you found the answer.

20. Extend Your Thinking Choose two fractions from the list that meet each condition.

$\frac{5}{8}$ $\frac{1}{10}$ $\frac{3}{4}$ $\frac{1}{5}$

a. Their sum is greater than 1.

b. Their difference is close to 0.

c. Their sum is between $\frac{1}{2}$ and 1.

> Use benchmark fractions. You can draw a number line to help.

© Pearson Education, Inc. 4

Another Look!

Jake ran $\frac{1}{9}$ of the distance to school and walked $\frac{2}{5}$ of the distance. Estimate what fraction of the distance he still needs to travel to get to school.

Use the benchmark fractions on the number line to help you.

What You Think

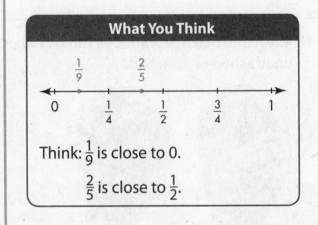

Think: $\frac{1}{9}$ is close to 0.

$\frac{2}{5}$ is close to $\frac{1}{2}$.

What You Write

$\frac{1}{9} + \frac{2}{5}$ is about $0 + \frac{1}{2} = \frac{1}{2}$.

The whole distance to school is $\frac{4}{4}$ or 1.

$1 - \frac{1}{2} = \frac{1}{2}$

Jake still needs to travel about $\frac{1}{2}$ of the distance to get to school.

In **1** through **6**, use benchmark fractions to decide if the sum or difference is reasonable or not reasonable.

1. $\frac{1}{5} + \frac{1}{2} > 1$

reasonable   not reasonable

2. $\frac{2}{5} + \frac{2}{3} > 1$

reasonable   not reasonable

3. $\frac{3}{7} + \frac{1}{3} < 1$

reasonable   not reasonable

4. $\frac{7}{10} - \frac{2}{5} < \frac{1}{2}$

reasonable   not reasonable

5. $\frac{9}{10} - \frac{1}{3} < \frac{1}{2}$

reasonable   not reasonable

6. $\frac{5}{6} - \frac{1}{4} > \frac{1}{2}$

reasonable   not reasonable

In **7** and **8**, estimate whether each sum or difference is reasonable. If it is not reasonable, estimate the sum or difference.

7. $\frac{1}{5} + \frac{4}{7}$ is about $\frac{3}{4}$.

8. $\frac{9}{10} - \frac{2}{5}$ is about $\frac{1}{4}$.

9. **Use Tools** Elena ate $\frac{2}{8}$ of a pizza and Dylan ate $\frac{1}{5}$ of the pizza. Use the number line to estimate about how much of the pizza Elena and Dylan ate in all. Explain.

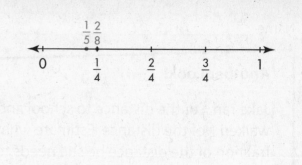

10. ⭐ Kara's grandmother is knitting a baby cap for charity. She knitted $\frac{1}{5}$ of the cap yesterday morning. By evening, she had knitted $\frac{7}{10}$ of the cap. Use benchmark fractions to estimate how much of the cap she knitted during the afternoon.

    A About $\frac{1}{4}$ of the cap

    B About $\frac{1}{2}$ of the cap

    C About $\frac{3}{4}$ of the cap

    D None of the above

11. **Math and Science** Earlobes can be either unattached or attached.

    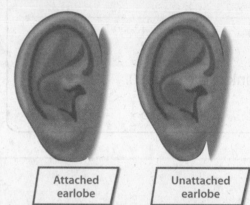

    Attached earlobe   Unattached earlobe

    In a class of 25 students, 15 have attached earlobes. What fraction of the students have unattached earlobes?

12. Carly made a beaded necklace. $\frac{4}{18}$ of the beads are blue and $\frac{1}{3}$ of the beads are green. Use benchmark fractions to estimate about what fraction of the beads in the necklace are blue or green. Explain.

13. **Extend Your Thinking** Jonathan saved money to have a party. If he spends $\frac{2}{8}$ of his money on food, $\frac{1}{5}$ of his money on prizes, and $\frac{2}{10}$ of his money on decorations, estimate what fraction of his money he will have left. Explain.

© Pearson Education, Inc. 4

Name _____

Solve & Share

Michelle rode her bike $\frac{3}{4}$ mile on Thursday, $\frac{3}{4}$ mile on Friday, and $\frac{2}{4}$ mile on Saturday. How far did she ride her bike in all? Draw a strip diagram and write an equation to solve the problem.

⭐ TEKS 4.1F Analyze mathematical relationships to connect and communicate mathematical ideas. Also, 4.3E. Mathematical Process Standards 4.1A, 4.1B, 4.1C, 4.1D, 4.1G

Digital Resources at PearsonTexas.com

Solve	Learn	Glossary	Check	Tools	Games

You can **analyze relationships**. How are equations and strip diagrams similar? *Show your work in the space above!*

Look Back!

Check for Reasonableness Is your answer reasonable? Explain.

Analyze

How Can You Analyze Relationships to Solve a Problem?

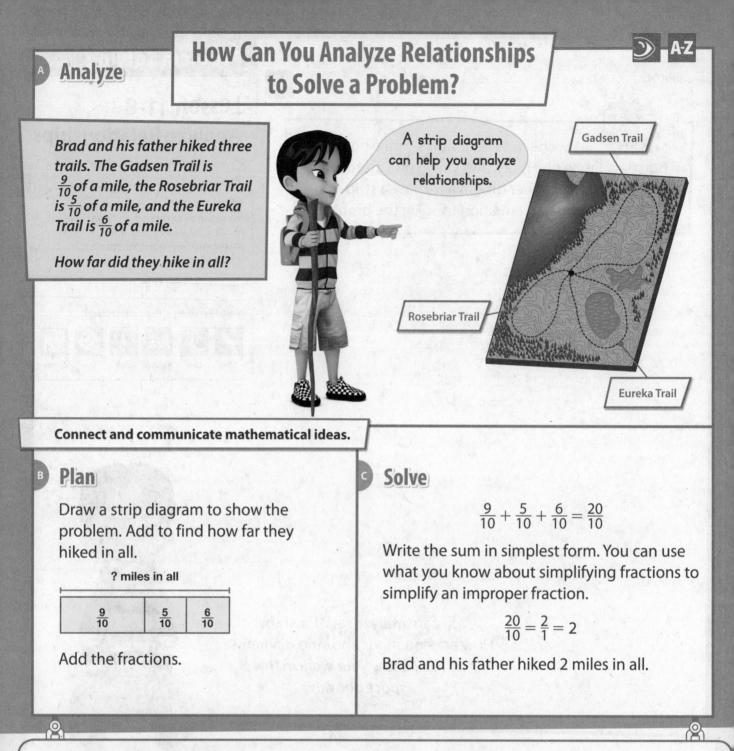

Brad and his father hiked three trails. The Gadsen Traïl is $\frac{9}{10}$ of a mile, the Rosebriar Trail is $\frac{5}{10}$ of a mile, and the Eureka Trail is $\frac{6}{10}$ of a mile.

How far did they hike in all?

A strip diagram can help you analyze relationships.

Gadsen Trail

Rosebriar Trail

Eureka Trail

Connect and communicate mathematical ideas.

B

Plan

Draw a strip diagram to show the problem. Add to find how far they hiked in all.

? miles in all

$\frac{9}{10}$	$\frac{5}{10}$	$\frac{6}{10}$

Add the fractions.

C

Solve

$$\frac{9}{10} + \frac{5}{10} + \frac{6}{10} = \frac{20}{10}$$

Write the sum in simplest form. You can use what you know about simplifying fractions to simplify an improper fraction.

$$\frac{20}{10} = \frac{2}{1} = 2$$

Brad and his father hiked 2 miles in all.

Do You Understand?

Convince Me! Alyssa hiked the Gadsen Trail and Joseph hiked the Rosebriar Trail. How much farther did Alyssa hike than Joseph? Draw a strip diagram and write an equation. Write your answer in simplest form.

© Pearson Education, Inc. 4

☆ Guided Practice ☆

> Draw a strip diagram and write an equation to solve.

1. Hannah ran $\frac{2}{3}$ mile. David ran $\frac{1}{3}$ mile. How much farther did Hannah run than David?

2. Number Sense Glenda wrote $\frac{1}{7}$ of her paper on Monday, $\frac{2}{7}$ of her paper on Tuesday, and $\frac{4}{7}$ of her paper on Wednesday. Her paper is due on Thursday. Did she complete it? Explain.

3. Write a problem that you can solve using a strip diagram and an equation.

☆ Independent Practice ☆

> **Leveled Practice** In **4** through **6**, use the strip diagram to write an equation to solve.

4. Connect Steve connected a $\frac{3}{8}$-foot wire extension to $\frac{5}{8}$-foot wire. How far will the wire and extension reach?

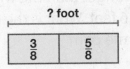

5. The smallest female spider measures about $\frac{3}{5}$ millimeter in length. The smallest male spider measures about $\frac{1}{5}$ millimeter in length. How much longer is the female spider than the male spider?

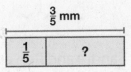

6. Analyze Information Felix bought $\frac{5}{6}$ pound of peanuts. He ate $\frac{3}{6}$ pound of the peanuts with his friends. How much did Felix have left?

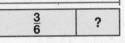

> Draw a strip diagram and write an equation to solve.

7. Susan mixed $\frac{1}{6}$ pound of grapes with $\frac{3}{6}$ pound of apple chunks to make a fruit salad. How much fruit salad did Susan make? Write your answer in simplest form.

Problem Solving

8. Use a Strip Diagram A recipe calls for 3 times as many cups of carrots as cups of peas. If Carmen used 2 cups of peas, how many cups of carrots will she use?

? cups of carrots

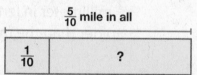

9. Explain Miguel has 8 comic books and 4 detective books. His sister says $\frac{2}{3}$ of his books are comic books. Miguel says that $\frac{8}{12}$ of his books are comic books. Who is correct?

10. Every Saturday, Jill spends 1 hour cleaning the kitchen, the living room, and the bedroom. She cleans the kitchen in $\frac{2}{5}$ hour and cleans the living room in $\frac{2}{5}$ hour. How much time does she spend cleaning the bedroom?

 A $\frac{4}{5}$ hour   C $\frac{2}{5}$ hour

 B $\frac{3}{5}$ hour   D $\frac{1}{5}$ hour

11. Draw a Picture Jack's dog has a rectangular pen. The length is two feet longer than the width. The width is 6 feet. What is the distance around the pen?

12. Joel walked $\frac{3}{8}$ mile to the store, $\frac{3}{8}$ mile to the library, and $\frac{1}{8}$ mile to the post office. How far did he walk in all? Write your answer in simplest form.

13. Sandra and Ron are hiking a trail. They have already hiked $\frac{1}{10}$ mile. How much farther do they have to travel to reach the $\frac{5}{10}$-mile marker? Write your answer in simplest form.

$\frac{5}{10}$ mile in all

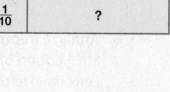

14. Extend Your Thinking If Sandra and Ron turn around and hike back $\frac{1}{10}$ mile, how far will they then need to hike to go to the $\frac{5}{10}$-mile marker?

A picture can help you organize your ideas.

© Pearson Education, Inc. 4

Name _____

Another Look!

Tina and Andy are building a model airplane together. Tina built $\frac{3}{5}$ of the model, and Andy built $\frac{1}{5}$ of the model. How much more has Tina built than Andy?

Remember to use a strip diagram to help you organize information.

Step 1	Step 2
Use a strip diagram to help you write an equation. $\frac{3}{5}$ of the model | $\frac{1}{5}$ | ? |	Write an equation to solve. $\frac{3}{5} - \frac{1}{5} = \frac{2}{5}$ Tina built $\frac{2}{5}$ more of the model than Andy.

In **1** and **2**, complete the strip diagram and write an equation to solve.

1. Isaiah filled $\frac{1}{8}$ of a jar with blue stones, $\frac{3}{8}$ of the jar with red stones, and $\frac{2}{8}$ of the jar with yellow stones. How much of the jar is filled in all?

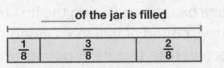

_____ of the jar is filled

\| $\frac{1}{8}$ \| $\frac{3}{8}$ \| $\frac{2}{8}$ \|

2. On Nick's playlist $\frac{6}{13}$ of the songs are instrumentals. What fraction of the songs are **NOT** instrumentals?

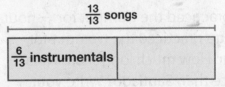

$\frac{13}{13}$ songs

\| $\frac{6}{13}$ instrumentals \| \|

In **3** and **4**, draw a picture and write an equation.

3. One day, a craft store sold $\frac{2}{9}$ yard of green felt. The store sold $\frac{1}{9}$ yard more purple felt than green felt. How many yards of purple felt did the store sell? Write your answer in simplest form.

4. Josh ran $\frac{2}{5}$ mile on Tuesday and $\frac{1}{5}$ mile on Thursday. How many more miles did Josh run on Tuesday than on Thursday?

5. Jamie bought $\frac{5}{8}$ pound of wheat flour. He also bought $\frac{2}{8}$ pound of white flour. How many pounds of flour did he buy?

6. Katie is $\frac{3}{5}$ of the way to Brianna's house. Larry is $\frac{1}{5}$ of the way to Brianna's house. How much closer to Brianna's house is Katie?

7. Extend Your Thinking Catalina has $\frac{7}{8}$ pound of sugar. First, she uses $\frac{1}{8}$ pound to make icing for a cake. Then, she uses $\frac{1}{4}$ pound to make lemonade. How much sugar does Catalina have left? Write your answer in simplest form.

Simplify your answer from the first step before solving the second step.

8. Ned caught $\frac{1}{3}$ pound of fish. Sarah caught $\frac{2}{3}$ pound of fish. Jessa caught $\frac{1}{3}$ pound of fish. Which strip diagram shows how to find how many pounds of fish they caught in all?

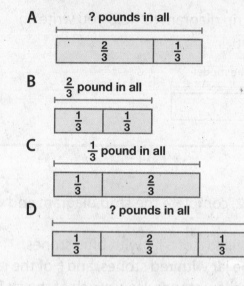

A ? pounds in all

$\frac{2}{3}$ $\frac{1}{3}$

B $\frac{2}{3}$ pound in all

$\frac{1}{3}$ $\frac{1}{3}$

C $\frac{1}{3}$ pound in all

$\frac{1}{3}$ $\frac{2}{3}$

D ? pounds in all

$\frac{1}{3}$ $\frac{2}{3}$ $\frac{1}{3}$

9. Nina practiced the trumpet for $\frac{7}{12}$ hour. Santiago practiced the trumpet for $\frac{3}{12}$ hour. How much longer did Nina practice than Santiago? Write your answer in simplest form.

10. Connect Betty bought $\frac{9}{16}$ pound of trail mix for a hiking trip. During the first hike, she ate $\frac{4}{16}$ pound of trail mix. During the second hike, she ate $\frac{3}{16}$ pound. How much trail mix does Betty have left?

A $\frac{9}{16}$ pound   C $\frac{5}{16}$ pound

B $\frac{6}{16}$ pound   D $\frac{2}{16}$ pound

11. Justify Ryan said that the difference of $\frac{9}{10}$ and $\frac{2}{5}$ is close to 0. Do you agree? Explain.

12. Draw a Picture Matt jogged $\frac{1}{8}$ mile. Thomas jogged $\frac{5}{8}$ mile. How much farther did Thomas jog? Draw a picture and write an equation to solve. Write your answer in simplest form.

© Pearson Education, Inc. 4

1. **Number Sense** Sam picked some apples. Tom ate $\frac{3}{10}$ of the apples and Sam ate $\frac{3}{10}$ of the apples. What fraction of the apples are left?

Applying Math Processes
- How does this problem connect to previous ones?
- What is my plan?
- How can I use tools?
- How can I use number sense?
- How can I communicate and represent my thinking?
- How can I organize and record information?
- How can I explain my work?
- How can I justify my answer?

2. **Reason** Gina jogged $\frac{3}{5}$ mile on Monday. Then she jogged $\frac{3}{5}$ mile on Tuesday. Has she jogged more than 1 mile? Explain.

3. **Extend Your Thinking** Find two fractions that have a sum of $\frac{9}{10}$. These same two fractions must also have a difference of $\frac{1}{2}$. What are the fractions?

Which denominator will you use to find the fractions?

4. **Tools** Chase makes a number line and divides it into eighths. From 0, he moves 7 spaces to the right. Then he moves 4 spaces to the left. He then moves 1 space to the right. At what point on the number line is Chase?

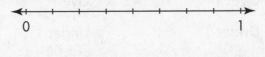

0   1

5. **Analyze Information** Ten campers set up their tents alongside a stream. Of the 10 tents, 3 tents are yellow and 2 tents are green. What fraction of the tents are either yellow or green? Show your work.

6. **Represent** Darla knitted an adult's scarf that was $\frac{11}{12}$ yard long and a child's scarf that was $\frac{8}{12}$ yard long. How much longer is the adult's scarf than the child's scarf?

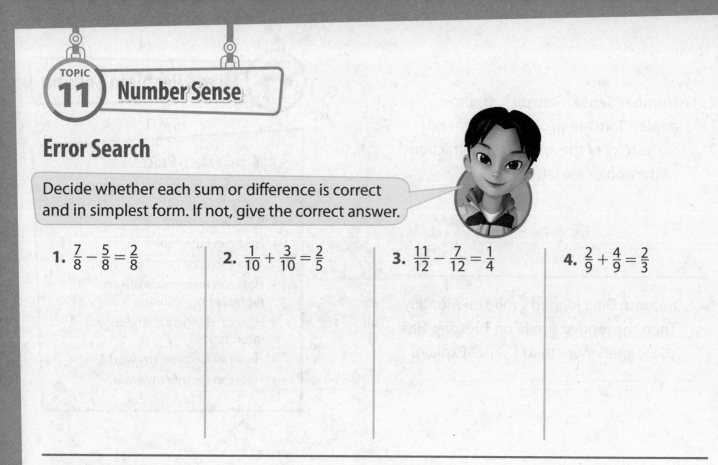

Error Search

Decide whether each sum or difference is correct and in simplest form. If not, give the correct answer.

1. $\frac{7}{8} - \frac{5}{8} = \frac{2}{8}$

2. $\frac{1}{10} + \frac{3}{10} = \frac{2}{5}$

3. $\frac{11}{12} - \frac{7}{12} = \frac{1}{4}$

4. $\frac{2}{9} + \frac{4}{9} = \frac{2}{3}$

Over or Under?

Decide whether the given sum is greater than (over) 1 or less than (under) 1. Circle your choice.

5. $\frac{2}{3} + \frac{2}{3}$

Over 1

Under 1

6. $\frac{1}{6} + \frac{3}{6}$

Over 1

Under 1

7. $\frac{7}{10} + \frac{4}{10}$

Over 1

Under 1

8. $\frac{3}{5} + \frac{1}{5}$

Over 1

Under 1

9. $\frac{5}{12} + \frac{5}{12}$

Over 1

Under 1

10. $\frac{3}{8} + \frac{7}{8}$

Over 1

Under 1

11. $\frac{1}{4} + \frac{2}{4}$

Over 1

Under 1

12. $\frac{3}{10} + \frac{9}{10}$

Over 1

Under 1

13. $\frac{7}{8} + \frac{2}{8}$

Over 1

Under 1

14. $\frac{7}{12} + \frac{2}{12}$

Over 1

Under 1

15. $\frac{1}{3} + \frac{1}{3}$

Over 1

Under 1

16. $\frac{4}{6} + \frac{3}{6}$

Over 1

Under 1

© Pearson Education, Inc. 4

Set A pages 557–562

While Ricardo's family was bird watching, they spotted eight loons. There were five in the water, one in the air, and two walking on land. What fraction of the loons did they see in the water or on land?

Add the fraction of the total loons that were in the water to the fraction of the total loons that were on land. Use objects such as fraction strips.

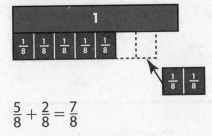

$$\frac{5}{8} + \frac{2}{8} = \frac{7}{8}$$

Reteaching

Remember to simplify the sum if possible.

Use fraction strips to add.

1. $\frac{2}{4} + \frac{2}{4}$

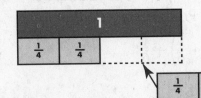

2. $\frac{3}{6} + \frac{2}{6}$

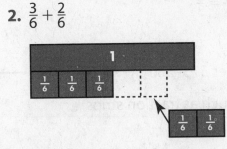

Set B pages 563–568

A zoo wants to keep $\frac{1}{8}$ of its habitat sections empty. Show two different ways they could fill the remaining habitat sections with monkeys, giraffes, and elephants.

$\frac{7}{8}$ of habitat sections occupied

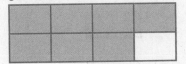

The zoo could put monkeys in $\frac{2}{8}$ of the habitat, giraffes in $\frac{3}{8}$, and elephants in $\frac{2}{8}$.

$$\frac{7}{8} = \frac{2}{8} + \frac{3}{8} + \frac{2}{8}$$

Or, they could put elephants in $\frac{4}{8}$ of the habitat, giraffes in $\frac{2}{8}$, and monkeys in $\frac{1}{8}$.

$$\frac{7}{8} = \frac{4}{8} + \frac{2}{8} + \frac{1}{8}$$

Remember that you can decompose fractions in different ways.

Write each fraction as a sum of two fractions. Use fraction strips to help.

1. $\frac{6}{8} =$ 2. $\frac{3}{4} =$

3. $\frac{5}{7} =$ 4. $\frac{6}{10} =$

5. $\frac{9}{13} =$ 6. $\frac{4}{5} =$

Write each fraction as a sum of three fractions. Use fraction strips to help.

7. $\frac{4}{6} =$ 8. $\frac{6}{14} =$

9. $\frac{5}{8} =$ 10. $\frac{10}{12} =$

Set C — pages 569–574

Add $\frac{4}{12} + \frac{5}{12}$. Write in simplest form.

Add the numerators; keep the like denominator. Simplify if possible.

$$\frac{4}{12} + \frac{5}{12} = \frac{9}{12} = \frac{3}{4}$$

Use properties of operations to add. Use the Associative Property of Addition.

$$\frac{2}{6} + \frac{1}{6} + \frac{1}{6} = \left(\frac{2}{6} + \frac{1}{6}\right) + \frac{1}{6}$$
$$= \frac{3}{6} + \frac{1}{6}$$
$$= \frac{4}{6} = \frac{2}{3}$$

Remember that you can use properties of operations to help you add fractions.

Add. Simplify, if possible.

1. $\frac{2}{5} + \frac{2}{5}$

2. $\frac{2}{4} + \frac{1}{4} + \frac{1}{4}$

3. $\frac{3}{8} + \frac{4}{8}$

4. $\frac{4}{10} + \frac{2}{10} + \frac{3}{10}$

5. $\frac{4}{9} + \frac{3}{9}$

6. $\left(\frac{4}{12} + \frac{3}{12}\right) + \frac{2}{12}$

7. $\frac{4}{6} + \frac{2}{6}$

8. $\frac{4}{11} + \frac{6}{11}$

Set D — pages 575–580

Use objects such as fraction strips to find $\frac{5}{8} - \frac{2}{8}$.

Use five $\frac{1}{8}$ strips to model $\frac{5}{8}$. Take two strips away.

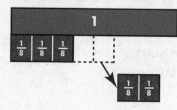

Three $\frac{1}{8}$ strips are left.

$$\frac{5}{8} - \frac{2}{8} = \frac{3}{8}$$

Use fraction strips to find $\frac{3}{4} - \frac{2}{4}$.

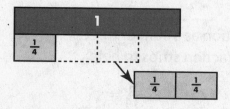

One $\frac{1}{4}$ strip is left.

$$\frac{3}{4} - \frac{2}{4} = \frac{1}{4}$$

Remember to simplify the difference if possible.

Use objects, such as fraction strips, to subtract.

1. $\frac{3}{3} - \frac{1}{3}$

2. $\frac{5}{6} - \frac{2}{6}$

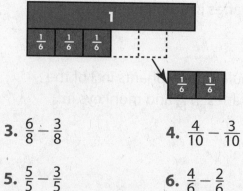

3. $\frac{6}{8} - \frac{3}{8}$

4. $\frac{4}{10} - \frac{3}{10}$

5. $\frac{5}{5} - \frac{3}{5}$

6. $\frac{4}{6} - \frac{2}{6}$

© Pearson Education, Inc. 4

Set E pages 581–586

Subtract $\frac{7}{8} - \frac{5}{8}$. Write in simplest form.

Subtract the numerators; keep the like denominator. Simplify if possible.

$\frac{7}{8} - \frac{5}{8} = \frac{2}{8} = \frac{1}{4}$

Use properties of operations to subtract:

$\frac{3}{10} - \frac{1}{10} = \left(\frac{1}{10} + \frac{1}{10} + \frac{1}{10}\right) - \frac{1}{10}$

$= \left(\frac{1}{10} + \frac{1}{10}\right) + \left(\frac{1}{10} - \frac{1}{10}\right)$

$= \frac{2}{10} + 0$

$= \frac{2}{10} = \frac{1}{5}$

Remember that you can subtract the numerators when the denominators are the same.

Subtract. Simplify, if possible.

1. $\frac{7}{10} - \frac{1}{10}$ 2. $\frac{10}{12} - \frac{3}{12}$

3. $\frac{4}{4} - \frac{2}{4}$ 4. $\frac{5}{6} - \frac{1}{6}$

5. $\frac{4}{8} - \frac{2}{8}$ 6. $\frac{4}{5} - \frac{1}{5}$

7. $\frac{2}{3} - \frac{1}{3}$ 8. $\frac{30}{100} - \frac{10}{100}$

Set F pages 587–592

Find the sum or difference shown on the number line. Write in simplest form, if possible.

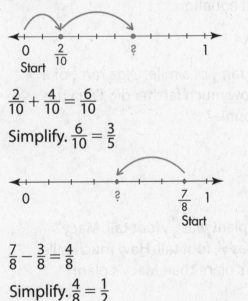

$\frac{2}{10} + \frac{4}{10} = \frac{6}{10}$

Simplify. $\frac{6}{10} = \frac{3}{5}$

$\frac{7}{8} - \frac{3}{8} = \frac{4}{8}$

Simplify. $\frac{4}{8} = \frac{1}{2}$

Remember that when adding or subtracting fractions with like denominators on a number line, the denominator does not change.

Write and solve the equation shown by each number line. Simplify, if possible.

1.

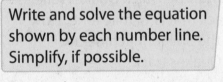

2.

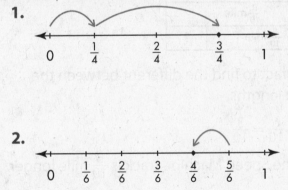

Stacy bought $\frac{7}{10}$ pound of cheddar cheese and bought $\frac{1}{5}$ pound of monterey jack cheese. Stacy said that she bought about one pound of cheese in all. Use estimation to determine if Stacy is correct.

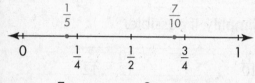

Think: $\frac{7}{10}$ is close to $\frac{3}{4}$.

$\frac{1}{5}$ is close to $\frac{1}{4}$.

Since $\frac{3}{4} + \frac{1}{4} = 1$, $\frac{7}{10} + \frac{1}{5}$ is about 1.

The statement is reasonable. Stacy bought about one pound in all.

Remember to use benchmark fractions, such as $\frac{1}{4}$, $\frac{1}{2}$, and $\frac{3}{4}$, to help you estimate the sums and differences of fractions.

1. Is $\frac{2}{5} + \frac{1}{2}$ about 1? Explain.

2. Is $\frac{7}{8} - \frac{2}{5}$ about 1? Explain.

3. Is $\frac{1}{5} + \frac{3}{8}$ greater than 1 or less than 1? Explain.

4. Is $\frac{3}{5} + \frac{3}{4}$ greater than 1 or less than 1? Explain.

The Speed Machine roller coaster has a track that is $\frac{9}{10}$ mile long. The Quick Quakes roller coaster has a track that is $\frac{6}{10}$ mile long. How much longer is the Speed Machine track than the Quick Quakes track?

$\frac{9}{10}$ mile	
$\frac{6}{10}$ mile	?

Subtract to find the different between the track lengths.

$\frac{9}{10} - \frac{6}{10} = \frac{3}{10}$

So, the Speed Machine track is $\frac{3}{10}$ mile longer.

Remember to draw a strip diagram to help you write an equation.

Solve.

1. Bonnie ran $\frac{1}{4}$ of a mile. Olga ran $\frac{3}{4}$ of a mile. How much farther did Olga run than Bonnie?

2. Linda's plant was $\frac{9}{12}$ foot tall. Macy's plant was $\frac{6}{12}$ foot tall. How much taller is Linda's plant than Macy's plant?

© Pearson Education, Inc. 4

Name _____

1. Paul found that $\frac{7}{8} = \frac{2}{8} + \frac{5}{8}$. Which of the following is another way to decompose $\frac{7}{8}$?

   A $\frac{7}{8} = \frac{3}{8} + \frac{3}{8}$

   B $\frac{7}{8} = \frac{1}{8} + \frac{3}{8} + \frac{4}{8}$

   C $\frac{7}{8} = \frac{3}{3} + \frac{4}{5}$

   D $\frac{7}{8} = \frac{1}{8} + \frac{3}{8} + \frac{3}{8}$

4. Which equation did Liz represent on the number line below?

   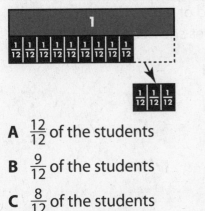

   A $\frac{6}{10} - \frac{2}{10} = \frac{4}{10}$

   B $\frac{6}{10} + \frac{2}{10} = \frac{8}{10}$

   C $\frac{6}{6} + \frac{2}{2} = \frac{8}{8}$

   D $\frac{10}{10} - \frac{8}{10} = \frac{2}{10}$

2. On Monday, $\frac{3}{12}$ of the students in class went on a field trip. What fraction of the students did **NOT** go on the field trip?

1

   $\frac{1}{12}$ $\frac{1}{12}$ $\frac{1}{12}$ $\frac{1}{12}$ $\frac{1}{12}$ $\frac{1}{12}$ $\frac{1}{12}$ $\frac{1}{12}$ $\frac{1}{12}$

   $\frac{1}{12}$ $\frac{1}{12}$ $\frac{1}{12}$

   A $\frac{12}{12}$ of the students

   B $\frac{9}{12}$ of the students

   C $\frac{8}{12}$ of the students

   D $\frac{3}{12}$ of the students

5. Jin ate $\frac{2}{10}$ of a bag of popcorn after school and $\frac{3}{10}$ of a bag of popcorn after dinner. Which of the following can be used to find how much of the bag of popcorn Jin ate?

   A Add $10 + 10$, and write the sum over 5. Simplify $\frac{20}{5}$ to get 4 bags.

   B Add $2 + 3$, and write the sum over $10 + 10$ to get $\frac{5}{20}$. Simplify $\frac{5}{20}$ to get $\frac{1}{4}$ of a bag.

   C Add $2 + 3$, and write the sum over 10 to get $\frac{5}{10}$. Simplify $\frac{5}{10}$ to get $\frac{1}{2}$ of a bag.

   D Subtract $3 - 2$, and write the difference over 10 to get $\frac{1}{10}$ of a bag.

3. Dean cut a strip of paper that was $\frac{5}{8}$ inch long. Terri cut a strip that was $\frac{3}{8}$ inch long. How much longer is Dean's strip of paper than Terri's strip of paper?

   A $\frac{1}{4}$ inch

   B $\frac{1}{2}$ inch

   C $\frac{3}{4}$ inch

   D 1 inch

6. Liam walked $\frac{3}{5}$ of a mile in the morning and $\frac{5}{8}$ of a mile in the afternoon. Which is the best estimate for the total distance he walked?

   A about $\frac{1}{4}$ mile

   B about $\frac{1}{2}$ mile

   C about $\frac{3}{4}$ mile

   D about 1 mile

7. Patrick measured a line that was $\frac{11}{16}$ inch long. Ellen measured a line that was $\frac{5}{16}$ inch long. How much longer was Patrick's line than Ellen's line?

A 1 inch longer

B $\frac{1}{2}$ inch longer

C $\frac{3}{8}$ inch longer

D $\frac{1}{4}$ inch longer

8. Riley planted flowers in $\frac{5}{9}$ of his garden, and he planted vegetables in $\frac{2}{9}$ of his garden. How much of his garden did he plant in all?

A $\frac{1}{3}$ of his garden

B $\frac{7}{18}$ of his garden

C $\frac{2}{3}$ of his garden

D $\frac{7}{9}$ of his garden

9. An adult Rough Green snake is $\frac{5}{6}$ yard long. An Eastern Garter snake is $\frac{4}{6}$ yard long. How much longer is the Rough Green snake than the Eastern Garter snake?

A $\frac{3}{2}$ yard longer

B 1 yard longer

C $\frac{2}{3}$ yard longer

D $\frac{1}{6}$ yard longer

10. Tyler is earning money to pay for a new game. He earned $\frac{2}{5}$ of the money he needed last week and $\frac{1}{5}$ of the money this week. What fraction of the money has he earned?

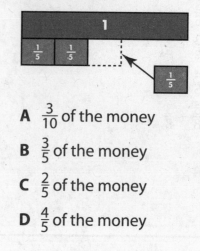

A $\frac{3}{10}$ of the money

B $\frac{3}{5}$ of the money

C $\frac{2}{5}$ of the money

D $\frac{4}{5}$ of the money

11. Sally needs $\frac{7}{8}$ yard of fabric. She already has $\frac{3}{8}$ yard of fabric. How much more fabric does she need?

A $\frac{1}{2}$ yard

B $\frac{3}{8}$ yard

C $\frac{7}{8}$ yard

D 1 yard

12. Roger found a way to decompose $1\frac{3}{5}$. He wrote $1\frac{3}{5} = \frac{2}{5} + \frac{3}{5} + \frac{3}{5}$. Is he correct? Explain.

612

© Pearson Education, Inc. 4

13. Josie bought $\frac{1}{4}$ pound of ham and $\frac{1}{4}$ pound of turkey. How much meat did Josie buy?

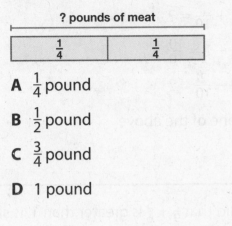

? pounds of meat

$\frac{1}{4}$ $\frac{1}{4}$

A $\frac{1}{4}$ pound

B $\frac{1}{2}$ pound

C $\frac{3}{4}$ pound

D 1 pound

14. Jasmin walked $\frac{1}{5}$ mile to the library, and then she walked $\frac{3}{5}$ mile to the store. How far did Jasmin walk in all?

A $\frac{2}{5}$ mile

B $\frac{4}{5}$ mile

C 1 mile

D $\frac{5}{4}$ mile

15. Tom said that the sum of $\frac{5}{12}$ and $\frac{1}{12}$ in simplest form is $\frac{6}{12}$. Is he correct? Explain.

16. Mrs. Garrison bought $\frac{7}{8}$ yard of fabric. She used $\frac{5}{8}$ yard to make a skirt. How much fabric does she have left?

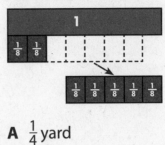

A $\frac{1}{4}$ yard

B $\frac{1}{3}$ yard

C $\frac{3}{4}$ yard

D $\frac{4}{3}$ yards

17. Amy bought $\frac{2}{3}$ quart of fruit salad and $\frac{1}{3}$ quart of three-bean salad. How much salad did she buy in all?

A 2 quarts

B 1 quart

C $\frac{1}{2}$ quart

D $\frac{1}{3}$ quart

18. Donna bought $\frac{3}{4}$ pound of cheddar cheese at the farmer's market. She used $\frac{1}{4}$ pound for a cheddar soup. How much cheddar cheese does Donna have left? Simplify your answer, if possible.

19. Tyler wrote the sum of $\frac{30}{100} + \frac{20}{100}$ in simplest form on the whiteboard. What did he write?

A $\frac{1}{10}$

B $\frac{10}{100}$

C $\frac{5}{10}$

D $\frac{1}{2}$

22. A pitcher had $\frac{9}{10}$ gallon of juice. Manuella drank $\frac{2}{10}$ gallon of juice. Which number sentence can be used to find how much juice was left?

A $\frac{9}{10} + \frac{2}{10} = ?$

B $\frac{9}{10} + ? = \frac{10}{10}$

C $\frac{9}{10} - \frac{2}{10} = ?$

D None of the above

20. Bella used $\frac{1}{8}$ cup of white flour and $\frac{7}{8}$ cup of wheat flour in a bread recipe. How much more wheat flour did she use than white flour?

A $\frac{3}{8}$ cup

B $\frac{1}{2}$ cup

C $\frac{3}{4}$ cup

D 1 cup

23. Kit said that $\frac{7}{9} + \frac{5}{6}$ is greater than 1. Is she correct? Explain.

21. Walt used $\frac{4}{6}$ yard of fabric. Lakota and Dallas each used $\frac{1}{6}$ yard of fabric. How many yards of fabric did they use in all?

24. Sasha found the sum of $\frac{3}{8}$ and $\frac{2}{8}$ in simplest form. What is the numerator of the sum?

614

Measurement Units and Conversions

Essential Questions:
What are customary measurement units, and how are they related?
What are metric measurement units, and how are they related?

Math and Science Project: Erosion and Measurement

Do Research Use the Internet or other sources to find information about how the Grand Canyon was formed.

Journal: Write a Report Include what you found. Also in your report:

- Tell about different ways to measure the size of the Grand Canyon.

- Look up the words *geology* and *geometry* in the dictionary. Write the definitions and explain how these words are related.

Name _____

Review What You Know

Vocabulary

Choose the best term from the box.
Write it on the blank.

- elapsed time
- length
- meter
- yard

1. The customary unit of length equal

to 3 feet or 36 inches is a _____.

2. The distance from one point to
another is a measurement of

_____.

3. A metric unit of length equal to

100 centimeters is a _____.

Multiplying 2-Digit Numbers

Find each product.

4. 14 × 3   **5.** 13 × 5

6. 25 × 6   **7.** 37 × 2

8. 42 × 4   **9.** 53 × 7

Dividing by 1-Digit Numbers

Find each quotient.

10. 80 ÷ 5   **11.** 112 ÷ 8

12. 117 ÷ 9   **13.** 78 ÷ 6

14. 42 ÷ 3   **15.** 126 ÷ 7

16. 96 ÷ 8   **17.** 72 ÷ 3

18. 92 ÷ 4   **19.** 96 ÷ 6

Problem Solving

20. Number Sense A league is a
nautical measurement equal to
3 miles. The deepest point in the
ocean is about 6.84 miles. About
how many leagues deep is the
ocean?

21. Connect A furlong is a unit of
length still used today in racing and
agriculture. A race that is 8 furlongs
is 1 mile. A furlong is 660 feet. How
many feet are in 1 mile?

Will you multiply
or divide?

© Pearson Education, Inc. 4

My Word Cards

Use the examples for each word on the front of the card to help complete the definitions on the back.

customary units of measure

cup ounce
teaspoon
Pound feet inch
Ton
Mile yard

mile (mi)

1 mile is about 4 times around this track.

capacity (liquid volume)

5 oz
4
3
2
1

80 ml
70
60
50
40
30
20
10

teaspoon (tsp)

tsp
TBSP

tablespoon (tbsp)

tsp
TBSP

fluid ounce (fl oz)

1 fl oz

weight

0 oz
10 0g 0
9 300 g 50
8 250 1
7 200 2
6 150 3
5 4

metric units of measure

centimeter LITER gram
kilogram
meter milliliter
kilometer

My Word Cards

Complete each definition. Extend learning by writing your own definitions.

A _____
is a customary unit of length equal to
5,280 feet or 1,760 yards.

Units of measure commonly used in the

United States are called _____

_____

_____.

A _____
is a customary unit of capacity equal to
$\frac{1}{3}$ tablespoon.

_____

_____
is the amount a container can hold,
measured in liquid units.

A _____

_____
is a customary unit of capacity equal to
2 tablespoons.

A _____
is a customary unit of capacity equal to
3 teaspoons.

Units of measure commonly used by

scientists are called _____

_____

_____.

_____
is how heavy an object is.

© Pearson Education, Inc. 4

My Word Cards

Use the examples for each word on the front of the card to help complete the definitions on the back.

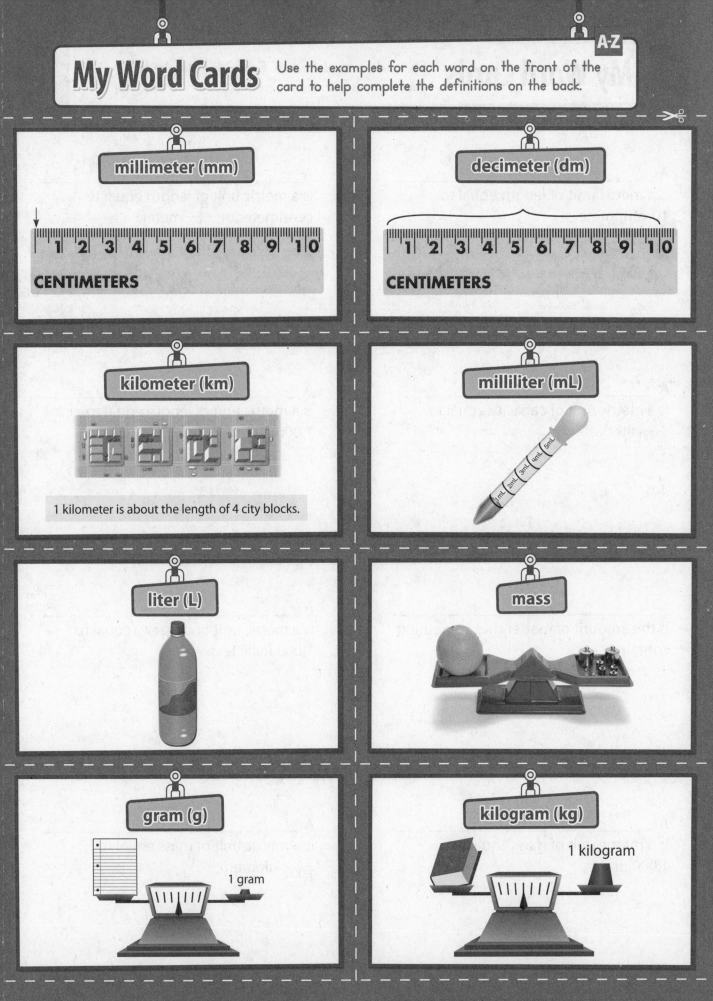

millimeter (mm)

1 2 3 4 5 6 7 8 9 10

CENTIMETERS

decimeter (dm)

1 2 3 4 5 6 7 8 9 10

CENTIMETERS

kilometer (km)

1 kilometer is about the length of 4 city blocks.

milliliter (mL)

1mL 2mL 3mL 4mL 5mL

liter (L)

mass

gram (g)

1 gram

kilogram (kg)

1 kilogram

My Word Cards

Complete each definition. Extend learning by writing your own definitions.

A _____ is a metric unit of length equal to 10 centimeters.

A _____ is a metric unit of length equal to $\frac{1}{10}$ centimeter or $\frac{1}{1,000}$ meter.

A _____ is a metric unit of capacity equal to $\frac{1}{1,000}$ liter.

A _____ is a metric unit of length equal to 1,000 meters.

_____ is the amount of matter that something contains.

A _____ is a metric unit of capacity equal to 1,000 milliliters.

A _____ is a metric unit of mass equal to 1,000 grams.

A _____ is a metric unit of mass equal to $\frac{1}{1,000}$ kilogram.

© Pearson Education, Inc. 4

My Word Cards

Use the examples for each word on the front of the card to help complete the definitions on the back.

leap year

February

S	M	T	W	T	F	S
		1	2	3	4	5
6	7	8	9	10	11	12
13	14	15	16	17	18	19
20	21	22	23	24	25	26
27	28	29				

decade

10 years

century

100 years

millennium (millennia)

1,000 years

Complete each definition. Extend learning by writing your own definitions.

A _____

is a unit of time equal to 10 years.

A _____

happens every four years when an extra day is added to the calendar in February.

A _____

is a unit of time equal to 1,000 years.

A _____

is a unit of time equal to 100 years.

© Pearson Education, Inc. 4

Name _____

☆ ☆
Solve & Share

Look around your classroom or school and list two objects that should be measured with inches, two objects that should be measured with feet, and two objects that should be measured with yards. **Solve this problem any way you choose.**

⭐ **TEKS 4.8A** Identify relative sizes of measurement units within the customary and metric systems. Also, 4.8. Mathematical Process Standards 4.1A, 4.1C, 4.1D, 4.1F, 4.1G

Digital Resources at PearsonTexas.com

Solve   Learn   Glossary   Check   Tools   Games

You can **analyze relationships**. Think about approximately how long each of these measurements is. **Show your work in the space below!**

Look Back!

Connect Name a situation where you may want to use an estimated measurement.

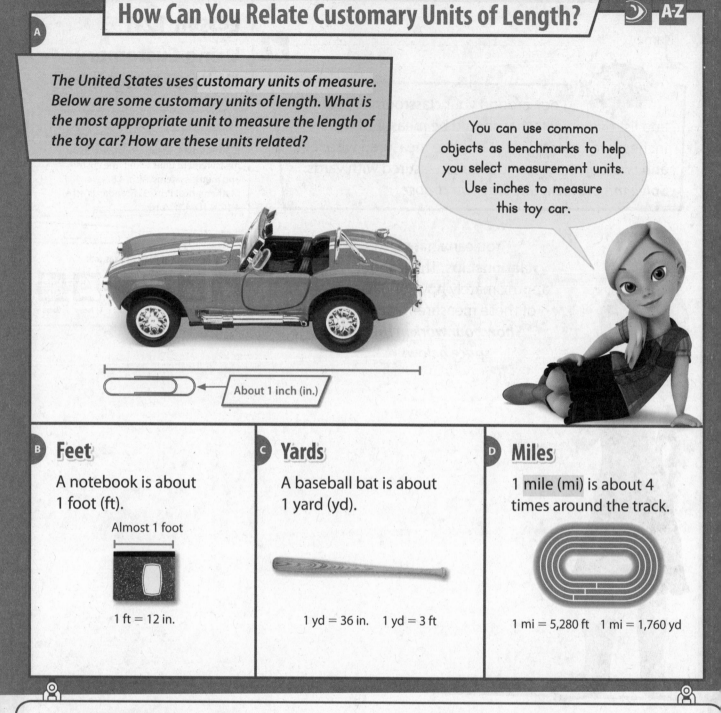

The United States uses customary units of measure. Below are some customary units of length. What is the most appropriate unit to measure the length of the toy car? How are these units related?

You can use common objects as benchmarks to help you select measurement units. Use inches to measure this toy car.

About 1 inch (in.)

Feet

A notebook is about 1 foot (ft).

Almost 1 foot

1 ft = 12 in.

Yards

A baseball bat is about 1 yard (yd).

1 yd = 36 in.   1 yd = 3 ft

Miles

1 mile (mi) is about 4 times around the track.

1 mi = 5,280 ft   1 mi = 1,760 yd

Do You Understand?

Convince Me! 1 mi = 5,280 ft. How can you use other relationships shown above to justify that this equation is correct?

© Pearson Education, Inc. 4

Name _____

Another Look!

Below are some customary units of length and examples that could be measured using those units.

Unit	Example
1 inch (in.)	width of a U.S. quarter
1 foot (ft) = 12 inches	gym shoes
1 yard (yd) = 3 feet	height of a desk
1 mile (mi) = 5,280 feet	distance between school and home

In **1** through **12**, choose the most appropriate unit to measure the length of each. Write in., ft, yd, or mi.

1. cat _____

2. lake _____

3. hallway _____

4. basketball court _____

5. boat _____

6. wallet _____

7. soccer field _____

8. finger bandage _____

9. computer cable _____

10. train route _____

11. nose _____

12. sea _____

13. Which unit would you most likely use to measure the length of a desktop?

14. Would you use the same unit to measure the height of the desk as you used to measure the length of the desktop? Explain.

---

15. ⭐ Which unit would be most appropriate for measuring the length of a barn?

   A inches
   B pounds
   C yards
   D miles

You can use more than one unit to measure. But sometimes one unit is more appropriate to use.

---

16. Which is greater, 20 feet or 7 yards? Complete the table to model the answer.

Yard	1						
Feet							

---

17. **Explain** Explain how you would decide which unit is best for measuring the length of the cover of your math book.

18. **Construct Arguments** When measuring the length of an object, how do you decide which unit of measure to use?

---

19. **Estimation** What unit would you use to measure the height of your classroom door? Explain.

20. **Extend Your Thinking** How much greater is 5 miles than 8,000 yards? Explain.

© Pearson Education, Inc. 4

Name _____

Solve & Share

Match the following items with the most appropriate unit of measurement. *Solve this problem any way you choose.*

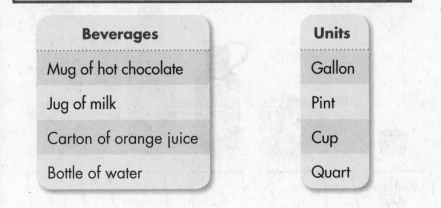

Beverages	Units
Mug of hot chocolate	Gallon
Jug of milk	Pint
Carton of orange juice	Cup
Bottle of water	Quart

TEKS 4.8A Identify relative sizes of measurement units within the customary and metric systems. Also, 4.8. Mathematical Process Standards 4.1A, 4.1C, 4.1D, 4.1F, 4.1G

Digital Resources at PearsonTexas.com

Solve   Learn   Glossary   Check   Tools   Games

You can **analyze relationships.** Think about ordering the items from least amount of liquid held to greatest amount of liquid held. *Show your work in the space above!*

Look Back!

Connect Give an example of a time when you would use each of the above units of capacity.

How Can You Relate Customary Units of Capacity?

A-Z

Capacity is the amount a container can hold, measured in liquid units. Here are some customary units for measuring capacity. How are they related? Which would be most appropriate to measure about how much water a kitchen sink holds?

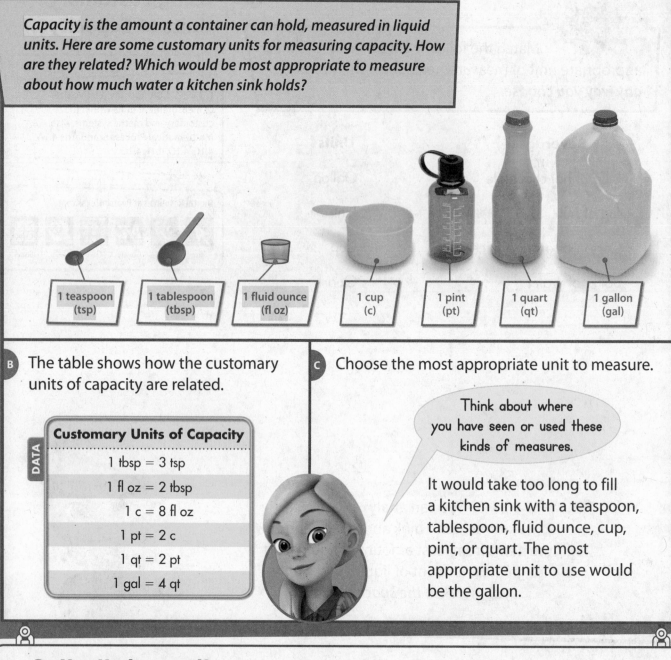

| 1 teaspoon (tsp) | 1 tablespoon (tbsp) | 1 fluid ounce (fl oz) | 1 cup (c) | 1 pint (pt) | 1 quart (qt) | 1 gallon (gal) |

B The table shows how the customary units of capacity are related.

Customary Units of Capacity
1 tbsp = 3 tsp
1 fl oz = 2 tbsp
1 c = 8 fl oz
1 pt = 2 c
1 qt = 2 pt
1 gal = 4 qt

DATA

C Choose the most appropriate unit to measure.

Think about where you have seen or used these kinds of measures.

It would take too long to fill a kitchen sink with a teaspoon, tablespoon, fluid ounce, cup, pint, or quart. The most appropriate unit to use would be the gallon.

Do You Understand?

Convince Me! How many cups are in 1 gallon? Use the data in the chart above to help you decide.

© Pearson Education, Inc. 4

Name _____

Another Look!

Capacity is the amount that a container can hold. Capacity can be measured in teaspoons, tablespoons, fluid ounces, cups, pints, quarts, and gallons, from smallest to largest.

Choose the most appropriate unit when working with customary measures of capacity.

A coffee cup is about 1 cup.

A small bottle of water is about 1 pint.

A carton of juice is about 1 quart.

A jug of milk is about 1 gallon.

In **1** through **6**, choose the best unit to measure the capacity.

1. water bottle _____

2. bathtub _____

3. milk carton _____

4. coffee pot _____

5. teacup _____

6. jug of juice _____

7. **Reason** Would a pint be a good tool for measuring the amount of water in a bathtub? Explain.

8. Are there more or less than 5 pt of blood in an adult human? Are there more or less than 5 gal of blood?

The adult human body contains about 5 qt of blood.

9. Connect Janice needs 1 pt of sour cream. Which size container should she buy? How many containers of that size does she need to purchase?

Sour Cream 2 C
Sour Cream 1 QT
Sour Cream 8 oz

10. Number Sense Would a teaspoon be a good way to measure the capacity of a milk carton? Explain.

11. Personal Financial Literacy A store sells 1 gallon of lemonade for $7, and 1 quart of lemonade for $2. Horace has $11 to buy 6 quarts of lemonade for a party. Explain whether he has enough money.

12. Which would be a better estimate of the capacity of the aquarium: 40 quarts or 400 quarts? Why?

Which unit has the greatest capacity?

A Tablespoon

B Quart

C Pint

D Teaspoon

14. Explain Cassidy says that capacity is the same as the amount. Do you agree? Explain.

15. w much water is Samuel most likely to k after soccer practice?

A fl oz

B c

C t

D al

16. Extend Your Thinking Kelly measured 12 teaspoons of a drink mix. She had a measuring cup showing fluid ounces. What equivalent amounts, in tablespoons and fluid ounces, could she have used?

© Pearson Education, Inc. 4

Name _____

Solve & Share

Name 3 animals: one that could have a weight less than 1 pound, one that could have a weight greater than 1 pound, and one that could have a weight of about 1 ton. *Solve this problem any way you choose.*

TEKS 4.8A Identify relative sizes of measurement units within the customary and metric systems. Also, 4.8. **Mathematical Process Standards 4.1A, 4.1C, 4.1D, 4.1G**

Digital Resources at PearsonTexas.com

Solve   Learn   Glossary   Check   Tools   Games

You can **reason.**
Think about different animals and what you know about ounces, pounds, and tons.

Look Back!

Connect Why are pounds used to measure a person's weight?

How Can You Relate Customary Units of Weight?

A-Z

Weight is how heavy an object is. Here are some customary units for measuring weight. How are they related? Which would be most appropriate to measure the weight of a peach?

1 ounce (oz)　　　1 pound (lb)　　　1 ton (T)

A key weighs about 1 ounce.

A kitten weighs about 1 pound.

A giraffe weighs about 1 ton.

B The table shows how the customary units of weight are related.

DATA

Units of Weight

1 lb = 16 oz
1 T = 2,000 lb

Compare the benchmark weights to the weight of a peach.

C Choose the most appropriate unit to measure. A peach weighs less than one pound.

So the most appropriate unit to use would be the ounce.

Do You Understand?

Convince Me! Name two objects that each weigh about the given amount.

10 ounces: _____ and _____

5 pounds: _____ and _____

2 tons: _____ and _____

© Pearson Education, Inc. 4

Name _____

Another Look!

There are 16 ounces (oz) in 1 pound (lb).

There are 2,000 lb in 1 ton (T).

> Choose the most appropriate unit when working with customary measures of weight.

You use ounces to weigh smaller things, like a tomato.

You use pounds to weigh things, like a heavy box.

You use tons to weigh very large or heavy things, like a rocket.

> In **1** through **6**, choose the most appropriate unit to measure the weight of each item. Write oz, lb, or T.

1. car _____

2. computer _____

3. bowling ball _____

4. onion _____

5. Tyrannosaurus rex _____

6. vacuum cleaner _____

---

7. Reason A hippo weighs about 5,000 lb. Does the same hippo weigh more or less than 5,000 oz?

8. Explain Would you most likely measure a leaf using ounces, pounds, or tons? Explain.

9. **Reason** Would a scale that is used to weigh food be the best tool to weigh concrete blocks? Explain.

10. **Connect** Jen wants to weigh her cat. What is the most appropriate unit she should use to weigh the cat: ounces, pounds, or tons?

11. What is the most appropriate unit you would use to measure the weight of a house?

12. **Explain** How are ounces and fluid ounces different?

13. **Justify** Dezi says that there are more ounces in 1 T than there are pounds. Do you agree? Explain.

14. **Use a Strip Diagram** One fluid ounce of water weighs about 1 ounce. About how many loaves of bread equal the weight of 1 gallon of water? Use a strip diagram to write an equation.

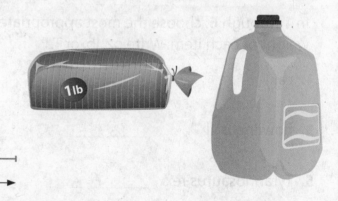

15. Which animal's weight would be best ⭐ measured in ounces?

   A Mouse
   B Elephant
   C Horse
   D Cow

16. **Extend Your Thinking** Mr. Johansson's truck weighs 3 tons. How many ounces does it weigh?

© Pearson Education, Inc. 4

Name _____

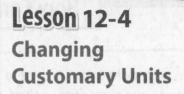
☆ **Solve & Share**

A soccer goal is 24 feet wide and 8 feet tall. What are the dimensions of a soccer goal when measured in inches? *Solve this problem any way you choose.*

⭐ TEKS 4.8B Convert measurements within the same measurement system… when given other equivalent measures represented in a table. Also, 4.8C. Mathematical Process Standards 4.1B, 4.1C, 4.1D, 4.1G

You can **formulate a plan**. Think about the relationship between feet and inches. *Show your work in the space below!*

Digital Resources at PearsonTexas.com

| Solve | Learn | Glossary | Check | Tools | Games |

Look Back!

Estimation How could you use estimation to check your answers for reasonableness?

How Can You Change Customary Units?

The table below can be used to change one customary unit of measure to another.

DATA

Customary Units

Length	Capacity	Weight
1 ft = 12 in.	1 tbsp = 3 tsp	1 lb = 16 oz
1 yd = 36 in.	1 fl oz = 2 tbsp	1 T = 2,000 lb
1 yd = 3 ft	1 c = 8 fl oz	
1 mi = 5,280 ft	1 pt = 2 c	
1 mi = 1,760 yd	1 qt = 2 pt	
	1 gal = 4 qt	

You can use multiplication or division to convert between units.

B How many pints are in five quarts?

To change larger units to smaller units, multiply.

5 qt = ? pt

1 qt = 2 pt

5 × 2 = 10

5 qt = 10 pt

There are 10 pints in five quarts.

C How many feet are equal to 84 inches?

To change smaller units to larger units, divide.

84 in. = ? ft

12 in. = 1 ft

84 ÷ 12 = 7

84 in. = 7 ft

There are 7 feet in 84 inches.

Do You Understand?

Convince Me! In the second example above, why do you divide 84 by 12?

© Pearson Education, Inc. 4

Another Example

Compare 2 gallons to 24 cups.

Step 1	Step 2
Change gallons into cups.	Compare.
1 gal = 4 qt, so 2 gal × 4 qt = 8 quarts.	32 c > 24 c
1 qt = 2 pt, so 8 qt × 2 pt = 16 pints.	So, 2 gal > 24 c.
1 pt = 2 c, so 16 pt × 2 c = 32 cups.	

☆ Guided Practice ☆

In **1** and **2**, find the missing number.

1. 7 lb = _____ oz   **2.** 3 yd = _____ in.

In **3** and **4**, compare. Write > or < for each ◯.

3. 2 tbsp ◯ 4 tsp   **4.** 16 fl oz ◯ 3 c

5. Explain In the first example on page 642, why do you multiply?

6. Formulate a Plan Do you multiply or divide to change inches to yards?

7. Explain Is a 4-foot stick longer or shorter than a 42-inch stick?

☆ Independent Practice ☆

In **8** through **11**, find each missing number.

8. 4 pt = ? qt   **9.** 18 tsp = ? tbsp   **10.** 2 c = ? fl oz   **11.** 4 tbsp = ? tsp

4 ÷ 2 = _____ qt   18 ÷ 3 = _____ tbsp   2 × 8 = _____ fl oz   4 × 3 = _____ tsp

In **12** through **15**, compare. Write > or < for each ◯.

12. 16 tbsp ◯ 2 c   **13.** 5 c ◯ 2 pt   **14.** 2 T ◯ 2,500 lb   **15.** 2 mi ◯ 2,000 yd

Problem Solving

In **16** through **18**, use the table at the right.

The weight of objects on other planets and the Moon is different than it is on Earth.

16. Analyze Information What is the approximate weight in ounces of a fourth grader on Venus?

17. Analyze Information What is the approximate weight in ounces of a fourth grader on the Moon?

18. Reason Would an adult weigh more on Earth or on Venus? Explain your reasoning.

Approximate Weight of a 4th-Grader

Earth	Jupiter	Venus	Moon
85 lb	215 lb	77 lb	14 lb

---

19. Reason Mr. Williams said that a giraffe's height is 180 inches, or 15 yards. What mistake did he make?

20. Communicate Which unit of measure would you use to measure the length of your shoe? Explain.

---

21. Mr. Kunkle uses a bowling ball that weighs 13 pounds. How many ounces does the bowling ball weigh?

  A 116 oz

  B 140 oz

  C 180 oz

  D 208 oz

22. Extend Your Thinking The longest tail feathers of any bird are those of the Argus Pheasant. The feathers measure 5 feet 7 inches in length. How many inches long are these feathers?

---

23. Number Sense Henry filled a bathtub with 15 gallons of water. How many quarts of water is this?

  A 20 qt   **C** 55 qt

  B 45 qt   **D** 60 qt

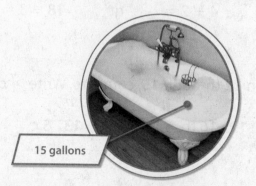

15 gallons

© Pearson Education, Inc. 4

Another Look!

Here is a table of the customary units of length, capacity, and weight. Use the table to change one customary unit of measure to another.

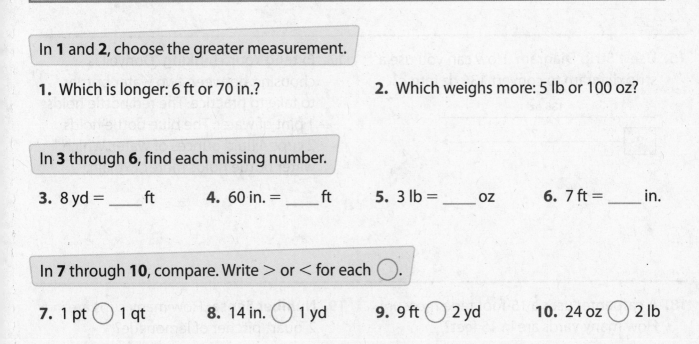

Customary Units		
Length	**Capacity**	**Weight**
1 ft = 12 in.	1 tbsp = 3 tsp	1 lb = 16 oz
1 yd = 36 in.	1 fl oz = 2 tbsp	1 T = 2,000 lb
1 yd = 3 ft	1 c = 8 fl oz	
1 mi = 5,280 ft	1 pt = 2 c	
1 mi = 1,760 yd	1 qt = 2 pt	
	1 gal = 4 qt	

To change smaller units to larger units, divide. To change larger units to smaller units, multiply.

Which distance is longer, 100 in. or 10 yd?

1 yd = 3 ft   1 ft = 12 in.

3 ft × 12 in. = 36 in.

10 yd × 36 in. = 360 in.

360 in. is greater than 100 in., so 10 yd is longer than 100 in.

In **1** and **2**, choose the greater measurement.

1. Which is longer: 6 ft or 70 in.?

2. Which weighs more: 5 lb or 100 oz?

In **3** through **6**, find each missing number.

3. 8 yd = ____ ft

4. 60 in. = ____ ft

5. 3 lb = ____ oz

6. 7 ft = ____ in.

In **7** through **10**, compare. Write > or < for each ◯.

7. 1 pt ◯ 1 qt

8. 14 in. ◯ 1 yd

9. 9 ft ◯ 2 yd

10. 24 oz ◯ 2 lb

11. Mrs. Brown buys this 5-pound bag of potatoes. There are 18 potatoes in the bag. How many ounces does the bag of potatoes weigh?

What information do you need to solve this problem?

12. Which measurement is NOT equal to 1 mile?

★

A 1,760 yd
B 5,280 yd
C 5,280 ft
D 63,360 in.

13. **Explain** A recipe calls for 4 tsp of baking soda and 1 fl oz of vanilla. Which measurement is greater? Explain.

14. A parking space is 20 feet long. A pickup truck is 6 yards long. How many inches longer is the parking space than the truck?

15. Liza is 4 feet 6 inches tall. How many inches tall is she?

★

A 46 in.
B 48 in.
C 54 in.
D 76 in.

16. **Use a Strip Diagram** How can you use a strip diagram to convert 136 oz into c?

136 oz

?   ?

17. **Extend Your Thinking** Donyell is choosing between two water bottles to take to practice. The red bottle holds 1 pint of water. The blue bottle holds 2 cups 4 fluid ounces of water. Which water bottle holds more? Explain.

18. A carpenter uses a 15-foot tape measure. How many yards are in 15 feet?

19. **Number Sense** How many cups are in a 2-quart pitcher of lemonade?

© Pearson Education, Inc. 4

Name _____

Solve & Share

Carson stood next to a tree that is 75 feet taller than she is. Carson is 52 inches tall. Jesse stood next to another tree that is 876 inches taller than he is. Jesse is 5 feet tall. How many inches tall is the tree next to Carson? **Solve this problem any way you choose.**

You can **formulate a plan.** Which information do you need to solve the problem? **Show your work in the space below!**

⭐ **TEKS 4.1B** Use a problem-solving model that incorporates analyzing given information, formulating a plan or strategy, determining a solution, justifying the solution, and evaluating the problem-solving process and the reasonableness of the solution. Also, 4.8B, 4.8C. **Mathematical Process Standards 4.1A, 4.1C, 4.1D, 4.1G**

Digital Resources at PearsonTexas.com

| Solve | Learn | Glossary | Check | Tools | Games |

Look Back!

Justify Which tree is taller? How do you know?

How Can Given Information Help You Solve a Problem?

Three students individually measured the width of their classroom. They recorded their data in the chart.

Which student made a mistake? Explain.

Think about how the answers are different and about ways to compare them.

Student	Measurement
Nancy	44 ft.
Matt	19 ft 6 in.
Mike	6 yd 1 ft 6 in.

DATA

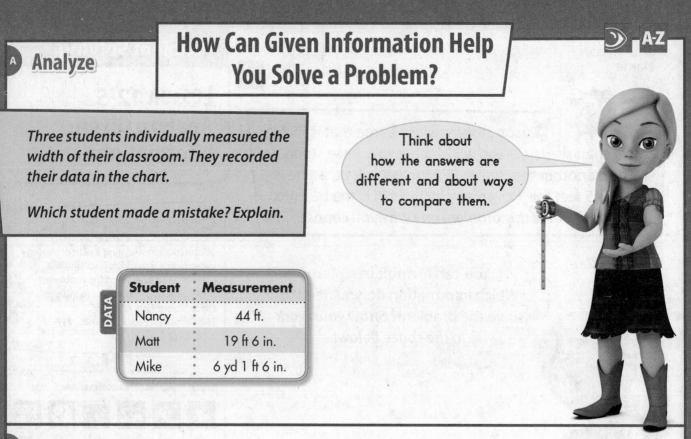

B Plan and Solve

Convert the students' measurements to inches and compare.

Nancy's measurement:
1 foot = 12 inches
44 × 12 = 528 inches

Matt's measurement:
1 foot = 12 inches
19 × 12 = 228 inches

19 feet = 228 inches
+   6 inches
234 inches

Mike's measurement:
1 yard = 36 inches
6 × 36 = 216 inches

6 yards = 216 inches
1 foot = 12 inches
+   6 inches
234 inches

Nancy's measurement is 528 inches. Both Mike's and Matt's measurements are 234 inches. Nancy must have made a mistake.

Do You Understand?

Convince Me! Amanda sent her pen pal some measurement facts. To make it fun, she changed some of the measurements to different units. Which facts seem reasonable and which facts do not seem reasonable? Explain.

Amanda's Facts

How far I walk to school	100in.
How much I weigh	160oz
Size of my fish aquarium	100qt
Length of my bedroom	4 yd

© Pearson Education, Inc. 4

☆ Guided Practice ☆

In **1** through **3**, solve each problem.

1. A bald eagle can have a wingspan of up to 7 feet 6 inches. A mallard duck can have a wingspan of about 32 inches. How much longer is the bald eagle's wingspan than the mallard duck's wingspan? Explain.

2. Explain why one yard is equal to 36 inches.

3. **Connect** Write a problem in which measurements are compared. Explain the relationship between those.

☆ Independent Practice ☆

In **4** through **7**, solve each problem.

4. A limousine is 240 inches long. A pick-up truck is 19 feet long. Which is longer?

5. Which container holds more: a gallon jug, a 3-quart pitcher, or a 5-pint bowl?

6. Julia and her brother went deep-sea fishing. They caught a spotted seatrout weighing 5 pounds 10 ounces, a snook weighing 8 pounds 4 ounces, and a redfish weighing 176 ounces. Which was the largest fish they caught?

7. **Explain** When converting ounces to pounds, you would have to divide the number of ounces by 16 to get the number of pounds. If you get a remainder when converting ounces to pounds, what does the remainder mean?

For another example, see Set E on page 692.

Problem Solving

Derek, Kitty, Eva, and Mercedes are measuring planks of wood for a tree house. Each plank must be 5 feet 10 inches long.

Plank Lengths	
Child	**Measurement**
Derek	2 yd − 2 in.
Kitty	1 yd + 34 in.
Eva	70 in.
Mercedes	60 in.

8. Derek said his planks measure 2 inches less than 2 yards. Did Derek measure correctly? Explain.

9. **Construct Arguments** Whose measurement is incorrect? Explain.

10. What is the perimeter in feet of this figure?

   A 48 ft
   B 24 ft
   C 4 ft
   D 2 ft

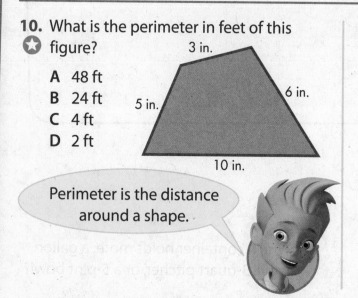

3 in.
6 in.
5 in.
10 in.

Perimeter is the distance around a shape.

11. **Extend Your Thinking** An ounce is related to a pound in the same way that a fluid ounce is related to what measure of capacity? Explain.

12. **Connect** How many feet would you run if you went twice around the inner track shown to the right? Explain.

One lap around the inner track is 440 yards

13. **Reason** How could you find out which weighs more: one ton of pillows or one ton of bowling balls?

14. **Formulate a Plan** Tony is 4 feet 4 inches. His little sister, Jillian, is half a foot shorter. Their father is 2 feet taller than Jillian. How tall is their father, in feet and inches?

© Pearson Education, Inc. 4

Another Look!

Jessy and Dean each weighed their pets. Jessy's dog weighed 12 pounds 2 ounces. Dean's cat weighed 128 ounces. Dean said his cat weighs more. Is he correct?

> Analyze given information to solve a problem.

Plan	First, I need to convert Jessy's measurement to ounces so I can compare the weights of her dog and Dean's cat.	Jessy's measurement: 12 pounds 2 ounces I remember that 1 pound = 16 ounces. 12 pounds × 16 ounces = 192 ounces. So, 12 pounds 2 ounces = 192 ounces + 2 ounces 192 + 2 = 194 ounces
Solve	Compare measurements. Dean's cat weighs 128 ounces. Jessy's dog weighs 194 ounces.	Dean was incorrect. His cat weighs 128 ounces and Jessy's dog weighs 194 ounces. Jessy's dog weighs more. Dean may not have remembered that each pound equals 16 ounces.

1. Raul measures the length of a hallway upstairs as 8 feet. His brother measures the length of a hallway downstairs as 96 inches. Which hallway is longer? Explain.

2. **Connect** A farmer is planning to create a new grazing field for his horses. He determines that he needs 280 yards of fencing for his new field. The fencing is sold by the foot. How many feet of fencing should the farmer buy? Explain.

> In order to compare, the units have to be the same.

3. Analyze Information ⭐ Maureen has a jump rope that is 62 inches long. Nancy's jump rope is 10 inches longer. How long is Nancy's jump rope?

A 4 ft, 4 in.
B 6 ft
C 6 ft, 4 in.
D 7 ft, 2 in.

4. The height of Ali's robot is 22 inches. Michael's robot is 6 inches taller than Ali's robot. What is the height of Michael's robot in feet and inches?

5. Number Sense An economy car weighs 400 pounds more than the compact car. How much does the economy car weigh?

Compact Car
1 Ton

6. Warren measured a rectangular window to find out how much wood he would need for a new frame. What is the total length of wood that Warren needs? Write your answer in feet and inches.

5 feet 6 inches

2 feet 9 inches

7. Extend Your Thinking Nikki uses two teaspoons of sugar in a recipe. Claire makes twice as much of the same recipe and then adds two more teaspoons of sugar. How many tablespoons of sugar does Claire use?

8. Explain Sam is 4 feet 5 inches tall. Karolyn is half a foot shorter. Meredith is two feet taller than Karolyn. Explain how to find each person's height in inches.

© Pearson Education, Inc. 4

Name _____

Solve & Share

A unit cube is 1 centimeter long, and 10 unit cubes, or a ten-rod, is a decimeter long. Choose an object in the classroom you could measure in decimeters and measure it. *Solve this problem any way you choose.*

★ TEKS 4.8A Identify relative sizes of measurement units within the customary and metric systems. Also, 4.8. Mathematical Process Standards 4.1A, 4.1C, 4.1D, 4.1G

Digital Resources at PearsonTexas.com

Solve   Learn   Glossary   Check   Tools   Games

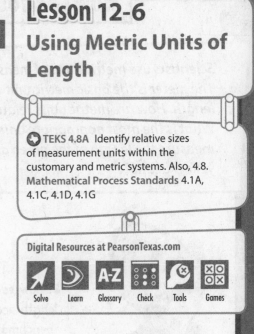

You can **use tools.** Select an object that can be measured with a ten-rod. *Show your work in the space above!*

Look Back!

Connect Name an object, besides a ten-rod, that has a length of about 1 decimeter.

How Can You Relate Metric Units of Length?

A-Z

Scientists use metric units of measure. The meter is the basic metric unit of length. How are metric units related? What is the most appropriate unit to measure the length of the green and yellow beetle?

DATA

Metric Units of Length

1 centimeter (cm) = 10 millimeters (mm)

1 decimeter (dm) = 10 centimeters (cm)

1 meter (m) = 100 centimeters (cm)

1 kilometer (km) = 1,000 meters (m)

The table shows how several metric units of length are related. Use common benchmarks to decide which to use to measure the beetle.

Use benchmark measures.

B

The thickness of a dime is about **1 millimeter**.

The length of a ladybug is about **1 centimeter**.

The width of a doorway is about **1 meter**.

The length of a train that has 60 cars is about **1 kilometer**.

The beetle is longer than a ladybug, but shorter than a doorway. So the most appropriate unit to use is the centimeter.

Do You Understand?

Convince Me! For each measurement unit below, name two objects in your classroom that are best measured using that unit.

Millimeters: _____ and _____

Centimeters: _____ and _____

Meters: _____ and _____

© Pearson Education, Inc. 4

Name _____

In **1** through **4**, choose the most appropriate unit of measure. Write mm, cm, dm, m, or km.

1. height of a house

2. length of a cat

3. width of a sunflower seed

4. distance traveled by plane

5. Which is a better unit to measure the width of this textbook: centimeter or meter?

6. Joni wants to measure the width of a narrow ribbon she is using to tie around the pinecone. Which metric unit should she use? Explain.

☆ **Independent Practice** *

In **7** through **9**, choose the most appropriate unit of measure. Write mm, cm, dm, m, or km.

7. length of a shoe

8. height of a tree

9. width of a strand of yarn

In **10** and **11**, estimate the length of each item.

10. Is the length of this feather, shown at actual size, closer to 2 cm or 2 dm?

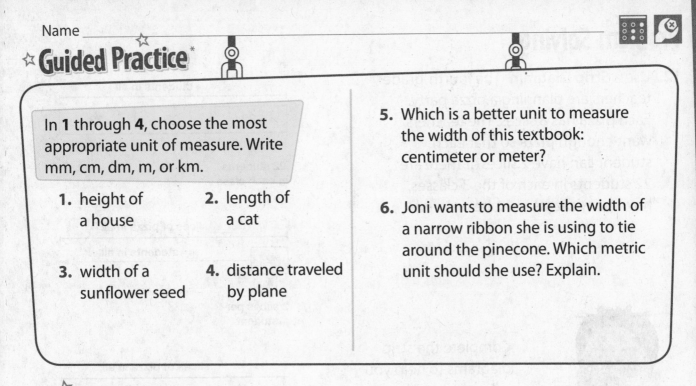

11. Is the length of this pinecone, shown at actual size, closer to 5 dm or 5 cm?

You can use your benchmarks to identify relative sizes of measurement units.

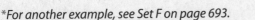

Problem Solving

12. Use a Strip Diagram The fourth-grade teachers are planning a pizza party. Each pizza has 8 slices. The teachers want enough pizza so that each student can have 2 slices. If there are 22 students in each of the 3 classes, how many pizzas must be ordered?

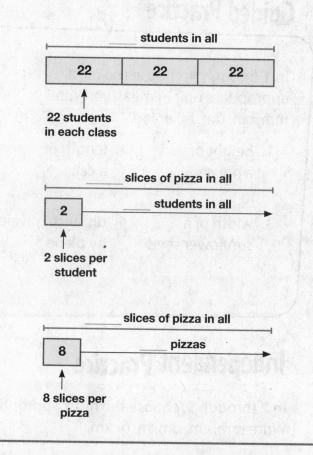

Complete the strip diagrams to help you solve this problem.

13. Connect Leonardo's road map shows that the distance between Dallas and Houston is 385 of some metric unit. However, the map has been torn, so Leonardo cannot read what the unit is. What is the unit for this distance?

14. Estimation In the year 2000, the world's largest Chinese dancing dragon was part of a celebration at the Great Wall of China. It took 3,200 people working inside the dragon to move it. Which is the best estimate of the length of the dragon?

A 3,048 mm
B 3,048 dm
C 3,048 cm
D 3,048 m

15. Extend Your Thinking How many beads are needed to make a string that is 5 dm long?

2 cm

16. Samuel has 3 objects of different lengths. One is 1 m, another is 1 cm, and the third one is 1 dm. Order the objects from longest to shortest.

© Pearson Education, Inc. 4

Name _____

Another Look!

Millimeters (mm), centimeters (cm), decimeters (dm), meters (m), and kilometers (km) can be used to measure length.

Metric units are used to estimate and measure length.

Metric Units of Length

1 cm = 10 mm

1 dm = 10 cm

1 m = 100 cm

1 km = 1,000 m

The thickness of a DVD is about 1 millimeter.

The width of a crayon is about 1 centimeter.

The width of your teacher's hand is about 1 decimeter.

The length of a baseball bat is about 1 meter.

In **1** through **6**, choose the most appropriate unit to measure each. Write mm, cm, dm, m, or km.

1. length of a finger

2. length of a football

3. width of a big toe

4. length of the lunchroom

5. distance between Paris and London

6. length of a soccer field

7. Is the length of this shell, shown at actual size, closer to 6 mm or 6 cm?

8. Number Sense Which would you be more likely to measure in centimeters: a fish tank or a swimming pool?

9. Math and Science In 2010, a glacier was 171 meters away from a road. Every year since then, it has moved 3 meters closer to the road. At this rate, in what year will the glacier meet the road?

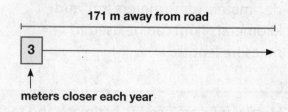

171 m away from road

3

meters closer each year

10. Number Sense The distance across a field is 200 m. Is the distance across the same field greater than or less than 20 km?

11. ⭐ Which is the most appropriate measure for the length of a skateboard?

    A 5 mm

    B 5 cm

    C 5 dm

    D 5 m

12. Explain Jill measured the length of her eraser. She wrote 5 on her paper without the unit. Which metric unit of measure should Jill include?

13. How much longer is a 12 cm pencil than a 1 dm pen?

14. ⭐ Which is the best unit of measure for determining the width of a house?

    A Centimeter

    B Decimeter

    C Meter

    D Kilometer

15. Extend Your Thinking Larry places five 20-centimeter long bricks end-to-end. What is the length, in meters, of the row of bricks? Explain.

© Pearson Education, Inc. 4

Name _____

☆ ☆
Solve & Share
  Liz has four containers filled with water: a soup can, a bleach bottle, a thimble, and a bucket. Which metric unit of capacity should Liz use to measure the amount of water in each container? Explain. **Solve this problem any way you choose.**

🔶 TEKS 4.8A Identify relative sizes of measurement units within the customary and metric systems. Also, 4.8. Mathematical Process Standards 4.1B, 4.1C, 4.1D, 4.1F, 4.1G

You can **analyze relationships.** Use capacity units that are less than the size of the container you want to measure. *Show your work in the space below!*

Digital Resources at PearsonTexas.com

Solve	Learn	Glossary	Check	Tools	Games

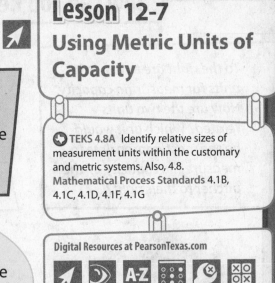

milliliter liter

Look Back!

Explain Why wouldn't liters be the most appropriate unit to measure the capacity of a juice glass?

How Can You Relate Metric Units of Capacity?

A

To the right are two metric units for measuring capacity. How are the two units related? Which unit would be the most appropriate to measure the capacity of the pitcher to their right?

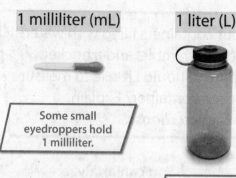

1 milliliter (mL)

Some small eyedroppers hold 1 milliliter.

1 liter (L)

Some water bottles hold 1 liter.

The liter is the basic metric unit of capacity.

B The table shows how the metric units of capacity are related.

DATA

Metric Units of Capacity

1 liter (L) = 1,000 milliliters (mL)

The prefix "milli" means *thousandths* for any metric measure.

C Choose the most appropriate unit to measure. The milliliter is a very small amount. The pitcher is larger than the water bottle.

So the liter would be the most appropriate unit to use.

Do You Understand?

Convince Me! The carton of milk at the right was full. For a cooking recipe, 250 mL of this milk were used. How many milliliters of milk are still in the carton? Explain.

MILK 1L

© Pearson Education, Inc. 4

☆ Guided Practice ☆

In **1** through **4**, choose which is the better estimate for capacity.

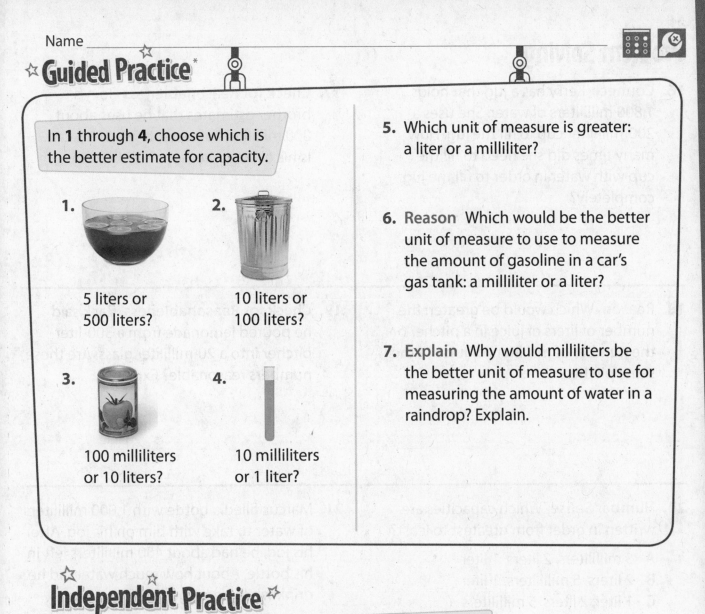

1. 5 liters or 500 liters?

2. 10 liters or 100 liters?

3. 100 milliliters or 10 liters?

4. 10 milliliters or 1 liter?

5. Which unit of measure is greater: a liter or a milliliter?

6. Reason Which would be the better unit of measure to use to measure the amount of gasoline in a car's gas tank: a milliliter or a liter?

7. Explain Why would milliliters be the better unit of measure to use for measuring the amount of water in a raindrop? Explain.

☆ Independent Practice ☆

In **8** through **11**, choose the more appropriate unit to measure the capacity. Write L or mL.

8. bucket

9. ink pen

10. juice glass

11. washing machine

In **12** through **15**, choose the better estimate for capacity.

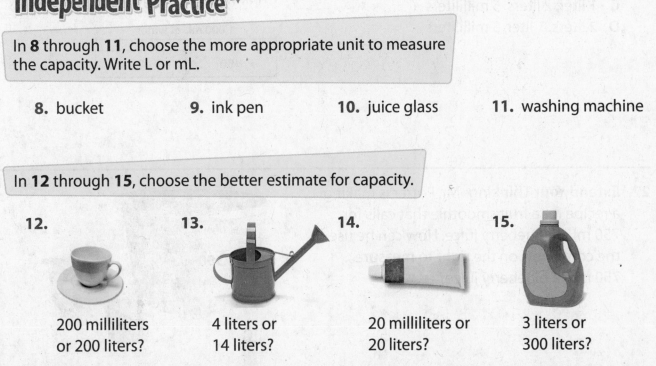

12. 200 milliliters or 200 liters?

13. 4 liters or 14 liters?

14. 20 milliliters or 20 liters?

15. 3 liters or 300 liters?

Problem Solving

16. Connect Kerry has a jug that holds 1,800 milliliters of water. She uses a 200-milliliter cup to fill the jug. How many times did she need to fill the cup with water in order to fill the jug completely?

17. Check for Reasonableness Joey's brother estimates that he uses about 800 milliliters of water to wash his car. Is his estimate reasonable? Explain.

18. Reason Which would be greater: the number of liters of juice in a pitcher or the number of milliliters of juice in the same pitcher?

19. Check for Reasonableness Zack said he poured lemonade from a 300-liter pitcher into a 20-milliliter glass. Are these numbers reasonable? Explain.

20. Number Sense Which capacities are written in order from greatest to least?

A 5 milliliters, 2 liters, 1 liter
B 2 liters, 5 milliliters, 1 liter
C 1 liter, 2 liters, 5 milliliters
D 2 liters, 1 liter, 5 milliliters

21. Marcus filled a bottle with 1,000 milliliters of water to take with him on his jog. After his jog, he had about 450 milliliters left in his bottle. About how much water did he drink while he jogged?

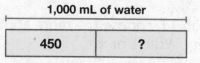

1,000 mL of water	
450	?

22. Extend Your Thinking Mr. Potter is making a recipe for a fruit smoothie that calls for 750 mL of blueberry juice. How can he use the containers on the right to measure 750 mL of blueberry juice?

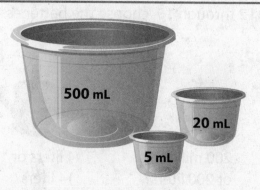

500 mL

20 mL

5 mL

© Pearson Education, Inc. 4

Name _____

Another Look!

Liters and milliliters are used when measuring capacity in metric units.

Capacity is the amount of liquid that an object can hold. The metric system of measurement uses the units liter (L) and milliliter (mL).

You would use liters to measure the amount of water in a water bottle or the amount of gasoline in a gas can.

A milliliter is a very small unit of measurement. You would use milliliters to measure small amounts of liquid, such as measuring an amount of liquid medicine.

1 L = 1,000 mL

In **1** through **8**, choose the more appropriate unit to measure the capacity. Write L or mL.

1. thimble

2. kitchen sink

3. coffee creamer container

4. bucket of water for a horse

5. squirt gun pistol

6. goldfish bowl

7. vase

8. wading pool

9. **Number Sense** A container holds 5 L of fluid. Does it hold more than or less than 500 mL of fluid?

10. A bottle is filled with saline solution for eyes. Is the bottle more likely to hold 15 mL of solution or 1 L of solution?

11. Number Sense Megan found that a bathtub contained 30 L of water. Then she measured the same amount of water and found that the capacity was 300 mL. Is the number of milliliters reasonable? Explain.

12. Estimation About how many mL of tomato juice does the smaller can hold?

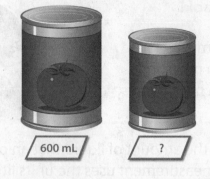

600 mL   ?

13. Explain Would you be more likely to measure the amount of water in your kitchen sink in liters or milliliters? Explain.

14. Connect A gallon of milk is about the same as 4 L of milk. About how many liters of milk are there in 10 gal?

15. Chris measures the amount of juice in a large bottle in liters. Is this unit of measure appropriate? Explain.

16. Sarah says she drinks 250 milliliters of water eight times each day. Which of the following is the best estimate for the amount of water Sarah drinks in one day?

A 2,000 L
B 250 L
C 2 L
D 2 mL

17. Phil needs to buy lemonade for a school party. Which container should he buy if he wants to get the most lemonade?

2 L   2000 mL

18. Extend Your Thinking Chef Tom's stew is too thin. To thicken the stew, he must add two teaspoons of liquid cornstarch every 10 minutes to make the stew thick enough. Chef Tom knows that a teaspoon is about the same as 5 mL. About how many mL of cornstarch will he add in 30 minutes?

© Pearson Education, Inc. 4

Name _____

Solve & Share

Order these different balls from the one with the least mass to the greatest mass: bowling ball, beach ball, ping-pong ball, and cannonball. Decide which unit of mass you would use to measure each. *Solve this problem any way you choose.*

⭐ **TEKS 4.8A** Identify relative sizes of measurement units within the customary and metric systems. Also, 4.8. **Mathematical Process Standards** 4.1B, 4.1C, 4.1D, 4.1F, 4.1G

Digital Resources at PearsonTexas.com

Solve   Learn   Glossary   Check   Tools   Games

You can use **reasoning**. A sheet of paper has a mass of about 1 gram. A textbook has a mass of about 1 kilogram. *Show your work in the space below!*

Look Back!

Connect Ideas For which metric measurement have you used the prefix "kilo" before?

A

Mass is the amount of matter that something contains. Below are two metric units for measuring mass. How are the two units related? Which unit would be the most appropriate to measure the mass of the red brick?

The kilogram is the basic metric unit of mass.

1 gram (g)

1 kilogram (kg)

A dollar bill has a mass of about 1 gram (g).

A cantaloupe has a mass of about 1 kilogram (kg).

B The table shows how the metric units of mass are related.

DATA

Metric Units of Mass

1 kilogram (kg) = 1,000 grams (g)

The prefix "kilo" means *thousand* for any metric measure.

C Choose the most appropriate unit to measure. The gram is a very small amount. A brick has a greater mass than a cantaloupe.

So the kilogram would be the most appropriate unit to use.

Do You Understand?

Convince Me! Which of the measurements in the table seem reasonable? Which do not seem reasonable? Explain.

Object	Mass
Hammer	1 kilogram
Book	20 grams
Comb	40 kilograms
Computer	2 kilograms
Dog	4 grams

DATA

© Pearson Education, Inc. 4

Another Example

How are weight and mass different?

The **weight** of an object is affected by gravity.

The weight of the red brick on the moon is not the same as its weight on Earth.

The **mass** of an object always stays the same.

A *pan balance* is used to measure mass. The mass of the red brick on the moon is the same as its mass on Earth, about 3 kg.

Pan balance

☆ Guided Practice *

In **1** and **2**, choose the more appropriate unit to measure the mass of each item. Write g or kg.

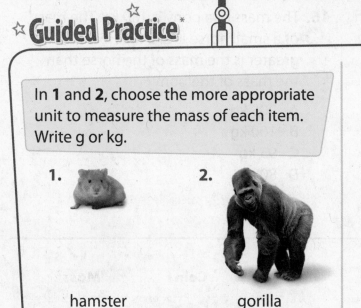

1. hamster

2. gorilla

3. Which number would be less, the mass of a grapefruit in grams or the mass of the same grapefruit in kilograms?

4. **Reason** Why is a pan balance a good tool to use to measure mass?

☆ Independent Practice ☆

In **5** through **12**, choose the more appropriate unit to measure the mass of each item. Write g or kg.

5. pencil

6. baseball player

7. baseball

8. car

9. strawberry

10. penguin

11. sailboat

12. dragonfly

Problem Solving

13. Explain Mandy says that she has a mass of 32 kg on Earth. What is her mass on the moon?

14. Number Sense Which is greater: the number of grams in the mass of a television, or the number of kilograms in the mass of the same television? Explain.

15. Use a Strip Diagram José needs $78 for a present. He has already saved $33. How much more does he need to save?

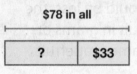

$78 in all

| ? | $33 |

16. ⭐ The mass of a pony is 180 kg. The mass of a small horse is 275 kg. How much greater is the mass of the horse than the mass of the pony?

   A 205 kg
   B 100 kg
   C 95 kg
   D 80 kg

17. Order the coins from least mass to greatest mass.

18. Reason There are 1,000 milligrams (mg) in 1 gram. How many milligrams are in one nickel?

19. Extend Your Thinking A roll of nickels contains 40 coins. What is the total mass of one roll of nickels? Would you use grams or kilograms to measure the mass of a roll of nickels? Explain.

Coin	Mass
	2.50 grams
	5.00 grams
	2.27 grams
	5.67 grams

© Pearson Education, Inc. 4

Name _____

Another Look!

Two metric units for mass are grams (g) and kilograms (kg).
1 kg = 1,000 g

A paperclip has a mass of about 1 gram.
A hardcover book has the mass of about 1 kilogram.

Which unit should you use to measure the mass of a bike?

How many paperclips would have the same mass as a bike? How many books?

The mass of a bike is much greater than the mass of a paperclip.
A kilogram is the most appropriate unit to measure a bike.

In **1** through **11**, choose the more appropriate unit to measure the mass of each item. Write g or kg.

1. The mass of a lawn mower is greater than the mass of a book.

   The most appropriate unit of measure for a lawn mower is _____.

2. The mass of a door key is less than the mass of a book.

   The most appropriate unit of measure for a door key is _____.

3. The mass of a pineapple is equal to the mass of a book.

   The most appropriate unit of measure is _____.

4. pumpkin   5. gold ring

6. robin's egg   7. cannonball

8. cement block   9. spool of thread

10. car tire   11. shoelace

12. Explain Would you be more likely to find the mass of a pen in grams or in kilograms? Explain.

13. The mass of a certain window is 18 kg. What is the mass of 5 of those windows?

14. Number Sense Which is a greater number, the mass of a cat in grams or the mass of the same cat in kilograms?

15. Bella has three different objects whose masses are 500 g, 125 g, and 375 g. Which is the sum of the masses of the objects?

A 1,000 kg   C 10 kg

B 100 kg   D 1 kg

16. The *Dromornis stirtoni* was once the largest living bird. It is now extinct. The ostrich is now the largest living bird. What is the difference in mass between the *Dromornis stirtoni* and the ostrich?

17. Which has a greater mass, an Andean condor or a Eurasian eagle owl? How much greater?

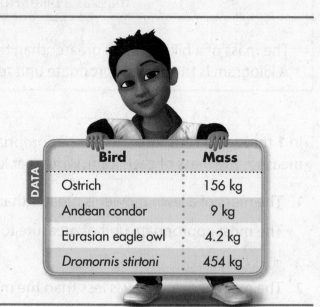

DATA

Bird	Mass
Ostrich	156 kg
Andean condor	9 kg
Eurasian eagle owl	4.2 kg
Dromornis stirtoni	454 kg

18. Personal Financial Literacy A drum set costs $78.39. Janice can buy it on credit by making 6 payments of $14. How much more does the drum set cost to buy on credit than to buy with cash? Tell how you found the answer.

19. Check for Reasonableness Is it reasonable to say that 10 marshmallows have a mass greater than 1 kilogram?

20. Extend Your Thinking Luis said that when his dog was born, she had a mass of 370 g and that when fully grown, his dog had a mass of 37 kg. Diego says that this is not possible, because the dog had a greater mass as a puppy than as an adult. Do you agree? If not, what mistake did Diego make? Explain.

A good explanation is clear, complete, and easy to understand.

© Pearson Education, Inc. 4

Name _____

Solve & Share

Maria is 156 centimeters tall. The average 10-year-old girl in the United States is 1 meter 430 millimeters tall. Is Maria taller than the average 10-year-old girl? **Solve this problem any way you choose.**

TEKS 4.8B Convert measurements within the same measurement system… from a smaller unit into a larger unit or a larger unit into a smaller unit when given other equivalent measures…. Also, 4.8C. Mathematical Process Standards 4.1C, 4.1D, 4.1F, 4.1G

You can **connect ideas.** Think about how meters, centimeters, and millimeters are connected. **Show your work in the space below!**

Digital Resources at PearsonTexas.com

Solve   Learn   Glossary   Check   Tools   Games

Look Back!

Communicate How could you have solved the problem a different way than you did?

How Can You Change Metric Units?

A

The table below can be used to change one metric unit of measure to another. Use the table to answer the questions.

> Metric units are easy to change because they are related by multiples of 10.

Metric Units		
Length	**Capacity**	**Mass**
1 m = 1,000 mm	1 L = 1,000 mL	1 g = 1,000 mg
1 cm = 10 mm		1 kg = 1,000 g
1 dm = 10 cm		
1 m = 100 cm		
1 km = 1,000 m		

DATA

B A large monarch butterfly's wingspan is about 10 centimeters. How long is this in millimeters?

To change larger units to smaller units, multiply.

10 cm = ? mm

1 cm = 10 mm

10 × 10 = 100

10 cm = 100 mm

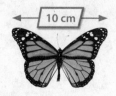
10 cm

A large monarch butterfly's wingspan is about 100 mm.

C A small monarch butterfly's wingspan is about 60 millimeters. How long is this in centimeters?

To change smaller units to larger units, divide.

60 mm = ? cm

10 mm = 1 cm

60 ÷ 10 = 6

60 mm = 6 cm

60 mm

A small monarch butterfly's wingspan is about 6 cm.

Do You Understand?

Convince Me! Explain how to change 600 mm to centimeters.

© Pearson Education, Inc. 4

Another Example

Compare 4,060 mL to 5 L.

Step 1

Change liters to milliliters.

1 L = 1,000 mL

5 × 1,000 = 5,000

5 L = 5,000 mL

Step 2

Compare.

4,060 mL < 5,000 mL

So, 4,060 mL < 5 L.

☆ Guided Practice *

In 1 through 4, find each missing number.

1. 1 kg = _____ g   **2.** 3 cm = _____ mm

3. 600 cm = _____ m **4.** 4 dm = _____ cm

In 5 through 8, compare. Write > or < for each ◯.

5. 3 m ◯ 200 cm   **6.** 4 L ◯ 7,000 mL

7. 1 kg ◯ 100 g   **8.** 1 km ◯ 3,000 m

9. How do you change centimeters to decimeters?

10. How do you change liters to milliliters?

11. Justify In Exercises 5 through 8, why did you change one of the units before comparing?

☆ Independent Practice ☆

In 12 through 14, find each missing number.

12. 8 kg = _____ g   **13.** 5 km = _____ m   **14.** 3,000 g = _____ kg

In 15 through 17, compare. Write > or < for each ◯.

15. 30 cm ◯ 30 mm   **16.** 2 km ◯ 200 m   **17.** 600 kg ◯ 6 g

Problem Solving

18. How many meters can a lion travel in one minute?

19. **Explain** Edgar says a giant tortoise is faster than a spider because 450 is greater than 31. Is he correct? Explain.

DATA

Distances Animals Can Travel in One Minute

Elephant	670 m
Giant Tortoise	450 cm
Spider	31 m
Lion	1 km 340 m

20. **Number Sense** Which measure is **NOT** equal to 6 meters?

- A 60 kilometers
- B 60 decimeters
- C 600 centimeters
- D 6,000 millimeters

21. **Reason** The mass of 5 tomatoes is about 1 kilogram. Estimate the mass of 1 tomato in grams.

22. **Use a Strip Diagram** A walking trail is 1 km long. Cecilia has walked the first 20 m. How much farther can she walk on the trail? Show your work.

1 km	
20 m	?

23. **Extend Your Thinking** There are about 5 milliliters in one teaspoon. There are 3 teaspoons in one tablespoon. About how many milliliters are there in 10 tablespoons? Show how you found the answer.

24. Roger walked 1 kilometer from his home to a park. In the park he walked 200 meters along a trail. Then he walked back along the trail and back to his home. How far did he walk in all?

- A 200 m
- B 400 m
- C 1,200 m
- D 2,400 m

© Pearson Education, Inc. 4

Name _____

Another Look!

Which has more mass: a kilogram of lead or 1,200 grams of bricks?

1 kg = 1,000 g
1,000 g of lead is less than 1,200 g of bricks.
The bricks have more mass.

Below are the conversion factors for metric units.

Remember: When converting from lesser to greater units, you divide. When converting from greater to lesser units, you multiply.

DATA	Metric Units		
	Length	**Capacity**	**Mass**
	1 m = 1,000 mm	1 L = 1,000 mL	1 g = 1,000 mg
	1 cm = 10 mm		1 kg = 1,000 g
	1 dm = 10 cm		
	1 m = 100 cm		
	1 km = 1,000 m		

In **1** through **6**, find each missing number.

1. 6 L = ? mL
6 × 1,000 = _____ mL

2. 8 m = ? cm
8 × 100 = _____ cm

3. 21,000 g = ? kg
21,000 ÷ 1,000 = _____ kg

4. 680 cm = _____ dm

5. 6 kg = _____ g

6. 9 L = _____ mL

In **7** through **14**, compare. Write >, <, or = for each ◯.

7. 4 m ◯ 400 dm

8. 4 dm ◯ 40 cm

9. 10 L ◯ 1,000 mL

10. 2 kg ◯ 1,500 g

11. 15 cm ◯ 150 mm

12. 1 km ◯ 999 m

13. 4,000 m ◯ 40 km

14. 2 dm ◯ 200 mm

15. Reason If 4 apples have a mass of 1 kg, about how many grams is each apple?

16. Maria drinks 400 mL of water every hour. How many hours will it take her to drink 2 L of water?

A 4 hours
B 5 hours
C 6 hours
D 8 hours

17. Tools Use the diagram to the right to write a subtraction sentence.

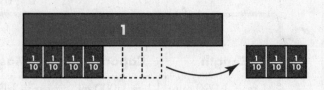

18. Explain A large zucchini has a mass of about 500 g. About how many kilograms of mass will 4 large zucchinis have? Explain.

19. Math and Science The mass of one boulder is about 4,600 kilograms. The mass of a second boulder is about 4,800,000 grams. Which boulder has a greater mass? Explain.

20. Extend Your Thinking If 5 potatoes together have a mass of 1 kilogram and 8 pears together have a mass of 1,200 grams, which has the greater mass, a potato or a pear? Explain.

21. During track practice, Jonathan ran 5 kilometers. Rob ran 4,250 meters. Who ran further? Explain.

© Pearson Education, Inc. 4

Name _____

Solve & Share

Allison skated for 2 hours on Saturday. Kylie skated for 100 minutes. Who skated longer? *Solve this problem any way you choose.*

TEKS 4.8C Solve problems that deal with … intervals of time … using addition, subtraction, multiplication, or division as appropriate. Also, 4.8B. Mathematical Process Standards 4.1A, 4.1B, 4.1C, 4.1D, 4.1G

Digital Resources at PearsonTexas.com

Solve   Learn   Glossary   Check   Tools   Games

You can use **mental math.** Think about how many minutes are in 1 hour. *Show your work in the space above!*

Look Back!

Construct Arguments Is it easier to change 100 minutes to hours or to change 2 hours to minutes? Explain.

How Can You Compare Units of Time?

On her birthday, Kara calculated that she was 108 months old. Her friend Jordan has the same birthday. If Jordan turned 8 years old, who is older, Kara or Jordan? You can convert different units of time in order to compare them.

Time can be expressed using different units that are related to each other.

DATA

Units of Time
1 minute = 60 seconds
1 hour = 60 minutes
1 day = 24 hours
1 week = 7 days
1 month = about 4 weeks
1 year = 52 weeks
1 year = 12 months
1 year = 365 days
1 leap year = 366 days
1 decade = 10 years
1 century = 100 years
1 millennium = 1,000 years

Change to common units to compare.

B Step 1

Change 8 years to months.
1 year = 12 months

To find the number of months in 8 years, multiply.
$8 \times 12 = 96$

So, 8 years = 96 months.

C Step 2

Compare the amounts.

Kara's age   Jordan's age

108 months ◯ **8 years**

108 months ⊘> **96 months**

So, Kara is older than Jordan.

Do You Understand?

Convince Me! In the example above, how many years old is Kara?

© Pearson Education, Inc. 4

Another Example

How much longer is a century than 3 decades 7 years?

Step 1	Step 2
Change time to years. 1 century = 100 years 3 decades 7 years = $(3 \times 10) + 7$ $= 30 + 7$ or 37 years	Subtract. $\begin{array}{r} 100 \\ -37 \\ \hline 63 \text{ years} \end{array}$

So, a century is 63 years longer.

Guided Practice

In **1** and **2**, write >, <, or = for each ◯.

1. $9 \times 4 =$ _____ weeks

9 months ◯ 27 weeks

2. $5 \times 60 =$ _____ seconds

5 minutes ◯ 300 seconds

3. Reason Do you multiply or divide if you want to change days to hours?

4. Reason Do you multiply or divide if you want to change months to years?

Independent Practice

Leveled Practice In **5** through **10**, write >, <, or = for each ◯.

5. $35 \times 7 =$ _____ days

35 weeks ◯ 340 days

6. $7 \times 24 =$ _____ hours

7 days ◯ 120 hours

7. $2 \times 365 =$ _____ days

2 years ◯ 730 days

8. 40 hours ◯ 2 days

9. 8 weeks ◯ 56 days

10. 12 months ◯ 40 weeks

In **11** through **16**, complete each number sentence.

11. 6 days = _____ hours

12. 2 years = _____ months

13. 6 minutes = _____ seconds

14. 3 decades = _____ years

15. 4 hours = _____ minutes

16. 4 centuries = _____ years

Problem Solving

17. Use a Strip Diagram It is believed that the Mayan pyramid of Kukulkan in Mexico was used as a calendar. It has 4 stairways leading to the top platform. Including the one extra step at the top, it has a total of 365 steps. How many steps are in each stairway?

> Each stairway has the same number of steps.

364 steps

4 stairways	?	?	?	?

> Subtract 1 from the total number of steps before you divide.

18. Connect Sara is watching a movie that is 1 hour 38 minutes long. She has already watched 48 minutes. If the time is 6:10 P.M., what time will the movie be over?

19. Trish is going to camp for 2 months. Which is greater than 2 months?

A 35 days

B 40 days

C 6 weeks

D 10 weeks

20. Reason Gina has 3 yards of fabric. She needs to cut 8 pieces, each 1 foot long. Does she have enough fabric? Explain.

21. Extend Your Thinking If you brush your teeth 10 minutes a day, about how many hours do you brush in a year?

22. Order the names in the table from the youngest person to the oldest person.

Family Member	Age
William	180 months
Kylie	520 weeks
Tyrese	2 decades

23. Explain How can you tell which is longer: 63 hours or 3 days? How much longer?

© Pearson Education, Inc. 4

Another Look!

You can use the information in the table to compare different lengths of time.

Which is longer: 3 years or 40 months?

1 year = 12 months

$3 \times 12 = 36$
3 years = 36 months

40 months > 36 months
40 months > 3 years

So, 40 months is longer than 3 years.

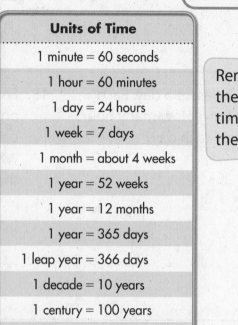

Units of Time

1 minute = 60 seconds	
1 hour = 60 minutes	
1 day = 24 hours	
1 week = 7 days	
1 month = about 4 weeks	
1 year = 52 weeks	
1 year = 12 months	
1 year = 365 days	
1 leap year = 366 days	
1 decade = 10 years	
1 century = 100 years	
1 millennium = 1,000 years	

Remember: Use the same units of time to compare the numbers.

In **1** through **12**, write >, <, or = for each ◯.

1. $7 \times 60 =$ ____ minutes
7 hours ◯ 380 minutes

2. $12 \times 7 =$ ____ days
68 days ◯ 12 weeks

3. 1 year ◯ 350 days

4. 25 months ◯ 2 years

5. 20 decades ◯ 2 centuries

6. 720 days ◯ 2 years

7. 8 decades ◯ 1 century

8. 72 hours ◯ 3 days

9. 240 minutes ◯ 3 hours

10. 3 years ◯ 120 months

11. 400 weeks ◯ 5 years

12. 3,000 days ◯ 1 decade

13. The table shows the length of time three books were listed on the Best Seller List. Which book was on the list for the longest time?

Book	Time on Best Seller List
Book 1	14 months
Book 2	420 days
Book 3	64 weeks

14. Mrs. Cash teaches 8 classes a day. Each ⭐ class is 45 minutes long. How many hours does Mrs. Cash teach each day?

A 6 hours

B 8 hours

C 60 hours

D 360 hours

15. **Formulate a Plan** A theater has 358 seats on the main level and 122 seats in the balcony. There are 6 shows each day. What is the greatest number of people the theater can seat in one day? Explain.

16. **Extend Your Thinking** John wants to find the age in months of everyone in his family. Complete the table.

Family Member	Age	Age in Months
John's father	4 decades	
John's mother	38 years	
John's brother	180 days	
John	500 weeks	

John's Family

17. **Analyze Information** Dave's goldfish lived for 2 years 8 months. Chris's goldfish lived for 35 months. Whose goldfish lived longer? How much longer?

18. Tree A lived for 6 decades and 5 years. Tree B lived for 58 years. Which tree lived longer? How much longer?

19. **Extend Your Thinking** How many minutes are in 1 week? Show your work.

20. **Explain** Which is longer: 180 seconds or 3 minutes? Explain how you decided.

© Pearson Education, Inc. 4

Name _____

Solve & Share

Between 6:00 A.M. and 7:00 A.M., the temperature outside rose 6°F. Between 7:00 A.M. and 8:00 A.M., the temperature rose 3°F. If the temperature at 8:00 A.M. is 73°F, what was the temperature at 6:00 A.M.? *Solve this problem any way you choose.*

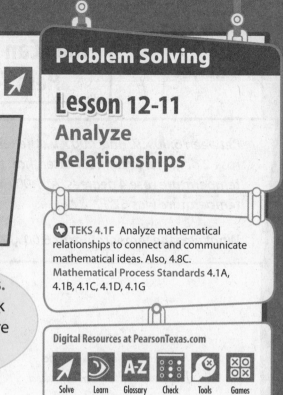

You can **analyze relationships.** Think about how you can work backward from the temperature at 8:00 A.M. *Show your work in the space below!*

⭐ TEKS 4.1F Analyze mathematical relationships to connect and communicate mathematical ideas. Also, 4.8C. Mathematical Process Standards 4.1A, 4.1B, 4.1C, 4.1D, 4.1G

Digital Resources at PearsonTexas.com

Solve Learn Glossary Check Tools Games

Look Back!

Explain What does it mean to work backward?

How Can Using Representations Help You Solve a Problem?

A Analyze

Between 6:00 A.M. and 7:00 A.M., the temperature rose 2 degrees. Every hour after that, the temperature rose 4 degrees. At 1:00 P.M., the temperature was 62°F.

What was the temperature at 6:00 A.M.?

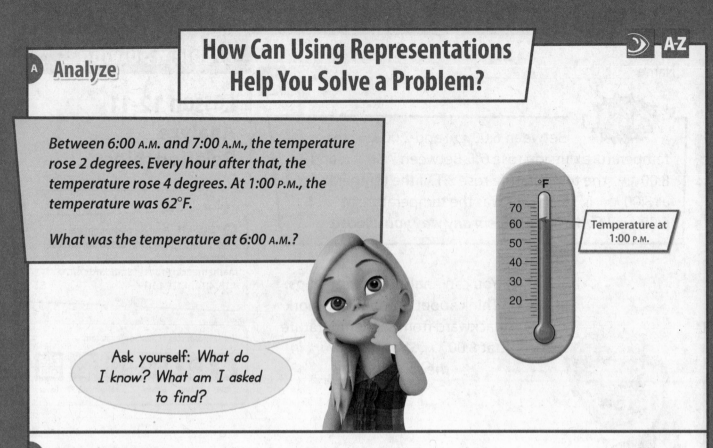

Temperature at 1:00 P.M.

Ask yourself: *What do I know? What am I asked to find?*

B Plan and Solve

You can use a representation to work backward, starting with the end result and reversing the steps to find the starting point.

Draw a picture to show each change. Work backward starting at 1:00 P.M.

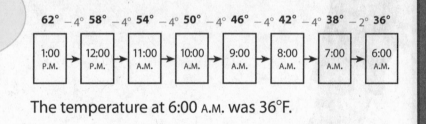

62° −4° **58°** −4° **54°** −4° **50°** −4° **46°** −4° **42°** −4° **38°** −2° **36°**

| 1:00 P.M. | | 12:00 P.M. | | 11:00 A.M. | | 10:00 A.M. | | 9:00 A.M. | | 8:00 A.M. | | 7:00 A.M. | | 6:00 A.M. |

The temperature at 6:00 A.M. was 36°F.

Do You Understand?

Convince Me! Show how you could check that the answer given to the example above is correct.

© Pearson Education, Inc. 4

Name _____

1. School starts at 7:45 A.M. It takes Fran 30 minutes to walk to school, 15 minutes to eat breakfast, and 20 minutes to get ready. What is the latest time Fran should get up?

2. **Check for Reasonableness** Check your answer to Problem 1. Show your work.

3. **Connect** Write a problem that uses working backward. Then answer your question.

Independent Practice ☆

In **4** through **6**, write the answer in a complete sentence.

4. **Draw a Picture** Wanda walked for 25 minutes from the mall to the train station. She waited 20 minutes for the train, and then had a 20 minute ride. She arrived home at 12:20 P.M. What time did she leave the mall?

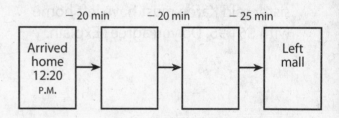

5. **Analyze Information** Art rode his bike from his house to Jay's house. The boys rode their bikes 3 miles to the park and then 4 miles to the mall. Art rode 9 miles in all. How many miles is Art's house from Jay's house?

6. **Reason** Sir John Franklin was an explorer who traveled in Canada and the United States. He was 33 years old when he began exploring northwestern Canada. In a second expedition 17 years later, he explored as far as Alaska. 11 years later, Franklin died in an expedition in search of a Northwest Passage in 1847. In what year was Franklin born?

Problem Solving

7. Use a Strip Diagram Sylvia had $43 after she went shopping. She spent $9 on pet food, $6 on salad items, $12 on soup, and $24 on vegetables. How much money did Sylvia start with?

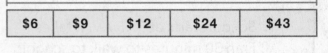

? money Sylvia started with				
$6	$9	$12	$24	$43

8. Analyze Information Nina walked 1 mile on Monday. She walked twice as far on Tuesday. On Wednesday, she walked three more miles than she did on Monday. On Thursday, she walked a mile less than she had walked on Wednesday. How many miles did Nina walk on Thursday?

9. Extend Your Thinking Georgette bought some craft items. The silk flowers cost three times as much as the ribbon. The ribbon cost two times what the foam cost. The vase cost $12, which was three times as much as the foam. How much did the silk flowers cost?

10. Construct Arguments Karen returned a pair of shoes to the store and received $44.95. Then she bought a sweater for $17.50 and a pair of jeans for $27.45. Karen had $7 when she got home. Her sister said Karen must have left home with $51.95. Do you agree? Explain.

11. ⭐ Laurie has band practice at 10:15 A.M. It takes her 20 minutes to get from home to practice and 5 minutes to warm up. By what time should she leave home to get to practice on time?

A 9:50 A.M.
B 9:55 A.M.
C 10:00 A.M.
D 10:10 A.M.

12. Formulate a Plan James is working at the school carnival. During the first half of the evening, he gives away all the prizes in 4 small boxes and 1 large box. During the second half of the evening, James gives away all the prizes in 2 small boxes and 3 large boxes. How many individual prizes did James give away?

25 prizes   75 prizes

13. Mrs. Harris is planning to drive her twin children to a soccer game at 6:00 P.M. They need to arrive 20 minutes early to warm up for the game. It takes 25 minutes to get to the soccer field. By what time do Mrs. Harris and the twins need to leave the house?

© Pearson Education, Inc. 4

Homework 12-11
Analyze Relationships

Another Look!

Brenda takes 30 minutes to get dressed for school. She eats breakfast for 20 minutes, then walks to school. It takes Brenda 15 minutes to walk to school. Brenda needs to be at school by 8:55 A.M. What time is the latest she should get out of bed in the morning?

> Start from the end point and work backward to the starting point.

Work backward from the end, doing the opposite of each step.

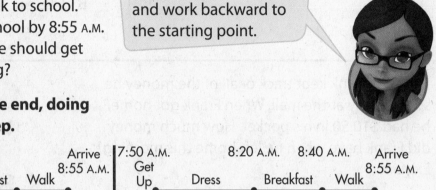

Brenda must get up by 7:50 A.M. to make it to school on time.

---

1. **Analyze Information** When Christopher Columbus was 41 years old, he sailed across the Atlantic Ocean for the first time. He went on his final expedition 10 years later, which took 2 years. He died 2 years after his final expedition ended, in 1506. What year was Columbus born?

2. **Formulate a Plan** The Declaration of Independence was signed in 1776. Three years earlier, the Boston Tea Party took place. Boston was settled 143 years before the Boston Tea Party. What year was Boston settled?

---

3. **Draw a Picture** After turning the television on, Jared watched 42 minutes of a nature program, saw 14 minutes of commercials, and spent 7 minutes in the kitchen fixing a snack. He turned the television off at 8:31 P.M. When did Jared turn the television on?

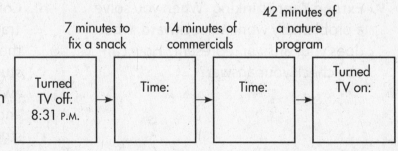

4. Formulate a Plan Leslie has 3 boxes of tea in her cupboard. Each box contains 11 tea bags. Each tea bag makes 3 cups of hot tea. How many cups of tea will Leslie make if she uses all the tea bags?

5. ⭐ Eunice has a soccer game at 7:00 P.M. She needs to be there 20 minutes early to warm up for the game, and it takes her 45 minutes to get to the soccer field. What time should she leave her house?

   A 5:55 P.M.   **C** 6:15 P.M.

   B 6:05 P.M.   **D** 6:40 P.M.

6. Explain Frank kept track of all of the money he spent today at the mall. When Frank got home, he had $10.50 in his pocket. How much money did Frank have when he left home this morning? Explain.

Lunch $5.60

Bus Fare $2.00

Shopping $6.50

7. Connect Veronica serves 24 cups of punch at a reception. Later, she makes another 48 cups of punch and serves 55 more cups to the guests. She has 17 cups of punch left over after the reception. How many gallons of punch did Veronica have at the beginning of the reception?

8. Connect Tessie has a volleyball game at 6:45 P.M. She needs to be there 15 minutes early to warm up for the game, and it takes her 40 minutes to get to the gym. What time should she leave her house?

9. Extend Your Thinking When you solve a problem by working backward, what does your answer represent? How can you check your answer?

10. Connect There were 21 students in Travis's fourth-grade class at the end of the school year. During the year, 4 new students joined his class, and 2 moved away. One student was transferred to another fourth-grade teacher. How many students were in Travis's class at the beginning of the school year?

 © Pearson Education, Inc. 4

Name _____

1. **Formulate a Plan** Hannah created the first 3 towers of a pattern using blocks. If she continues the pattern, how many blocks will she need to create the 8th tower?

Applying Math Processes

- How does this problem connect to previous ones?
- What is my plan?
- How can I use tools?
- How can I use number sense?
- How can I communicate and represent my thinking?
- How can I organize and record information?
- How can I explain my work?
- How can I justify my answer?

2. **Number Sense** An art teacher is preparing for her class. She wants to divide 1 gallon of paint into 4-oz jars. How many jars can she fill?

3. **Draw a Picture** Tricia set up 2 tables end to end. The tables are rectangles that can fit 4 chairs on each long side and 2 chairs on each short side. The 2 tables are joined at their short sides. How many chairs can be set? Draw a diagram to show your solution.

4. **Extend Your Thinking** Thomas has 2 objects of equal mass. He places two 1-kg units on one side of a pan balance scale. He places the 2 objects and a 200-gram unit on the other side. If the scale is level, what would be the mass of each of the objects? Show how you found your answer.

5. **Analyze Information** The lengths of three hiking trails are shown in the table. Order the trails from longest to shortest.

DATA	Trail	Length
	Eagle Loop	1 mile
	Cypress Point	5,800 feet
	River Trail	1,250 yards

6. **Estimation** Sophia is making picture frames for eight of her friends. Each frame needs 25 inches of wood trim. She buys 15 feet of wood trim. Use estimation to decide if she bought enough material to make 8 frames. Explain your reasoning.

Error Search

Find each problem that is not correct. Circle the incorrect part and replace it so it is correct.

1. 8 ft = 96 yd

2. 18 lb > 120 oz

3. 540 cm < 54 dm

4. 300 kg > 3,000 g

5. 6 qt > 2 gal

6. 2 L = 2,000 mL

7. 80 km > 9,000 m

8. 120 days < 15 weeks

9. 400 minutes = 5 hours

Compatible Numbers

Mental Math Draw loops around two or more numbers next to each other, across, or down, with a product of 48 and 120. Look for compatible numbers (numbers that are easy to compute with mentally).

10. Find products of 48.

2	2	12	16	4
6	4	12	3	3
8	4	2	6	4
12	4	3	2	8
2	24	3	4	4

11. Find products of 120.

3	6	20	40	3
20	12	10	30	4
2	5	2	3	4
2	60	6	2	10
5	4	6	24	5

© Pearson Education, Inc. 4

Reteaching

Set A pages 623–628

Which is the most appropriate unit to use to measure the height of the desk? Use either inches, feet, yards, or miles.

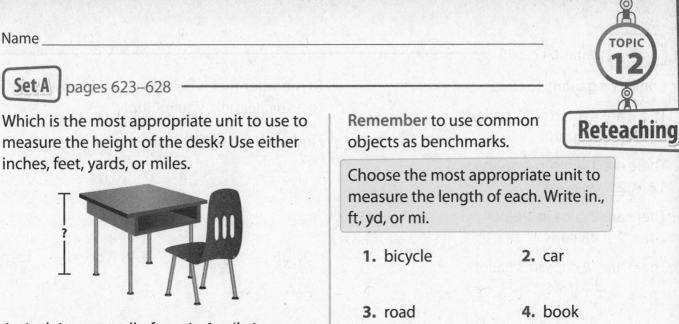

An inch is too small of a unit. A mile is too large of a unit. So, either feet or yards would be an appropriate unit.

Remember to use common objects as benchmarks.

Choose the most appropriate unit to measure the length of each. Write in., ft, yd, or mi.

1. bicycle   **2.** car

3. road   **4.** book

5. flagpole   **6.** crayon

Set B pages 629–634

Which is the better estimate for the capacity of the bucket?

2 pints or 2 gallons?

The pint is too small of a unit. The better unit to use is the gallon.

The better estimate is 2 gallons.

Remember that a cup is a smaller unit of measure than a pint.

Which is the better estimate for the capacity of each item?

1.

2 cups or 20 cups?

2.

1 gallon or 8 gallons?

Set C pages 635–640

Which is the better unit to measure the weight of a pear?

Most pears weigh less than a pound.

So, the better unit to use would be the ounce.

Remember to use common objects as benchmarks.

Give the best unit to measure the weight of each item. Write oz, lb, or T.

1. a whale   **2.** an apple

3. a puppy   **4.** a baseball

5. a box of books   **6.** a hippopotamus

Convert 3 gallons to cups.

There are 4 quarts in 1 gallon.
$3 \times 4 = 12$ quarts

There are 2 pints in 1 quart.
$12 \times 2 = 24$ pints

There are 2 cups in 1 pint.
$24 \times 2 = 48$ cups

There are 48 cups in 3 gallons.

Remember that when changing from a larger to a smaller unit, you multiply.

Find each missing measure.

1. 5 T = _____ lb   **2.** 10 mi = _____ ft

3. 36 c = ____ qt   **4.** 8 fl oz = ____ tbsp

5. 4 yd = ____ in.   **6.** 16 pt = ____ gal

Linda, Barbara, and Christina measured the width of their playground. One of their measurements is incorrect. Who do you think measured incorrectly? Why?

Student	Measurement
Linda	12 yd 1 ft 3 in.
Barbara	400 ft
Christina	37 ft 3 in.

DATA

Convert each measurement to feet and compare.

Linda = 36 ft + 1 ft + 3 in. = 37 ft 3 in.

Barbara = 400 ft

Christina = 37 ft 3 in.

Barbara's measurement is incorrect because the other two measurements are equal.

Remember to explain your answer.

Solve each problem.

1. A bag of apples weighs 5 pounds. A bag of grapefruit weighs 12 pounds. How many more ounces does the bag of grapefruit weigh than the bag of apples? Explain your answer.

2. Mr. Gibson wants to make his driveway longer. It is currently 8 yards long. If the maximum length of a driveway is 30 feet long, how many more yards can he add to his driveway? Explain your answer.

© Pearson Education, Inc. 4

Name _____

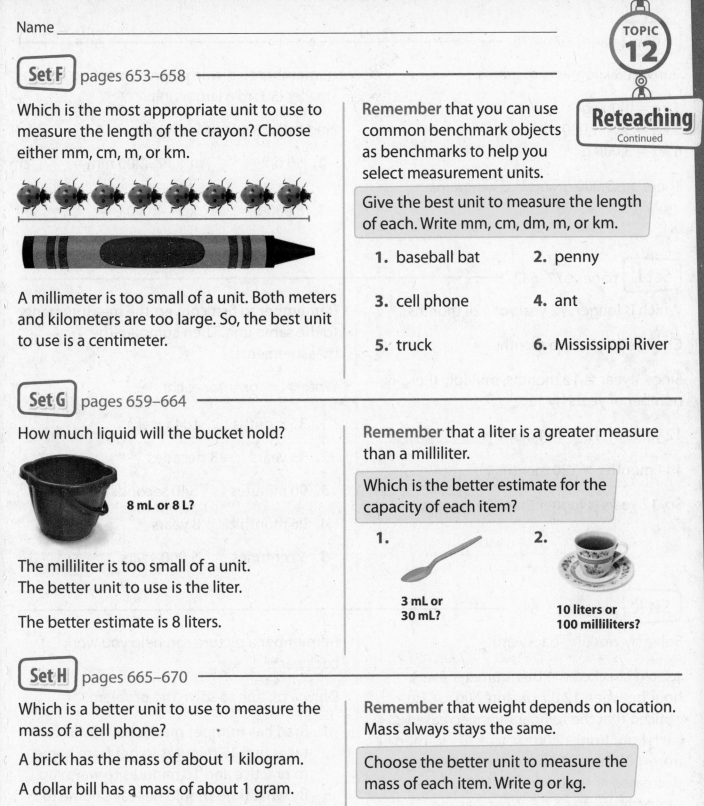

TOPIC 12

Reteaching
Continued

Set F pages 653–658

Which is the most appropriate unit to use to measure the length of the crayon? Choose either mm, cm, m, or km.

A millimeter is too small of a unit. Both meters and kilometers are too large. So, the best unit to use is a centimeter.

Remember that you can use common benchmark objects as benchmarks to help you select measurement units.

Give the best unit to measure the length of each. Write mm, cm, dm, m, or km.

1. baseball bat   2. penny

3. cell phone   4. ant

5. truck   6. Mississippi River

Set G pages 659–664

How much liquid will the bucket hold?

8 mL or 8 L?

The milliliter is too small of a unit.
The better unit to use is the liter.

The better estimate is 8 liters.

Remember that a liter is a greater measure than a milliliter.

Which is the better estimate for the capacity of each item?

1.   2.

3 mL or   10 liters or
30 mL?   100 milliliters?

Set H pages 665–670

Which is a better unit to use to measure the mass of a cell phone?

A brick has the mass of about 1 kilogram.

A dollar bill has a mass of about 1 gram.

The mass of a brick is much greater than the mass of a cell phone. So, grams would be a better unit to use to measure the mass of a cell phone.

Remember that weight depends on location. Mass always stays the same.

Choose the better unit to measure the mass of each item. Write g or kg.

1. crayon   2. watermelon

3. carrot   4. wallet

5. bicycle   6. table

7. penny   8. paper clip

Topic 12 | Reteaching   **693**

Convert 3 kilograms to grams.

1 kg = 1,000 g
3 kg = 3 × 1,000 g
3 kg = 3,000 g

There are 3,000 grams in 3 kilograms.

Remember to divide when converting from a smaller unit to a larger unit.

Find each missing measure.

1. 50 dm = _____ m   **2.** 200 mm = _____ cm

3. 8,000 g = _____ kg   **4.** 90 L = _____ mL

Which is longer: 12 years or 120 months?

Change 12 years to months.

Since 1 year = 12 months, multiply the number of years by 12.

12 years × 12 = 144 months

144 months > 120 months

So, 12 years is longer than 120 months.

Remember to first convert the measurements to the same unit. Then compare the measurements.

Write >, <, or = for each $\bigcirc$.

1. 36 months $\bigcirc$ 104 weeks

2. 33 years $\bigcirc$ 3 decades

3. 90 minutes $\bigcirc$ 540 seconds

4. 96 months $\bigcirc$ 8 years

5. 5 centuries $\bigcirc$ 5,000 years

Solve by working backward.

Jerrold checked the thermometer every hour between 12:00 P.M. and 7:00 P.M. He noticed that the temperature decreased 3° each hour from 12:00 P.M. to 4:00 P.M. Then from 4:00 P.M. to 7:00 P.M., the temperature decreased 4° each hour. At 7:00 P.M., the temperature was 57°F. What was the temperature at 12:00 P.M.?

57° + 4→**61°** + 4→**65°** + 4→**69°** + 3→**72°** + 3→**75°** + 3→**78°** + 3→**81°**

| 7:00 P.M. | 6:00 P.M. | 5:00 P.M. | 4:00 P.M. | 3:00 P.M. | 2:00 P.M. | 1:00 P.M. | 12:00 P.M. |

The temperature at 12:00 P.M. was 81°F.

Remember a picture can help you work backward.

Draw a picture to solve the problem.

1. Brad has trumpet practice at 10:45 A.M. It takes him 15 minutes to get from home to practice and 10 minutes to warm up. By what time should he leave home to get to practice on time?

© Pearson Education, Inc. 4

1. Which is the most appropriate unit to use to measure the length of an earthworm?

A Feet

B Yards

C Miles

D Inches

2. Which is the most appropriate unit to use to measure the capacity of a swimming pool?

A Gallons

B Cups

C Pints

D Tablespoons

3. Morgan rode her bike 2 kilometers from her house to her friend's house. From her friend's house, she rode 600 meters in all going to and from the library. Then she rode back home. How many meters did she ride her bike in all?

4. Which is the best estimate of the mass of a football?

A 400 grams

B 400 kilograms

C 4 grams

D 4 kilograms

5. Rob's backpack weighs 80 ounces. How many pounds does his backpack weigh?

A 3 pounds

B 4 pounds

C 5 pounds

D 1,280 pounds

6. On Monday, Matt hiked from the start of the Lodge Trail to the end of the Blue Ridge Trail where a friend picked him up. He told his friend that he had hiked 7,200 meters in one day. Is Matt correct? Explain.

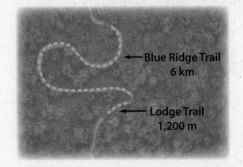

Blue Ridge Trail
6 km

Lodge Trail
1,200 m

7. Which of the following holds about 2 liters of water?

A Bathtub

B Drinking glass

C Pitcher

D Eye dropper

8. Three friends each measured the capacity of a goldfish bowl. Which friend most likely measured incorrectly?

Student	Measurement
Janell	28 cups
Leah	10 pints
Kathleen	5 quarts

DATA

9. Which shows the lengths of rope in order from least to greatest?

A 80 inches, 2 yards, 5 feet

B 5 feet, 2 yards, 80 inches

C 2 yards, 5 feet, 80 inches

D 5 feet, 80 inches, 2 yards

10. It takes a guinea pig about 68 days to develop completely before it is born. Which is about the same amount of time as 68 days?

A 100 hours

B 6 months

C 10 weeks

D All of the above

11. Which is the most appropriate unit to use to measure the length of a school hallway?

A Millimeters

B Centimeters

C Meters

D Kilometers

12. Devon has a Kennedy half-dollar coin. What is the width of the half-dollar coin in millimeters?

3 cm

© Pearson Education, Inc. 4

13. Which is the most appropriate unit to measure the weight of a pair of scissors?

A Ounces

B Inches

C Pounds

D Tons

14. Mrs. Warren bought 6,000 milliliters of lemonade for a party. How many liters of lemonade did she buy?

A 6 L

B 12 L

C 30 L

D 60 L

15. Kara is 6 years old. How many months are in 6 years?

16. Luis is leaving for vacation in 5 hours. Which is the same length of time as 5 hours?

A 500 minutes

B 300 minutes

C 300 seconds

D 1,800 seconds

17. Andrea ran 400 meters in gym class. Which of the following is **NOT** equal to the distance she ran?

A 40 km

B 4,000 dm

C 40,000 cm

D 400,000 mm

18. A window is 60 inches long. What is the length of the window in feet?

19. Which capacity is the greatest amount?

A 24 fluid ounces

B 5 cups

C 2 pints

D 1 quart

22. In 2009, Hawaii celebrated 50 years as a state. How many months are in 50 years?

A 120 months

B 350 months

C 600 months

D 2,600 months

---

20. At 4:30 P.M., the thermometer outside of Yasmine's window read 40°C. It had risen 8°C between noon and 4:30 P.M. and 5°C between 7:00 A.M. and noon. What was the temperature at 7:00 A.M.?

A 13°C

B 27°C

C 33°C

D 53°C

23. Michael had $22 left after he went to the fair. He spent $8 on food, $5 on games, and $4 for admission. How much money did Michael start with?

A $5

B $29

C $39

D $45

---

21. An adult male gorilla ate 4,000 pounds of food over the summer. How many tons of food did he eat during the summer?

A 1 T

B 2 T

C 3 T

D 4 T

24. Elsie has 5 pounds of trail mix. She wants to divide it into 8 smaller bags. How many ounces will each bag contain?

A 1 ounce

B 3 ounces

C 5 ounces

D 10 ounces

© Pearson Education, Inc. 4

Solving Measurement Problems

Essential Questions:
What do area and perimeter mean and how can each be found?
How can measurements be converted to solve problems?

Some objects are magnetic and some are not. Magnetism is a physical property of matter.

Maglev trains are high-tech trains that use electromagnets to float above a magnetic field.

Fasten your seat belts! Here's a project on maglev trains and measurement.

Math and Science Project: Magnets and Measurement

Do Research Using the Internet, research maglev trains in the United States and other countries. Compare the speeds and travel times of these trains with traditional trains.

Journal: Write a Report Include what you found. Also in your report:

• What is the greatest speed reached by a maglev train?

• What is the normal traveling speed of a maglev train?

• Compare the trip times on a maglev train to trip times on traditional trains.

Name _____

Review What You Know

Vocabulary

Choose the best term from the box.
Write it on the blank.

- mass
- inches
- capacity
- square unit

1. The amount of liquid a container can

   hold is called its _____.

2. _____ is the amount of
   matter that something contains.

3. A _____ is a square
   with sides that are each 1 unit long.

Multiplication Facts

Find each product.

4. 6 × 5   **5.** 7 × 9

6. 8 × 8   **7.** 7 × 4

8. 3 × 6   **9.** 5 × 4

10. 4 × 9   **11.** 8 × 5

12. 9 × 6   **13.** 8 × 4

14. 3 × 9   **15.** 8 × 7

Unit Conversions

Find the missing number.

16. 8 yd = _____ ft

17. 60 in. = _____ ft

18. 3 lb = _____ oz

19. 7 ft = _____ in.

20. 8 km = _____ m

21. 6 L = _____ mL

22. 2 kg = _____ g

23. 300 cm = _____ m

Money

Count the bills and coins and write
the amount.

24.

25.

26. Explain Can you make $1.55 with
less than 10 coins, using quarters,
dimes, and nickels? Explain which
tool—a digital tool, objects,
manipulatives, or paper and
pencil—you would select to solve
this problem. Then solve.

© Pearson Education, Inc. 4

My Word Cards

Use the examples for each word on the front of the card to help complete the definitions on the back.

A-Z

perimeter

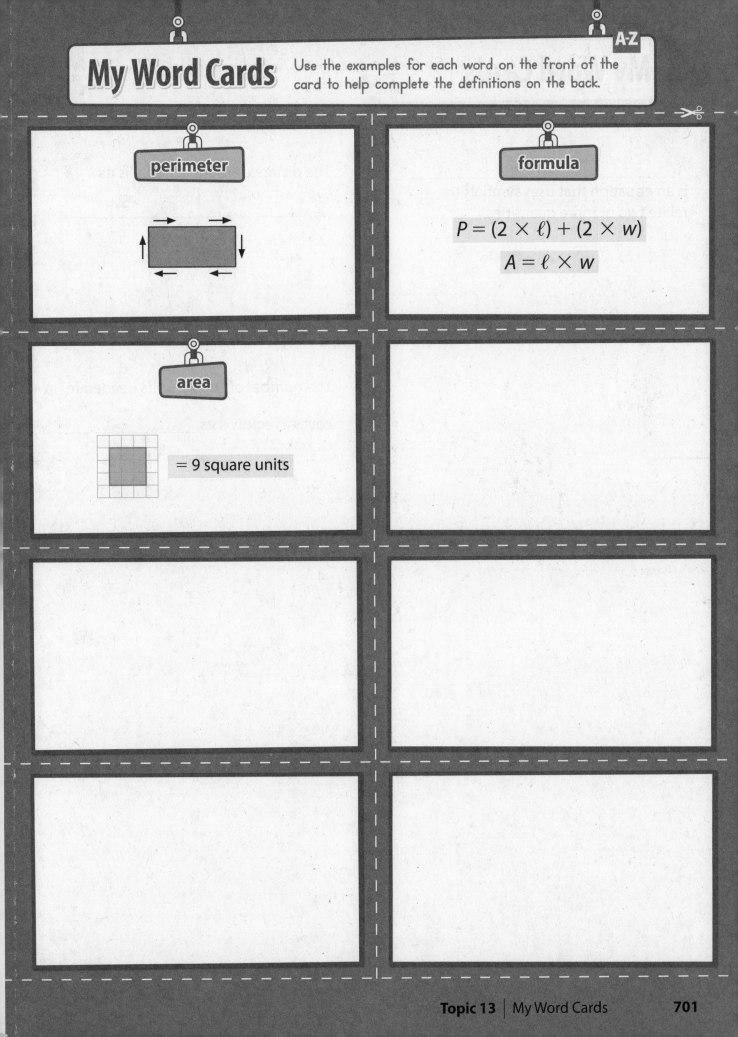

formula

$$P = (2 \times \ell) + (2 \times w)$$
$$A = \ell \times w$$

area

= 9 square units

My Word Cards

Complete each definition. Extend learning by writing your own definitions.

A _____ is an equation that uses symbols to relate two or more quantities.

The distance around a figure is its _____.

The number of square units needed to cover a region is its _____.

© Pearson Education, Inc. 4

Name _____

☆ ☆
Solve & Share

At a community vegetable garden, the organizers want to install a fence around the garden. The garden is rectangular and measures 12 feet by 15 feet. How many feet of fencing do they need? *Solve this problem any way you choose.*

⚡ TEKS 4.5C Use models to determine the formulas for the perimeter of a rectangle ($\ell + w + \ell + w$ or $2\ell + 2w$), including the special form for perimeter of a square (4s) .... Also, 4.5D. Mathematical Process Standards 4.1B, 4.1D, 4.1E, 4.1F, 4.1G

You can **create and use a representation**. A picture can help you model this problem. *Show your work in the space below!*

Digital Resources at PearsonTexas.com
Solve   Learn   Glossary   Check   Tools   Games

Look Back!

Connect Ideas You know that 1 yd = 3 ft. How many yards of fence are needed for the garden above?

How Can You Use a Formula to Calculate Perimeter?

A

Perimeter is the distance around a figure.

What formula can you use to find the perimeter of any rectangle? What is the perimeter of the rectangle below?

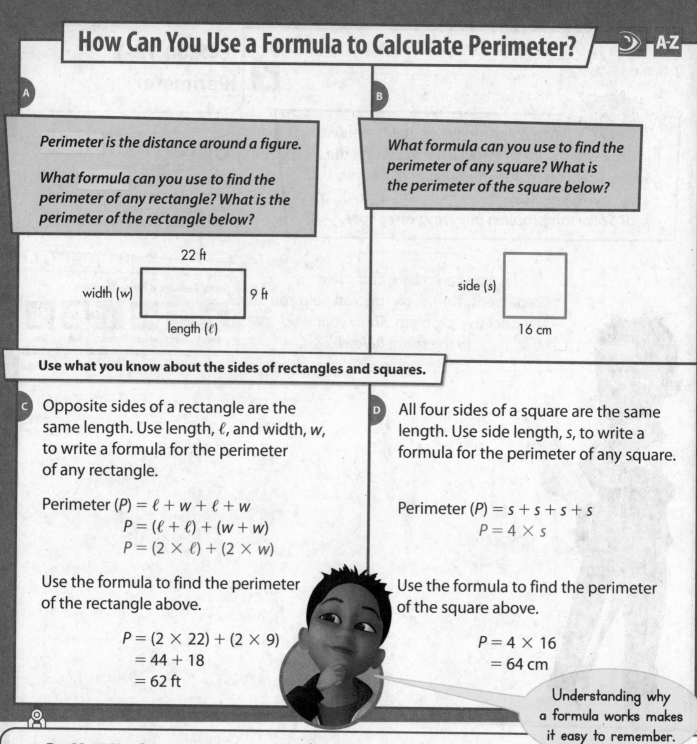

22 ft

width (w)   9 ft

length (ℓ)

B

What formula can you use to find the perimeter of any square? What is the perimeter of the square below?

side (s)

16 cm

Use what you know about the sides of rectangles and squares.

C Opposite sides of a rectangle are the same length. Use length, ℓ, and width, w, to write a formula for the perimeter of any rectangle.

Perimeter $(P) = \ell + w + \ell + w$

$P = (\ell + \ell) + (w + w)$

$P = (2 \times \ell) + (2 \times w)$

Use the formula to find the perimeter of the rectangle above.

$P = (2 \times 22) + (2 \times 9)$

$= 44 + 18$

$= 62$ ft

D All four sides of a square are the same length. Use side length, s, to write a formula for the perimeter of any square.

Perimeter $(P) = s + s + s + s$

$P = 4 \times s$

Use the formula to find the perimeter of the square above.

$P = 4 \times 16$

$= 64$ cm

Understanding why a formula works makes it easy to remember.

Do You Understand?

Convince Me! How can you estimate to see if the value you found for the perimeter of the rectangle above is reasonable?

© Pearson Education, Inc. 4

Name _Ben_

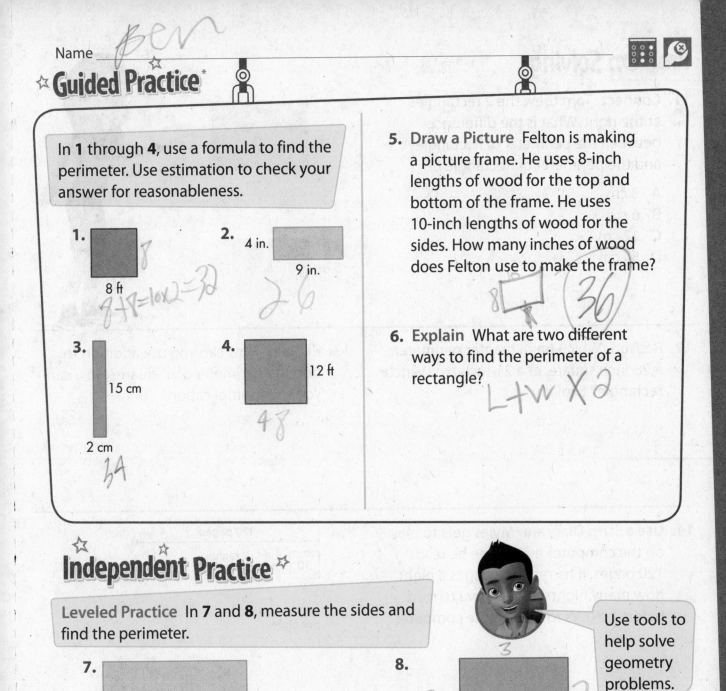

In **1** through **4**, use a formula to find the perimeter. Use estimation to check your answer for reasonableness.

1.
8

8 ft

$8+8=10\times2=32$

2.
4 in.

9 in.

26

3.
15 cm

2 cm

34

4.
12 ft

48

5. Draw a Picture Felton is making a picture frame. He uses 8-inch lengths of wood for the top and bottom of the frame. He uses 10-inch lengths of wood for the sides. How many inches of wood does Felton use to make the frame?

8

36

6. Explain What are two different ways to find the perimeter of a rectangle?

$L+w\times2$

☆ **Independent Practice** ☆

Leveled Practice In **7** and **8**, measure the sides and find the perimeter.

7.
4

15 cm

9

8.
3

3 cm

2

2 cm

Use tools to help solve geometry problems.

In **9** and **10**, estimate, and then use a formula to find the perimeter.

9. A square 22 in. long on each side

88

10. A rectangle 13 ft long and 38 ft wide

102

13
38
51

Problem Solving

11. Connect Tom drew the 2 rectangles at the right. What is the difference between the perimeter of Rectangle *A* and the perimeter of Rectangle *B*?

  A 3 cm
  B 6 cm
  C 12 cm
  D 54 cm

6 cm   *A*

9 cm

5 cm   *B*

7 cm

---

12. Reason Which has a greater perimeter: a 28-inch square, or a 21-inch by 31-inch rectangle? Explain.

13. Explain How can you use addition to find the perimeter of a square? How can you use multiplication?

---

14. Use a Strip Diagram Myles gets to play on the computer every time he reads 120 pages. If he reads 10 pages a night, how many nights will he have to read before he gets to play on the computer?

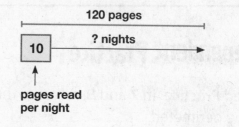

120 pages

10   ? nights

pages read
per night

---

15. Connect Use the Distributive Property to write the formula for the perimeter of a rectangle in an equivalent way.

16. Extend Your Thinking James wants to draw a rectangle with a perimeter of 42 units and a length of 13 units. What is the width? Explain.

© Pearson Education, Inc. 4

Another Look!

Perimeter is the distance around a figure. When a figure has sides of equal length, you can use multiplication to find the perimeter.

The formula for the perimeter of a rectangle is $P = (2 \times \ell) + (2 \times w)$.

ℓ is the length of the rectangle.
w is the width of the rectangle.

In the figure below, $\ell = 11$ and $w = 3$.

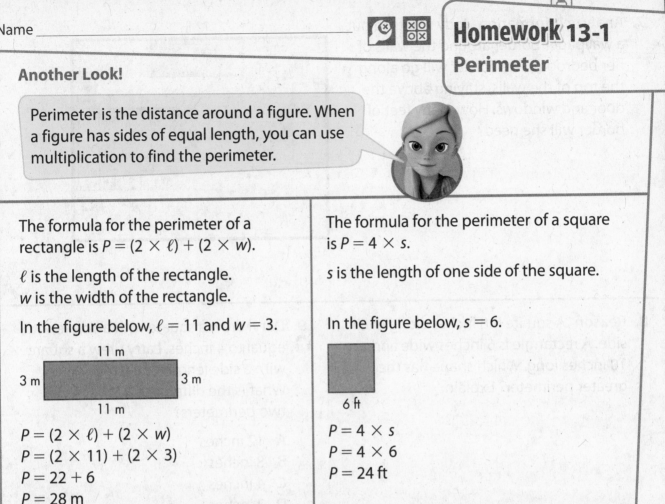

11 m
3 m   3 m
11 m

$P = (2 \times \ell) + (2 \times w)$
$P = (2 \times 11) + (2 \times 3)$
$P = 22 + 6$
$P = 28$ m

The formula for the perimeter of a square is $P = 4 \times s$.

s is the length of one side of the square.

In the figure below, $s = 6$.

6 ft

$P = 4 \times s$
$P = 4 \times 6$
$P = 24$ ft

In **1** through **6**, use a formula to find the perimeter. Use estimation to check the reasonableness of your solution.

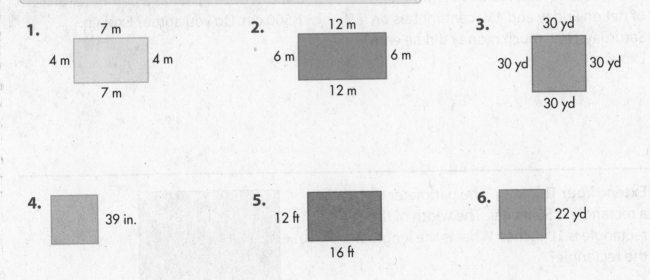

1.
7 m
4 m   4 m
7 m

2.
12 m
6 m   6 m
12 m

3.
30 yd
30 yd   30 yd
30 yd

4.
39 in.

5.
12 ft
16 ft

6.
22 yd

7. Analyze Information Jody wants to put a wallpaper border around the walls of her bedroom. The border will go along the top of the walls, staying above the door and windows. How many feet of border will she need?

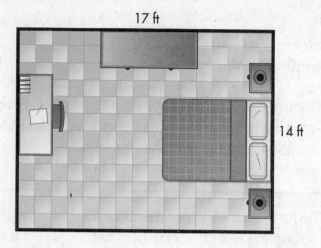

17 ft

14 ft

8. Reason A square is 8 inches along each side. A rectangle is 6 inches wide and 10 inches long. Which shape has the greater perimeter? Explain.

9. Daryl drew a square with a side length equal to 4 inches. Larry drew a square with a side length equal to 5 inches. What is the difference between the two perimeters?

A 12 inches

B 8 inches

C 4 inches

D 2 inches

10. Personal Financial Literacy Trevor earns $6 for each meter of fishing net he repairs. He repaired 250 centimeters of net on Friday and 450 centimeters on Saturday. How much money did he earn? Explain.

11. Check for Reasonableness Clark says a rectangle with a length of 309 cm and a width of 249 cm has a perimeter of 1,500 cm. Do you agree? Explain.

12. Extend Your Thinking The perimeter of a rectangle is 50 inches. The width of the rectangle is 10 inches. What is the length of the rectangle?

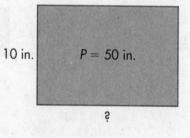

10 in. $P = 50$ in.

?

© Pearson Education, Inc. 4

Name _____

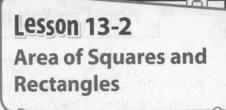

Lesson 13-2
Area of Squares and Rectangles

Solve & Share

Jorge is carpeting a room that is shaped like a square. One wall of the room is 6 yards long. How many square yards of carpet will Jorge need? *Solve this problem any way you choose.*

TEKS 4.5C Use models to determine the formulas for … the area of a rectangle ($\ell \times w$). Also, 4.5D.
Mathematical Process Standards 4.1A, 4.1C, 4.1D, 4.1F, 4.1G

You can use tools. A grid can help you model this problem. *Show your work in the space below!*

Digital Resources at PearsonTexas.com

| Solve | Learn | Glossary | Check | Tools | Games |

Look Back!

Connect Ideas How is finding the area of a square similar to finding a perfect square number?

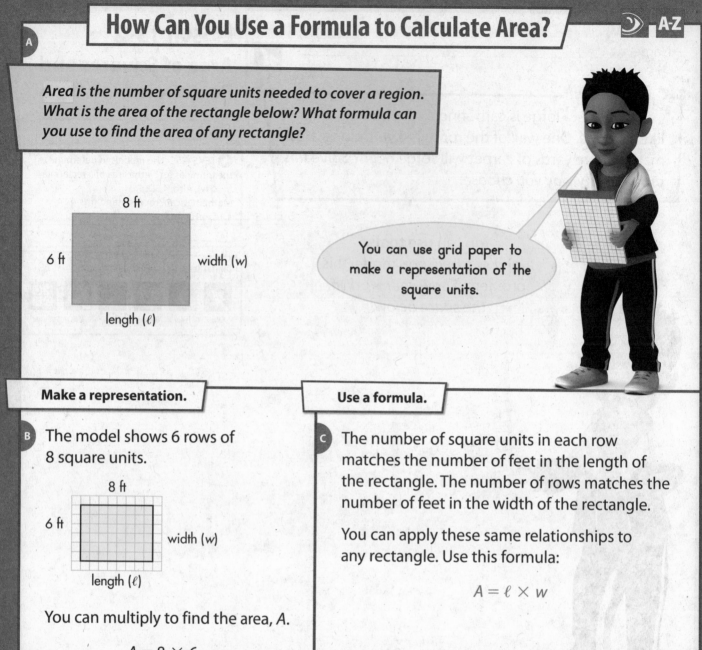

A

Area is the number of square units needed to cover a region. What is the area of the rectangle below? What formula can you use to find the area of any rectangle?

8 ft

6 ft

width (w)

length (ℓ)

> You can use grid paper to make a representation of the square units.

Make a representation.

B The model shows 6 rows of 8 square units.

8 ft

6 ft

width (w)

length (ℓ)

You can multiply to find the area, A.

$A = 8 \times 6$
$A = 48$ square feet

Use a formula.

C The number of square units in each row matches the number of feet in the length of the rectangle. The number of rows matches the number of feet in the width of the rectangle.

You can apply these same relationships to any rectangle. Use this formula:

$$A = \ell \times w$$

Do You Understand?

Convince Me! What is the formula for the area of a square? Explain.

© Pearson Education, Inc. 4

Name _____

☆ **Guided Practice** ☆

In **1** through **4**, use the formula to find the area.

1. 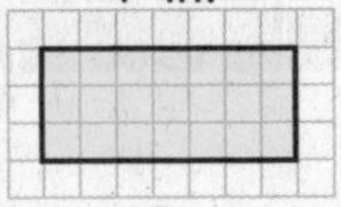 7 in.

3 in.

21

2. 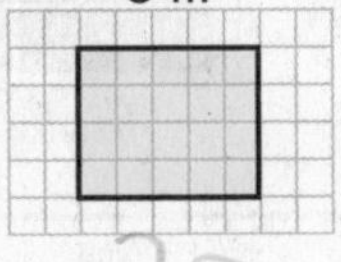 5 m

4 m

20

3. 14 ft

8 ft

14 8 112
112

4. 9 cm

9 8

5. Reason If the figure in Exercise 3 were drawn on grid paper, how many rows would be in the figure? How many square units would there be in each row? *110 vs*
14 sq

6. Connect A wall in Mike's bedroom is 12 feet long and 8 feet tall. He wants to paint the entire wall blue. How much area does Mike have to paint? *12 8 96* *96*

☆ **Independent Practice** ☆

Leveled Practice In **7** through **9**, count the units to find the length and the width. Then, use the formula to find the area.

7. 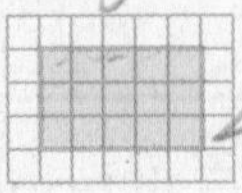 *5 3* *15*

8. 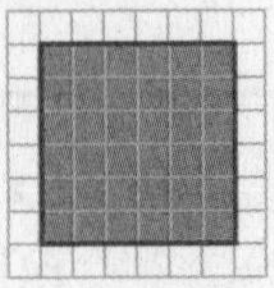 *36*

9. 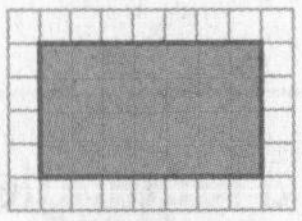 *7 4 28*

In **10** through **13**, use the formula to find the area.

10. 4 ft

9 ft

36

11. 13 mm

9 mm

13 9 117 *117*

12. 5 in.

7 in.

35

13. 4 yd

16

For another example, see Set A on page 747.   **Topic 13** | Lesson 13-2   **711**

Problem Solving

14. Connect Mr. Chen tiled his kitchen floor, as shown by the diagram at the right. Each tile measures 1 square foot and cost $5. How much did it cost Mr. Chen to tile his kitchen floor?

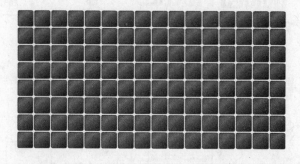

15. Connect What is the area of a square that has a perimeter of 40 feet? Explain your reasoning.

16. Number Sense Kirsten ran 1,200 meters in 5 minutes, running at the same pace the entire way. How many meters did she run each minute?

17. Extend Your Thinking A landscaper plants a flowerbed around a rectangular fishpond. What is the area of the flowerbed?

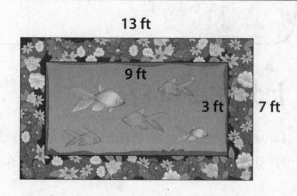

13 ft

9 ft

3 ft   7 ft

18. ⭐ The area of a rectangle is 50 square feet. What could be the dimensions of the rectangle?

A   10 ft by 40 ft
B   10 ft by 20 ft
C   10 ft by 15 ft
D   10 ft by 5 ft

A picture can help you visualize a problem.

19. Extend Your Thinking Gail bought 60 feet of fencing to enclose a rectangular garden plot. What could be the possible dimensions of the garden? Explain how you found those dimensions. What would be the area given those dimensions?

© Pearson Education, Inc. 4

Name _____

Another Look!

The formula for the area of a rectangle is area = length × width, or $A = \ell \times w$.

5 ft

8 ft

What is the area of the rectangle?

Step 1	Step 2	Step 3
Write the formula for the area of a rectangle. $A = \ell \times w$	Identify ℓ and w in the rectangle. $\ell = 8$ and $w = 5$	Calculate the area of the rectangle. $A = 8 \times 5$ $A = 40$ The area is 40 sq ft.

You can label an area in "square units" if there are no units given in the problem.

In **1** through **6**, use the formula to find the area.

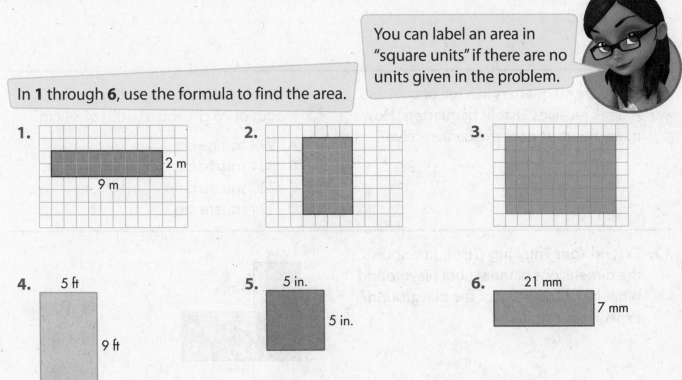

1.
2 m
9 m

2.

3.

4.
5 ft
9 ft

5.
5 in.
5 in.

6.
21 mm
7 mm

7. Connect Mindy wants to paint one wall in her bedroom. What would be the area of the painted wall?

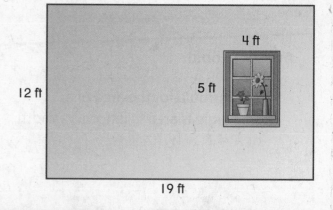

12 ft

4 ft

5 ft

19 ft

8. Explain A storefront window has 154 square feet of glass. The window is 7 feet tall. What is the perimeter of the window? Explain.

9. Construct Arguments Yasemin is trying to find the area of a square. She uses the formula $A = s \times s$ and finds that the area is 121 sq dm. Do you agree with Yasemin? Explain.

11 dm

10. There are 40 quarters in a roll of quarters. A bank receives 38 rolls of quarters. How many quarters does the bank receive?

11. Which is the area of a rectangle with a length of 26 cm and a width of 34 cm?

A 992 square cm
B 884 square cm
C 720 square cm
D 324 square cm

12. Extend Your Thinking The figure shows the dimensions of the school playground. What is the total area of the playground? Explain your strategy.

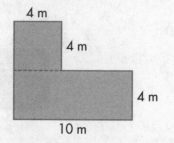

4 m

4 m

4 m

10 m

© Pearson Education, Inc. 4

Name _____

Solve & Share

A can of paint is used to cover all 224 square feet of a wall. The wall is 8 feet high. Tape is placed along the top, bottom, and sides of the wall. What is the length of the wall? How much tape is needed? *Solve this problem any way you choose.*

TEKS 4.5D Solve problems related to perimeter and area of rectangles where dimensions are whole numbers. Mathematical Process Standards 4.1A, 4.1B, 4.1C, 4.1D, 4.1G

Digital Resources at PearsonTexas.com

Solve   Learn   Glossary   Check   Tools   Games

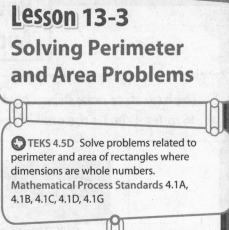

You can **formulate a plan.** What information do you need to find an area? What do you need to find a perimeter? *Show your work in the space above!*

Look Back!

Justify What formula could you use to help you explain how you solved this problem?

How Can You Use Perimeter And Area to Solve Problems?

The new state park shown below has a perimeter of 36 miles. What is the area of the new state park?

width = 7 mi

length = ?

Look for a hidden question that you will need to answer.

Use rectangle length and width relationships.

You know that the perimeter is 36 miles and the width is 7 miles. The hidden question is:

What is the length of the park?

The opposite sides of a rectangle are the same length, so multiply the width by 2. $7 \times 2 = 14$

Subtract 14 from perimeter. $36 - 14 = 22$

This difference is twice the length of the park, so divide 22 by 2. $22 \div 2 = 11$

So, the length of the park is 11 miles.

Use the answer to the hidden question to answer the original question.

$\ell = 11$ miles
$w = 7$ miles
$A = \ell \times w$
$\quad = 11 \times 7$
$\quad = 77$ sq mi

7 miles

11 miles

The area of the park is 77 square miles.

Do You Understand?

Convince Me! If the perimeter of the park above was 48 miles instead of 36 miles, then what would the length of the park be?

© Pearson Education, Inc. 4

Name _____

1. Find the length.

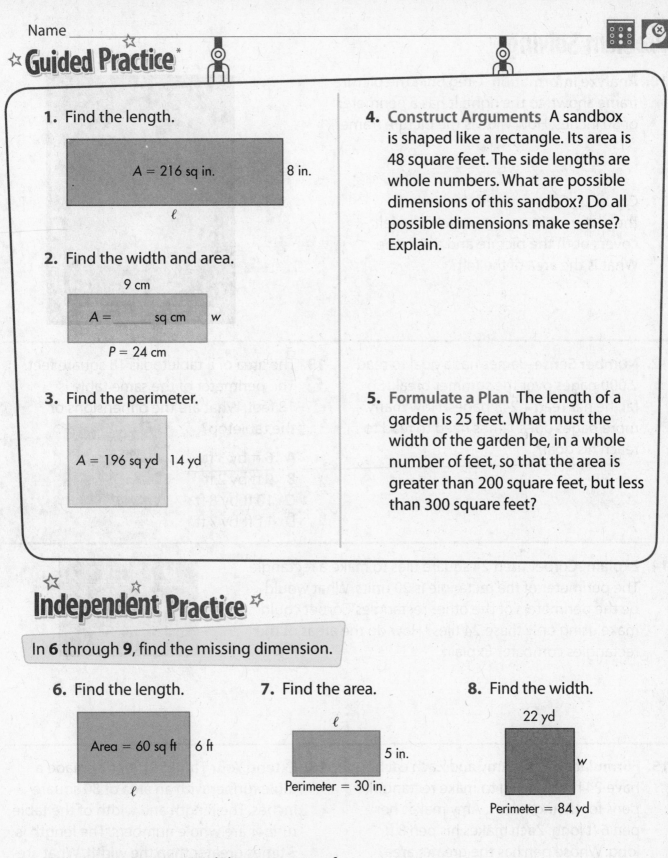

A = 216 sq in.   8 in.

ℓ

2. Find the width and area.

9 cm

A = _____ sq cm   w

P = 24 cm

3. Find the perimeter.

A = 196 sq yd   14 yd

4. Construct Arguments A sandbox is shaped like a rectangle. Its area is 48 square feet. The side lengths are whole numbers. What are possible dimensions of this sandbox? Do all possible dimensions make sense? Explain.

5. Formulate a Plan The length of a garden is 25 feet. What must the width of the garden be, in a whole number of feet, so that the area is greater than 200 square feet, but less than 300 square feet?

☆ **Independent Practice** ☆

In **6** through **9**, find the missing dimension.

6. Find the length.

Area = 60 sq ft   6 ft

ℓ

7. Find the area.

ℓ

5 in.

Perimeter = 30 in.

8. Find the width.

22 yd

w

Perimeter = 84 yd

9. Draw a Picture Find the perimeter of a rectangle with a 9 mm width and an area of 270 sq mm.

Problem Solving

10. Analyze Information Greg built the picture frame shown to the right. It has a perimeter of 50 inches. How wide is the picture frame?

11. Connect Greg covered the back of the picture with a piece of felt. The felt covers both the picture and the frame. What is the area of the felt?

$\ell = 14$ in.

12. Number Sense James has a goal to read 2,000 pages over the summer break. So far, he has read 1,248 pages. How many more pages does James need to read to reach his goal?

13. ⭐ The area of a tabletop is 18 square feet. The perimeter of the same table is 18 feet. What are the dimensions of the tabletop?

    A 6 ft by 3 ft
    B 9 ft by 2 ft
    C 10 ft by 8 ft
    D 11 ft by 7 ft

14. Explain Corbet used 24 square tiles to make a rectangle. The perimeter of the rectangle is 20 units. What would be the perimeters of the other rectangles Corbet could make using only these 24 tiles? How do the areas of the rectangles compare? Explain.

15. Formulate a Plan Amy and Zach each have 24 ft of fencing to make rectangular pens for their gardens. Amy makes her pen 6 ft long. Zach makes his pen 8 ft long. Whose pen has the greater area? How much greater?

16. Extend Your Thinking Nancy made a table runner with an area of 80 square inches. The length and width of the table runner are whole numbers. The length is 5 times greater than the width. What are the dimensions of the table runner?

© Pearson Education, Inc. 4

Name _____

Another Look!

Find the perimeter of the rectangle.

The length and width of a rectangle are used to find both the perimeter and the area of the figure.

Step 1

Use the formula for the area of a rectangle to find the length.

$A = \ell \times w$

$28 = \ell \times 4$ Substitute the numbers you know.

$\ell = 7$ cm

The length of the rectangle is 7 cm.

4 cm | Area = 28 sq cm
ℓ

Step 2

Use the formula to find the perimeter of the rectangle.

$P = (2 \times \ell) + (2 \times w)$

$P = (2 \times 7) + (2 \times 4)$ Substitute the numbers you know.

$P = (14) + (8) = 22$ cm

The perimeter of the rectangle is 22 cm.

In **1** through **4**, use the formulas for perimeter and area to solve each problem.

1. Find the length.

2 ft | ℓ Area = 28 sq ft

2. Find the width.

w | Perimeter = 86 in.
25 in.

3. Find the length. Then find the perimeter.

3 ft | Area = 33 sq ft
ℓ

4. Find the width. Then find the area.

w | Perimeter = 40 in.
12 in.

5. Formulate a Plan The length of the flower garden is 3 times as great as the width. What are the dimensions of the flower garden?

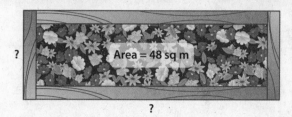

? Area = 48 sq m

?

---

6. The perimeter of a quilt is 34 ft. If the quilt ⭐ is 8 ft long, what is its area?

A 18 sq ft
B 72 sq ft
C 144 sq ft
D 292 sq ft

7. Number Sense The Green Darner is one of the largest dragonflies. It weighs about four hundredths of an ounce. Write four hundredths in standard form.

---

8. The sides of each square in the potholder measure 1 inch. What are the perimeter and area of the potholder?

---

9. Draw a Picture Julie planted a rectangular garden that is 20 feet long. She placed 56 feet of fencing around her garden. Draw and label a sketch of her garden. What is the width of her garden? What is the area?

10. Extend Your Thinking An art class is planning to paint a rectangular mural with an area of 60 square feet. It has to be at least 4 feet high but no more than 6 feet high. The length and width have to be whole numbers. List all possible lengths for the mural.

© Pearson Education, Inc. 4

Name _____

Solve & Share

A wild bird feeder holds 8 cups of birdseed. How many times can this feeder be filled from a 3-gallon container of birdseed? *Solve this problem any way you choose.*

TEKS 4.8C Solve problems that deal with measurements of length, intervals of time, liquid volumes, mass, and money using addition, subtraction, multiplication, or division as appropriate. Mathematical Process Standards 4.1A, 4.1B, 4.1C, 4.1D, 4.1F, 4.1G

Digital Resources at PearsonTexas.com

Solve Learn Glossary Check Tools Games

You can **analyze relationships.** Which operations can you use to convert between units? *Show your work in the space below!*

DATA

1 gallon = 4 quarts
1 quart = 2 pints
1 pint = 2 cups

Look Back!

Justify How can you check your work?

How Can You Solve Measurement Problems?

A

Andy is using a roll of fabric to make a sofa cushion like the one shown. He will use 1 yard of fabric for the front and back parts of the cushion.

What is the total length of fabric Andy needs to make the cushion?

Each edge = 15 in.

Some measurement problems can be solved using models. Remember: 1 yard = 36 inches.

Use a model.

B Draw a number line to show the information given in the problem. Andy will use 1 yard of fabric for the front and back.

0	1 yd	2 yd	3 yd

0	36 in.	72 in.	108 in.

$3 \times 15 = 45$ in.

Each edge is 15 inches long, so he will need 3 times 15 inches for the sides.

C Use the model to combine the units. You can use inches as a common unit.

Fabric for front and back	36 in.
Fabric for sides	+ 45 in.
Total length of fabric	81 in.

You can write 81 inches in mixed units.

1 yd = 36 in. 2 yd = 72 in.

81 in. − 72 in. = 9 in.

So, Andy needs 2 yards 9 inches of fabric.

Do You Understand?

Convince Me! To solve some measurement problems, you need to convert measurements to fractions. What fraction of 1 foot is 9 inches? What fraction of 1 yard is 9 inches? Tell how you decided.

© Pearson Education, Inc. 4

☆ **Guided Practice**

Use the model to solve.

1. A teacher's desk is 5 feet 4 inches long. How long is the desk in inches?

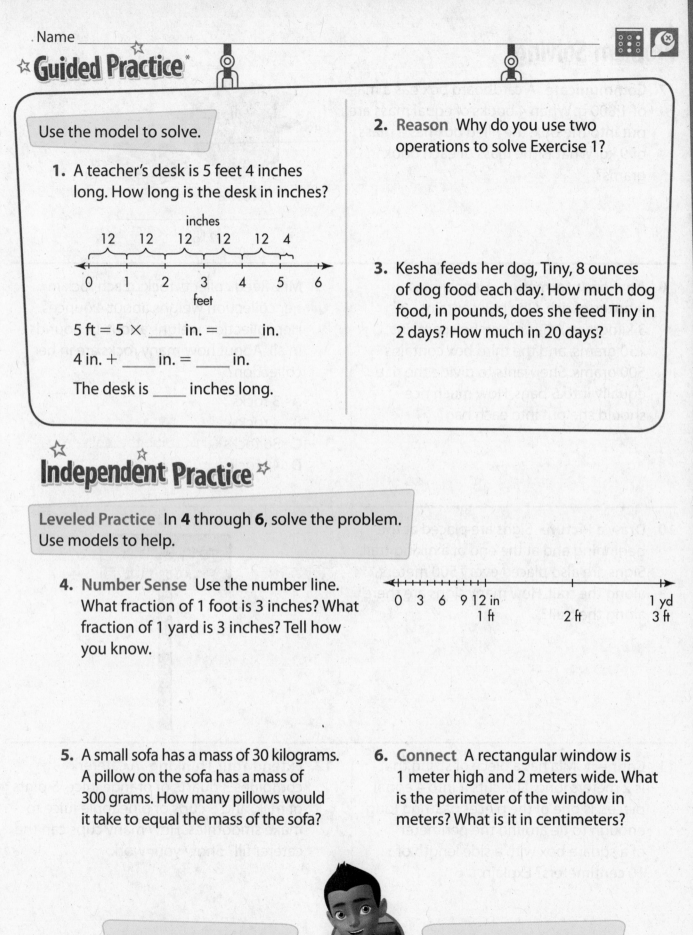

inches

12   12   12   12   12   4

0   1   2   3   4   5   6
feet

5 ft = 5 × _____ in. = _____ in.

4 in. + _____ in. = _____ in.

The desk is _____ inches long.

2. **Reason** Why do you use two operations to solve Exercise 1?

3. Kesha feeds her dog, Tiny, 8 ounces of dog food each day. How much dog food, in pounds, does she feed Tiny in 2 days? How much in 20 days?

☆ **Independent Practice** ☆

Leveled Practice In **4** through **6**, solve the problem. Use models to help.

4. **Number Sense** Use the number line. What fraction of 1 foot is 3 inches? What fraction of 1 yard is 3 inches? Tell how you know.

0   3   6   9 12 in
          1 ft   2 ft

1 yd
3 ft

5. A small sofa has a mass of 30 kilograms. A pillow on the sofa has a mass of 300 grams. How many pillows would it take to equal the mass of the sofa?

6. **Connect** A rectangular window is 1 meter high and 2 meters wide. What is the perimeter of the window in meters? What is it in centimeters?

1 kilogram = 1,000 grams

1 meter = 100 centimeters

Problem Solving

7. Communicate A cardboard box has a mass of 1,800 g. When 4 books of equal mass are put into the box, the filled box has a mass of 9 kg. What is the mass of each book in grams?

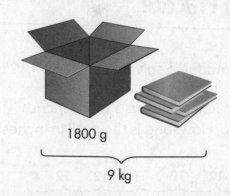

1800 g

9 kg

---

8. Analyze Information Hannah has 3 boxes of rice. One box contains 3 kilograms, the second box contains 150 grams, and the third box contains 500 grams. She wants to divide the rice equally into 5 bags. How much rice should she put into each bag?

9. ⭐ Mrs. Reed collects rocks. Each rock in her collection weighs about 4 ounces. Her collection weighs about 12 pounds in all. About how many rocks are in her collection?

A 3 rocks

B 4 rocks

C 36 rocks

D 48 rocks

---

10. Draw a Picture Signs are placed at the beginning and at the end of a hiking trail. Signs are also placed every 500 meters along the trail. How many signs are there along the trail?

3 KILOMETERS
END OF TRAIL

---

11. Connect Mia has a piece of string that is 2 meters long. She cuts it into 4 equal pieces. Is one of the pieces of string long enough to tie around the perimeter of a square box with a side length of 16 centimeters? Explain.

12. Extend Your Thinking A caterer combines 3 quarts of orange juice, 5 pints of milk, and 5 cups of pineapple juice to make smoothies. How many cups can the caterer fill? Show your work.

© Pearson Education, Inc. 4

Another Look!

Lance has a 5-gallon aquarium. He fills the aquarium using a 2-quart container. How many times will he have to fill the 2-quart container to fill the aquarium?

You can use models to help you solve measurement problems.

4 qt = 1 gal

1 gal			
1 qt	1 qt	1 qt	1 qt
1 container		1 container	

So, Lance has to fill the container 2 times to fill one gallon in the aquarium.

Since there are 5 gallons, he must fill the container 2 × 5, or 10 times.

In **1** through **4**, solve the problem.

1. The mass of a tiger at a zoo is 135 kilograms. Randy's cat has a mass of 5,000 grams. How many times greater is the mass of the tiger than the mass of Randy's cat?

2. Rob has a 2-liter bottle of iced tea. He plans to pour the iced tea into 250-milliliter containers. How many containers can he fill?

3. Susan bought a 2-kilogram bag of grapes. On the way home, she ate 125 grams of the grapes. How many grams of grapes did Susan have left?

4. A car with a 20-gallon gas tank can go 25 miles on 1 gallon of gas. If the tank is full at the beginning of a trip, how many times does the driver have to refill the gas tank on a 725-mile trip?

5. Reason Jeremy uses 18 inches of twine for each box he packs for shipping. How many yards of twine does he need to wrap 5 boxes?

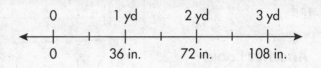

6. Estimation Students hike 16,900 feet one morning and 14,850 feet in the afternoon. Estimate the total number of miles they hiked that day. Explain.

7. Lou cuts 3 yards from a 9-yard roll of fabric. Then he cuts 4 more feet from the roll. How much fabric is left on the roll?

8. Draw a Picture Janice needs 3 gallons of lemonade for a party. She has 4 quarts, 6 pints, and 4 cups of lemonade already made. How much more lemonade does she need to make?

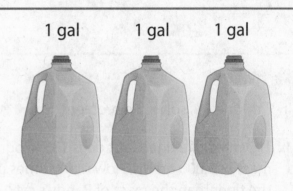

9. A yellow ribbon is 56 centimeters long. It is twice as long as a green ribbon. A brown ribbon is 4 times as long as the green ribbon. What is the length of the brown ribbon?

A 28 centimeters

B 56 centimeters

C 1 meter 12 centimeters

D 112 meters

10. Extend Your Thinking Dave is packing fruit in boxes. He wants to put the same number of apples, pears, and oranges in each box. An apple has a mass of 250 grams, a pear has a mass of 350 grams, and an orange has a mass of 400 grams. The filled boxes must have a mass no greater than 5 kilograms. How many of each fruit can Dave put in each box without exceeding 5 kilograms?

© Pearson Education, Inc. 4

Name _____

Solve & Share

A certain flash drive costs $24.35, including tax. A customer gives the cashier two $20 bills. How much change should the cashier give back to the customer? *Solve this problem any way you choose.*

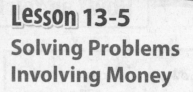

TEKS 4.8C Solve problems that deal with measurements of length, intervals of time, liquid volumes, mass, and money using addition, subtraction, multiplication, or division as appropriate. **Mathematical Process Standards 4.1A, 4.1B, 4.1C, 4.1D, 4.1G**

You can **connect** decimals to real-world problems involving money. *Show your work in the space below!*

Digital Resources at PearsonTexas.com

Solve   Learn   Glossary   Check   Tools   Games

Look Back!

Estimation Use estimation to check whether your answer is reasonable.

How Can You Use Counting to Make Change?

A-Z

How can you count to make change from a $20 bill used to buy the toy airplane?

Making change is often easiest by counting up from the smaller amount.

penny
1¢

nickel
5¢

dime
10¢

quarter
25¢

half dollar
50¢

$8.36

B One way

Start with $8.36. Count up using the fewest coins.

Give this		Get this
4 pennies	⟶	$8.40
1 dime	⟶	$8.50
1 half dollar	⟶	$9
1 $1 bill	⟶	$10
1 $10 bill	⟶	$20

C Another way

Start with $8.36. Count up a different way.

Give this		Get this
4 pennies	⟶	$8.40
2 nickels	⟶	$8.50
2 quarters	⟶	$9
1 $1 bill	⟶	$10
2 $5 bills	⟶	$20

The change is the total amount given, $11.64.

Do You Understand?

Convince Me! In the example above, how could mental math be used to find the amount of change, rather than counting up with coins?

© Pearson Education, Inc. 4

☆ Guided Practice *

In **1** and **2**, tell the amount of change for each situation.

1. You give the salesperson a $10 bill and three $5 bills to buy two movie tickets. How much change should you get?

MOVIE TICKET
$11.25

2. A new jacket costs $65.89. How much change should you get if you give the salesperson four $20 bills?

3. **Mental Math** How would the amount of change in Exercise 2 be different if you gave the salesperson one $50 bill and one $20 bill?

4. **Reason** If an item costs $19.54, why might someone give the sales clerk a $20 bill and 4 pennies?

Independent Practice ☆

Leveled Practice In **5** through **7**, tell the amount of change needed for each situation.

5.

$24.86

6. **Connect** Carlos buys some knee pads and elbow pads. The total cost of the pads is $14.38. How much change should Carlos receive if he pays for the pads with two $10 bills?

Give this	**Get this**
_____ pennies ⟶	$24.90
1 dime ⟶	$_____
1 $____ bill ⟶	$30.00
1 $____ bill ⟶	$_____
$_____ in change	

7. **Connect** A new drawing pad costs $6.89. How much change should you get if you give the salesperson a $20 bill?

Problem Solving

8. Reason Leo went to lunch with his parents. The bill was $17.85. Complete the table to show two different combinations of coins and bills that can be used to make this amount.

One Way		Another Way	
Give this	Get this	Give this	Get this
Total	$17.85	Total	$17.85

9. Reason Lucy buys a magazine for $4.19. She gives the sales clerk a $5 bill and two dimes. What is her change?

10. Connect Marco used a $10 bill to pay for a jump rope. He received $3.08 in change. How much did the jump rope cost?

11. Mr. Edwards bought seven concert tickets for a total of $168. What is the cost of one concert ticket?

Which operation will you use?

12. Rajeev bought a skateboard that cost $37.74. How much change did he get back if he paid with four $10 bills?

A $2.26
B $3.26
C $2.74
D $3.74

13. Construct Arguments Matthew buys a video game for $34.28. He pays for the game using two $20 bills. Matthew thinks he should receive $6.72 in change. Is he correct? Explain.

14. Extend Your Thinking Jenna bought a book for $12.19. She gave the sales clerk one $20 bill and one quarter. How can you find Jenna's change?

© Pearson Education, Inc. 4

Name _____

Another Look!

Christine buys a loaf of bread from the bakery that costs $3.59. She pays for the loaf with a $5 bill. What is Christine's change?

First, start with the cost of the bread. Use coins and bills until you reach the amount Christine paid.

$3.59 → $3.60 → $3.65 → $3.75 → $4.00 → $5.00

penny   nickel   dime   quarter
1¢   5¢   10¢   25¢

Then, count the change. Count coins and bills in reverse order.

$1.00 → $1.25 → $1.35 → $1.40 → $1.41

Christine's change is $1.41.

1. Mr. Jackson buys a pair of shoes for $41.12. He hands the clerk a $50 bill.

   a. Complete the table using the least number of coins and bills.

   b. Count the value of the coins and bills to find the amount of change.

   Total cost = $41.12

Give this	Get this
	$41.15
	$41.25
3 quarters	$
	$
	$50.00

2. Mrs. Hargrove takes her dog to the veterinarian. She owes the doctor $34.56, and she pays with a $50 bill.

   a. List the change using the least number of coins and bills.

   b. What is the total amount of change she should receive?

3. Emma buys a game for $26.84. She pays for the game with a $20 bill and two $5 bills. How much change should she receive? List the change in coins and bills.

4. **Connect** Three friends combine their money to buy tickets for a baseball game. If they share the change evenly, how much change will each friend receive?

$12
$12
$12

---

5. The cost to rent a ski boat is $174.83. Six friends each pay $34. How much change will the group of friends receive?

6. A DVD costs $27.55. How much money should you give the cashier to receive $2.50 in change?

A $35.45
B $32.50
C $30.05
D $29.40

---

7. **Extend Your Thinking** Julia and Carl buy 2 sandwiches, 1 salad, 1 piece of fruit, and 2 drinks for lunch. They gave the cashier $20.03. What coins and bills could they receive in change?

Menu	
Sandwich	$3.96
Chips	$0.79
Fruit	$1.24
Salad	$2.17
Drink	$1.55

---

8. **Analyze Information** Jessica is 115 months old. Jared is 9 years 270 days old. Who is older? How much older?

Use an average of 30 days in each month to solve this problem.

9. **Math and Science** A lodestone is a natural magnet that attracts iron and steel. The force required to pull a magnet free from a steel plate is called "pull force." A certain magnet has a pull force of 2.2 pounds. Write this pull force as a mixed number.

© Pearson Education, Inc. 4

Name _____

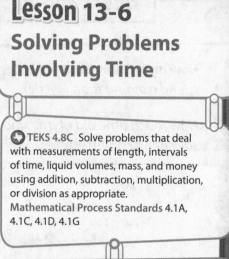

Solve & Share

The Big Sur International Marathon is run on the California coast each spring. How much less time did it take the overall women's winner than the women's winner in the Ages 70–74 group? Tell how you decided. *Solve this problem any way you choose.*

🟢 TEKS 4.8C Solve problems that deal with measurements of length, intervals of time, liquid volumes, mass, and money using addition, subtraction, multiplication, or division as appropriate. Mathematical Process Standards 4.1A, 4.1C, 4.1D, 4.1G

DATA	Men	Women
Overall	2 h 23 min	2 h 50 min
Ages 65–69	3 h 34 min	3 h 58 min
Ages 70–74	4 h 20 min	4 h 34 min

Digital Resources at PearsonTexas.com

Solve	Learn	Glossary	Check	Tools	Games

You can **select** and **use tools** to think about time differences. *Show your work in the space above!*

Look Back!

Number Sense Was the difference in the overall men's winner and the men's winner in the Ages 70–74 group more or less than 2 hours? How do you know by just looking at the data?

How Can You Solve Problems Involving Time?

How much more time did Birsen spend training than Myrtle?

How much time did Myrtle and Joy spend combined?

Training Times	
Name	**Time**
Myrtle	2 hours 32 minutes
Birsen	5 hours 8 minutes
Joy	3 hours 40 minutes

DATA

You can use strip diagrams to model the problems.

Remember, 1 hour = 60 minutes.

B Find how much more time Birsen spent training than Myrtle did.

5 h 8 min

2 h 32 min	x

Find $x = $ 5 h 8 min − 2 h 32 min.

Write the subtraction in a column.

$$\overset{4}{\cancel{5}} \text{ h } \overset{68}{\cancel{8}} \text{ min}$$
$$- 2 \text{ h } 32 \text{ min}$$
$$\overline{2 \text{ h } 36 \text{ min}}$$

Since 8 min < 32 min, regroup 1 h as 60 min.

So, $x = $ 2 h 36 min.

Birsen spent 2 hours 36 minutes more time training than Myrtle.

C Find how much time Myrtle and Joy spent training combined.

y	
2 h 32 min	3 h 40 min

Find $y = $ 2 h 32 min + 3 h 40 min.

Write the addition in a column.

$$2 \text{ h } 32 \text{ min}$$
$$+ 3 \text{ h } 40 \text{ min}$$
$$\overline{5 \text{ h } 72 \text{ min}}$$
$$= 6 \text{ h } 12 \text{ min}$$

Since 72 min > 1 h, regroup 60 min as 1 h.

So, $y = $ 6 h 12 min.

Myrtle and Joy spent 6 hours 12 minutes training combined.

Do You Understand?

Convince Me! Ellie said, "When you add two times like those above, it's easy to tell when you have to regroup the minutes." What does she mean?

Name _____

☆ Guided Practice ☆

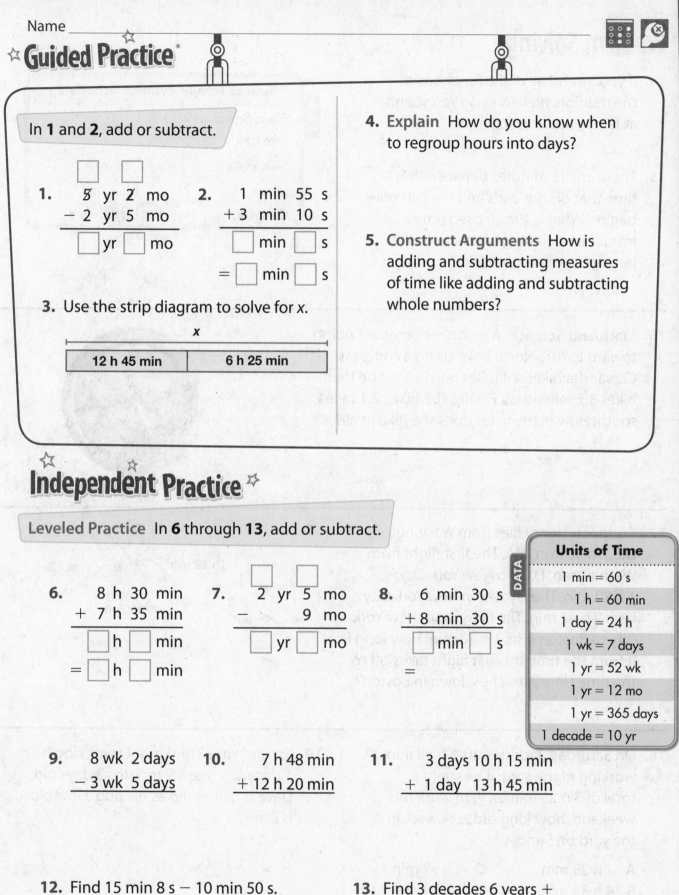

In **1** and **2**, add or subtract.

1. ☐ ☐
    3̶ yr 2̶ mo
    − 2 yr 5 mo
    ──────────
    ☐ yr ☐ mo

2. 1 min 55 s
    + 3 min 10 s
    ──────────
    ☐ min ☐ s
    = ☐ min ☐ s

3. Use the strip diagram to solve for *x*.

    | *x* |
    | 12 h 45 min | 6 h 25 min |

4. **Explain** How do you know when to regroup hours into days?

5. **Construct Arguments** How is adding and subtracting measures of time like adding and subtracting whole numbers?

☆ Independent Practice ☆

Leveled Practice In **6** through **13**, add or subtract.

6. 8 h 30 min
    + 7 h 35 min
    ──────────
    ☐ h ☐ min
    = ☐ h ☐ min

7. ☐ ☐
    2 yr 5 mo
    −   9 mo
    ──────────
    ☐ yr ☐ mo

8. 6 min 30 s
    + 8 min 30 s
    ──────────
    ☐ min ☐ s
    =

Units of Time
1 min = 60 s
1 h = 60 min
1 day = 24 h
1 wk = 7 days
1 yr = 52 wk
1 yr = 12 mo
1 yr = 365 days
1 decade = 10 yr

9. 8 wk 2 days
    − 3 wk 5 days

10. 7 h 48 min
    + 12 h 20 min

11. 3 days 10 h 15 min
    + 1 day 13 h 45 min

12. Find 15 min 8 s − 10 min 50 s.

13. Find 3 decades 6 years + 1 decade 9 years.

Problem Solving

14. If you attend all of the functions of the reunion, how long do you spend at family reunion activities?

DATA

Suarez Family Reunion Schedule	
Trip to Scenic Lake Park	4 h 15 min
Slide show	55 min
Dinner	1 h 30 min
Campfire	1 h 35 min

15. There are 55 minutes between the time that dinner ends and the campfire begins. What is the elapsed time from the beginning of dinner to the beginning of the campfire?

16. **Math and Science** A magnetic compass points toward Earth's North Pole. Using a compass, Cassandra hikes 4.4 miles northeast. She then hikes 3.2 miles east. Finally, she hikes 2.1 miles south. How many miles does she hike in all?

17. **Connect** Henry flies from Washington, D.C., to Boston, MA. The first flight from Washington, D.C., to New York City is 1 h 12 min. The layover in New York City lasts 2 h 41 min. The flight from New York City to Boston lasts 1 h 10 min. How long is it from the time the first flight takes off to the time Henry touches down in Boston?

1h 10 min Boston

1h 12 min New York City

Washington, DC

18. On Saturday, Jack spends 1 h 58 min working in the yard. If he spent a total of 5 h 25 min on yard work this weekend, how long did Jack work in the yard on Sunday?

A 7 h 23 min **C** 3 h 27 min

B 4 h 33 min **D** 3 h 23 min

19. **Extend Your Thinking** Dave's dog is 1 decade 2 years 9 months 3 days old. Dave is half as old as his dog. How old is Dave?

© Pearson Education, Inc. 4

Name _____

Another Look!

You can add and subtract measures of time. Remember to regroup as needed.

Find 5 years 8 months + 3 years 7 months.	Find 5 min 18 s − 3 min 45 s.
Step 1 Add the months. 8 + 7 = 15 months	**Step 1** Subtract the seconds. Since 18 < 45, regroup 1 min as 60 s. 5 min 18 s = 4 min 78 s 78 s − 45 s = 33 s
Step 2 Regroup 12 months as 1 year. 15 months = 1 year 3 months	
Step 3 Add the years. 5 + 3 + 1 = 9 years	**Step 2** Subtract the minutes. 4 − 3 = 1 min
5 years 8 months + 3 years 7 months = 9 years 3 months	5 min 18 s − 3 min 45 s = 1 min 33 s

In **1** through **5**, add or subtract.

1.   8 h 12 min
   + 3 h 15 min

2.   9 wk 5 days
   − 1 wk 6 days

3.   1 decade 8 yr
   −   9 yr

4.   3 h 6 min 45 s
   + 8 h 55 min 20 s

5.   5 decades 4 yr 3 mo
   − 2 decades 5 yr 6 mo

Units of Time
1 min = 60 s
1 h = 60 min
1 day = 24 h
1 wk = 7 days
1 yr = 52 wk
1 yr = 12 mo
1 yr = 365 days
1 decade = 10 yr

DATA

6. **Represent** Draw a strip diagram to model 5 h 8 min − 3 h 12 min. Write an equation and find the difference.

7. The Baltimore Marathon features a relay race. The times for each leg run by a winning team are shown in the table at the right. What is the total time it took this team to run the marathon?

DATA

Baltimore Marathon Winner Results	
Leg of Race	Time Run
Leg 1	32 min 56 s
Leg 2	42 min 28 s
Leg 3	34 min 34 s
Leg 4	39 min 2 s

8. Use a Strip Diagram Group tours of the Luray Caverns in Luray, VA, begin about every 20 minutes. The first group toured the caverns from 9:00 A.M. to 10:12 A.M. The second group of the day toured from 9:20 A.M. to 10:35 A.M. Complete the strip diagram to model how much longer the second tour was than the first tour. Then solve for *x*.

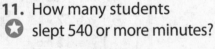

9. Uma is 12 years 9 months 5 days old. Her brother is 10 months 1 day old. How much older is Uma than her brother?

10. Extend Your Thinking Mr. Kent teaches 7 classes that are 50 minutes each. He also has a 30-minute lunch break. How long does Mr. Kent spend teaching class and at lunch?

11. How many students slept 540 or more minutes?

A 9 students
B 8 students
C 18 students
D 26 students

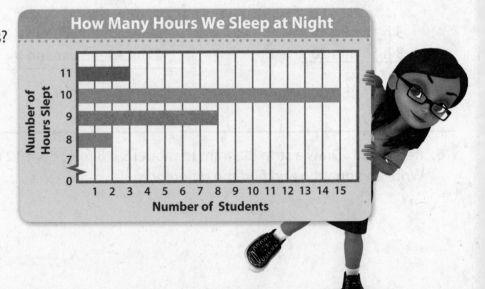

© Pearson Education, Inc. 4

Name _____

☆ **Solve & Share** ☆

Three girls and four boys went to an amusement park. The total cost of their tickets was $140. What was the cost of each ticket? *Solve this problem any way you choose.*

You can **formulate a plan.** You may have to solve a smaller problem as a first step. This will give you enough information to then solve the entire problem. *Show your work in the space below!*

⭐ TEKS 4.1A Apply mathematics to problems arising in everyday life, society, and the workplace.
TEKS 4.1C Select … techniques, including mental math, estimation, and number sense as appropriate, to solve problems. Also, 4.5A, 4.8C.
Mathematical Process Standards 4.1B, 4.1D, 4.1F, 4.1G

Digital Resources at PearsonTexas.com

Solve   Learn   Glossary   Check   Tools   Games

Look Back!

Mental Math Explain how you could use mental math to help solve this problem.

What Steps Can You Use to Solve a Problem?

A Analyze

A museum collection of 36 dragonflies and 54 butterflies will be used in two new displays. There will be the same number of insects in both displays. How many insects will be in each display?

> Look for a hidden question to be answered before you can solve the problem.

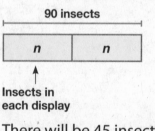

36 dragonflies

54 butterflies

B Plan and Solve

First, you need to find the total number of insects in the collection.

Let t = total number of insects

t insects in all	
36 dragonflies	54 butterflies

$$t = 36 + 54 = 90$$

There are 90 insects in all.

C Plan and Solve

Use the total number of insects to find how many insects will be in each display case.

Let n = number of insects in each case

90 insects	
n	n

↑
Insects in each display

$$90 \div 2 = n$$
$$45 = n$$

There will be 45 insects in each display case.

Do You Understand?

Convince Me! In the example above, suppose 5 of the dragonflies and 8 of the butterflies were given to another museum before making the displays. Could the remaining dragonflies and butterflies still be evenly divided between two displays? Explain.

© Pearson Education, Inc. 4

Name _____

1. **Analyze Information** Twelve friends went camping. All except 4 of the friends went on a hike. The hikers carried 32 water bottles. Each hiker carried the same number of water bottles. How many water bottles did each hiker carry?

2. **Communicate** What hidden question did you have to answer first to find the solution to Exercise 1?

3. Write a word problem that can be solved by finding and answering a hidden question.

In Exercise 3, write information for a simple problem. Then add more information and ask a question that will require answering the simple problem first.

☆ **Independent Practice** ☆

In **4** through **6**, solve. Remember to look for a hidden question to answer first.

4. **Formulate a Plan** Mrs. Lum bought 12 rolls of pink ribbon and some rolls of yellow ribbon. The total cost of the rolls of ribbon is $45. Each roll costs $3. How many rolls of yellow ribbon did Mrs. Lum buy?

5. **Analyze Information** Mr. Alton wants to buy tickets for a show. The tickets are for seats in 3 rows with 3 seats in each row. The total cost of the tickets is $108. Each ticket costs the same. What is the cost of one ticket?

6. **Mental Math** A store has boxed sets of DVDs for sale. Each boxed set has 2 rows with 3 DVDs in each row. The total cost of a boxed set is $60. Each DVD costs the same. How many DVDs are in a boxed set? What is the cost of one DVD?

Problem Solving

7. Tools Vanya bought 5 medium packages of buttons and 3 small packages of beads. What was the total number of buttons she bought?

Number of Items in Package			
Item	Small	Medium	Large
Beads	32	64	96
Buttons	18	38	56

8. Number Sense Victor cleaned $\frac{4}{18}$ of the auditorium. Chas and Tamara each cleaned $\frac{3}{18}$ of the auditorium. James cleaned the rest. What fraction of the auditorium did James clean? Write your answer in simplest form.

9. Estimation Each stripe of the world's largest American flag is more than 19 feet wide. There are 7 red stripes and 6 white stripes. Each stripe is the same width. About how wide is this flag? Explain your answer.

10. Tools Mrs. Casey bought one adult admission ticket and one child admission ticket. Then she bought one adult ticket and one child ticket for a boat ride. What was the total amount Mrs. Casey spent?

County Fair		
Kind of Ticket	Adult	Child
Admission	$8	$4
Boat Rides	$2	$1

11. Martin raked 3 lawns last week and 4 lawns this week. He earned a total of $168. He earned the same amount for each lawn. How much did he earn for each lawn he raked?

A $1,176
B $56
C $42
D $24

12. Extend Your Thinking Read the problem below. Then show two different ways to find the answer.

Dog and cat food are sold in 20-pound bags. There are 7 bags of dog food and 9 bags of cat food on the store shelves. How many pounds of dog and cat food are on the shelves?

742

Name _____

Another Look!

When solving a multi-step problem, you may need to answer one or more hidden questions before you can answer the question that is asked.

Read the problem.

There are 48 students in the band. The boys and girls are in separate rows. There are 6 students in each row. There are 3 rows of boys. How many rows of girls are there?

What do you know?	**What do you need to find out?**
• There are 48 students in the band.	• **Not asked:** How many boys are in the band? **Solve:** 3 rows of boys $\times$ 6 students in each row = 18 boys
• The boys and girls are in separate rows.	• **Not asked:** How many girls are in the band? **Solve:** 48 students − 18 boys = 30 girls
• There are 6 students in each row.	• **Asked:** How many rows of girls are there? **Solve:** 30 girls ÷ 6 students in each row = 5 rows of girls
• There are 3 rows of boys.	

In **1** and **2**, answer hidden questions to help solve the problem.

1. Marcus counted a total of 40 wheels from bicycles and tricycles while sitting on a park bench. Marcus counted 11 bicycles. How many tricycles did Marcus count?

   a. How many of the wheels belong to bicycles?

   ____ bicycles $\times$ ____ wheels on each = ____ bicycle wheels

   b. How many wheels belong to tricycles?

   ____ total wheels − ____ bicycle wheels = ____ tricycle wheels

   c. How many tricycles did Marcus count?

   ____ tricycle wheels ÷ ____ wheels on each = ____ tricycles

2. Julie bought 15 baseballs and some softballs. The total cost of the balls is $90. Each ball costs $5. How many softballs did Julie buy?

3. Explain Friday night, a pizza parlor sold 5 large pizzas and some medium pizzas. The pizza parlor made a total of $291. How many medium pizzas were sold?

PIZZA

Medium $9   Large $15

4. Kendra is using 27 blue pieces and some ☆ white pieces to make a quilt. The quilt has a total area of 540 square inches. Each piece of the quilt has an area of 5 square inches. How much of the area of the quilt is white?

A 81 sq in.
B 108 sq in.
C 405 sq in.
D 513 sq in.

5. Connect Bert bought 4 books for $7 each and a magazine for $5.57. He paid with a $50 bill. How much change did Bert receive? List the least number of coins and bills Bert could have received.

6. Explain There were 24 students in a class. All of the students, except 2, went bowling. What is the total cost the students paid if each person who went bowling paid $5?

7. Personal Financial Literacy Opal saves $7 a week for 16 weeks. Her brother Grant saves $27 a month for 4 months. Who saves more money? Explain.

8. Extend Your Thinking Maurice and Trina both solve the problem at the right. Maurice plans to add first and then multiply. Trina plans to multiply first and then add. Who is correct? Use a property of operations to justify your answer.

A tree farm has 45 maple trees and 27 pine trees for sale. Each tree sells for $56. How much will the tree farm earn from selling all the trees?

© Pearson Education, Inc. 4

Name _____

1. **Connect** An airplane needed 4 hours 12 minutes for a flight to the west coast. The return flight took only 3 hours 43 minutes. How much shorter was the return flight?

Applying Math Processes
- How does this problem connect to previous ones?
- What is my plan?
- How can I use tools?
- How can I use number sense?
- How can I communicate and represent my thinking?
- How can I organize and record information?
- How can I explain my work?
- How can I justify my answer?

2. **Number Sense** A baseball team bought 8 boxes of baseballs. If the team spent a total of $1,664, what was the cost of 1 box of baseballs?

3. **Connect** A certain recipe for a bowl of fruit punch calls for 2 quarts of fruit juice. Georgia has 5 gallons of fruit juice. How many bowls of fruit punch can she make?

4. **Draw a Picture** The Portman's kitchen table is rectangular. The table is 4 feet wide, and has a perimeter of 24 feet. Mrs. Portman wants to buy a tablecloth. The package says that the tablecloth will cover up to 36 square feet. What is the area of the kitchen table?

1 gallon equals 4 quarts.

5. **Extend Your Thinking** What is the area of the rectangle? How does the area of the triangle compare to the area of the rectangle? What is the area of the triangle?

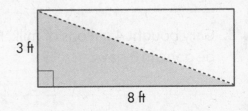

3 ft

8 ft

Error Search

Decide whether the information for each figure is correct. If not, change one number so that the information is correct.

1. Perimeter of rectangle = 42 in.

Length = 30 in.

Width = 12 in.

2. Area of square = 81 sq ft

Length = 9 ft

3. Area of rectangle = 48 sq m

Length = 12 m

Width = 6 m

4. Perimeter of square = 64 cm

Length = 8 cm

Reasoning

Write whether each statement is true or false. If you write false, change the numbers or words so that the statement is true.

5. The area of a square that has a side length of 10 inches is 40 square inches.

6. Harry has a $10 bill and two $5 bills. He cannot buy 4 books that cost $5.25 each.

7. Tammy bought a shirt for $6.85. She paid with a $10 bill. She received more than $3 in change.

8. Gary bought 4 gallons of milk. His children drink 6 quarts of milk each day. The milk will not be gone in 3 days.

9. A football team had 1 yard to go before scoring a touchdown. This is less than 20 inches.

10. Along the course for a 5-kilometer race, there is water available every 400 meters. There are more than 10 places where water is available.

Set A pages 703–714

Use formulas to find the perimeter and area.

Remember you can add the lengths of each side to find the perimeter and count the square units to find the area.

$P = (2 \times \ell) + (2 \times w)$ $A = \ell \times w$
$P = (2 \times 14) + (2 \times 6)$ $A = 14 \times 6$
$P = 28 + 12$ $A = 84$
$P = 40$

The perimeter of the rectangle is 40 meters.
The area of the rectangle is 84 square meters.

Find the perimeter and area of each figure.

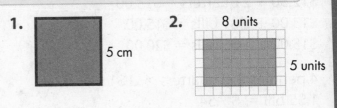

Set B pages 715–720

Manuel built a picture frame using 20 inches of wood. The frame has a length of 6 inches. What is the width of the picture frame? What is the area enclosed by the picture frame?

$6 + 6 = 12$ Add the two known sides.

$20 - 12 = 8$ Subtract the total of the two known sides from the perimeter to find the total of the two unknown sides.

$8 \div 2 = 4$ Divide to find the width of one side.

The width of the picture frame is 4 inches.

$A = \ell \times w = 6 \times 4 = 24$
The area is 24 square inches.

Remember that some problems have hidden questions that need to be answered first.

1. Sally used 20 feet of fencing to enclose her garden. The garden has a length of 5 feet. What is the area of Sally's garden?

2. A bulletin board is 3 feet wide. Its area is 15 square feet. What is the perimeter of the bulletin board?

Set C pages 721–726

Jan uses 2 quarts of orange juice, 4 pints of yogurt, and 5 cups of lemonade to make a smoothie. How many cups of smoothies does she make?

1 qt = 2 pt   1 pt = 2 c
2 c = 1 pt   **4 pt = 8 c**
4 c = 1 qt

So, Jan makes 8 c + 8 c + 5 c = 21 cups of smoothies.

Remember that you can use diagrams and number lines to solve many measurement problems.

1. Jaina and Steven walked to earn money for a fundraising event. Jaina walked 2 kilometers. Steven walked 1,800 meters. Who walked farther? Show your work.

You buy lunch for yourself and a friend that costs $12.46. How much change should you get if you give the cashier a $20 bill?

Count up to $20 using coins and bills.

$12.46 + 4 pennies = $12.50
$12.50 + 2 quarters = $13.00
$13.00 + 2 $1 bills = $15.00
$15.00 + 1 $5 bills = $20.00

4 pennies + 2 quarters + 2 $1 bills + 1 $5 bill = $ 7.54

Remember that you can use different combinations of money to make change.

1. Gary buys three tickets to a movie for a total of $26.25. He pays with a $20 bill and a $10 bill. How much change should he get back?

2. A carpenter buys a tool box and hand tools for a total of $32.56. How much change will the carpenter receive if he pays with two $20 bills?

The ride to the beach took 2 hours 13 minutes. The ride home took 1 hour 47 minutes. How much longer was the ride to the beach than the ride home?

2 h 13 min = 1 h 73 min
1 h 73 min − 1 h 47 min = 26 minutes

The ride to the beach took 26 minutes longer.

Remember that time measures must be in the same unit before you can add or subtract them.

1. A movie is showing at the local theater every 2 hours 40 minutes. The movie lasts 1 hour 50 minutes. How long after the movie ends does it start again?

There are 13 girls and 14 boys that will form volleyball teams. Each team needs 6 players. Extra players will be alternates. How many teams can be formed? How many players will be alternates?

Step 1

13 + 14 = 27   Find the total number of children.

Step 2

$$\begin{array}{r} 4\ R3 \\ 6\overline{)27} \\ -24 \\ \hline 3 \end{array}$$ Divide 27 by 6 to find the number of teams.

There will be 4 teams with 3 players left to be alternates.

Remember to answer the hidden question and use the answer to solve the problem.

1. Three friends ordered 2 pizzas. Each pizza was cut into 8 slices. If each person ate the same number of slices, how many slices did each person eat? How many slices were left over?

2. Mark's mother spent $79 on 3 shirts and a package of socks for him. If each shirt cost $24, how much did the package of socks cost?

© Pearson Education, Inc. 4

Name _____

1. Pepper's dog pen measures 4 meters wide and 5 meters long. What is the perimeter of the pen?

   A 20 meters

   B 18 meters

   C 14 meters

   D 11 meters

2. A picnic table is 9 feet long and 3 feet wide. What is the area of the rectangular surface of the table?

   A 24 square feet

   B 27 square feet

   C 36 square feet

   D 54 square feet

3. Which statement is true about the bedrooms in the drawings below?

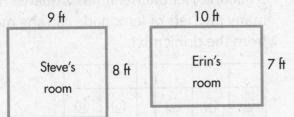

9 ft   10 ft

Steve's room   8 ft

Erin's room   7 ft

   A Erin's room has a greater area than Steve's room.

   B Steve's room has a greater perimeter than Erin's room.

   C They both have the same perimeter.

   D None of the above

4. Nicole buys three juices to share with her friends. The total cost is $5.25. She pays with a $20 bill. How much change should she get back?

   A $14.25

   B $14.75

   C $16.50

   D $18.25

5. Terry bought $89 in clothing. He spent $32 on jeans and the rest on 3 shirts that each cost the same amount. Which equation would you **NOT** use when finding the cost, c, of each shirt?

   A $57 \div 3 = c$

   B $32 + c = 89$

   C $89 - 32 = 57$

   D $c = 19$

6. Ed is retiling a pool that is 12 feet long and 7 feet wide. What is the area of the floor of the pool?

   A 19 square feet

   B 42 square feet

   C 72 square feet

   D 84 square feet

7. Ben played at a friend's house for 2 hours 35 minutes. Later he played at a park. He played for a total of 3 hours 52 minutes that day. How long did he play at the park?

A 6 hours 27 minutes

B 2 hours 17 minutes

C 1 hour 17 minutes

D 17 minutes

8. Lisa buys 4 postcards, a T-shirt, and a button from a gift shop in Washington, D.C. The items cost a total of $23.19. She paid for them with three $10 bills. How much change should she get back?

9. A square picture frame measures 6 inches on a side. What is the perimeter of the frame in inches?

⓪	⓪	⓪	•	⓪	⓪
①	①	①		①	①
②	②	②		②	②
③	③	③		③	③
④	④	④		④	④
⑤	⑤	⑤		⑤	⑤
⑥	⑥	⑥		⑥	⑥
⑦	⑦	⑦		⑦	⑦
⑧	⑧	⑧		⑧	⑧
⑨	⑨	⑨		⑨	⑨

10. The perimeter of a rectangle is 26 inches. The width of the rectangle is 5 inches. What is the area of the rectangle?

A 40 square inches

B 26 square inches

C 16 square inches

D 8 square inches

11. The measurements of Norton's computer monitor are shown below. What is the perimeter of his monitor? Show your work.

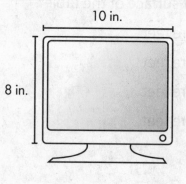

10 in.

8 in.

12. Belinda has a can of drink mix that makes 3 gallons. Her pitcher holds 2 quarts. How many pitchers of lemonade can she make from the drink mix?

⓪	⓪	⓪	•	⓪	⓪
①	①	①		①	①
②	②	②		②	②
③	③	③		③	③
④	④	④		④	④
⑤	⑤	⑤		⑤	⑤
⑥	⑥	⑥		⑥	⑥
⑦	⑦	⑦		⑦	⑦
⑧	⑧	⑧		⑧	⑧
⑨	⑨	⑨		⑨	⑨

© Pearson Education, Inc. 4

Lines, Angles, and Shapes

Essential Questions:
How can lines, angles, and shapes be described, analyzed, and classified?
How are angles measured, added, and subtracted?

All living things are classified as producers, consumers, or decomposers.

Producers make food. Consumers use the food producers make or eat other organisms.

We are consumers! Here's a project on food webs and angles.

Math and Science Project: Food Webs

Do Research Use the Internet or other sources to find information about producers and consumers.

Journal: Write a Report Include what you found. Also in your report:

• What do producers need to survive? What do consumers need to survive?

• Give at least three examples of both producers and consumers.

• Find a food web picture that uses arrows to connect producers and consumers. Identify different types of triangles and quadrilaterals formed by the arrows of the food web.

Name _____

Review What You Know

Vocabulary

Choose the best term from the box.
Write it on the blank.

- triangle
- polygon
- quadrilateral
- angle

1. A polygon with four sides is a

   _____.

2. A polygon with three sides is a

   _____.

3. A(n) _____ is formed by two
   rays with the same endpoint.

Solids

Name the solid figure that each object
looks like.

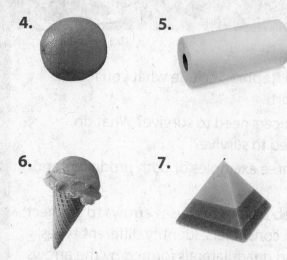

4.

5.

6.

7.

Addition

Solve.

8. 35 + 39

9. 72 + 109

10. 44 + 12

11. 145 + 238

12. 642 + 8

13. 99 + 41

14. 984 + 984

15. 22 + 888

16. 72 + 391

17. 43 + 294

Problem Solving

18. **Explain** There are 525,600 minutes in
    most years. How many minutes are in
    a leap year?

Every fourth year is a leap year.
Leap years are easy to remember
because they are always a multiple
of 4: 2012, 2016, 2020, and so on.

© Pearson Education, Inc. 4

My Word Cards

Use the examples for each word on the front of the card to help complete the definitions on the back.

A-Z

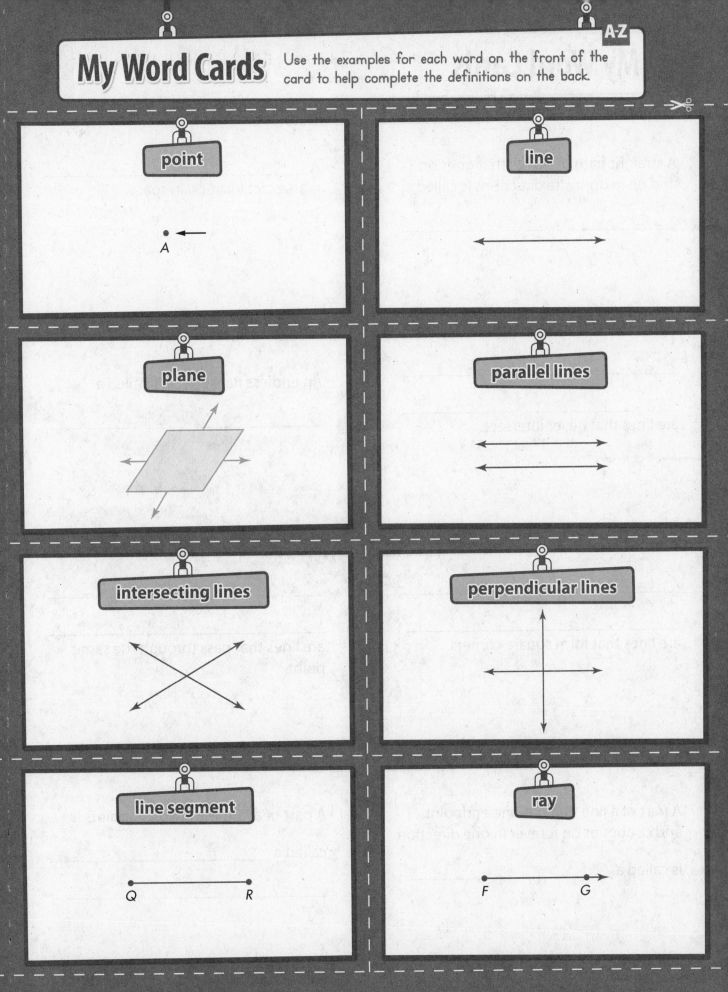

point

A

line

plane

parallel lines

intersecting lines

perpendicular lines

line segment

Q   R

ray

F   G

My Word Cards

Complete each definition. Extend learning by writing your own definitions.

A straight path of points that goes on and on in opposite directions is called a

_____.

A _____
is an exact location in space.

_____

_____

are lines that never intersect.

An endless flat surface is called a

_____.

_____

_____

are lines that form square corners.

_____

_____

are lines that pass through the same point.

A part of a line that has one endpoint and continues on forever in one direction

is called a _____.

A part of a line with two endpoints is

called a _____

_____.

© Pearson Education, Inc. 4

My Word Cards

Use the examples for each word on the front of the card to help complete the definitions on the back.

A-Z

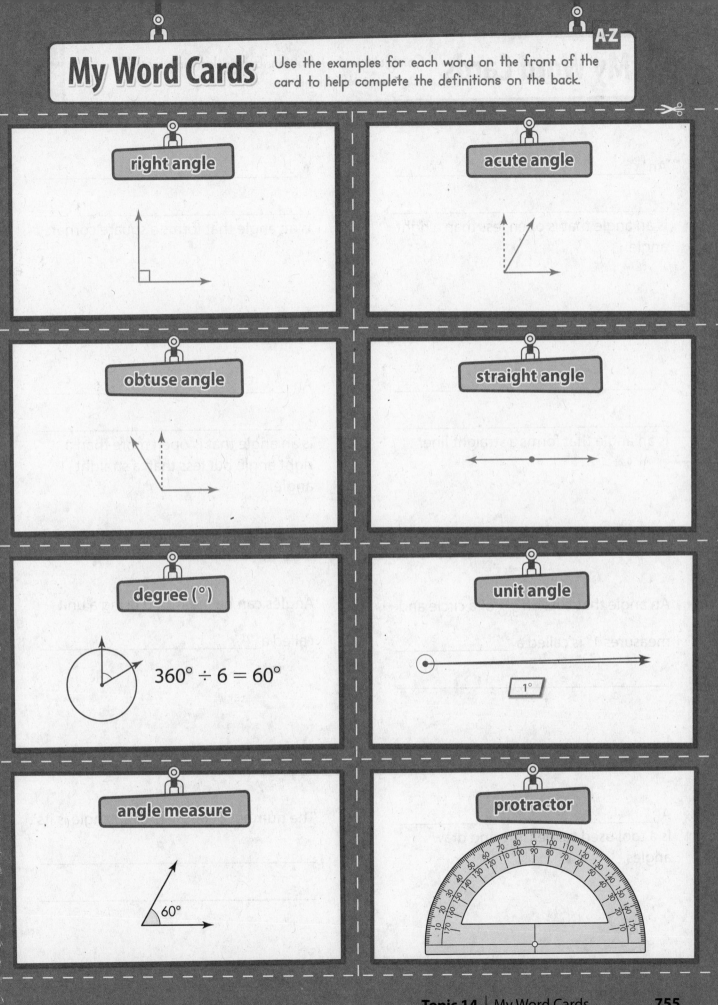

right angle

acute angle

obtuse angle

straight angle

degree (°)

$360° \div 6 = 60°$

unit angle

1°

angle measure

60°

protractor

My Word Cards

Complete each definition. Extend learning by writing your own definitions.

An _____

_____

is an angle that is open less than a right angle.

A _____

_____

is an angle that forms a square corner.

A _____

_____

is an angle that forms a straight line.

An _____

_____

is an angle that is open more than a right angle but less than a straight angle.

An angle that cuts off $\frac{1}{360}$ of a circle and

measures 1° is called a _____

_____.

Angles can be measured using a unit

called a _____.

A _____

is a tool used to measure and draw angles.

The number of degrees of an angle is its

_____

_____.

756

© Pearson Education, Inc. 4

My Word Cards

Use the examples for each word on the front of the card to help complete the definitions on the back.

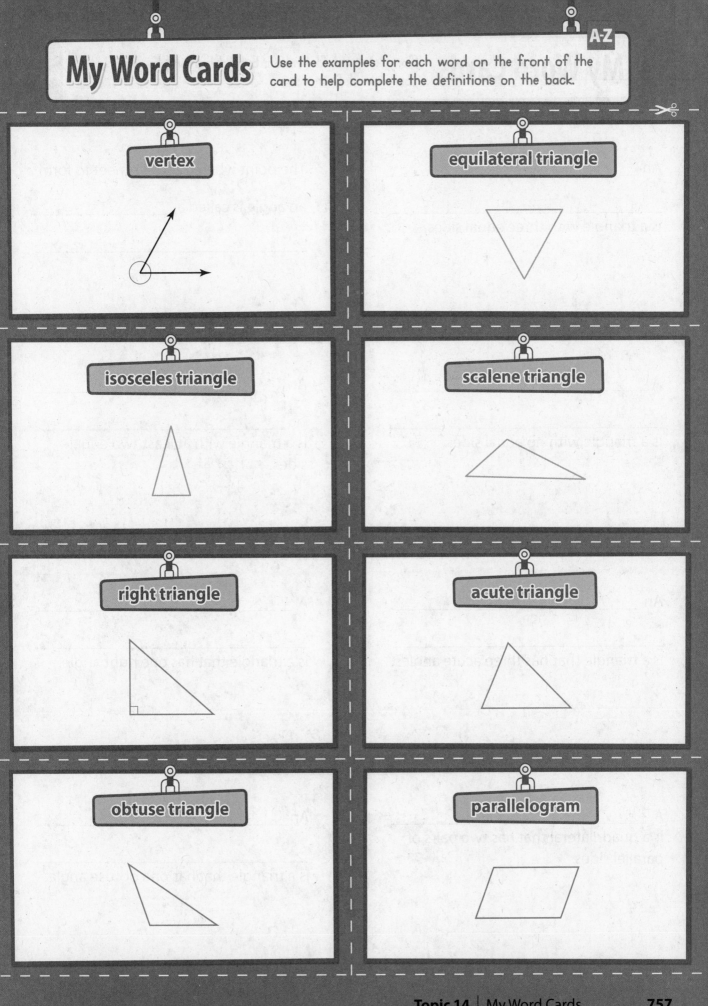

vertex

equilateral triangle

isosceles triangle

scalene triangle

right triangle

acute triangle

obtuse triangle

parallelogram

My Word Cards

Complete each definition. Extend learning by writing your own definitions.

An _____

_____
is a triangle with three equal sides.

The point where two rays meet to form

an angle is called a _____

_____.

A _____

_____
is a triangle with no equal sides.

An _____

_____
is a triangle with at least two equal sides.

An _____

_____
is a triangle that has three acute angles.

A _____

_____
is a triangle that has one right angle.

A _____
is a quadrilateral that has two pairs of parallel sides.

An _____

_____
is a triangle that has one obtuse angle.

© Pearson Education, Inc. 4

My Word Cards

Use the examples for each word on the front of the card to help complete the definitions on the back.

A-Z

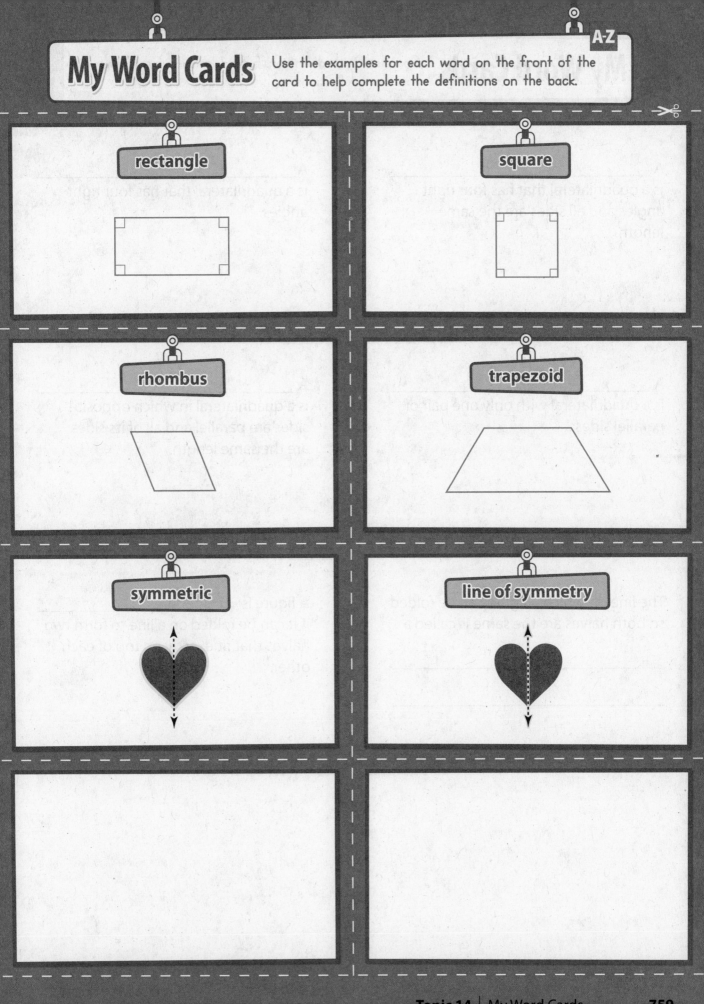

rectangle

square

rhombus

trapezoid

symmetric

line of symmetry

My Word Cards

Complete each definition. Extend learning by writing your own definitions.

A _____
is a quadrilateral that has four right angles and all sides are the same length.

A _____
is a quadrilateral that has four right angles.

A _____
is a quadrilateral with only one pair of parallel sides.

A _____
is a quadrilateral in which opposite sides are parallel and all of its sides are the same length.

The line on which a figure can be folded so both halves are the same is called a

_____

_____ .

A figure is _____
if it can be folded on a line to form two halves that fit exactly on top of each other.

© Pearson Education, Inc. 4

Name _____

Solve & Share

In math, a line goes on forever in a straight path in two directions. Draw two lines. Describe how this pair of lines is related to each other. *Solve this problem any way you choose.*

⭐ TEKS 4.6A Identify points, lines, line segments, rays, angles, and perpendicular and parallel lines. Also, 4.6. **Mathematical Process Standards** 4.1A, 4.1D, 4.1E, 4.1G

You can **communicate**. Think of and use math language you already know. *Show your work in the space below!*

Digital Resources at PearsonTexas.com

| Solve | Learn | Glossary | Check | Tools | Games |

Look Back!

Create and Use Representations Draw a second pair of lines that are related to each other in a different way. Describe how these lines are related.

What Are Some Important Geometric Terms?

Point, line, and plane are basic terms used to relate objects in space. These terms also can be related to real-world situations.

A point is an exact location in space.

$\dot{z}$

A line is a straight path of points that goes on and on in opposite directions.

A plane is an endless flat surface.

B Pairs of lines are given special names depending on their relationship.

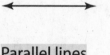

Parallel lines never intersect.

Intersecting lines pass through the same point.

Perpendicular lines are lines that form square corners.

Do You Understand?

Convince Me! Find examples in your classroom where you can imagine parallel lines, intersecting lines, and perpendicular lines. Tell how you decided.

© Pearson Education, Inc. 4

Name _____

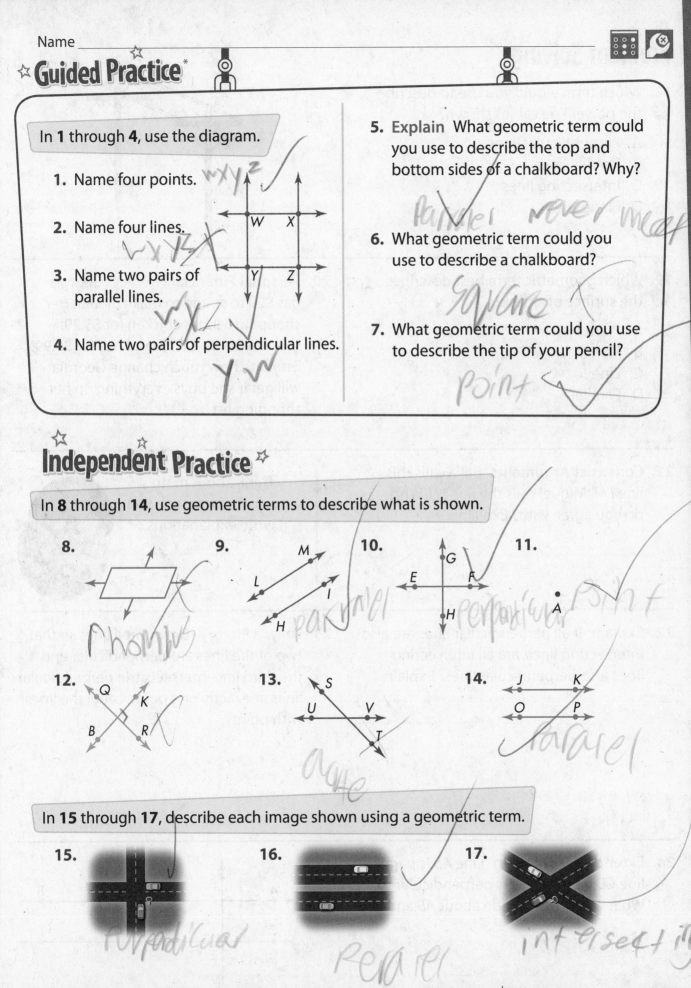

In **1** through **4**, use the diagram.

1. Name four points.

2. Name four lines.

3. Name two pairs of parallel lines.

4. Name two pairs of perpendicular lines.

5. **Explain** What geometric term could you use to describe the top and bottom sides of a chalkboard? Why?

parallel never meet

6. What geometric term could you use to describe a chalkboard?

square

7. What geometric term could you use to describe the tip of your pencil?

point

☆ **Independent Practice** ☆

In **8** through **14**, use geometric terms to describe what is shown.

8. *rhombus*

9. *parallel*

10. *perpendicular*

11. *point*

12.

13. *acute*

14. *parallel*

In **15** through **17**, describe each image shown using a geometric term.

15. *perpendicular*

16. *parallel*

17. *intersecting*

Problem Solving

18. Which term would you use to describe the power line cables shown?

   A Perpendicular lines
   B Parallel lines
   C Intersecting lines
   D Plane

19. Which geometric term best describes the surface of a desk?

   A Point
   B Plane
   C Line
   D Parallel

20. Personal Financial Literacy Georgia has $20 to spend to make dinner. Her shopping list has chicken for $5.29, salad items for $8.73, and rice for $1.99. Estimate how much change Georgia will get if she buys everything on her shopping list.

21. Construct Arguments Bella calls this line *LM*. Miguel calls the line *LN*. Who do you agree with? Explain.

Think about math vocabulary when you write explanations.

22. Explain If all perpendicular lines are also intersecting lines, are all intersecting lines also perpendicular lines? Explain.

23. Draw a Picture Draw three lines so that two of the lines are perpendicular and the third line intersects the perpendicular lines at exactly one point. Label the lines with points.

24. Extend Your Thinking Line *AB* is parallel to line *CD*, and line *CD* is perpendicular to line *EF*. What can you conclude about *AB* and *EF*?

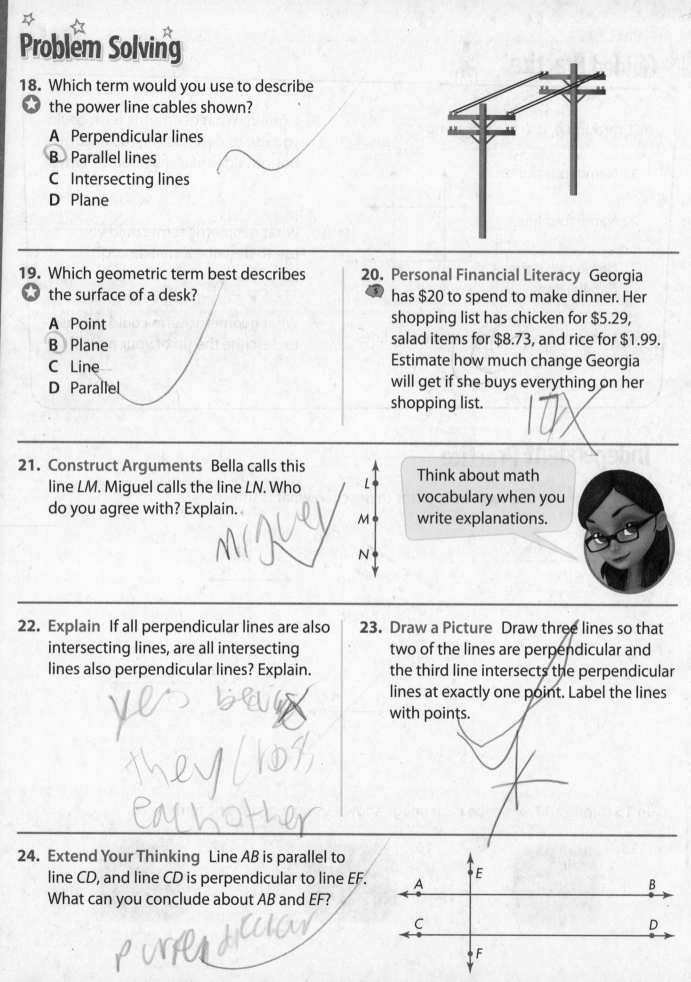

© Pearson Education, Inc. 4

Another Look!

Here are some important geometric terms.

X
•

Point
A point is an exact location in space. This is point *X*.

A ←————•————•————→ B

Line
A line is a straight path of points that goes on and on in both directions. This is line *AB*.

Parallel lines
Parallel lines never intersect.

Intersecting lines
Intersecting lines pass through the same point.

Perpendicular lines
Perpendicular lines form right angles.

In **1** through **3**, use geometric terms to describe what is shown. Be as specific as possible.

1.

2.

3. ←—•————•————•—→

4. Name three different lines.

5. Name a pair of parallel lines.

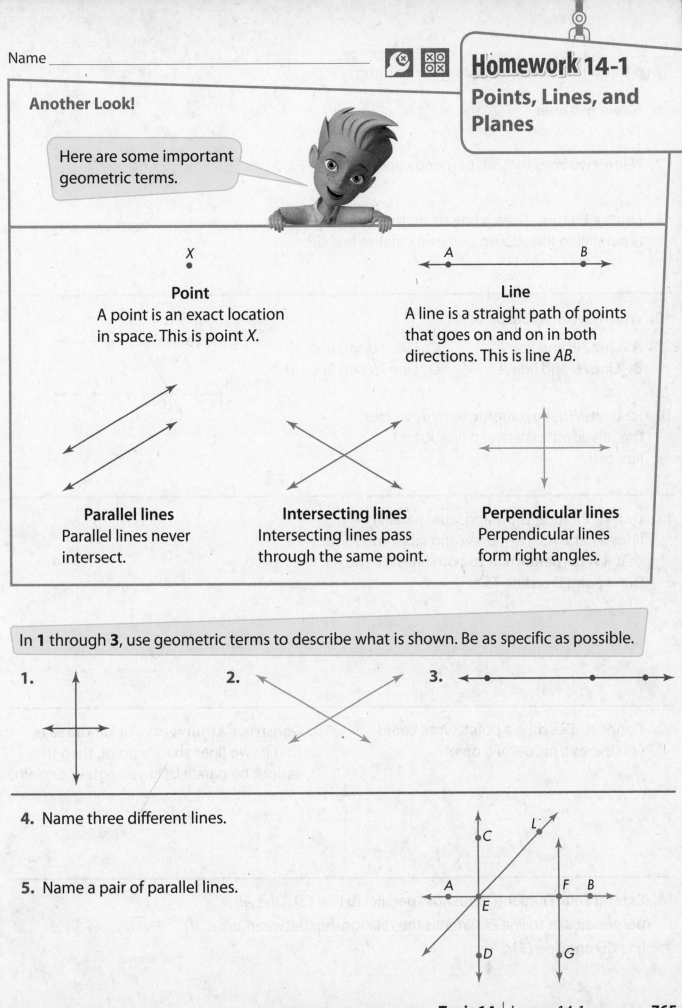

6. Name two lines.

7. Name two lines that are perpendicular.

8. Draw a Picture Draw a line *HF* on the diagram that is parallel to line *AE* and perpendicular to line *GF*.

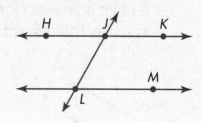

---

9. Which two lines are parallel?

   A Line *HK* and line *JL*   **C** Line *HJ* and line *JK*
   B Line *HJ* and line *JL*   **D** Line *HJ* and line *LM*

10. Reason What geometric term describes the relationship between line *JL* and line *LM*?

---

11. Draw a Picture Draw and label parallel lines *XY* and *RS*. Then draw and label line *TS* so that it is perpendicular to both lines *XY* and *RS*. Draw point *Z* on line *TS*.

---

12. Connect Describe a point. What could you use as a model of a point?

13. Construct Arguments Alexandra says that if two lines share a point, then they cannot be parallel. Do you agree? Explain.

---

14. Extend Your Thinking Line *AB* is parallel to line *CD*. Line *AB* is perpendicular to line *EF*. What is the relationship between line *CD* and line *EF*?

© Pearson Education, Inc. 4

Name _____

Solve & Share

A right angle forms a square corner, like the one shown below. Draw two more angles that are open less than the right angle. *Solve this problem any way you choose.*

⭐ TEKS 4.6A Identify points, lines, line segments, rays, angles, and perpendicular and parallel lines. Also, 4.6. **Mathematical Process Standards** 4.1A, 4.1B, 4.1D, 4.1E, 4.1F, 4.1G

You can **create representations**. The measure of an angle is less if the sides of the angle are closer together. *Show your work in the space below!*

Digital Resources at PearsonTexas.com

Solve   Learn   Glossary   Check   Tools   Games

Look Back!

Connect Ideas Draw an angle that is open more than the right angle.

What Geometric Terms Are Used to Describe Parts of Lines and Angles?

A

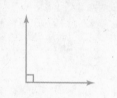

Line segments and rays are sets of points that describe parts of lines.

A line segment is a part of a line with two endpoints.

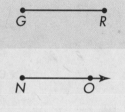
G   R

A ray is a part of a line that has one endpoint and continues on forever in one direction.

N   O

Angles are formed by two intersecting lines or by rays that have the same endpoint. Angles are given special names depending on their measure.

B

A **right angle** is a square corner.

An **acute angle** is open less than a right angle.

An **obtuse angle** is open more than a right angle but less than a straight angle.

A **straight angle** forms a straight line.

Do You Understand?

Convince Me! Complete each figure to show the given angle.

Obtuse angle   Straight angle   Acute angle   Right angle

© Pearson Education, Inc. 4

☆ Guided Practice ☆

In **1** through **4**, use geometric terms to describe what is shown.

1. 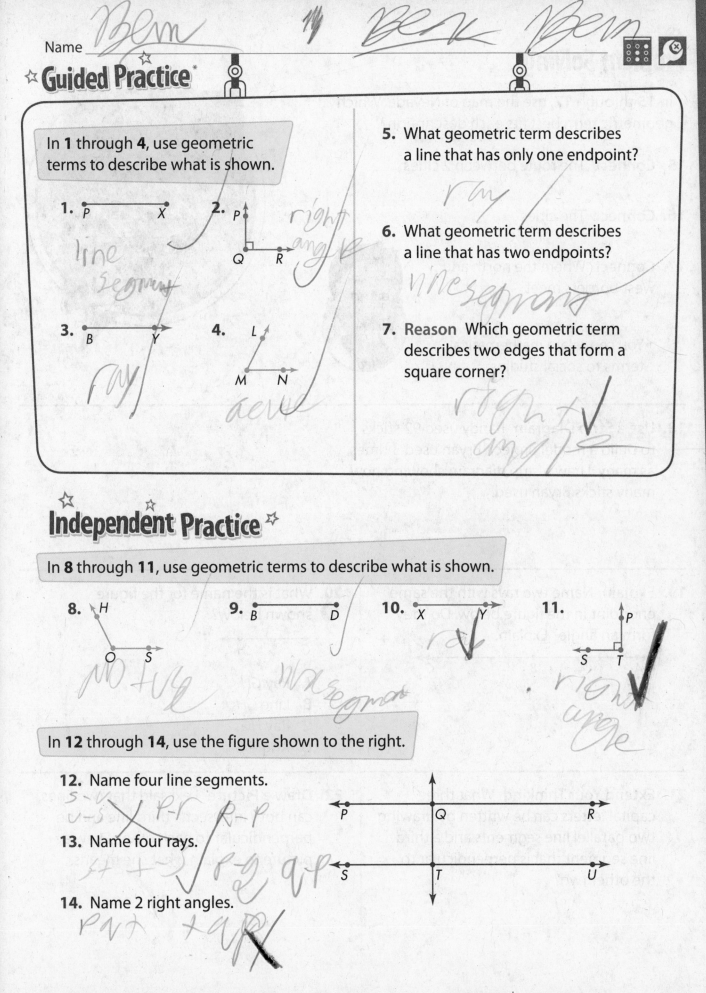 P———X   *line segment*

2. P↑ Q—R   *right angle*

3. B•——•Y→   *ray*

4. L↑ M•——•N→   *acute*

5. What geometric term describes a line that has only one endpoint?

    ray

6. What geometric term describes a line that has two endpoints?

    line segment

7. **Reason** Which geometric term describes two edges that form a square corner?

    right angle ✓

Independent Practice ☆

In **8** through **11**, use geometric terms to describe what is shown.

8. H↑ O•——•S→   *motion*

9. B•——•D   *line segment*

10. X•——•Y→   ✓

11. P↑ S←—•T   *right angle* ✓

In **12** through **14**, use the figure shown to the right.

12. Name four line segments.
    S–V P–R R–P
    U–S ✗

13. Name four rays.
    ✓

14. Name 2 right angles.
    PVT +QPV ✗

Problem Solving

In **15** through **17**, use the map of Nevada. Which geometric term best fits each description?

15. Connect The route between 2 cities

16. Connect The cities

~~vegas~~ ~~laughlin~~ ~~line segment~~
~~line segment~~

17. Connect Where the north and west borders meet

~~above~~

You can relate mathematical terms to social studies.

---

18. Use a Strip Diagram Randy used 92 sticks to build a model project. Bryan used 3 times as many. Draw a strip diagram showing how many sticks Bryan used.

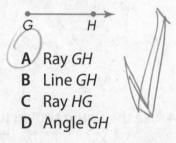

---

19. Explain Name two rays with the same endpoint in the figure below. Do they form an angle? Explain.

A   *B*   *C*

No because its a point

20. What is the name for the figure shown below?

G   *H*

A Ray *GH*
B Line *GH*
C Ray *HG*
D Angle *GH*

---

21. Extend Your Thinking What three capital letters can be written by drawing two parallel line segments and a third line segment that is perpendicular to the other two?

G H A

22. Draw a Picture Lexi said that two lines can both intersect a third line and be perpendicular to each other. Draw a picture to explain what she means.

770   © Pearson Education, Inc. 4

Name _____

Another Look!

Here are some important geometric terms.

Homework 14-2
Line Segments, Rays, and Angles

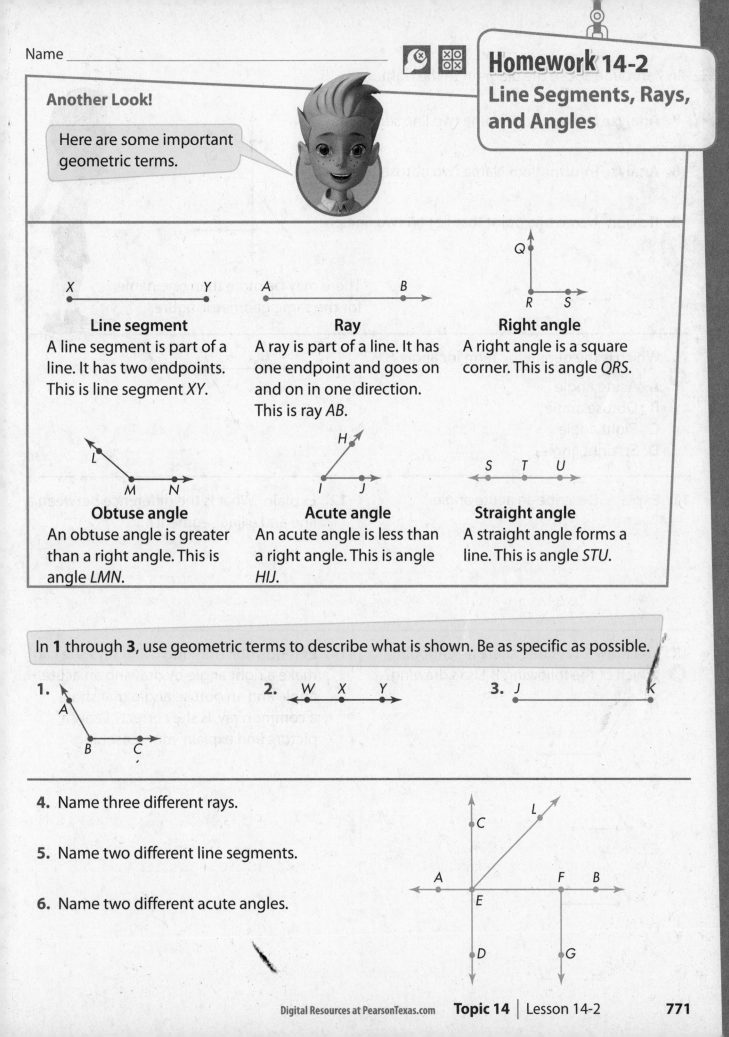

Line segment
A line segment is part of a line. It has two endpoints. This is line segment *XY*.

Ray
A ray is part of a line. It has one endpoint and goes on and on in one direction. This is ray *AB*.

Right angle
A right angle is a square corner. This is angle *QRS*.

Obtuse angle
An obtuse angle is greater than a right angle. This is angle *LMN*.

Acute angle
An acute angle is less than a right angle. This is angle *HIJ*.

Straight angle
A straight angle forms a line. This is angle *STU*.

In **1** through **3**, use geometric terms to describe what is shown. Be as specific as possible.

1.

2. W   X   Y

3. J   K

4. Name three different rays.

5. Name two different line segments.

6. Name two different acute angles.

Digital Resources at PearsonTexas.com **Topic 14** | Lesson 14-2 **771**

7. Analyze Information Name two line segments.

8. Analyze Information Name two obtuse angles.

9. Reason Name one point that lies on two lines.

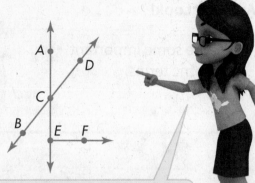

There may be more than one name for the same geometric figure.

---

10. Which is the geometric term for angle *HJK*?

⭐

   A Acute angle

   B Obtuse angle

   C Right angle

   D Straight angle

---

11. Explain Describe an acute angle.

12. Explain What is the difference between a line and a line segment?

---

13. Lisa drew 2 rays that share an endpoint. Which of the following is Lisa's drawing?

⭐

   A

   B

   C

   D

14. Extend Your Thinking Nina says she can make a right angle by drawing an acute angle and an obtuse angle that share a common ray. Is she correct? Draw a picture and explain your reasoning.

© Pearson Education, Inc. 4

Name _____

Solve & Share

It is 9:00. How could you describe the angle made by the two hands of a clock? *Solve this problem any way you choose.*

You can communicate the size of an angle using units called degrees. There are 360 degrees in a full circle. *Show your work in the space below!*

TEKS 4.7A Illustrate the measure of an angle as the part of a circle whose center is at the vertex of the angle that is "cut out" by the rays of the angle…. TEKS 4.7B Illustrate degrees as the units used to measure an angle…. Also, 4.7. Mathematical Process Standards 4.1B, 4.1D, 4.1E, 4.1F, 4.1G

Digital Resources at PearsonTexas.com

Solve | Learn | Glossary | Check | Tools | Games

Look Back!

Connect Ideas What two fractions do the hands divide the clock into?

What Is the Unit Used to Measure Angles?

A

Jill drew a right angle and wants to find its measurement. Angles can be measured in units called degrees (°). A unit angle is an angle that cuts off $\frac{1}{360}$ of a circle and measures 1°. When you find the degrees of an angle, you find its angle measure.

The measure of an angle depends on the fraction of a circle cut off by its rays.

$1° = \frac{1}{360}$ of a circle

B Divide to find the angle measure of a right angle.

Right angles divide a circle into 4 equal parts.

$360° ÷ 4 = 90°$

The angle measure of a right angle is 90°.

C What is the angle measure of a straight angle?

A straight angle divides a circle into 2 equal parts.

$360° ÷ 2 = 180°$

The angle measure of a straight angle is 180°.

D Find the measure of an angle that cuts off $\frac{1}{6}$ of a circle.

Remember, $\frac{1}{6}$ means 1 of 6 equal parts, so divide by 6 to find the angle measure.

$360° ÷ 6 = 60°$

The angle measure is 60°.

Do You Understand?

Convince Me! Susan thinks the measure of angle *B* is greater than the measure of angle *A*. Do you agree? Explain.

© Pearson Education, Inc. 4

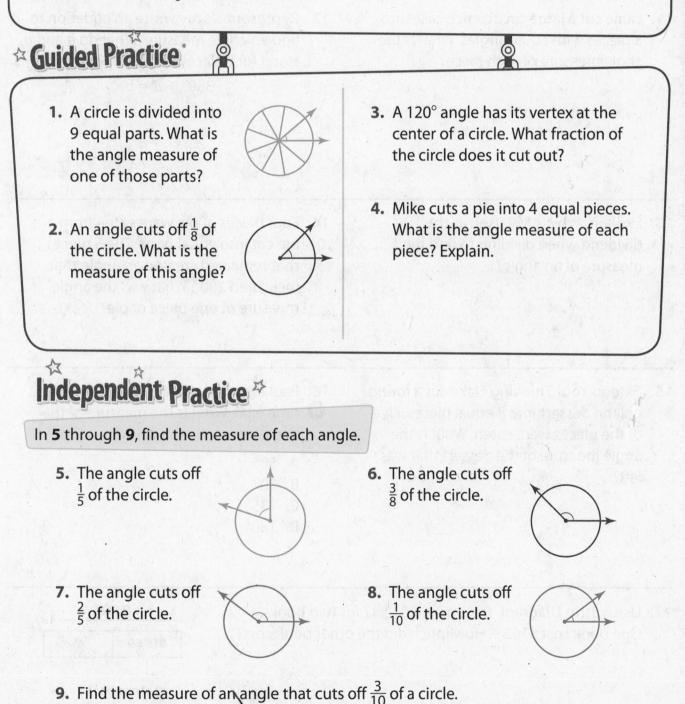

Another Example

Find the measure of an angle that cuts off $\frac{2}{6}$ of a circle.

Remember that $\frac{2}{6} = \frac{1}{6} + \frac{1}{6}$. So, you can add to find the measure of $\frac{2}{6}$ of a circle.

$$60° + 60° = 120°$$

The angle measure of $\frac{2}{6}$ of a circle is 120°.

$\frac{1}{6} = 60°$ $\frac{2}{6} = ?$

☆Guided Practice *

1. A circle is divided into 9 equal parts. What is the angle measure of one of those parts?

2. An angle cuts off $\frac{1}{8}$ of the circle. What is the measure of this angle?

3. A 120° angle has its vertex at the center of a circle. What fraction of the circle does it cut out?

4. Mike cuts a pie into 4 equal pieces. What is the angle measure of each piece? Explain.

Independent Practice ☆

In **5** through **9**, find the measure of each angle.

5. The angle cuts off $\frac{1}{5}$ of the circle.

6. The angle cuts off $\frac{3}{8}$ of the circle.

7. The angle cuts off $\frac{2}{5}$ of the circle.

8. The angle cuts off $\frac{1}{10}$ of the circle.

9. Find the measure of an angle that cuts off $\frac{3}{10}$ of a circle.

Problem Solving

10. What is the measure of the angle created when the clock shows 3:00?

---

11. Lanie cut a large circular rice cake into 3 pieces with equal angles. What is the angle measure of each piece?

12. Represent Jacey wrote an equation to find an angle measure. What do *a* and *b* stand for in Jacey's equation?

$$360° \div a = b$$

---

13. Explain Why is 360 used as the dividend when dividing to find the measure of an angle?

14. Four pieces of pie were eaten from a pie cut into equal parts. The 5 pieces that remained created an angle that measured 200°. What was the angle measure of one piece of pie?

---

15. Extend Your Thinking Jake cut a round gelatin dessert into 8 equal pieces. Five of the pieces were eaten. What is the angle measure of the dessert that was left?

16. Paul drew a clock face that showed the time 6:00. What is the measure of the angle shown on the clock?

    A 50°
    B 90°
    C 135°
    D 180°

---

17. Use a Strip Diagram Devon paid $32.37 for two books. One book cost $16.59. How much did the other book cost?

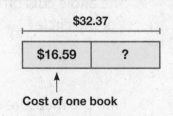

© Pearson Education, Inc. 4

Name _____

Another Look!

Fractions of a circle can help with the understanding of angle measures.

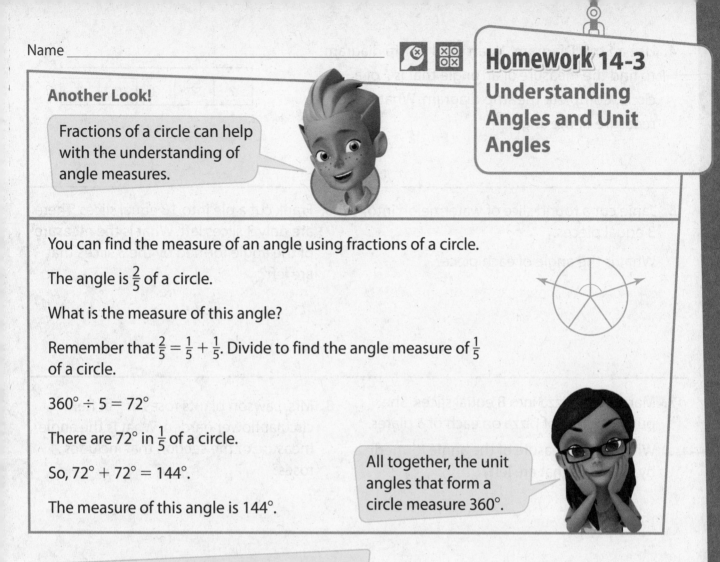

You can find the measure of an angle using fractions of a circle.

The angle is $\frac{2}{5}$ of a circle.

What is the measure of this angle?

Remember that $\frac{2}{5} = \frac{1}{5} + \frac{1}{5}$. Divide to find the angle measure of $\frac{1}{5}$ of a circle.

$360° \div 5 = 72°$

There are 72° in $\frac{1}{5}$ of a circle.

So, $72° + 72° = 144°$.

The measure of this angle is 144°.

All together, the unit angles that form a circle measure 360°.

In **1** through **3**, find the measure of each angle.

1. **Formulate a Plan** A circle is divided into 9 equal parts.

   What is the measure of the angle?

   _____ ÷ _____ = _____

   The measure of the angle is _____ degrees.

2. A circle is divided into 9 equal parts. What is the angle measure of three of those parts?

   _____ degrees

3. A circle is divided into 10 equal parts. What is the angle measure of four of those parts?

   _____ degrees

4. **Use a Strip Diagram** Noah used a strip diagram to find the measure of an angle that is $\frac{1}{5}$ of a circle. Complete the strip diagram. What is the measure of the angle?

| ? | ? | ? | ? | ? |

↑
Angle measure

---

5. Janie cut a round slice of watermelon into 3 equal pieces.

   What is the angle of each piece?

6. Frank cut a pie into 10 equal slices. There are only 3 slices left. What is the measure of the angle formed by the 3 slices that are left?

---

7. Maria cut a pizza into 8 equal slices. She put two slices of pizza on each of 3 plates.

   What is the measure of the angle formed by the slices that are left?

8. Mrs. Lawson plants roses in $\frac{2}{9}$ of her circular flower garden. What is the angle measure of the section that includes roses?

---

9. **Personal Financial Literacy** Wendy's older brother is buying a car. He must make 24 payments of $95 each. How much does he have to pay in all?

10. **Extend Your Thinking** Sam cut a pie into equal slices. There are only 3 slices left. The angle measure for the three slices is 72°. How many slices did Sam cut the pie into?

---

11. **Extend Your Thinking** A circle is divided into 18 equal parts. How many degrees is the angle for each part? How many degrees is the angle for 5 parts? Explain.

12. Brian cut an extra large round pizza into 8 pieces. Seven of the pieces were eaten. What angle measure of pizza is left?

    A 30°   C 45°

    B 40°   D 90°

© Pearson Education, Inc. 4

Name _____

The smaller angles of the tan pattern block measure 30°. What is the measure of the angle below? *Solve this problem any way you choose.*

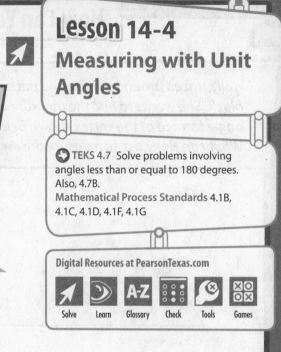

?

You can **use tools.** You can use angles that you already know to help you measure other angles. *Show your work in the space above!*

Lesson 14-4
Measuring with Unit Angles

⭐ **TEKS 4.7** Solve problems involving angles less than or equal to 180 degrees. Also, 4.7B.
Mathematical Process Standards 4.1B, 4.1C, 4.1D, 4.1F, 4.1G

Digital Resources at PearsonTexas.com

| Solve | Learn | Glossary | Check | Tools | Games |

Look Back!

Reason If the angle above was divided into two equal angles, what would be the measure of these two angles?

How Can You Measure Angles?

A

Holly traced around a trapezoid pattern block. She wants to find the measure of the angle formed at the vertex shown below. What can Holly use to measure the angle?

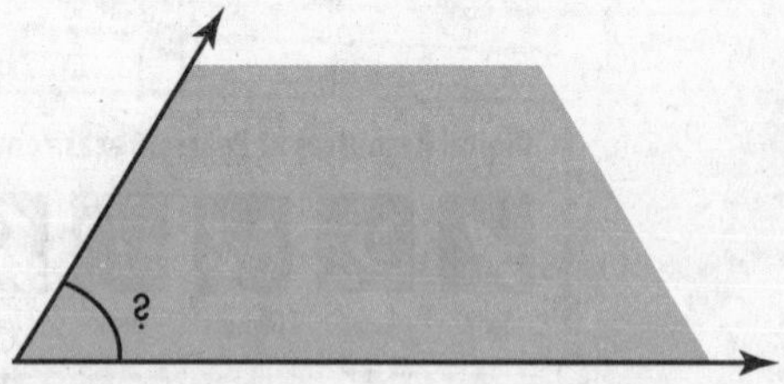
?

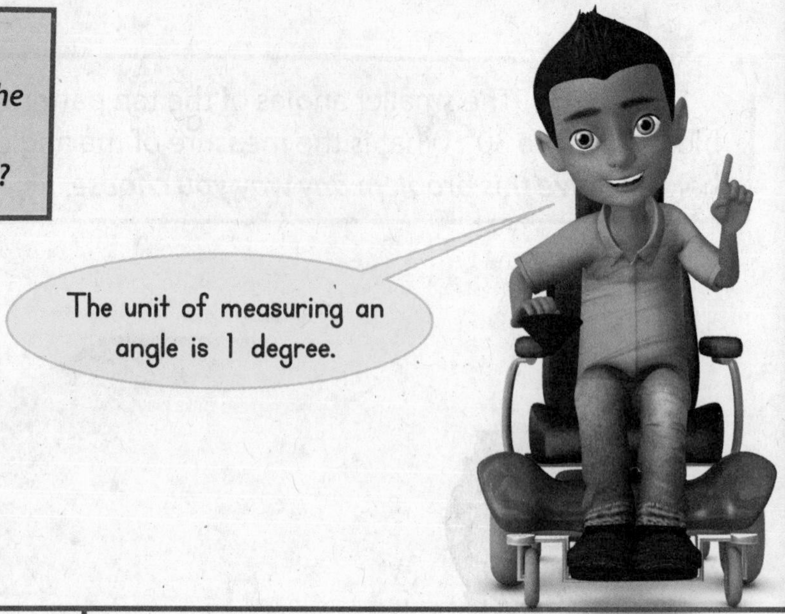
The unit of measuring an angle is 1 degree.

Use pattern blocks.

B Use an angle you know to find the measure of another angle.

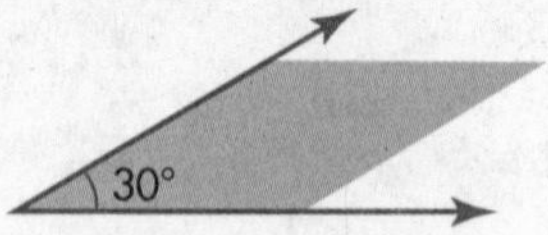
30°

The smaller angle of the tan pattern block measures 30°.

It turns through 30 unit angles of 1°.

C The smaller angle of the trapezoid pattern block matches two of the smaller angles of the tan pattern block. Each smaller angle is 30°.

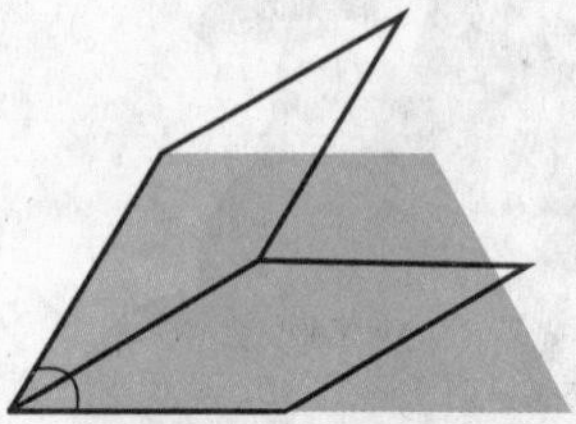

$2 \times 30° = 60°$

The measure of the angle is 60°.

Do You Understand?

Convince Me! How many 45° angles are there in a 180° angle? Tell how you decided.

© Pearson Education, Inc. 4

Name _____

In **1** and **2**, use angles you know to find the measure of each angle. Explain how the angles in the square can help.

1.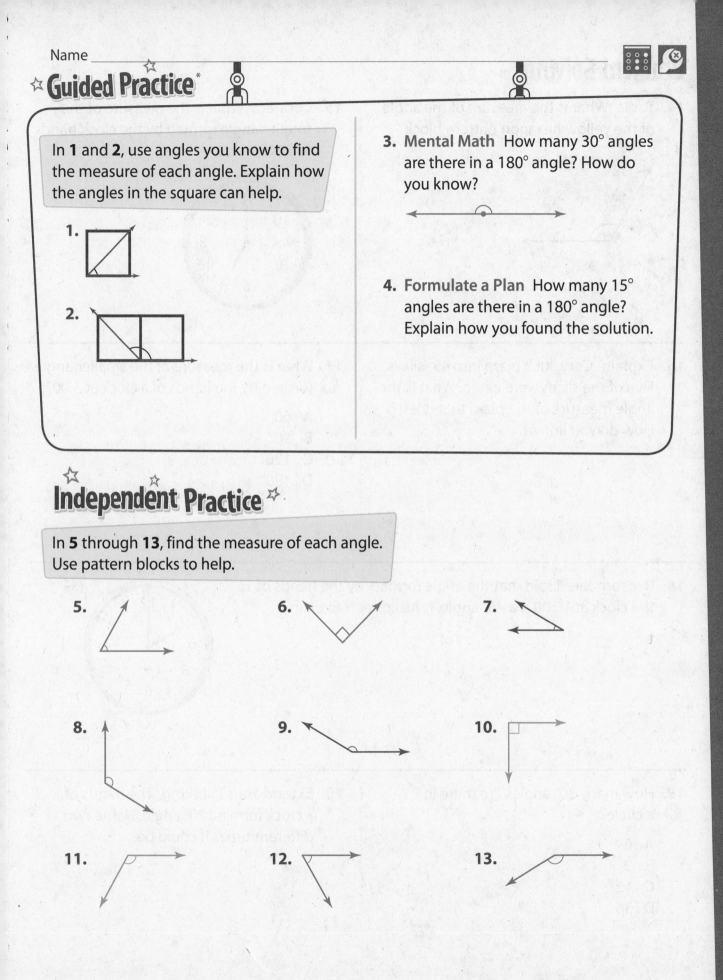

2.

3. **Mental Math** How many 30° angles are there in a 180° angle? How do you know?

4. **Formulate a Plan** How many 15° angles are there in a 180° angle? Explain how you found the solution.

☆ **Independent Practice** ☆

In **5** through **13**, find the measure of each angle. Use pattern blocks to help.

5.

6.

7.

8.

9.

10.

11.

12.

13.

Problem Solving

14. Tools What is the measure of the angle of the yellow hexagon pattern block?

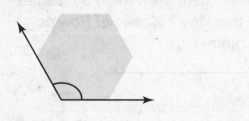

15. Connect What is the measure of the smaller angle formed by the clock hands at 5:00?

16. Explain Cory cut a pizza into 45° slices. Five of the slices were eaten. What is the angle measure of the pizza that is left? How do you know?

17. What is the measure of the smaller angle formed by the hands of a clock at 3:00?

- **A** 60°
- **B** 90°
- **C** 120°
- **D** 180°

18. Reason Jared said that the angle formed by the hands of the clock at 10:00 is a 45° angle. Is he correct? Explain.

19. How many 30° angles are there in a circle?

- **A** 6
- **B** 9
- **C** 12
- **D** 36

20. Extend Your Thinking The hands of a clock form a 120° angle. Name two different times it could be.

© Pearson Education, Inc. 4

Another Look!

Use the smaller angle of the tan pattern block.
It has a measure of 30°.

Find the measure of the angle below.

Two of the 30° angles will fit into the angle.

You can use an angle you know to find the measure of an angle you do not know.

Add: 30° + 30° = 60°. The measure of this angle is 60°.

In **1** through **3**, find the measure of each angle. Use pattern blocks to help.

120°

60°

150°   30°

1.

2.

3.

4. Choose 2 pattern blocks and place them next to each other. Trace two of their sides that form an angle. Label that angle's measure.

5. Extend Your Thinking A Ferris wheel has 12 cars that are equally spaced around the center. What is the measure of the angle formed between each of the arms that hold the Ferris wheel cars? Explain.

Remember that right angles divide a circle into 4 equal parts.

6. Construct Arguments A round classroom table top is made from 5 identical wedges. What is the measure of each angle formed on the inside of the classroom table? How do you know?

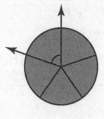

7. Draw a Picture How many 30° angles are there in a 150° angle? Draw a picture and justify your solution.

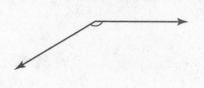

8. Mario cut a pizza into 9 equal slices. He put a slice of pizza on each of 5 plates. What is the measure for the angle of the slices that are left?

9. What is the measure of this angle?

A 105°
B 120°
C 135°
D 150°

© Pearson Education, Inc. 4

Name _____

Solve & Share

Find the measure of angle *ABC*.
Solve this problem any way you choose.

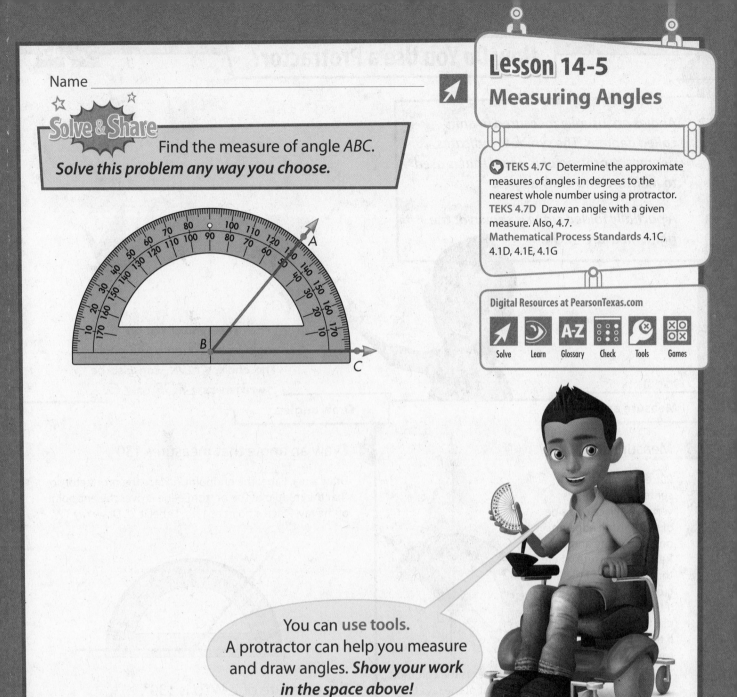

⊕ **TEKS 4.7C** Determine the approximate measures of angles in degrees to the nearest whole number using a protractor. **TEKS 4.7D** Draw an angle with a given measure. Also, 4.7. **Mathematical Process Standards** 4.1C, 4.1D, 4.1E, 4.1G

Digital Resources at PearsonTexas.com

Solve	Learn	Glossary	Check	Tools	Games

You can **use tools.**
A protractor can help you measure and draw angles. *Show your work in the space above!*

Look Back!

Select and Use Tools Use the protractor at the right to draw an angle that measures 110°.

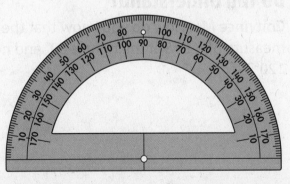

How Do You Use a Protractor?

Angles are usually measured in units called degrees. The symbol ° indicates degrees. A protractor is a tool that is used to measure and draw angles.

A partially folded crane is shown at the right. Measure ∠PQR.

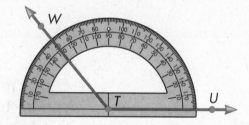

The symbol for an angle looks like an acute angle. The angle, ∠PQR, can also be written as ∠RQP or ∠Q.

Measure angles.

B Measure ∠PQR.

Place the protractor's center on the angle's vertex, Q. Place one side of the bottom edge on one side of the angle. Read the measure where the other side of the angle crosses the protractor. If the angle is acute, use the lesser number. If the angle is obtuse, use the greater number.

The measure of ∠PQR is 45°.

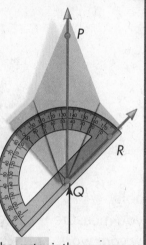

The vertex is the common endpoint of the rays that form the angle.

Draw angles.

C Draw an angle that measures 130°.

Draw a ray. Label the endpoint T. Place the protractor so that the middle of the bottom edge is over the endpoint of the ray. Place a point at 130°. Label it W. Draw ray TW.

The measure of ∠WTU is 130°.

Do You Understand?

Convince Me! How do you know that the measure of ∠UTS at the right is 60° and not 120°?

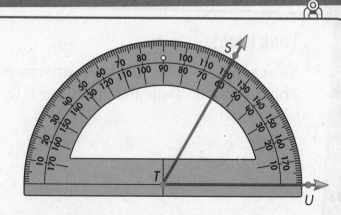

© Pearson Education, Inc. 4

Name _____

In **1** and **2**, use a protractor to measure each angle.

1. 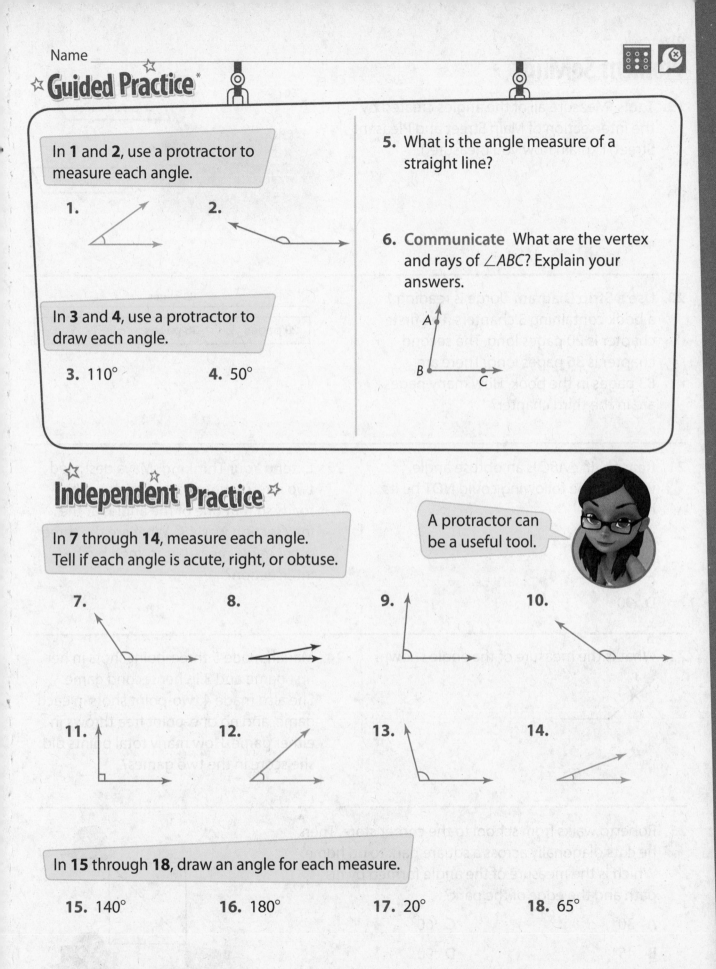   **2.**

In **3** and **4**, use a protractor to draw each angle.

3. 110°   **4.** 50°

5. What is the angle measure of a straight line?

6. Communicate What are the vertex and rays of ∠*ABC*? Explain your answers.

☆ **Independent Practice** ☆

In **7** through **14**, measure each angle. Tell if each angle is acute, right, or obtuse.

A protractor can be a useful tool.

7.   **8.**   **9.**   **10.**

11.   **12.**   **13.**   **14.**

In **15** through **18**, draw an angle for each measure.

15. 140°   **16.** 180°   **17.** 20°   **18.** 65°

Problem Solving

19. **Tools** Measure all of the angles created by the intersection of Main Street and Pleasant Street. Explain how you measured.

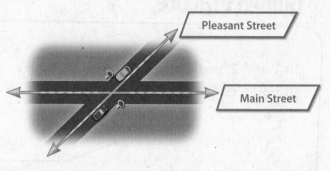

20. **Use a Strip Diagram** Jorge is reading a book containing 3 chapters. The first chapter is 20 pages long. The second chapter is 36 pages long. There are 83 pages in the book. How many pages are in the third chapter?

83 pages		
20 pages	36 pages	?

21. **Reason** If ∠ABC is an obtuse angle, which of the following could **NOT** be its measure?

A 140°
B 95°
C 105°
D 90°

22. **Extend Your Thinking** Maya designed two intersecting roads. She drew the roads so that one of the angles at the intersection was 45°. What are the three other angle measures formed by the intersection?

23. What is the measure of the angle shown?

24. Mariah made 5 three-point shots in her first game and 3 in her second game. She also made 4 two-point shots in each game, and no one-point free throws in either game. How many total points did she score in the two games?

25. Roberto walks from school to the corner store. Then he cuts diagonally across a square park to go home. Which is the measure of the angle formed by his path and the edge of the park?

A 30°   C 60°

B 45°   D 90°

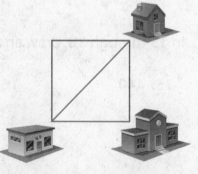

© Pearson Education, Inc. 4

Name _____

Another Look!

Use a protractor to measure or draw angles.

To measure an angle:

Place the protractor's center on the vertex of the angle, and the 0° mark on one of the angle's rays. Read the number in degrees where the other ray of the angle crosses the protractor. If the angle is acute, use the lesser number. If the angle is obtuse, use the greater number.

To draw an angle:

Draw a dot to show the vertex of the angle. Place the center of the protractor on the vertex point. Draw another point at the 0° mark and another point at the angle degree mark. Draw rays from the vertex through the other points.

In **1** through **3**, use a protractor to measure the angles.

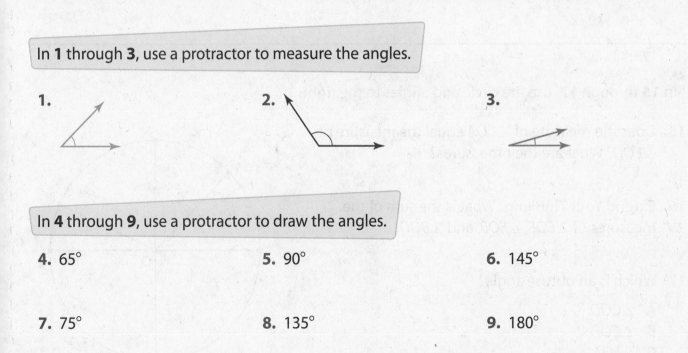

1.

2.

3.

In **4** through **9**, use a protractor to draw the angles.

4. 65°   **5.** 90°   **6.** 145°

7. 75°   **8.** 135°   **9.** 180°

10. Reason The angle is $\frac{1}{5}$ of the circle. What is the measure of the angle?

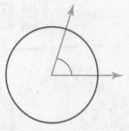

There are multiple ways to determine an angle's measure.

---

11. Rich sliced 3 pieces of pizza. Each piece of pizza forms a 20° angle. If all of the pieces were placed together, what would the measure of the angle be?

12. Stuart, Sam, Sue, and Sally have equal-sized pieces of pie. When the 4 pieces are put together, they form a 100° angle. What is the angle measure of each piece?

  A 100°
  B 50°
  C 25°
  D 15°

---

13. Explain Gail and 3 friends share half a pie. Each piece of pie is the same size. Gail believes each piece of pie has an angle measure of 25°. Is Gail correct? Explain.

14. Represent Joanie is making a map of the trails in the community park. Two of the trails start at the same point and form a 40° angle. Use a protractor to draw the angle that she will use on her map.

In **15** through **17**, use the circle and angles to the right.

15. Does the measure of ∠COA equal the measure of ∠EOD? What are their measures?

16. Extend Your Thinking What is the sum of the measures of ∠EOF, ∠FOB, and ∠BOC?

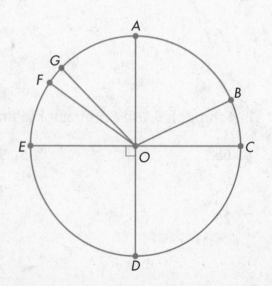

17. Which is an obtuse angle?

  A ∠COD
  B ∠COF
  C ∠FOA
  D ∠BOC

© Pearson Education, Inc. 4

Name _____

☆ ☆
Solve & Share

Draw a ray BC that divides ∠ABD. Measure each angle. **Solve this problem any way you choose.**

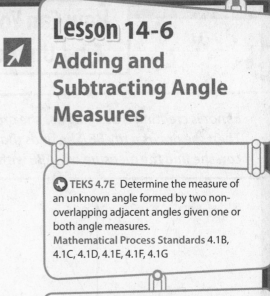

🟉 TEKS 4.7E Determine the measure of an unknown angle formed by two non-overlapping adjacent angles given one or both angle measures.
Mathematical Process Standards 4.1B, 4.1C, 4.1D, 4.1E, 4.1F, 4.1G

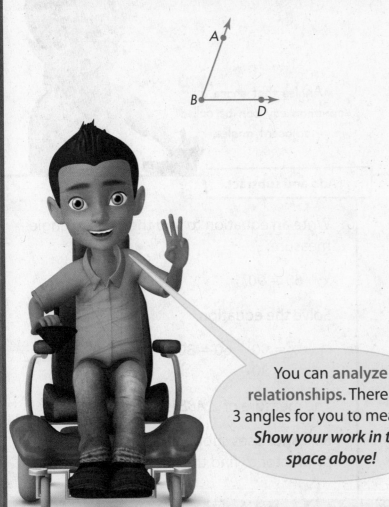

Digital Resources at PearsonTexas.com

Solve   Learn   Glossary   Check   Tools   Games

You can **analyze relationships.** There are 3 angles for you to measure. **Show your work in the space above!**

Look Back!

Create and Use Representations How can you relate the measures of the three angles above using an equation?

How Can You Add and Subtract to Find Unknown Angle Measures?

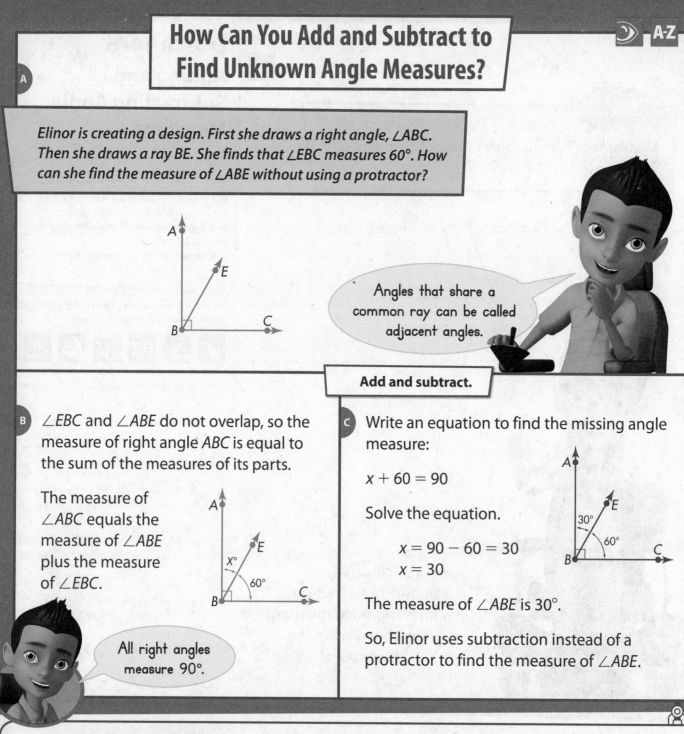

Elinor is creating a design. First she draws a right angle, ∠ABC. Then she draws a ray BE. She finds that ∠EBC measures 60°. How can she find the measure of ∠ABE without using a protractor?

Angles that share a common ray can be called adjacent angles.

Add and subtract.

B ∠EBC and ∠ABE do not overlap, so the measure of right angle ABC is equal to the sum of the measures of its parts.

The measure of ∠ABC equals the measure of ∠ABE plus the measure of ∠EBC.

All right angles measure 90°.

C Write an equation to find the missing angle measure:

$x + 60 = 90$

Solve the equation.

$x = 90 - 60 = 30$
$x = 30$

The measure of ∠ABE is 30°.

So, Elinor uses subtraction instead of a protractor to find the measure of ∠ABE.

Do You Understand?

Convince Me! What is the measure of ∠ABC if the measure of ∠DBC is 115°? How did you decide?

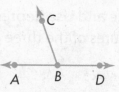

© Pearson Education, Inc. 4

☆ Guided Practice *

In **1** and **2**, use the diagram next to each exercise. Add or subtract to find the missing angle measure.

1. What is the measure of angle *EBC* if angle *ABE* measures 25°?

2. What is the measure of angle *AEB* if angle *CEB* measures 68°?

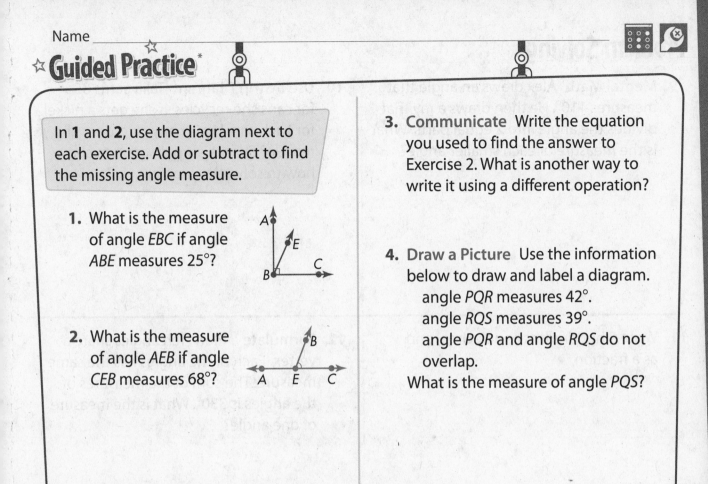

3. **Communicate** Write the equation you used to find the answer to Exercise 2. What is another way to write it using a different operation?

4. **Draw a Picture** Use the information below to draw and label a diagram.
   angle *PQR* measures 42°.
   angle *RQS* measures 39°.
   angle *PQR* and angle *RQS* do not overlap.
   What is the measure of angle *PQS*?

Independent Practice ☆

In **5** and **6**, use the diagram to the right.

5. What is the measure of angle *FGJ* if angle *JGH* measures 22°?

6. What is the measure of angle *KGF* if angle *EGK* measures 59°?

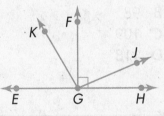

In **7** and **8**, use the diagram to the right.

7. Joe makes a design by turning quadrilateral *ABCD* 72° about point *A*. He rotates it 72° about point *A* again. What is the measure of angle *DAZ*?

8. The measure of angle *YAD* is 72°. The measure of angle *YAB* is 93°. What is the measure of angle *DAB*?

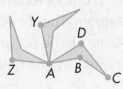

Problem Solving

9. Mental Math Alex draws an angle that measures 110°. He then draws a ray that divides the angle into 2 equal parts. What is the measure of each smaller angle?

10. Use a Strip Diagram Talia earns 85¢ for cans she recycles. If she gets a nickel for each can, how many cans does she recycle? Draw a strip diagram to show how to solve the problem.

11. Write 5 hundredths as a decimal and as a fraction.

12. Formulate a Plan Ten angles share a vertex. Each of the angles has the same measure. The sum of the measures of the angles is 330°. What is the measure of one angle?

13. Reason Angle *EFG* is divided into 2 smaller angles by a ray. One of the smaller angles formed is an obtuse angle and the other is an acute angle. Which of the following could **NOT** be the measure of angle *EFG*?

A 89°

B 98°

C 109°

D 118°

14. Check for Reasonableness Carla drew two acute adjacent angles labeled angle *JLK* and angle *KLM*. The two angles have different measures. Carla says angle *JLM* is greater than a right angle. Is it possible for Carla to be correct? Explain.

15. Extend Your Thinking Li uses pattern blocks to make a design. He puts 5 pattern blocks together, as shown in the diagram. The measure of angle *LJK* is 30°. Name all the 60° angles shown that have point *J* as a vertex.

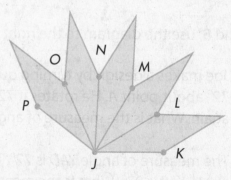

© Pearson Education, Inc. 4

Another Look!

You can add or subtract angle measures.

You can add to find angle measures.

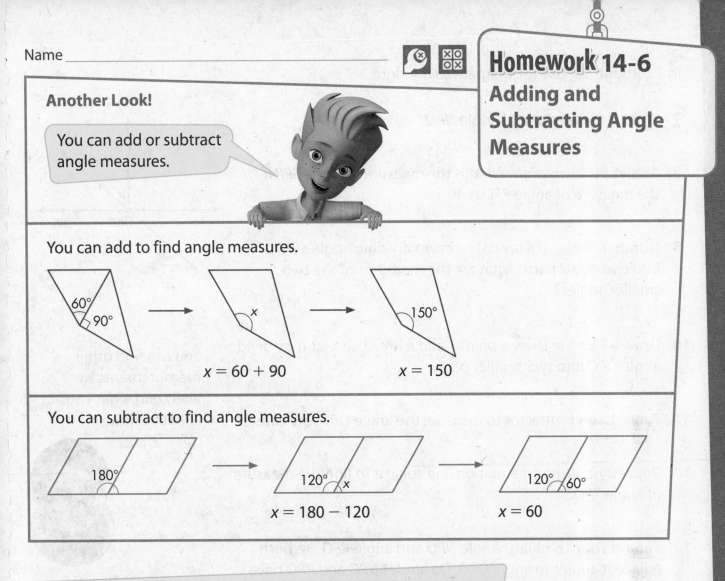

$x = 60 + 90$

$x = 150$

You can subtract to find angle measures.

$x = 180 - 120$

$x = 60$

In **1** through **5**, add or subtract to find the missing angle measure.

Angle *TUW* and angle *WUV* are adjacent angles. Together, they form angle *TUV*.

A diagram can help you see the relationships between angles.

	Angle Measure (°)		
	∠TUW	∠WUV	∠TUV
1.	120	45	
2.	105		155
3.	100		170
4.		25	150
5.	112	36	

6. **Reason** Jody places two tiles as shown to the right. She needs a third tile to fill the space between these two pieces. What angle measure does the third tile need to have in order to fill the space with no gaps?

60° 60°

7. What is the measure of angle *NPO*?

8. Analyze Information What is the measure of angle *SPR* if the measure of angle *RPQ* is 40°?

9. Number Sense If a ray *PM* is drawn dividing angle *SPN* into two equal parts, what are the measures of the two smaller angles?

10. Draw a Picture Draw a point *T* and a ray *PT* so that they divide angle *OPQ* into two smaller parts.

11. Tools Use a protractor to measure the angle *OPT* you formed.

12. Represent Write an equation and solve it to find the measure of angle *TPQ*.

13. Extend Your Thinking Angle *NPO* and angle *RPQ* are both adjacent angles to angle *QPO*. Do angles *NPO* and *RPQ* have the same measure? How do you know?

You can find other measurements by analyzing what you already know.

---

14. Angle *CMW* and angle *WML* together form angle *CML*. Angle *CMW* is a right angle. Which must be true about angle *CML*?

    A It is an acute angle.
    B It is a straight angle.
    C Its measure is greater than 90°.
    D Its measure is greater than 180°.

15. Explain Shane says a straight angle always has 180° degrees. Is he correct? Explain.

Name _____

☆ **Solve & Share** ☆

Sort the triangles shown in the workspace into two or more groups. Explain how you sorted them. **Solve this problem any way you choose.**

⭐ **TEKS 4.6C** Apply knowledge of right angles to identify acute, right, and obtuse triangles. Also, 4.6D.
Mathematical Process Standards 4.1A, 4.1D, 4.1G

Digital Resources at PearsonTexas.com

Solve	Learn	A-Z Glossary	Check	Tools	Games

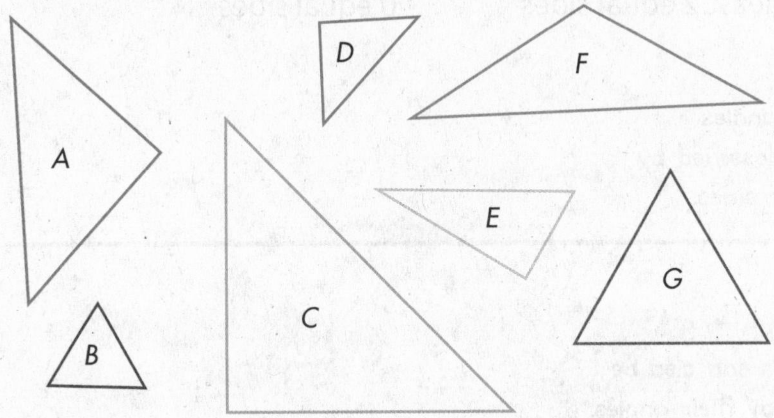

A

D

F

E

C

G

B

You can **construct arguments.** There are different ways of classifying triangles. **Show your work in the space above!**

Look Back!

Reason What is true about all 7 triangles that you sorted?

How Can You Classify Triangles?

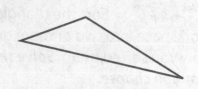

Equilateral triangle
3 equal sides

Isosceles triangle
At least 2 equal sides

Scalene triangle
0 equal sides

Triangles can be classified by their sides.

B

Triangles can also be classified by their angles.

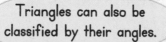

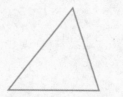

A right triangle has one right angle.

An acute triangle has three acute angles.
All of its angles measure less than a right angle.

An obtuse triangle has one obtuse angle.
One angle has a measure greater than a right angle.

Do You Understand?

Convince Me! Can a triangle have more than one obtuse angle? Explain.

© Pearson Education, Inc. 4

Name _____

In **1** through **4**, classify each triangle by its sides and then by its angles.

1.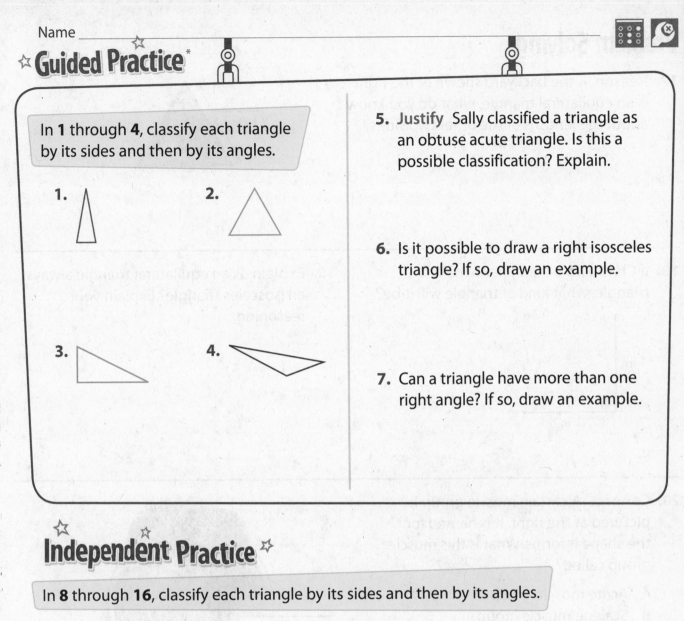

2.

3.

4.

5. **Justify** Sally classified a triangle as an obtuse acute triangle. Is this a possible classification? Explain.

6. Is it possible to draw a right isosceles triangle? If so, draw an example.

7. Can a triangle have more than one right angle? If so, draw an example.

Independent Practice ☆

In **8** through **16**, classify each triangle by its sides and then by its angles.

8.

9.

10.

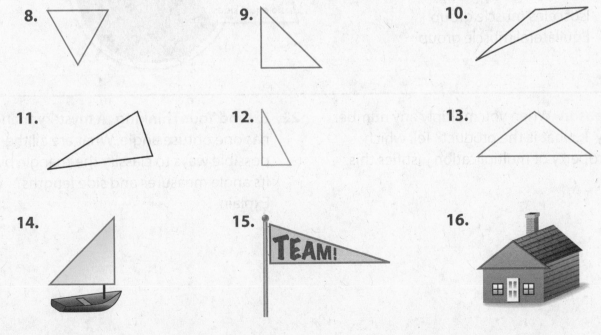

11.

12.

13.

14.

15.

16.

Problem Solving

17. Reason If the backyard shown at the right is an equilateral triangle, what do you know about the lengths of the other two sides?

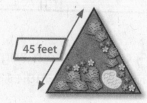
45 feet

---

18. If Chris uses a third line to make a triangle, what kind of triangle will it be?

1 in.

1 in.

19. Explain Is an equilateral triangle always an isosceles triangle? Explain your reasoning.

---

20. Connect A certain muscle group is pictured at the right. It is named for the shape it forms. What is this muscle group called?

A Acute muscle group
B Scalene muscle group
C Isosceles muscle group
D Equilateral muscle group

no equal sides

---

21. Reason When you multiply any number by 1, what is the product? Tell which property of multiplication justifies this.

22. Extend Your Thinking A mystery triangle has one obtuse angle. What are all the possible ways to classify the triangle by its angle measures and side lengths? Explain.

© Pearson Education, Inc. 4

Another Look!

Triangles can be classified by their angle measures, side lengths, or both!

Equilateral triangle
All sides are the same length.

Isosceles triangle
At least two sides are the same length.

Scalene triangle
No sides are the same length.

Right triangle
One angle is a right angle.

Acute triangle
All three angles are acute angles.

Obtuse triangle
One angle is an obtuse angle.

In **1** through **5**, classify each triangle by its sides and then by its angles.

1.

2.

3.

4.

5.

You can use tools to help you classify shapes.

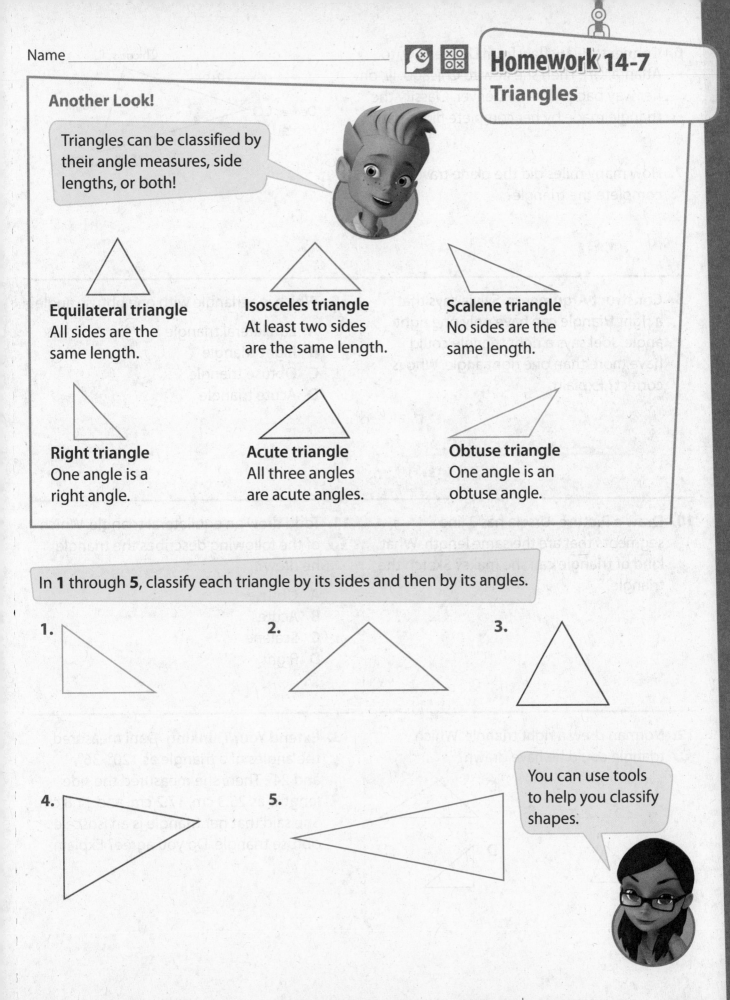

6. Connect Hilary flew from Denver, CO, to Atlanta, GA. Then she flew to Chicago, IL, on her way back home to Denver. Classify the triangle made by her complete flight path.

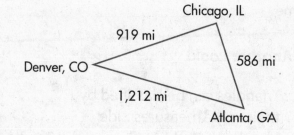

Chicago, IL
919 mi
586 mi
Denver, CO
1,212 mi
Atlanta, GA

7. How many miles did the plane travel to complete the triangle?

---

8. Construct Arguments Sylvia says that a right triangle can have only one right angle. Joel says a right triangle could have more than one right angle. Who is correct? Explain.

9. Which is a triangle with one obtuse angle?

A Equilateral triangle
B Right triangle
C Obtuse triangle
D Acute triangle

---

10. Draw a Picture Ursula has 3 line segments that are the same length. What kind of triangle can she make? Sketch the triangle.

11. Todd drew an equilateral triangle. Which of the following describes the triangle he drew?

A Obtuse
B Acute
C Scalene
D Right

---

12. Norman drew a right triangle. Which triangle could he have drawn?

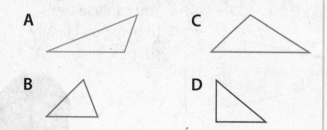

A

C

B

D

13. Extend Your Thinking Dani measured the angles of a triangle as 120°, 36°, and 24°. Then, she measured the side lengths as 25.3 cm, 17.2 cm, and 11.8 cm. She said that her triangle is an isosceles obtuse triangle. Do you agree? Explain.

© Pearson Education, Inc. 4

Name _____

Solve & Share

Draw three differently-shaped quadrilaterals that have opposite sides that are parallel. *Solve this problem any way you choose.*

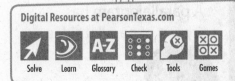

⭐ TEKS 4.6D Classify two-dimensional figures based on the presence or absence of parallel or perpendicular lines or the presence or absence of angles of a specified size.
Mathematical Process Standards 4.1B, 4.1D, 4.1E, 4.1F, 4.1G

Digital Resources at PearsonTexas.com

| Solve | Learn | Glossary | Check | Tools | Games |

You can **connect ideas**. You can use what you know about parallel lines and angles to draw shapes. *Show your work in the space above!*

Look Back!

Communicate What are names for the quadrilaterals you drew?

Quadrilaterals can be classified by their angles or pairs of sides. Which of the quadrilaterals shown have only one pair of parallel sides? Which have two pairs of parallel sides?

A parallelogram has 2 pairs of parallel sides.

A rectangle has 4 right angles. It is also a parallelogram.

A square has 4 right angles and all sides are the same length. It is a parallelogram, rectangle, and rhombus.

Quadrilaterals have properties that make them different from one another.

B

A rhombus is a quadrilateral that has opposite sides that are parallel and all of its sides are the same length.

A trapezoid is a quadrilateral with only one pair of parallel sides.

Trapezoids have only one pair of parallel sides. Parallelograms, rectangles, squares, and rhombuses all have two pairs of parallel sides.

Do You Understand?

Convince Me! Why is a trapezoid not a parallelogram? Explain.

© Pearson Education, Inc. 4

Another Example

Can a trapezoid have perpendicular sides?

Perpendicular sides form right angles. A trapezoid can have two right angles that form perpendicular sides. A trapezoid with two right angles is called a right trapezoid.

☆ Guided Practice *

In **1** through **4**, write all the names you can use for each quadrilateral.

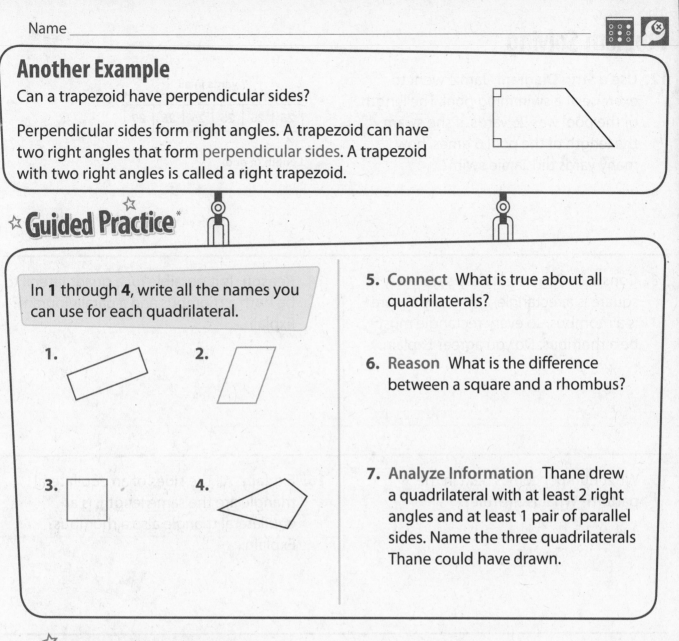

1.

2.

3.

4.

5. **Connect** What is true about all quadrilaterals?

6. **Reason** What is the difference between a square and a rhombus?

7. **Analyze Information** Thane drew a quadrilateral with at least 2 right angles and at least 1 pair of parallel sides. Name the three quadrilaterals Thane could have drawn.

Independent Practice *

In **8** through **11**, write all the names you can use for each quadrilateral.

8.

9.

10.

11.

HOME   0 10 20 30 40 50 40 30 20 10 0   AWAY

*For another example, see Set H on page 826.

Problem Solving

12. Use a Strip Diagram Jamie went to exercise at a swimming pool. The length of the pool was 25 yards. If she swam the length of the pool 6 times, how many yards did Jamie swim?

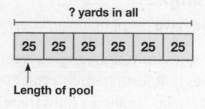

? yards in all

| 25 | 25 | 25 | 25 | 25 | 25 |

Length of pool

---

13. Construct Arguments Tia says every square is a rectangle, and every square is a rhombus, so every rectangle must be a rhombus. Do you agree? Explain.

14. Reason Is it possible for a quadrilateral to be both a rhombus and a parallelogram? Explain.

---

15. What number comes next in the pattern? What is the rule?

1, 4, 9, 16, ■

16. Explain All the sides of an equilateral triangle are the same length. Is an equilateral triangle also a rhombus? Explain.

---

17. In math class, Mr. Meyer drew a quadrilateral on the board. It had only one set of parallel sides and no right angles. Which shape was it?

A Square
B Rhombus
C Rectangle
D Trapezoid

18. Extend Your Thinking Could you use the formula for finding the perimeter of a square to find the perimeter of any other quadrilateral? Explain.

The formula for perimeter of a square is $P = 4 \times s$.

© Pearson Education, Inc. 4

Name _____

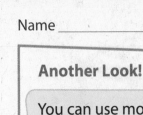
Another Look!

You can use more than one of these names for some quadrilaterals.

Quadrilateral
A polygon with 4 sides.

Rectangle
There are four right angles.

Parallelogram
Opposite sides are parallel.

Square
There are four right angles. All sides are the same length.

Rhombus
Opposite sides are parallel and all sides are the same length.

Trapezoid
There is only one pair of parallel sides.

In **1** through **4**, write the most specific name for each quadrilateral.

1.

2.

3.

4.

In **5** through **7**, write all the names you can use for each quadrilateral.

5.

6.

7.

8. **Represent** The figure at the right is called an Escher cube. It is named after the Dutch artist M. C. Escher. Look at the 7 white shapes created by this drawing. Tell what they are.

9. Which is **NOT** a parallelogram?
   ⭐
   A Rhombus
   B Rectangle
   C Square
   D Trapezoid

10. **Explain** Why can a square never be a trapezoid?

11. **Math and Science** Most plants use sunlight, water, and carbon dioxide to make their own food. This process is called photosynthesis and takes place mainly in the leaves of a plant. The leaves of a giant water lily can grow to be 8 feet across the center. How many inches is this?

8 feet across

12. **Justify** Rick drew a rhombus. What other names might describe the figure Rick drew based on what you know about quadrilaterals? Explain.

13. **Extend Your Thinking** Hannah has 11 toothpicks that are the same length. Name the types of triangles and quadrilaterals Hannah can make if she uses only one toothpick for each side of each figure.

© Pearson Education, Inc. 4

Lesson 14-9
Line Symmetry

TEKS 4.6B Identify and draw one or more lines of symmetry, if they exist, for a two-dimensional figure.
Mathematical Process Standards 4.1C, 4.1D, 4.1F, 4.1G

Digital Resources at PearsonTexas.com

Solve Learn Glossary Check Tools Games

...ways can you fold a square ...y on top of the other half? ...ay you choose.

...an use tools. ...quare piece of paper ...ve this problem? Show ...k in the space below!

no

...ationships What shapes can you form when you fold ...half?

What Is Line Symmetry?

A figure is symmetric if it can be folded on a line to form two halves that fit exactly on top of each other. The fold line is called a line of symmetry. The picture of the truck at the right has one line of symmetry.

How many lines of symmetry do other figures have?

Consider all the different ways a figure can be folded.

B A figure can have more than one line of symmetry.

C A figure can have many lines of symmetry.

D A figure can have lines of symmetry

Do You Understand?

Convince Me! Find two capital letters that have exactly one line of symmetry. Find two capital letters that have exactly two lines of symmetry.

© Pearson Education, Inc. 4

Name _____

In **1** and **2**, tell if each line is a line of symmetry.

1.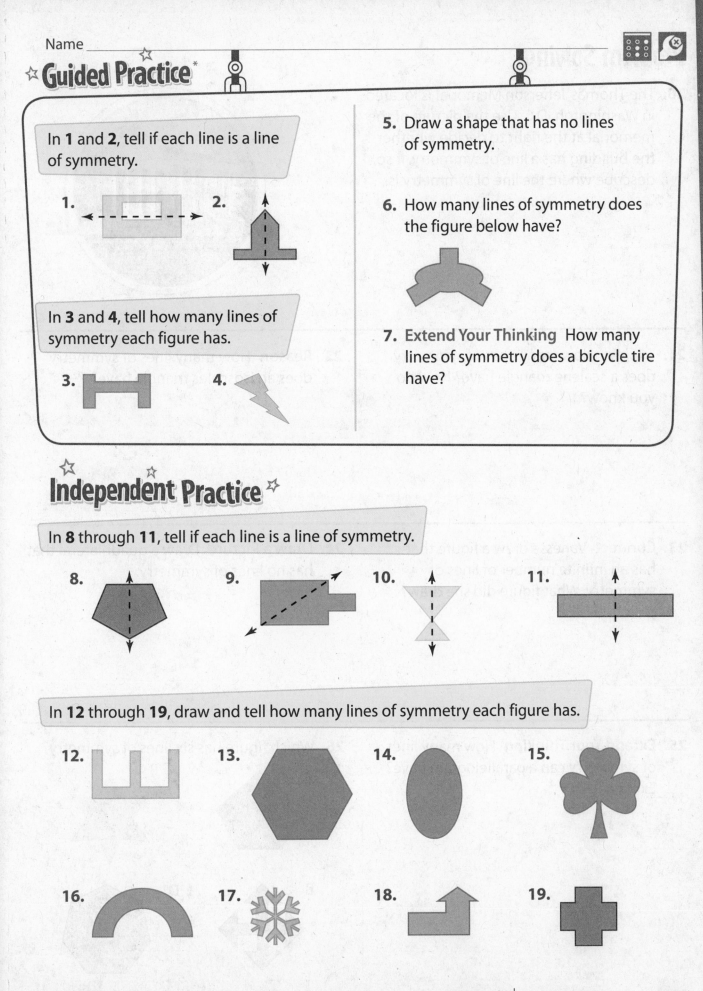

2.

5. Draw a shape that has no lines of symmetry.

6. How many lines of symmetry does the figure below have?

In **3** and **4**, tell how many lines of symmetry each figure has.

3.

4.

7. Extend Your Thinking How many lines of symmetry does a bicycle tire have?

Independent Practice ☆

In **8** through **11**, tell if each line is a line of symmetry.

8.

9.

10.

11.

In **12** through **19**, draw and tell how many lines of symmetry each figure has.

12.

13.

14.

15.

16.

17.

18.

19.

Problem Solving

20. The Thomas Jefferson Memorial is located in Washington, D.C. Use the picture of the memorial at the right to decide whether the building has a line of symmetry. If so, describe where the line of symmetry is.

21. Explain How many lines of symmetry does a scalene triangle have? How do you know?

22. Reason How many lines of symmetry does an isosceles triangle have?

23. Connect Vanessa drew a figure that has an infinite number of lines of symmetry. What figure did she draw?

24. Draw a Picture Draw a quadrilateral that has no lines of symmetry.

25. Extend Your Thinking How many lines of symmetry can a parallelogram have? Explain.

26. Which figure has six lines of symmetry?

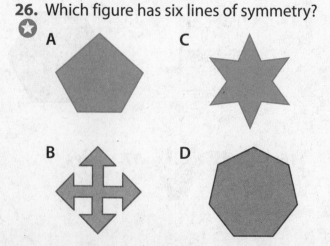

A   C

B   D

© Pearson Education, Inc. 4

Another Look!

Symmetric figures are figures that can be folded to make two halves that match each other.

How many lines of symmetry does a square have?

Step 1

If you fold the square along any of the 4 dashed lines, the two halves will lie on top of each other.

Step 2

A square has 4 lines of symmetry.

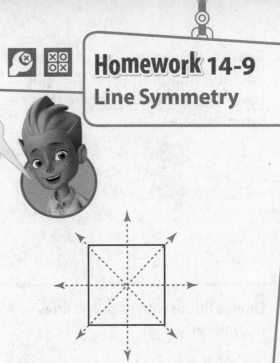

In **1** through **4**, tell how many lines of symmetry each figure has.

1.

2.

3.

4.

5. **Reason** How many lines of symmetry does the letter R have?

6. Draw all of the lines of symmetry for the figure.

7. **Draw a Picture** Complete the drawing so that the figure is symmetric.

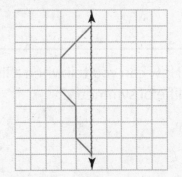

8. Reason How many lines of symmetry does the wagon wheel at the right have? Draw or explain where the lines of symmetry are.

9. Draw a figure with exactly 2 lines of symmetry.

Think about what the word "exactly" means.

10. Math and Science Animals are consumers in a food web. Animals depend on plants or other animals for food. Elephants are called herbivores because they eat only plants. An adult elephant in the wild may eat 150 kilograms of grass and other plants in one day. How many grams is this?

11. Which of the letters has exactly 2 lines of symmetry?

  A M
  B A
  C T
  D H

12. Extend Your Thinking Regular polygons have sides that are all the same length and angles that all have the same measure. An equilateral triangle and a square are regular polygons. How does the number of sides of a regular polygon relate to the number of lines of symmetry the figure has?

13. Explain How can you tell when a line is **NOT** a line of symmetry?

14. Personal Financial Literacy Stewart wants to buy two tickets to a soccer match. The tickets cost $15.75 each. Stewart has $25.73. How much more money does he need? Tell how you found the answer.

© Pearson Education, Inc. 4

Name ____________________

Solve & Share

True or False: **All right triangles have two sides of the same length.** Explain your answer. ***Solve this problem any way you choose.***

Problem Solving

Lesson 14-10
Use Reasoning

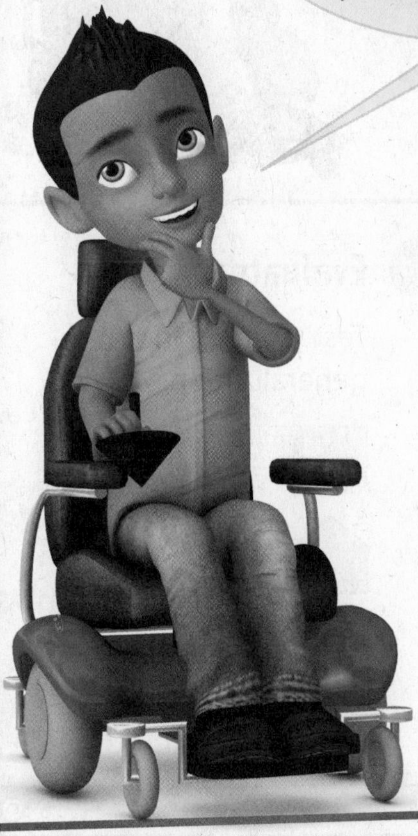

TEKS 4.1G Display, explain, and justify mathematical ideas and arguments using precise mathematical language in written or oral communication. Also, 4.6. Mathematical Process Standards 4.1B, 4.1C, 4.1D, 4.1F

Digital Resources at PearsonTexas.com

Solve | Learn | Glossary | Check | Tools | Games

You can formulate a plan. In math, if you can find one exception to a rule, then the rule is not true. ***Show your work in the space below!***

Look Back!

Construct Arguments True or False: **All right triangles have two acute angles.** Explain your answer.

How Can You Make and Test Generalizations?

A Analyze

What is true about all of these shapes?

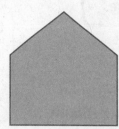

Use reasoning and look for things these shapes have in common.

B Analyze and Plan

Make a generalization:
The number of sides in each shape is the same as the number of angles.

Make another generalization:
They each have 2 right angles.

C Justify

Test your first generalization.

4 sides and 4 angles

5 sides and 5 angles

3 sides and 3 angles

It works.

D Evaluate

Test your second generalization.

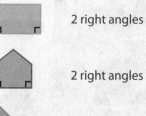

2 right angles

2 right angles

1 right angle

It is not correct.

Do You Understand?

Convince Me! Is the generalization that every four-sided polygon has at least one right angle correct? If not, draw a picture to show why not.

© Pearson Education, Inc. 4

☆ Guided Practice ☆

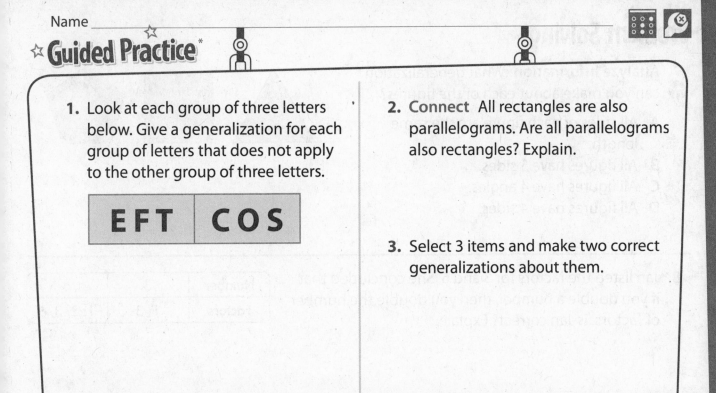

1. Look at each group of three letters below. Give a generalization for each group of letters that does not apply to the other group of three letters.

E F T | **C O S**

2. **Connect** All rectangles are also parallelograms. Are all parallelograms also rectangles? Explain.

3. Select 3 items and make two correct generalizations about them.

Independent Practice ☆

Solve.

4. **Communicate** Look at each group of numbers below. Compare the factors to each product. What generalization can you make about factors and products for counting numbers?

   $6 \times 8 = 48$ $46 \times 5 = 230$ $1 \times 243 = 243$

5. Write the factors for 8, 16, and 20. What generalization can you make about all multiples of 4?

6. Analyze the figures to the right. What connections can you make among the three figures?

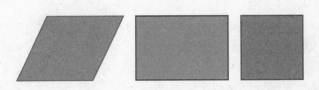

Problem Solving

7. Analyze Information What generalization can you make about each of the figures?

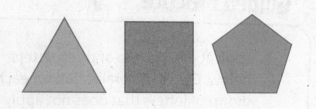

A All sides of each figure are the same length.

B All figures have 5 sides.

C All figures have 4 angles.

D All figures have 4 sides.

---

8. Jan listed the factors for 3 and 6. She concluded that if you double a number, then you double the number of factors. Is Jan correct? Explain.

Number	3	6
Factors	1, 3	1, 2, 3, 6

---

9. Which generalization about these figures is **NOT** true?

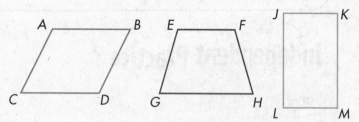

A Each figure is a quadrilateral.

B Each figure has two pairs of parallel sides.

C Each figure has at least two sides of equal length.

D Each figure has at least one line of symmetry.

---

10. Construct Arguments Susan said that all squares are rectangles and therefore all rectangles are squares. Is Susan correct? Explain.

11. Extend Your Thinking Draw a right triangle and an equilateral triangle. Describe how the angles in each are similar and how they are different.

© Pearson Education, Inc. 4

Another Look!

You can use reasoning to make generalizations about lines, angles, shapes, and other mathematical ideas. When you make a generalization, it is important to test it to see if it is correct.

Two lines on a plane will always intersect if they are not parallel.

Test: Lines go on and on in two directions, so extend the lines.

It's true. Any two lines on a plane that are not parallel will eventually intersect.

1. **Number Sense** Make a generalization about the sum of three odd numbers. Then test your generalization. Is it true?

If you can find one example of a generalization that is not true, then the generalization is not true.

2. Ronnie says that if all of the sides of a polygon have equal lengths, then all of the angles will have equal measures. He drew the figures below.

Is his generalization true? Explain.

3. **Construct Arguments** Write down five consecutive multiples of 5. What generalization can you make about all multiples of 5?

4. Which generalization is true about triangles?

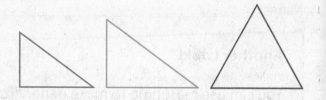

  A All triangles have 1 right angle.
  B All triangles have 3 angles and 3 sides.
  C All sides of a triangle are equal in length.
  D All the angles of a triangle are equal.

---

5. **Draw a Picture** Look at the pattern below. Draw the shape that would come next.

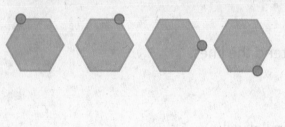

6. **Communicate** What generalization could be made about the triangles below?

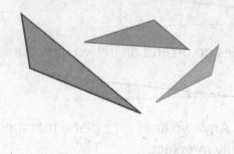

---

7. **Explain** Today, Mike flew from New York to Chicago. Last week, Brittany flew from New York to Los Angeles. On Tuesday, Lucinda flew from New York to Miami. Can you make a connection among the three friends and the flights they took?

8. **Extend Your Thinking** How can analyzing information and making a generalization help you identify a pattern?

---

9. **Justify** What generalization can you make about all the figures shown? Explain why your generalization is correct.

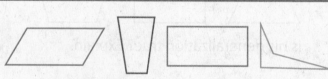

© Pearson Education, Inc. 4

Name _____

1. **Analyze Information** Angle *ABD* and angle *DBC* are adjacent right angles. Together, they form angle *ABC*. What type of angle is angle *ABC*?

Applying Math Processes
- How does this problem connect to previous ones?
- What is my plan?
- How can I use tools?
- How can I use number sense?
- How can I communicate and represent my thinking?
- How can I organize and record information?
- How can I explain my work?
- How can I justify my answer?

2. **Reason** Donny drew a quadrilateral. Donny's quadrilateral had two pairs of parallel sides. All four sides were of equal length and the angles connecting the sides were not right angles. What quadrilateral did Donny draw?

3. **Draw a Picture** A clock shows that the time is 5 o'clock. What type of angle is formed by the hands on the clock?

4. **Number Sense** Two adjacent angles form a 74° angle. The smaller angle measures 27°. What is the measure of the larger angle?

5. **Communicate** What are three geometric names that could be used to classify the figure below?

6. **Extend Your Thinking** Ashley drew a ray to divide a 124° angle into two acute angles. What are the measures of the smallest and largest angles she may have created when she drew the ray?

Error Search

Find each problem that is not correct. Circle what is wrong and rewrite the problem so it is correct.

1.	2.	3.	4.
29°	118°	180°	103°
+ 42°	+ 53°	− 115°	− 14°
61°	171°	75°	89°

Over or Under

Tools Circle the correct answer. Use a protractor where needed.

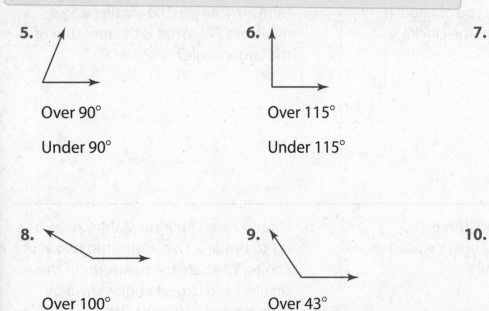

5.

Over 90°

Under 90°

6.

Over 115°

Under 115°

7.

Over 45°

Under 45°

8.

Over 100°

Under 100°

9.

Over 43°

Under 43°

10.

Over 51°

Under 51°

© Pearson Education, Inc. 4

Set A pages 761–766

Pairs of lines are given special names.

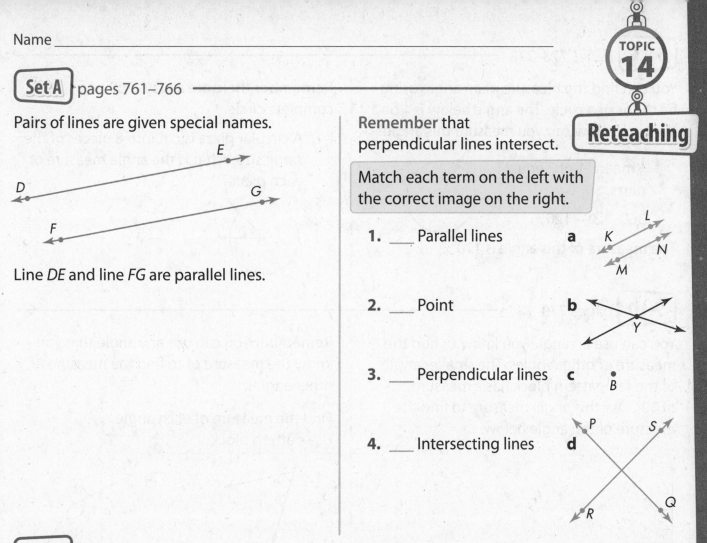

Line *DE* and line *FG* are parallel lines.

Remember that perpendicular lines intersect.

Match each term on the left with the correct image on the right.

1. ___ Parallel lines   **a**

2. ___ Point   **b**

3. ___ Perpendicular lines   **c**

4. ___ Intersecting lines   **d**

Set B pages 767–772

Geometric terms are used to describe figures.

A ray has one endpoint and continues on forever in one direction.

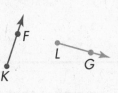

An angle is formed by intersecting lines or by two rays with a common endpoint.

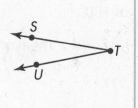

Remember that a line segment does not continue beyond its endpoints.

Use geometric terms to describe what is shown.

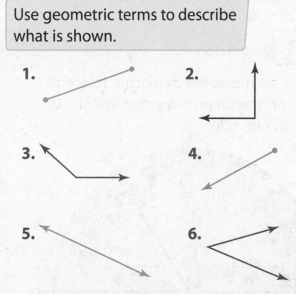

1.   2.

3.   4.

5.   6.

Set C pages 773–778

You can find the measure of an angle using fractions of a circle. The angle below is $\frac{1}{3}$ of the circle. How can you measure this angle?

$\frac{1}{3}$ means 1 of 3 equal parts.

$360 \div 3 = 120$

The measure of this angle is 120°.

Remember there are always 360° in a complete circle.

1. A circular pizza is cut into 8 pieces of the same size. What is the angle measure of each piece?

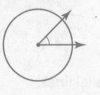

Set D pages 779–784

You can use an angle you know to find the measure of other angles. The smaller angle of the tan pattern block has a measure of 30°. Use this angle measure to find the measure of the angle below.

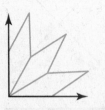

Three of the 30° angles will fit into the angle. Add: $30° + 30° + 30° = 90°$.

The measure of this angle is 90°.

Remember you can use any angle that you know the measure of to find the measure of other angles.

Find the measure of each angle. Use pattern blocks.

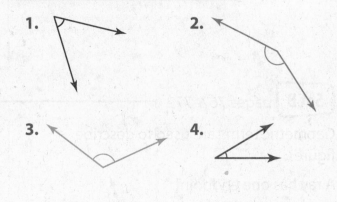

1.

2.

3.

4.

Set E pages 785–790

Angles are measured by placing the center of the protractor on the vertex and the 0° mark on one side.

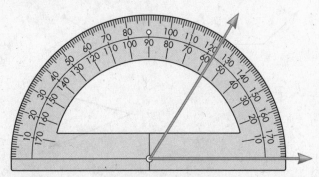

The measure of this angle is 57°.

Remember that a straight line forms an angle of 180°.

In **1** and **2**, measure the angles.

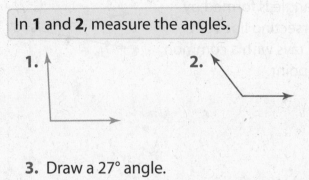

1.

2.

3. Draw a 27° angle.

© Pearson Education, Inc. 4

Reteaching
Continued

Set F pages 791–796

If two angles share a ray, then the sum of the measures of the angles is equal to the measure of the larger angle that is made up by the two angles.

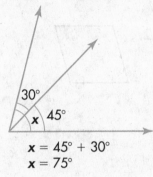

$x = 45° + 30°$
$x = 75°$

You can use subtraction to find the measure of the missing angle in the figure shown below.

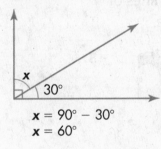

$x = 90° - 30°$
$x = 60°$

Remember you can subtract to find angle measures.

1. Angle *ABC* and angle *CBD* together make the larger angle *ABD*. Complete the table for different measures of angle *ABD*.

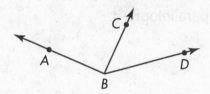

Angle Measure (degrees)		
∠ABC	∠CBD	∠ABD
100°	45°	
95°		155°
105°		170°
	25°	140°
122°	36°	

2. A ray is drawn that splits a right angle into two smaller angles. One angle measures 27°. What is the measure of the other angle?

Set G pages 797–802

Triangles can be classified by their sides and angles.

Two sides are the same length, and each angle measures less than a right angle. It is an isoceles, acute triangle.

Remember that scalene triangles have no equal sides.

Classify each triangle by its sides and then by its angles.

1.   2.

Set H pages 803–808

Name the quadrilateral.

Opposite sides are parallel. There are no right angles. All sides are not the same length. It is a parallelogram.

Remember that a quadrilateral can be a rectangle, square, trapezoid, parallelogram, or rhombus.

Write all the names you can use for each quadrilateral.

1.    2.

Set I pages 809–814

How many lines of symmetry does the figure have?

Fold the figure along the dashed line. The two halves are equal and fit one on top of the other.

It has 1 line of symmetry.

Remember that figures can have many lines of symmetry.

Draw and tell how many lines of symmetry for each figure.

1.   2. **C**   3.

Set J pages 815–820

What is true about all of these shapes?

The number of sides in each is the same as the number of angles. Test your generalization.

4 sides,   3 sides,   4 sides,
4 angles   3 angles   4 angles

Remember to test your generalizations.

1. Look at each group of numbers below. Give a generalization for each group of numbers that does not apply to the other group of three numbers.

1 4   **3**
  7   **6 9**

© Pearson Education, Inc. 4

Name _____

1. Which type of triangle has no equal sides?

   A Isosceles

   B Scalene

   C Equilateral

   D None of the above

4. Which geometric term best describes the light that shines from a flashlight?

   A Point   **C** Line segment

   B Ray   **D** Plane

---

2. $\angle ABC$ has a measure of 40°. $\angle CBD$ has a measure of 23°. The angles share a ray and form $\angle ABD$. Which is the measure of $\angle ABD$?

   A 17°

   B 27°

   C 63°

   D 73°

5. Which quadrilateral has only one pair of parallel sides?

   A Square

   B Parallelogram

   C Trapezoid

   D Rhombus

---

3. Laney used drinking straws in art to form a figure that had perpendicular sides. Which could be her figure?

   A

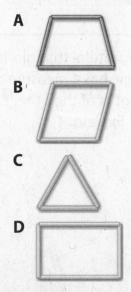

   B

   C

   D

6. Thomas chose these shapes.

He said that the following shapes did not belong with the ones he chose.

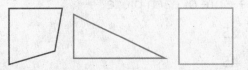

What generalization can you make about the shapes Thomas chose?

7. Which stick is parallel to stick *S*?

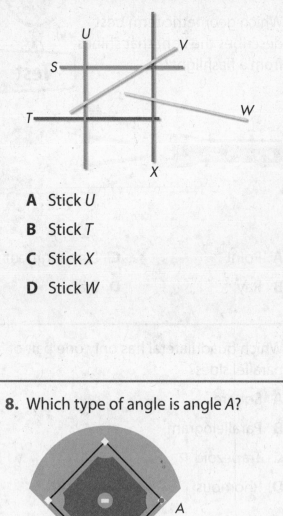

A Stick *U*

B Stick *T*

C Stick *X*

D Stick *W*

---

8. Which type of angle is angle *A*?

A

A Obtuse   **C** Right

B Acute   **D** Straight

---

9. Gisela cuts an apple pie into 8 pieces of the same size. Which is the angle measure of each piece?

A 25°

B 45°

C 80°

D 90°

---

10. Four of Mrs. Li's students decorated a bulletin board with the shapes shown below. Who made a shape with 8 lines of symmetry?

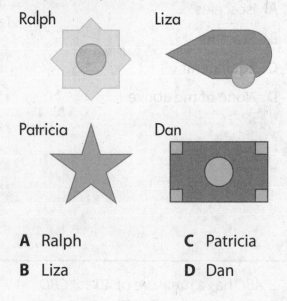

Ralph   Liza

Patricia   Dan

A Ralph   **C** Patricia

B Liza   **D** Dan

---

11. Two wooden roof beams in a barn meet at a 60° angle. Draw an angle to represent how the beams meet.

---

12. Triangle *ABC* is an equilateral triangle. If one side of the triangle has a measure of 4 ft, what are the lengths of the other two sides of the triangle? Explain.

© Pearson Education, Inc. 4

13. Terry is measuring an angle using pattern blocks. The smaller angle of each of the pattern blocks shown below measures 30°. What is the measure of the angle shown?

16. Anthony cuts a round pizza into 6 equal slices. He eats 4 slices. Which is the angle measure of the remaining portion of the pizza?

A 30°

B 60°

C 90°

D 120°

14. What is the measure of the angle shown below?

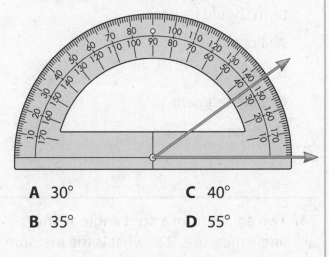

A 30°   **C** 40°

B 35°   **D** 55°

17. Daphne thinks that a square is an example of every other type of quadrilateral. Daphne is incorrect. Which quadrilateral can **NOT** be a square?

A Rectangle

B Parallelogram

C Trapezoid

D Rhombus

15. Suzi is trying to determine which types of angles can be used to form a triangle. Which set of angles could form a triangle?

A Two right angles, one acute angle

B One obtuse angle, one right angle, one acute angle

C Two obtuse angles, one acute angle

D One right angle, two acute angles

18. Which is the measure of an angle that cuts off $\frac{1}{4}$ of a circle?

A 40°

B 45°

C 60°

D 90°

19. If the measure of ∠WXZ is 33°, what is the measure of ∠ZXY?

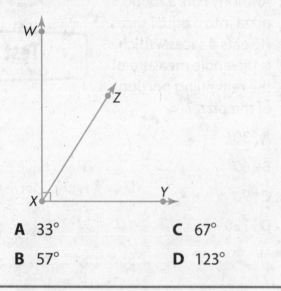

A 33°   **C** 67°

B 57°   **D** 123°

20. Juanita measures the angles of a triangle. She determines that all three are acute angles. Which could be the largest angle in the triangle Juanita measured?

A 76°

B 90°

C 96°

D 120°

21. The blueprint for the new North High School shows the first floor in the shape of a rectangle. What is the measure, in degrees, of each angle formed by the outer walls of the school?

22. Angle ABD is a right angle. Ray BC divides angle ABD into two equal angles. Which is the measure of angle ABC?

A 30°

B 45°

C 50°

D 60°

23. David's teacher asks him to describe his desktop using a geometric term. Which term should he use?

A Point

B Line

C Line segment

D Plane

24. Two angles form a right angle. If one angle measures 22°, what is the measure, in degrees, of the other angle?

© Pearson Education, Inc. 4

Data Analysis

Essential Questions:
What are ways to display data?
How can graphs be used to display data and answer questions?

Adaptations enable organisms to survive in their environment.

The insect in this picture is hiding to avoid being eaten.

It's like playing hide-and-seek! Here's a project on adaptations and data analysis.

Math and Science Project: Animal Adaptations

Do Research Use the Internet or other sources to find information about how some plants and animals adapt to survive.

Journal: Write a Report Include what you found. Also in your report:

- Include an example of an insect that uses camouflage.

- Describe an example of how a plant's leaves are adapted to help it live.

- Include an example of a data display you saw while researching.

Name _____

Review What You Know

Vocabulary

Choose the best term from the box.
Write it on the blank.

> • decimal
>
> • fraction
>
> • mixed number
>
> • whole number

1. A _____ has a whole number and a fraction.

2. A _____ uses place value to show parts less than one whole.

3. A _____ has a numerator and a denominator.

Comparing Units of Time

In **4** through **7**, write >, <, or = in the ◯.

4. 50 weeks ◯ 1 year

5. 3 years ◯ 365 days

6. 4 weeks ◯ 40 days

7. 48 hours ◯ 2 days

Measuring Angles

In **8** and **9**, tell the measure of the angle created by the clock hands.

8.   **9.**

Interpreting Graphs

In **10** and **11**, use the bar graph.

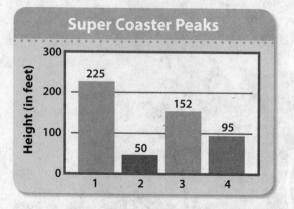

Super Coaster Peaks

10. What is the difference between the heights of Peak 1 and Peak 3?

11. **Explain** Why is this statement incorrect? The heights of Peak 2 and Peak 4 have the greatest difference.

© Pearson Education, Inc. 4

My Word Cards

Use the examples for each word on the front of the card to help complete the definitions on the back.

frequency table

Age	Tally	Frequency
8	卌 /	6
9	卌 卌	10
10	卌	5
11	//	2

frequency

Age	Tally	Frequency
8	卌 /	6
9	卌 卌	10
10	卌	5
11	//	2

dot plot

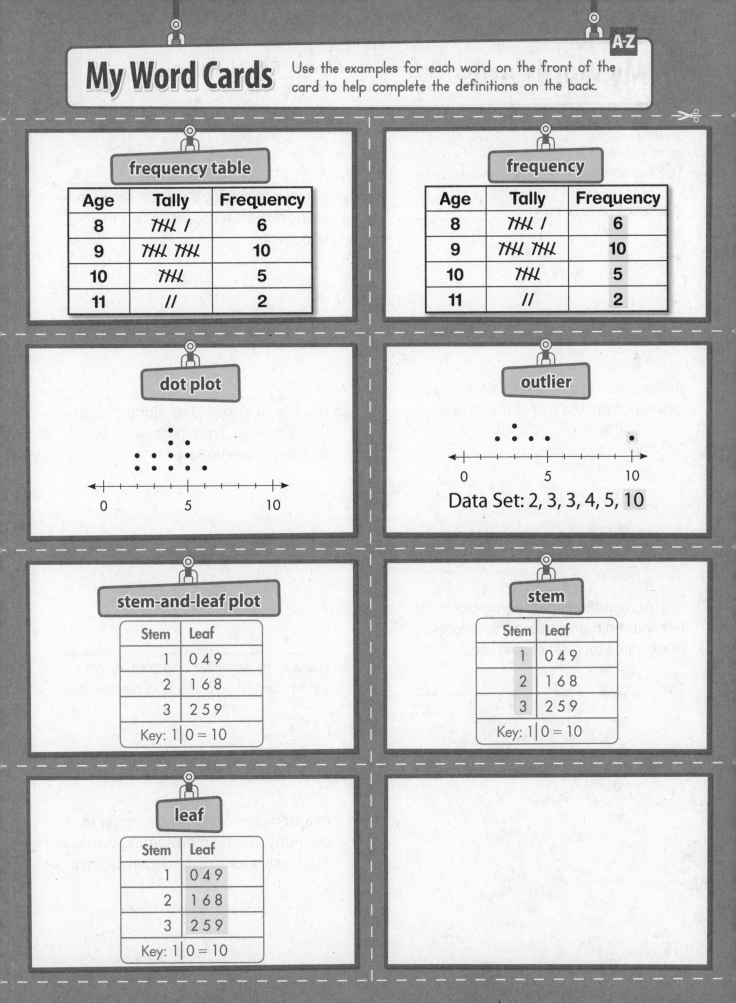

outlier

Data Set: 2, 3, 3, 4, 5, 10

stem-and-leaf plot

Stem	Leaf
1	0 4 9
2	1 6 8
3	2 5 9
Key: 1	0 = 10

stem

Stem	Leaf
1	0 4 9
2	1 6 8
3	2 5 9
Key: 1	0 = 10

leaf

Stem	Leaf
1	0 4 9
2	1 6 8
3	2 5 9
Key: 1	0 = 10

My Word Cards

Complete each definition. Extend learning by writing your own definitions.

The number of times a response occurs in a set of data is its _____.

A _____ is a way to display data that shows how many times a response occurs in a set of data.

Any number in a data set that is very different from the rest of the numbers is called an _____.

A _____ is a way to display data along a number line, where each dot represents one number in a set of data.

In a stem-and-leaf plot, a number in the left column representing the greatest place value for a set of data is called the _____.

A _____

_____ is a way to organize and display data using numerical order and place value.

In a stem-and-leaf plot, a number in the right column representing the least place value for a set of data is called a _____.

© Pearson Education, Inc. 4

☆ Guided Practice*

In **1** and **2**, use the frequency table of hours worked by students in a class to complete a project.

Hours	Tally	Frequency
$2\frac{1}{2}$	⁊⁊⁊⁊ ///	8
$2\frac{3}{4}$	⁊⁊⁊⁊ //	7
3	//	2
$3\frac{1}{4}$	⁊⁊⁊⁊ /	6
$3\frac{1}{2}$	////	4

1. How much time was most often needed to complete the project?

   $2\frac{1}{2}$ ✓

2. How many students are in the class?

   27 ✓

3. **Communicate** When making a frequency table that uses whole numbers and fractions, how can you organize the numbers?

   Lau as

   X

4. **Explain** Look at the fish lengths caught by Rafa's class on the previous page. How does organizing the data in a frequency table help you answer the question asked?

   you know what it is

☆ Independent Practice ☆

Leveled Practice In **5** through **8**, use the data about the amount of flour used in different cookie recipes.

5. Complete the frequency table below the data.

6. How many cookie recipes are represented in the data table?

   15

7. Which amount of flour is most often used in the cookie recipes shown?

   3 cups X

8. How many recipes shown use more than 2 cups of flour?

   7 ✓

Flour Used in Cookie Recipes

$1\frac{3}{4}$ cups	$2\frac{1}{2}$ cups	3 cups
$2\frac{1}{2}$ cups	3 cups	$1\frac{3}{4}$ cups
3 cups	$1\frac{3}{4}$ cups	$1\frac{3}{4}$ cups
$1\frac{3}{4}$ cups	$1\frac{3}{4}$ cups	3 cups
$1\frac{3}{4}$ cups	$2\frac{1}{2}$ cups	$1\frac{3}{4}$ cups

Flour Used	Tally	Frequency
$1\frac{3}{4}$	⊔⊔X I	7 X
$2\frac{1}{2}$	///	3 ✓
3	⁊⁊⁊⁊	5 X

Problem Solving

9. Analyze Information
Make a frequency table to organize the data shown at the right. What is the most common age when children are required to be in school for the states shown?

DATA	Ages at Which Some State Laws Require Children to Be in School									
	State	**Age**	**State**	**Age**	**State**	**Age**	**State**	**Age**	**State**	**Age**
	CA	6	KS	7	MO	7	NH	6	TX	6
	DE	5	MA	6	MT	7	OH	6	UT	6
	FL	6	MD	5	NC	7	OR	7	VA	5
	ID	7	ME	7	ND	7	PA	8	WA	8
	IN	7	MN	7	NE	7	TN	6	WI	6

10. Which is more common: states that require children to be in school at age 5, or age 8?

11. How many more states require children to be in school at either age 6 or age 7 than other ages?

12. Represent What number is shown by the tally marks 𝈫𝈫 ////?

A 5
B 7
C 8
D 9

13. Estimation Jorge collects sports cards. He displays his cards in an album. There are 63 pages in the album that each hold 9 cards. Use compatible numbers to estimate the number of cards in the album if all of the pages are full.

14. Students in Ms. Johnson's class have shoe sizes shown in the table to the right. Complete the missing parts of the table. Which is the most common shoe size?

15. Which is the least common shoe size of those shown?

16. Extend Your Thinking Two more students said that they wear a size 6 shoe. Including these students in the data, which is the most common shoe size?

Shoe Size	Tally	Frequency
4	/	
$4\frac{1}{2}$		2
5	//	
$5\frac{1}{2}$		5
6		3
$6\frac{1}{2}$	//	
7	///	
$7\frac{1}{2}$	//	
9		2

© Pearson Education, Inc. 4

Another Look!

The table below shows the actual weights of bags of oranges on a shelf in a supermarket.

DATA

Weights of Bags of Oranges				
4 pounds	$3\frac{7}{8}$ pounds	$4\frac{1}{8}$ pounds	$3\frac{7}{8}$ pounds	4 pounds
$4\frac{1}{8}$ pounds	$4\frac{1}{4}$ pounds	$3\frac{7}{8}$ pounds	$4\frac{1}{8}$ pounds	$3\frac{7}{8}$ pounds
$3\frac{7}{8}$ pounds	$3\frac{7}{8}$ pounds	$3\frac{7}{8}$ pounds	$3\frac{7}{8}$ pounds	$4\frac{1}{8}$ pounds
$4\frac{1}{8}$ pounds	$4\frac{1}{4}$ pounds	$4\frac{1}{8}$ pounds	$4\frac{1}{4}$ pounds	$3\frac{7}{8}$ pounds
$4\frac{1}{8}$ pounds	$4\frac{1}{8}$ pounds	$4\frac{1}{8}$ pounds	$4\frac{1}{8}$ pounds	4 pounds

You can make a tally chart of the data. Each tally represents 1 bag of oranges. Then you can add a frequency column to complete a frequency table.

Frequency tables can help organize data and solve problems.

Bags of Oranges		
Weight	**Tally**	**Frequency**
$3\frac{7}{8}$ pounds	卌 ////	9
4 pounds	///	3
$4\frac{1}{8}$ pounds	卌 卌	10
$4\frac{1}{4}$ pounds	///	3

1. The prices of items at a concession stand are listed below. Use the information to complete the frequency table to the right.

   $1.00 $1.50 $1.25 $0.75 $2.50 $3.00
   $1.50 $0.75 $1.50 $2.00 $1.50 $1.25

Price	Tally	Frequency
$0.75		
$1.00		
$1.25		
$1.50		
$2.00		
$2.50		
$3.00		

2. Which price is most common for the items sold at the concession stand?

3. How many different items are sold at the concession stand?

4. How many times as many $1.50 items are there as $0.75 items?

5. Analyze Information The heights of all the players on the South High School basketball team are shown in the frequency table at the right. Which statement is true?

A There are more players taller than 6 feet than there are players shorter than 6 feet.

B The most common height of a player is 6 feet.

C There are no players $6\frac{1}{2}$ feet tall.

D All of the above.

Height	Tally	Frequency
$5\frac{5}{6}$ ft	//	2
$5\frac{11}{12}$ ft	//	2
6 ft	THL	5
$6\frac{1}{6}$ ft	///	3
$6\frac{1}{4}$ ft	/	1
$6\frac{5}{12}$ ft	/	1

6. Explain How does making a frequency table help you organize data?

7. Represent Which number is represented by THL THL THL ////?

Video Game Prices

$42.49	$35.00	$54.99	$29.99
$42.49	$44.99	$44.99	$49.99
$39.99	$42.49	$44.99	$49.99
$44.99	$49.99	$42.49	$44.99
$42.49	$46.90	$44.99	$49.99
$54.99	$56.99	$36.99	$39.99
$54.99	$39.99	$39.99	

Price	Tally	Frequency
$29.99		
$35.00		
$36.99		
$39.99		
$42.49		
$44.99		
$46.90		
$49.99		
$54.99		
$56.99		

8. Complete the frequency table for the data of video game prices.

9. What is the lowest-priced game?

10. What is the most common price of a game?

11. Extend Your Thinking The letters *a, e, i, o, u* are vowels. All other letters are consonants. How many letters in the words *United States Constitution* are vowels? How many are consonants? Make a frequency table to find out.

© Pearson Education, Inc. 4

Name _____

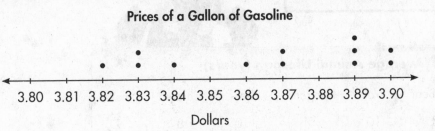

Solve & Share   Emily took a survey of 12 gas stations in her town. She plotted the cost of a gallon of gasoline in the dot plot shown below. What is the difference between the most expensive and the least expensive gallon of gas? *Solve this problem any way you choose.*

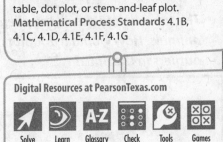
⭐ **TEKS 4.9B** Solve one- and two-step problems using data in whole number, decimal, and fraction form in a frequency table, dot plot, or stem-and-leaf plot. Mathematical Process Standards 4.1B, 4.1C, 4.1D, 4.1E, 4.1F, 4.1G

Prices of a Gallon of Gasoline

```
                      •
         •            •        •       •
    •    •    •       •    •   •   •   •
 ───┼────┼────┼────┼────┼────┼────┼────┼────┼────┼────┼──►
  3.80 3.81 3.82 3.83 3.84 3.85 3.86 3.87 3.88 3.89 3.90
                      Dollars
```

Digital Resources at PearsonTexas.com

| Solve | Learn | Glossary | Check | Tools | Games |

You can **use representations.** A dot plot can help organize data along a number line. *Show your work in the space above!*

Look Back!

Number Sense What was the most frequent price of a gallon of gas in the survey?

How Can You Use Data in a Dot Plot to Solve Problems? A-Z

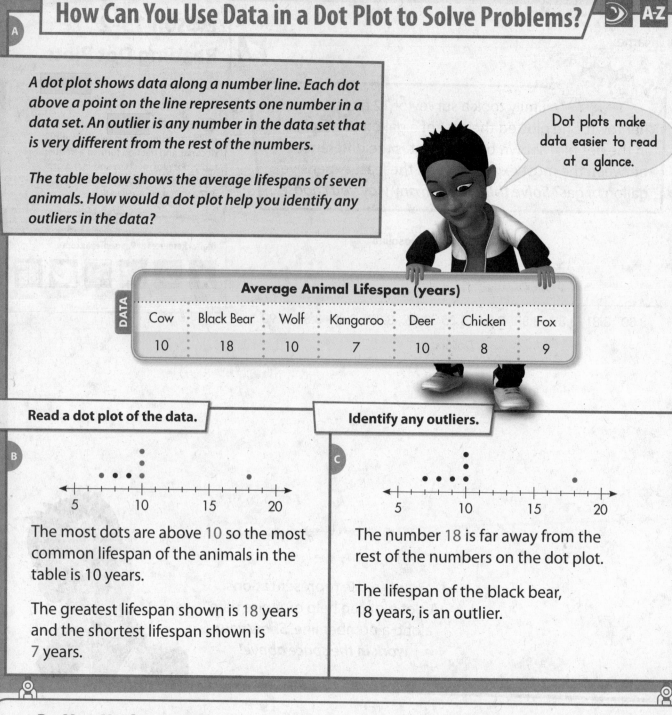

A dot plot shows data along a number line. Each dot above a point on the line represents one number in a data set. An outlier is any number in the data set that is very different from the rest of the numbers.

The table below shows the average lifespans of seven animals. How would a dot plot help you identify any outliers in the data?

Dot plots make data easier to read at a glance.

DATA

Average Animal Lifespan (years)						
Cow	Black Bear	Wolf	Kangaroo	Deer	Chicken	Fox
10	18	10	7	10	8	9

Read a dot plot of the data.

The most dots are above 10 so the most common lifespan of the animals in the table is 10 years.

The greatest lifespan shown is 18 years and the shortest lifespan shown is 7 years.

Identify any outliers.

The number 18 is far away from the rest of the numbers on the dot plot.

The lifespan of the black bear, 18 years, is an outlier.

Do You Understand?

Convince Me! Put 4 more dots on the dot plot below so 18 is not an outlier. How did you decide?

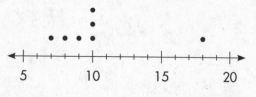

© Pearson Education, Inc. 4

☆ Guided Practice*

In **1** through **4**, use the dot plot below.

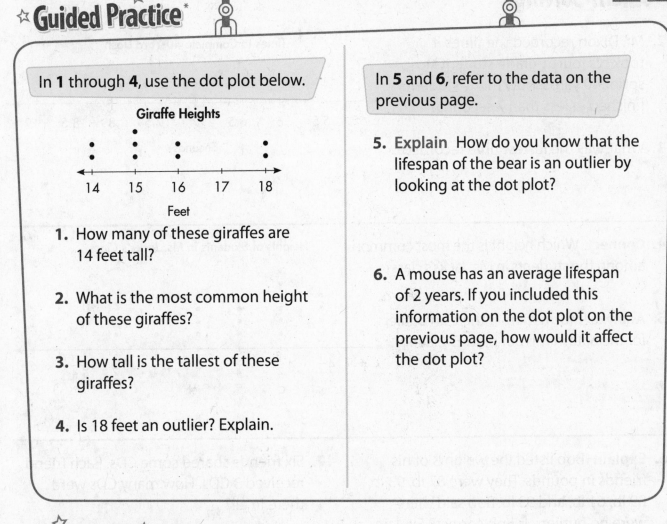

Giraffe Heights

14   15   16   17   18

Feet

1. How many of these giraffes are 14 feet tall?

2. What is the most common height of these giraffes?

3. How tall is the tallest of these giraffes?

4. Is 18 feet an outlier? Explain.

In **5** and **6**, refer to the data on the previous page.

5. **Explain** How do you know that the lifespan of the bear is an outlier by looking at the dot plot?

6. A mouse has an average lifespan of 2 years. If you included this information on the dot plot on the previous page, how would it affect the dot plot?

☆ Independent Practice ☆

In **7** through **11**, use the dot plot to the right.

7. How many people ran the 100-meter sprint?

8. Which time was the most common?

9. Which time is an outlier?

10. How many more people ran 100 meters in 10.6 seconds than 10.1 seconds?

11. Curtis said that more than half the people ran 100 meters in less than 10.4 seconds. Do you agree? Explain.

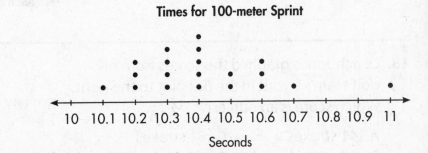

Times for 100-meter Sprint

10   10.1 10.2 10.3 10.4 10.5 10.6 10.7 10.8 10.9 11

Seconds

Problem Solving

12. Mr. Dixon recorded the times it took his fourth-grade students to sprint 40 yards. How many students finished in less than 7 seconds?

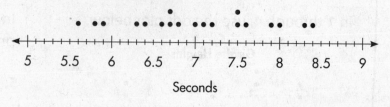

Times to Complete 40-Yard Dash

Seconds

13. What was the fastest time recorded?

---

14. Connect Which height is the most common among the students in Ms. Jacks's class?

15. Analyze Information Is there an outlier for the data in this dot plot? Explain.

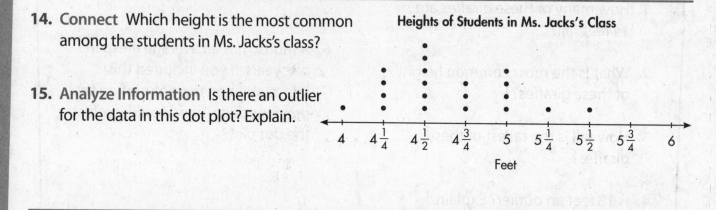

Heights of Students in Ms. Jacks's Class

Feet

---

16. Explain Bob listed the weights of his friends in pounds. They were 87 lb, 93 lb, 89 lb, 61 lb, and 93 lb. Bob said there were no outliers. Is Bob correct? Explain.

17. Six friends shared some CDs. Each friend received 3 CDs. How many CDs were there in all?

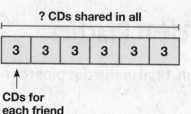

? CDs shared in all

| 3 | 3 | 3 | 3 | 3 | 3 |

CDs for each friend

---

18. Coach Jones graphed the scores from his ⭐ golf team's tryout in the dot plot to the right. Which score is an outlier?

   A 41 strokes   **C** 51 strokes

   B 44 strokes   **D** 67 strokes

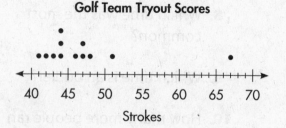

Golf Team Tryout Scores

Strokes

19. Extend Your Thinking What are five scores that, if added to the list, would eliminate the presence of an outlier?

© Pearson Education, Inc. 4

Name _____

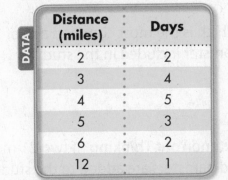
Another Look!

The data table shows the distances Freda ran over a period of days.

A dot plot shows data along a number line. On the dot plot, each dot represents 1 day. An outlier is a data point that is very different from the rest of the data.

DATA	Distance (miles)	Days
	2	2
	3	4
	4	5
	5	3
	6	2
	12	1

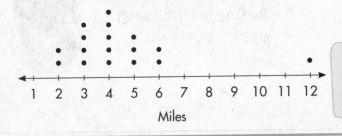

Freda's Daily Running Distance

Miles

12 miles is an outlier because it is not close to the distances she ran on the other days.

In **1** through **4**, use the dot plot at the right.

1. Identify the outlier in the data set.

2. Which weight is the most common?

3. How many more puppies weighed 3 pounds than 7 pounds?

4. How many puppies weighed less than 7 pounds?

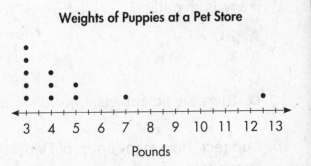

Weights of Puppies at a Pet Store

Pounds

5. **Connect** What is the total weight of all the puppies? Explain how you found your answer.

A dot plot includes a number line. Do you remember how to locate points on a number line that are not whole numbers?

6. Analyze Information How many hamsters are included in the study shown?

7. Which is the most common age of a hamster included in the study?

8. Extend Your Thinking If two 21-month old hamsters are added to the study, how does that change the data?

Ages of Hamsters

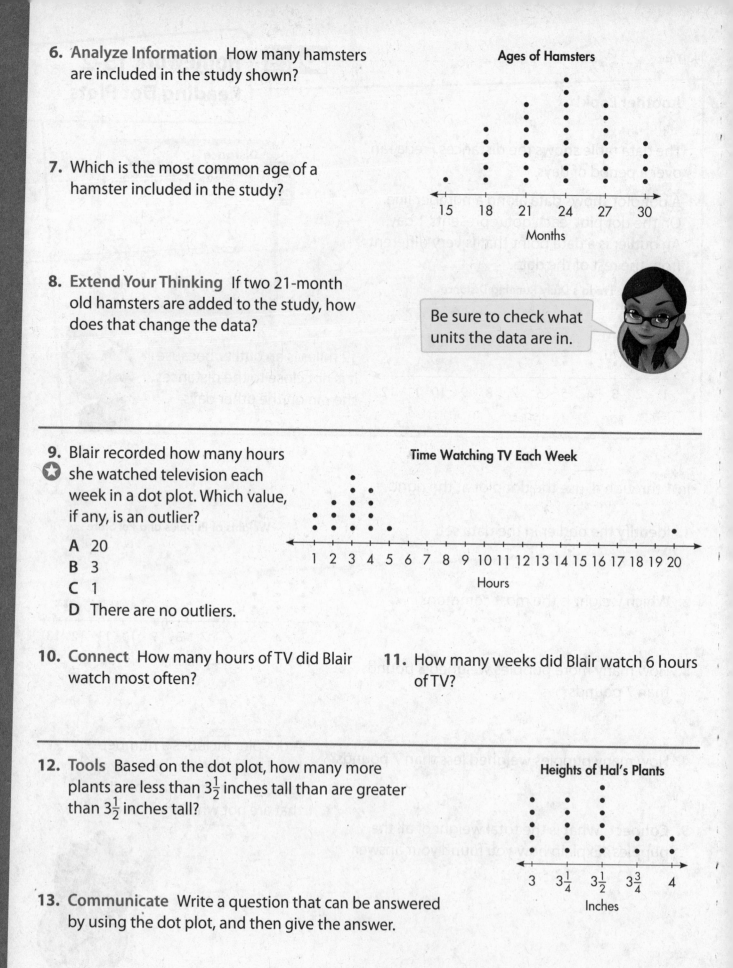

Months

Be sure to check what units the data are in.

---

9. ★ Blair recorded how many hours she watched television each week in a dot plot. Which value, if any, is an outlier?

  A 20
  B 3
  C 1
  D There are no outliers.

Time Watching TV Each Week

Hours

10. Connect How many hours of TV did Blair watch most often?

11. How many weeks did Blair watch 6 hours of TV?

---

12. Tools Based on the dot plot, how many more plants are less than $3\frac{1}{2}$ inches tall than are greater than $3\frac{1}{2}$ inches tall?

Heights of Hal's Plants

$3 \quad 3\frac{1}{4} \quad 3\frac{1}{2} \quad 3\frac{3}{4} \quad 4$

Inches

13. Communicate Write a question that can be answered by using the dot plot, and then give the answer.

© Pearson Education, Inc. 4

☆ **Solve & Share** ☆

In a class of 27 students, five students have 1 pet. Three students have 2 pets. Four students have 3 pets. Two students have 4 pets. One student has 8 pets. The remaining twelve students do not have any pets. Are there any outliers in this set of data? Explain. *Solve this problem any way you choose.*

⭐ TEKS 4.9A Represent data on a frequency table, dot plot, or stem-and-leaf plot marked with whole numbers and fractions. Also, 4.9, 4.9B. Mathematical Process Standards 4.1D, 4.1E, 4.1G

Digital Resources at PearsonTexas.com

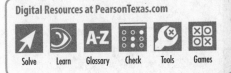

Solve   Learn   Glossary   Check   Tools   Games

You can **create representations.** A dot plot can help you organize data. *Show your work in the space below!*

Look Back!

Communicate How can you use a dot plot to find the most frequently occurring data?

How Can You Make Dot Plots That Include Fractions?

Serena measured the lengths of the pencils in her pencil box. How can she make a dot plot to show these lengths?

DATA

Lengths of Serena's Pencils

Color	Length
Red	6 in.
Blue	$4\frac{3}{4}$ in.
Green	$4\frac{3}{4}$ in.
Purple	$5\frac{1}{2}$ in.
Orange	$4\frac{3}{4}$ in.
Yellow	$4\frac{3}{4}$ in.

You can think of $\frac{1}{2}$ as $\frac{2}{4}$.

Include fractions on the number line.

B

Draw a number line and choose a scale based on the lengths in the table. Mark halves and fourths.

The scale should show data values from the least to greatest.

Write a title for the dot plot, and write a label to tell what the numbers represent.

Draw a dot for each length.

The dot plot shows the lengths of her pencils.

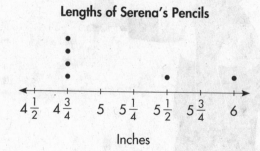

Lengths of Serena's Pencils

$4\frac{1}{2}$ $4\frac{3}{4}$ 5 $5\frac{1}{4}$ $5\frac{1}{2}$ $5\frac{3}{4}$ 6

Inches

Do You Understand?

Convince Me! Use the data to the right to complete the dot plot below. What statements can you make about the data using the dot plot?

Shoe Sizes

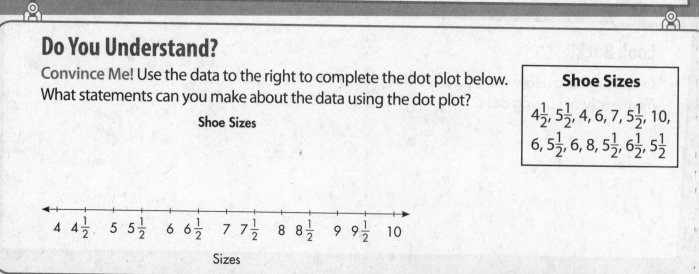

Shoe Sizes

$4\frac{1}{2}$, $5\frac{1}{2}$, 4, 6, 7, $5\frac{1}{2}$, 10, 6, $5\frac{1}{2}$, 6, 8, $5\frac{1}{2}$, $6\frac{1}{2}$, $5\frac{1}{2}$

4 $4\frac{1}{2}$ 5 $5\frac{1}{2}$ 6 $6\frac{1}{2}$ 7 $7\frac{1}{2}$ 8 $8\frac{1}{2}$ 9 $9\frac{1}{2}$ 10

Sizes

© Pearson Education, Inc. 4

☆ Guided Practice *

1. Complete the dot plot.

Lengths of Sandy's Pencils

DATA

Color	Length
Red	$6\frac{1}{4}$ in.
Blue	$5\frac{1}{4}$ in.
Green	$6\frac{3}{4}$ in.
Purple	$5\frac{3}{4}$ in.
Orange	$6\frac{3}{4}$ in.
Yellow	$6\frac{1}{2}$ in.

Lengths of Sandy's Pencils

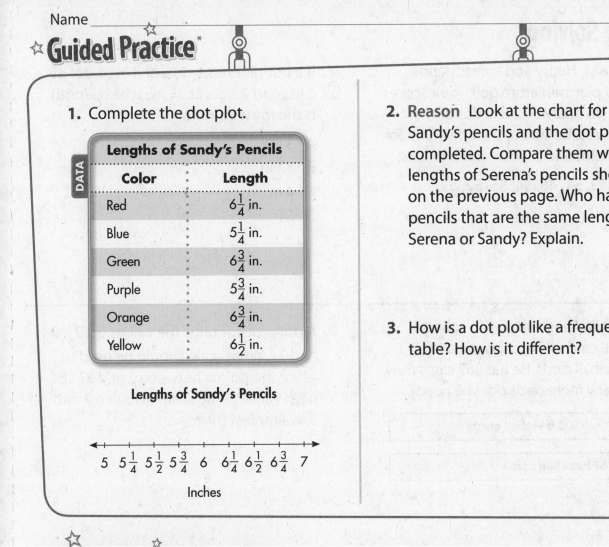

$5 \quad 5\frac{1}{4} \quad 5\frac{1}{2} \quad 5\frac{3}{4} \quad 6 \quad 6\frac{1}{4} \quad 6\frac{1}{2} \quad 6\frac{3}{4} \quad 7$

Inches

2. **Reason** Look at the chart for Sandy's pencils and the dot plot you completed. Compare them with the lengths of Serena's pencils shown on the previous page. Who has more pencils that are the same length, Serena or Sandy? Explain.

3. How is a dot plot like a frequency table? How is it different?

☆ Independent Practice ☆

Leveled Practice In **4** and **5**, use the table to the right.

4. Rico wants to organize his collection of paper chains. Use the data the chart to complete the dot plot.

Lengths of Rico's Paper Chains

Paper Chain Lengths	
8 in.	$8\frac{1}{2}$ in.
$6\frac{1}{2}$ in.	8 in.
$7\frac{1}{2}$ in.	$6\frac{1}{2}$ in.
8 in.	$7\frac{1}{2}$ in.
$6\frac{1}{2}$ in.	8 in.

$6 \quad 6\frac{1}{2} \quad 7 \quad 7\frac{1}{2} \quad 8 \quad 8\frac{1}{2} \quad 9$

Inches

5. What is the length of the longest paper chain? What is the shortest length?

*For another example, see Set B on page 873.

Problem Solving

6. **Represent** Henry and some friends went to play miniature golf. Their scores are shown below. Make a dot plot of their scores. Be sure to include a title for the dot plot and a label for the values.

   51, 70, 52, 51, 48, 54, 55, 52, 52

7. If a dot plot has 3 dots at 4 in., 1 dot at 5 in., and 2 dots at $3\frac{1}{2}$ in., which length is the most common?

   A 3 in.

   B $3\frac{1}{2}$ in.

   C 4 in.

   D 5 in.

8. **Use a Strip Diagram** Gavin collects baseball cards. His goal is to have 500 baseball cards. He has 367 cards now. How many more cards does he need?

500 baseball cards	
367 baseball cards	?

9. A dot plot contains the values $2\frac{1}{8}$, $2\frac{1}{4}$, $2\frac{1}{2}$ and $2\frac{5}{8}$. What scale should be used to place the points between 2 and 3? List each value of the scale between 2 and 3 in simplest form.

10. Trisha's swimming coach recorded the times it took her to swim one lap each day last week. Make a dot plot of Trisha's lap times. Be sure to include a title for the dot plot and a label for the values.

11. **Extend Your Thinking** If you made a dot plot of Trisha's time using 0 and 5 minutes as the boundaries, would the outlier be more or less obvious than if the boundaries of your dot plot were 50 and 75 seconds? Explain.

DATA

Day	Time
Monday	55 seconds
Tuesday	57 seconds
Wednesday	51 seconds
Thursday	72 seconds
Friday	51 seconds

© Pearson Education, Inc. 4

Another Look!

Dorothy measured the lengths of the fingers on her left hand. She also measured the length of her thumb. Dorothy wants to make a dot plot to show the measurements.

Follow these steps to create a dot plot.

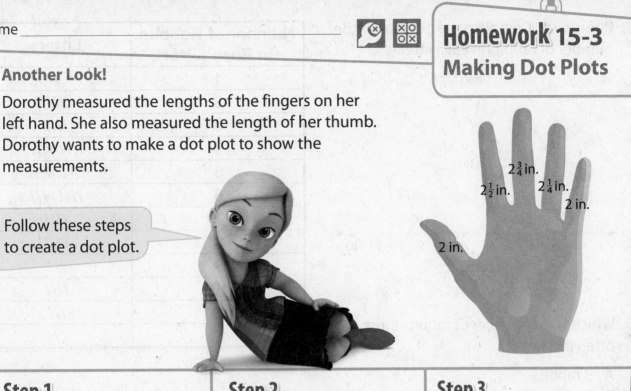

$2\frac{3}{4}$ in.

$2\frac{1}{2}$ in. $2\frac{1}{4}$ in.

2 in.

2 in.

Step 1	**Step 2**	**Step 3**
Draw a number line and choose a scale based on the data collected. The scale should show data values from least to greatest.	Write a title for the dot plot and a label for the numbers.	Draw a dot for each length.

Step 1

2   $2\frac{1}{4}$ $2\frac{1}{2}$ $2\frac{3}{4}$

Step 2

Lengths of Dorothy's Fingers

2   $2\frac{1}{4}$ $2\frac{1}{2}$ $2\frac{3}{4}$

Inches

Step 3

Lengths of Dorothy's Fingers

2   $2\frac{1}{4}$ $2\frac{1}{2}$ $2\frac{3}{4}$

Inches

1. Aiden has two toy cars that measure $2\frac{1}{2}$ in., three that measure $2\frac{3}{4}$ in., one that measures $2\frac{1}{4}$ in., one that measures $3\frac{1}{2}$ in., and one that measures $3\frac{3}{4}$ in. Use this data to complete the dot plot below.

Lengths of Aiden's Cars

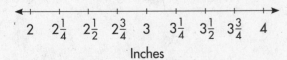

2   $2\frac{1}{4}$ $2\frac{1}{2}$ $2\frac{3}{4}$ 3 $3\frac{1}{4}$ $3\frac{1}{2}$ $3\frac{3}{4}$ 4

Inches

2. How long is the longest car?

3. Which length appears most often on the dot plot?

4. **Explain** Are more cars shorter or longer than 3 inches? How do you know?

5. Represent Complete the dot plot of the number of rabbits in each litter.

Litters

1 2 3 4 5 6 7 8 9 10 11 12
Rabbits

Number of Rabbits in Each Litter	Litters
1	/
2	///
3	THL
4	THL ////
5	THL THL
6	THL ///
7	////
8	////
9	///
10	THL
11	///
12	/

6. Which is the number of rabbits most often in a litter?

A 3 rabbits
B 4 rabbits
C 5 rabbits
D 6 rabbits

7. Explain Is the 1-rabbit litter an outlier? Explain.

8. How many litters of rabbits are included in the data?

9. Class members read the following number of pages over the weekend:

9, 11, 7, 10, 9, 8, 7, 13, 2, 12, 10, 9, 8, 10, 11, 12

Which number is an outlier?

10. Extend Your Thinking Tony wants to make a dot plot of the distances he rode his bike last week. He rode the following distances in miles:

3, 4.7, 6, 3, 5.5, 3, 5.5

Draw a dot plot for Tony.

Making a dot plot can help you find outliers.

© Pearson Education, Inc. 4

Name _____

Solve & Share

Maggie received the following scores on her spelling tests this year: 87, 72, 93, 78, 88, 84, 82, 87, and 92. She received a grade of B for each test score between 80 and 89. Organize the data so that it is easy to find how many B grades Maggie has received. **Solve this problem any way you choose.**

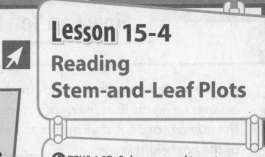

TEKS 4.9B Solve one- and two-step problems using data in whole number, decimal, and fraction form in a frequency table, dot plot, or stem-and-leaf plot. Mathematical Process Standards 4.1B, 4.1D, 4.1F, 4.1G

Digital Resources at PearsonTexas.com

Solve   Learn   Glossary   Check   Tools   Games

You can **connect ideas.** Place value can help you organize data. **Show your work in the space below!**

Look Back!

Communicate Explain how you could have used a different way to organize the data to find your answer.

How Can You Read a Stem-and-Leaf Plot?

A-Z

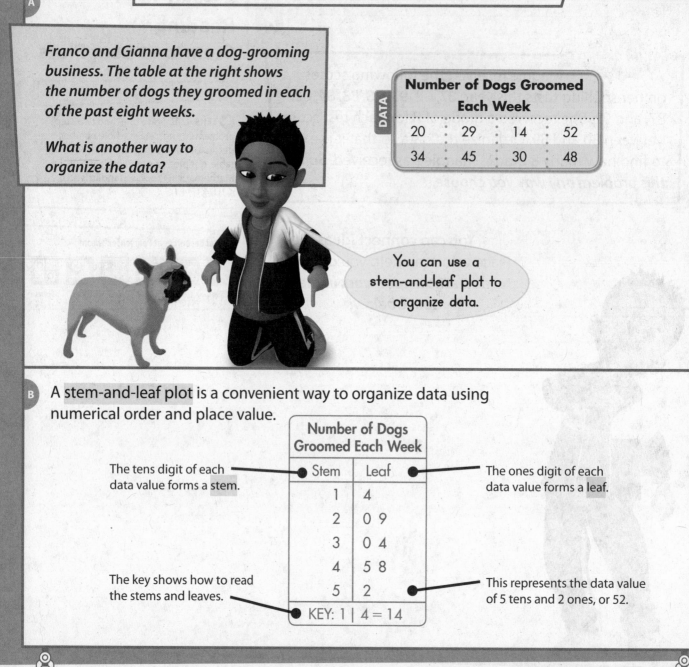

A

Franco and Gianna have a dog-grooming business. The table at the right shows the number of dogs they groomed in each of the past eight weeks.

What is another way to organize the data?

Number of Dogs Groomed Each Week			
20	29	14	52
34	45	30	48

You can use a stem-and-leaf plot to organize data.

B

A stem-and-leaf plot is a convenient way to organize data using numerical order and place value.

Number of Dogs Groomed Each Week

Stem	Leaf
1	4
2	0 9
3	0 4
4	5 8
5	2

KEY: 1 | 4 = 14

The tens digit of each data value forms a stem.

The ones digit of each data value forms a leaf.

The key shows how to read the stems and leaves.

This represents the data value of 5 tens and 2 ones, or 52.

Do You Understand?

Convince Me! In the example above, describe how the stem-and-leaf plot would change if in the ninth week they groomed 8 dogs.

854

© Pearson Education, Inc. 4

Name _____

Another Example

Some stem-and-leaf plots use decimal values as leaves.

How much farther did Kim swim during her longest workout than she did during her shortest workout?

Kim's shortest workout was 0.5 mi. Her longest workout was 2.0 mi. 2.0 − 0.5 = 1.5, so Kim swam 1.5 miles farther during her longest workout.

Miles Kim Swam Each Workout

Stem	Leaf
0	5 5
1	0 0 2 5
2	0

KEY: 0|5 = 0.5

☆ Guided Practice ☆

In **1** and **2**, use the stem-and-leaf plot.

Points Scored

Stem	Leaf
1	2 5 8 9
2	0 4 7
3	0 4 6 6 8
4	3 5

KEY: 1|2 = 12

1. What is the least number of points scored?

2. What is the greatest number of points scored?

3. **Explain** What is the meaning of this key at the bottom of a stem-and-leaf plot?

KEY: 1 | 7 = 17

4. In Another Example above, how many times did Kim swim 1 mile as her workout?

Independent Practice ☆

In **5** through **8**, use the stem-and-leaf plot to the right.

5. What is the greatest number of points scored? The least number?

6. Which point value occurs most often?

7. How many point values are less than 29 points?

8. How many point values are greater than 35 points?

Points Scored

Stem	Leaf
1	8
2	1 6 7 8 9
3	0 5 5
4	1 4 6

KEY: 1|8 = 18

For another example, see Set C on page 874. **Topic 15** | Lesson 15-4 **855**

Problem Solving

9. Analyze Information Which data value occurs most often in this stem-and-leaf plot?

A 6 hours   C 26 hours
B 20 hours   D 36 hours

Hours Spent Volunteering Last Month

Stem	Leaf
1	6 7 9
2	0 6 6 7 9
3	1 5 6 7

KEY: 1|6 = 16

10. What is the difference between the greatest value and the sum of the two least data values?

11. Reason Suppose there are 15 leaves on a stem-and-leaf plot. How many values are in this data set?

12. Explain How do you find the least and greatest data values on a stem-and-leaf plot?

13. Justify Jamie says that there were more times that the basketball team scored between 70 and 80 points than between 60 and 70 points. Do you agree? Explain.

Basketball Team Scores

Stem	Leaf
4	9
5	2 4 6 6
6	1 1 2 3 8 8 9
7	0 3 3 3 5 7 8
8	6
9	4

KEY: 4|9 = 49

14. Extend Your Thinking During the last game of the season, the basketball team scores 102 points. How would you place 102 on this stem-and-leaf plot?

© Pearson Education, Inc. 4

om
ears)

Ar of students
rds for a two-
n-and-leaf plot

lot?

Students Absent Each Day

Stem	Leaf
1	2 5 6 9
2	1 4 7 8
3	0 3

KEY: 1|2 = 12

The key shows that each stem-leaf combination represents a two-digit number.

The stems in this plot represent the tens digits: 0, 20, and 30.

The leaves in this plot represent the ones digits: 1, 2, 3, 4, 5, 6, 7, 8, and 9.

ow many
needed to list
stem-and-leaf

36
43
34

ot at the right.

f birthday cards
he stem-and-leaf

0?

Birthday Cards Sold Each Day

Stem	Leaf
2	1 5 6 7 8 9 9
3	0 3
4	2 2 3 4 9

KEY: 2|1 = 21

(centimeters)

e plot?

6

in one day?

old in one day?

5. How many people are swimming during this time?

6. Analyze Information How many swimmers are younger than 30?

7. Which age group has the greatest number of swimmers?

8. Reason Look at the two 5s as leaves next to the stem 6. What do they represent?

Ages of Swimmers f	
6:00 A.M. to 7:00 A.M.	
Stem	Leaf
0	9
1	1
2	3 9
3	
4	7
5	5 7 7 9
6	5 5 6 6 7 8
7	0 1
KEY: 0|9 = 9	

---

9. The key to a stem-and-leaf plot reads:

$$Key: 8\,|\,3 = 8.3$$

What does 7 | 2 mean in the same stem-and-leaf plot?

A 2.1

B 2.7

C 7.2

D 72

10. Extend Your Thinking H different stems would b the following values in a plot? List the stems.

42	34	47
41	45	31
62	45	36

---

11. Analyze Information The heights of different seedlings are shown in the stem-and-leaf plot. What is the difference in height between the tallest seedling and the shortest seedling?

12. Connect What is the most common seedling height, in millimeters?

Heights of Seedling	
Stem	Leaf
1	5 5 9
2	2 3 3 3
3	0 4 7
4	2 2 8
5	1 2
KEY: 1|5 = 1.5	

© Pearson Education, Inc. 4

Another Look!

A school keeps track of the number of students that are absent each day. The records for a two-week period are shown in the stem-and-leaf plot to the right.

How do you read a stem-and-leaf plot?

A stem-and-leaf plot is a convenient way to organize data.

Students Absent Each Day	
Stem	Leaf
1	2 5 6 9
2	1 4 7 8
3	0 3
KEY: 1│2 = 12	

Step 1	Read the key.	The key shows that each stem-leaf combination represents a two-digit number.
Step 2	Identify the stem for each data value.	The stems in this plot represent the tens digits: 10, 20, and 30.
Step 3	Identify the leaf for each data value.	The leaves in this plot represent the ones digits: 0, 1, 2, 3, 4, 5, 6, 7, 8, and 9.

In **1** through **4**, use the stem-and-leaf plot at the right.

A small card shop records the number of birthday cards sold each day. The data is displayed in the stem-and-leaf plot to the right.

Birthday Cards Sold Each Day	
Stem	Leaf
2	1 5 6 7 8 9 9
3	0 3
4	2 2 3 4 9
KEY: 2│1 = 21	

1. Using the key, what is the value of 3 | 0?

2. How many days are represented by the plot?

3. What is the least number of cards sold in one day?

4. What is the greatest number of cards sold in one day?

5. How many people are swimming during this time?

Ages of Swimmers from 6:00 A.M. to 7:00 A.M. (years)	
Stem	Leaf
0	9
1	1
2	3 9
3	
4	7
5	5 7 7 9
6	5 5 6 6 7 8 9
7	0 1

KEY: 0 | 9 = 9

6. Analyze Information How many swimmers are younger than 30?

7. Which age group has the greatest number of swimmers?

8. Reason Look at the two 5s as leaves next to the stem 6. What do they represent?

---

9. The key to a stem-and-leaf plot reads:

⭐

Key: 8 | 3 = 8.3

What does 7 | 2 mean in the same stem-and-leaf plot?

A 2.1

B 2.7

C 7.2

D 72

10. Extend Your Thinking How many different stems would be needed to list the following values in a stem-and-leaf plot? List the stems.

42	34	47	36
41	45	31	43
62	45	36	34

---

11. Analyze Information The heights of different seedlings are shown in the stem-and-leaf plot. What is the difference in height between the tallest seedling and the shortest seedling?

Heights of Seedlings (centimeters)	
Stem	Leaf
1	5 5 9
2	2 3 3 3 3 6
3	0 4 7
4	2 2 8
5	1 2

KEY: 1 | 5 = 1.5

12. Connect What is the most common seedling height, in millimeters?

© Pearson Education, Inc. 4

Name _____

Solve & Share

After school, José has a dog-walking service for his neighbors. For ten weeks, he walks a different number of dogs each week: 23, 11, 30, 12, 41, 13, 17, 42, 11, and 24. Organize this set of data. *Solve this problem any way you choose.*

⭐ TEKS 4.9A Represent data on a frequency table, dot plot, or stem-and-leaf plot marked with whole numbers and fractions. Also, 4.9, 4.9B. Mathematical Process Standards 4.1D, 4.1E, 4.1G

Digital Resources at PearsonTexas.com

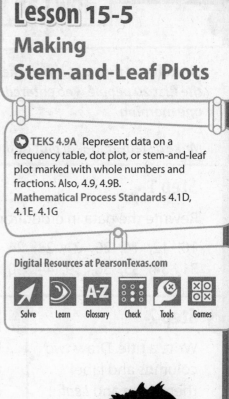

Solve   Learn   Glossary   Check   Tools   Games

You can **create representations.** A stem-and-leaf plot can help you organize data. *Show your work in the space above!*

Look Back!

Create and Use Representations How many weeks did José walk more than 20 dogs?

How Can You Make a Stem-and-Leaf Plot?

The table at the right shows the ages of the first 20 people who entered a library one morning.

Make a stem-and-leaf plot of the data.

Ages (in years) of Twenty Library Users				
21	12	31	23	20
14	58	35	78	34
50	24	28	10	44
25	29	39	58	36

Step 1

Rewrite the data in order from least to greatest.

10, 12, 14, 20, 21, 23, 24, 25, 28, 29,
31, 34, 35, 36, 39, 44, 50, 58, 58, 78

The first step is to make an organized list of the data.

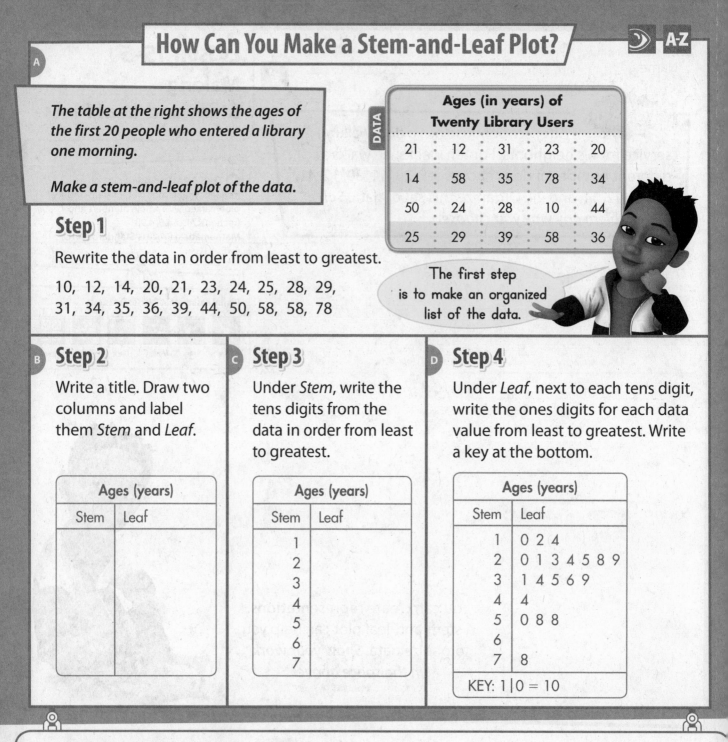

Step 2

Write a title. Draw two columns and label them *Stem* and *Leaf*.

Ages (years)

Stem	Leaf

Step 3

Under *Stem*, write the tens digits from the data in order from least to greatest.

Ages (years)

Stem	Leaf
1	
2	
3	
4	
5	
6	
7	

Step 4

Under *Leaf*, next to each tens digit, write the ones digits for each data value from least to greatest. Write a key at the bottom.

Ages (years)

Stem	Leaf
1	0 2 4
2	0 1 3 4 5 8 9
3	1 4 5 6 9
4	4
5	0 8 8
6	
7	8

KEY: 1|0 = 10

Do You Understand?

Convince Me! Write three conclusions you can make by looking at the stem-and-leaf plot for the ages of library users.

© Pearson Education, Inc. 4

☆ Guided Practice ☆

1. Complete the stem-and-leaf plot to show the following ages, in years, for people in a store:

   27 13 64 46 18 39 10 22
   41 70 16 32 15 46 60 17

Ages of People in a Store (years)	
Stem	Leaf
1	0, 3, 5, 6, 8 ✓
2	2, 7 ✗
3	2, ✗
4	1, 6, 6 ✓
6	0 ✗

   KEY: 3|0 = 30

2. **Justify** Compare the listing of ages in Exercise 1 with the stem-and-leaf plot you created. Why is the stem-and-leaf plot a better way to display the data?

   easier to read

3. How should you organize the list of values from a table before putting it in a stem-and-leaf plot?

   ✓ *frequency table*

4. **Explain** Is it possible for a stem to have no leaves? Explain.

   ✓ *no, because then it's just a list a stem plott*

☆ Independent Practice ☆

Leveled Practice In **5** and **6**, use the data to complete the stem-and-leaf plot.

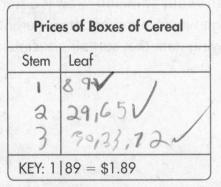

You can use 2-digit leaves to represent cents.

5. **Weights of Pumpkins (pounds)**

   35 29 21 29 32 16 38 38

   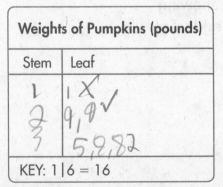

Weights of Pumpkins (pounds)	
Stem	Leaf
1	1 ✗ ✓
2	9, 9 ✓
3	5, 9, 8, 2

   KEY: 1|6 = 16

6. **Prices of Boxes of Cereal**

   $3.30, $1.89, $2.65, $3.72, $2.29, $3.33

Prices of Boxes of Cereal	
Stem	Leaf
1	8 9 ✓
2	29, 65 ✓
3	30, 33, 72 ✓

   KEY: 1|89 = $1.89

Problem Solving

Handwritten at top: key 1|0=10

7. Represent Make a stem-and-leaf plot of the weights. Be sure to include a title and a key.

Handwritten stem-and-leaf plot:

```
0 | 7
2 | 0,0,7
7 | 1,5,5
8 | 1
6 | 7
```

Handwritten: Leaf plot, 1|0 X

Weights of 13 Dogs in a Show (pounds)	
Breed	**Weight**
Beagle	20
Boxer	71
Chihuahua	7
German Shepherd	81
Golden Retriever	75
Labrador Retriever	67
Miniature Dachshund	20
Miniature Poodle	13
Shih Tzu	17
Standard Dachshund	27
Standard Poodle	75
Toy Poodle	10
Yorkshire Terrier	7

Side label: DATA

8. Construct Arguments Noah said that over half of the dogs weighed more then 50 pounds. Do you agree? Explain.

Handwritten: No, Over 50 ✓

9. Math and Science Hummingbirds have long, slender beaks that are adapted for sipping nectar from flowers. The beak of a ruby-throated hummingbird is 20 mm long. How long is this beak in centimeters?

Handwritten: 200

10. ⭐ Which data value occurs most often in this stem-and-leaf plot?

A 6
B 20
C 26
D 36

Handwritten: B circled

Hours Spent Volunteering Last Month	
Stem	Leaf
1	6 7 9
2	0 6 6 7 9
3	1 5 6 7
KEY: 1|6 = 16	

11. Extend Your Thinking How is a stem-and-leaf plot showing 2-digit whole-number data different from a stem-and-leaf plot showing data that contains decimals to the tenths?

862

© Pearson Education, Inc. 4

Homework 15-5
Making Stem-and-Leaf Plots

Another Look!

A stem-and-leaf plot is a convenient way to organize data.

Johnny kept track of the yardage gained on each pass completion by the football team in last week's game. Create a stem-and-leaf plot for the data he tracked.

Passing Yardage Gained
14, 12, 8, 2, 1, 9, 12, 8, 23, 13, 41, 40, 5, 19, 5, 37, 10, 20, 7, 13

Put the data in order. 1 2 5 5 7 8 8 9 10 12 12 13 13 14 19 20 23 37 40 41

Decide which stems to use. Use 0 for values under 10.

Write a title.

Complete the leaves.

Yardage Gained on Pass Plays

Stem	Leaf
0	1 2 5 5 7 8 8 9
1	0 2 2 3 3 4 9
2	0 3
3	7
4	0 1

Make a key. ——— KEY: 0 | 1 = 1

1. Use the data below to complete the stem-and-leaf plot to the right.

Number of Pushups			
10	45	20	20
37	24	21	9

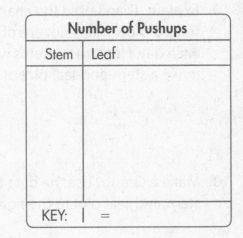

Number of Pushups	
Stem	Leaf
KEY:	=

2. Which stem has the greatest number of leaves?

   A 0   **B** 1   **C** 2   **D** 3

3. What is the difference between the greatest number and the least number of pushups?

4. What is a way to compare the greatest number of pushups to the least number of pushups, other than as a difference?

5. Maurice is making a stem-and-leaf plot of a set of data that includes the decimal values 5.2, 6.3, 7.4 and 5.9. Which key could he use?

   A KEY: 5 | 2 = 52
   B KEY: 5. | 2 = 5.2
   C KEY: 5 | 2 = 5.2
   D KEY: .5 | 2 = .52

6. Represent The lengths of eight crayons, in centimeters, are shown below. Make a stem-and-leaf plot of the data.

   7.4   8.7   8.9   9.1   9.2   9.6   7.2   8.7

7. Personal Financial Literacy At a certain clothing store, all shirts are on sale for the same price. Mr. Chan bought 6 shirts and paid a total of $62.99, including sales tax. If the sales tax was $2.99, what was the price of one shirt?

8. Construct Arguments Peeta says that because there are 5,280 feet in 1 mile, there are more than 25,000 feet in 5 miles. Is Peeta correct? Explain.

9. Explain Diana used the chart to the right to keep track of how many dozens of ears of corn she sold each day. How many stems will Diana need to make a stem-and-leaf plot of the data? Explain.

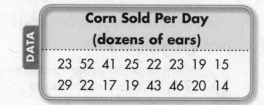

DATA	Corn Sold Per Day (dozens of ears)
	23 52 41 25 22 23 19 15
	29 22 17 19 43 46 20 14

10. Make a Graph Use the data to complete the stem-and-leaf plot to the right.

11. Which stem has the most leaves?

12. Extend Your Thinking There are 12 units in a dozen. How many ears of corn did Diana sell in total on her two busiest days?

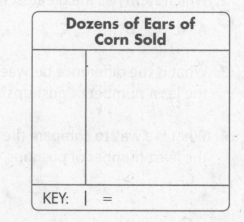

Dozens of Ears of Corn Sold

KEY: | =

© Pearson Education, Inc. 4

Name _____

☆ Solve & Share ☆

Five pairs of students perform an experiment. One partner closes her eyes and says "go," then says "stop" when she thinks one minute has passed. The other partner records the number of seconds between "go" and "stop." The seconds recorded for those students are shown below.

49   67   51   34   45   63   51   47   72   44

Do the experiment with a partner and add your data to the data above. Then create a representation that shows the data. *Solve this problem anyway you choose.*

⭐ TEKS 4.1E Create and use representations to organize, record, and communicate mathematical ideas. Also, 4.9B.
Mathematical Process Standards 4.1B, 4.1D, 4.1G

Digital Resources at PearsonTexas.com

Solve   Learn   Glossary   Check   Tools   Games

You can **create and use representations.** Would a stem-and-leaf plot work? *Show your work in the space above!*

Look Back!

Communicate Look at your representation. Write three statements that describe the data.

How Do You Use Data to Solve Problems?

A Analyze

A class gets $5 for each magazine subscription that students sell. Was the total amount raised by the students who sold 15 subscriptions more than or less than the total amount raised by the students who sold 45 subscriptions? How much more or less?

Magazine Subscriptions Sold

You can find information you need to solve the problem by reading the dot plot.

B Plan and Solve

Find and solve the hidden questions.

What is the total amount raised by the students who sold 15 subscriptions?

$5 \times 8 \times 15 = \$600$

What is the total amount raised by the students who sold 45 subscriptions?

$5 \times 2 \times 45 = \$450$

C Plan and Solve

Answer the main questions.

The 8 students who sold 15 subscriptions raised a greater total ($600) than the 2 students who sold 45 subscriptions ($450).

$\$600 - \$450 = \$150$

The students who sold 15 subscriptions raised $150 more.

Do You Understand?

Convince Me! Does the dot plot above show that most students sold fewer than 25 subscriptions? Explain.

© Pearson Education, Inc. 4

☆ Guided Practice *

In **1** through **5**, use the dot plot.

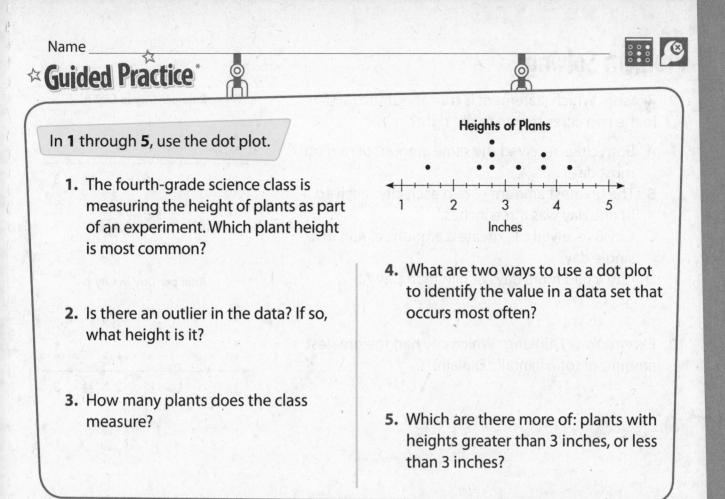

Heights of Plants

Inches

1. The fourth-grade science class is measuring the height of plants as part of an experiment. Which plant height is most common?

2. Is there an outlier in the data? If so, what height is it?

3. How many plants does the class measure?

4. What are two ways to use a dot plot to identify the value in a data set that occurs most often?

5. Which are there more of: plants with heights greater than 3 inches, or less than 3 inches?

☆ Independent Practice ☆

In **6** through **8**, use the stem-and-leaf plot.

6. The two youngest guests are Lisa's brothers. How old are they?

7. Lisa's age is the same as the age of the greatest number of her guests. How old is she?

8. Are the combined ages of the guests who are younger than 20 less than or greater than the combined ages of the guests who are older than 60? How much more or less?

Ages of Lisa's Party Guests (in years)	
Stem	Leaf
0	7 8
1	0 0 0 0 0 1 1
2	2
3	6 8 9
4	2
5	
6	2 3
KEY: 0|7 = 7	

Problem Solving

9. Reason Which statement is true about the rainfall in the two cities shown to the right?

   A Both cities received the same amount of rain on most days.

   B The greatest amount of rain each city received in one day was three inches.

   C City B received the greatest amount of rain in a single day.

   D City B had more days of rain than City A.

10. Extend Your Thinking Which city had the greatest amount of total rainfall? Explain.

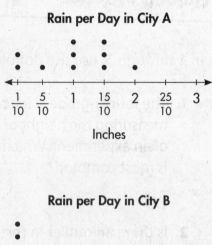

Rain per Day in City A

Inches

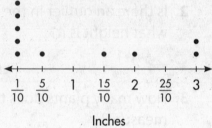

Rain per Day in City B

Inches

---

11. Holly collected information about the number of residents in several homes. Below is a list of the data she collected:

3 7 4 5 3 4 3 5   2 3 6
4 5 3 5 7 3 6 12 3 5 4

What is the outlier in her data?

  A 2   **C** 7
  B 5   **D** 12

12. Explain How do you determine the boundaries when creating a dot plot?

---

13. Math and Science A cuttlefish has adapted to change its skin color and texture to blend in with its surroundings. Some scientists estimate that cuttlefish have as many as 10 million colored cells in their skin. Write 10 million in standard form.

14. What stems are needed in a stem-and-leaf plot of the values below?

15 19 17 15 21 22 24
18 23   9 31 15 17 32

© Pearson Education, Inc. 4

Another Look!

Dot plots, frequency tables, and stem-and-leaf plots can be used to organize data to help you solve problems.

Marvis listed the points scored in each game by the Washington Middle School basketball team.

Points Scored in Basketball Games							
36	31	32	39	43	27	31	34
28	27	56	25	31	28	33	35

Next, Marvis made an organized list of the points scored in each game.

Points Scored in Basketball Games							
25	27	27	28	28	31	31	31
32	33	34	35	36	39	43	56

Lastly, Marvis used the organized list to make a dot plot of the data.

Points Scored in Basketball Games

```
                    •
        • ••   ••••••  •      •                    •
   +--+--+--+--+--+--+--+--+--+--+--+--+--+--+--+--+--+
   20    25    30    35    40    45    50    55    60
```

1. Use the data above to complete a stem-and-leaf plot of the points scored in basketball games.

Points Scored in Basketball Games	
Stem	Leaf
KEY:	

2. Use the stem-and-leaf plot from Exercise 1. When were more total points scored: when the team scored less than 30 points, or when the team scored more than 40 points? How many more?

3. Represent Josie took a survey of the hourly rate for babysitting. Her data are in the table to the right. Use the data to complete the frequency table.

Babysitting Hourly Rates ($)		
6.00	5.30	5.25
5.00	5.75	5.25
5.15	5.50	5.00
5.75	5.75	5.50

4. ⭐ If Josie wants to use the rate that is most common among the other babysitters, what should she charge per hour?

A $5.00

B $5.25

C $5.75

D $6.00

5. Tomorrow, Josie is going to babysit for 6 hours. How much more would she make by charging the greatest hourly rate listed rather than the least hourly rate?

Rate ($)	Tally	Frequency
5.00		
5.15		
5.25		
5.30		
5.50		
5.75		
6.00		

6. Analyze Information The number of bagels sold at the coffee shop each day this week is shown in the table. Which day is an outlier for this data set?

Bagels Sold Each Day	
Sunday	23
Monday	16
Tuesday	7
Wednesday	19
Thursday	17
Friday	22
Saturday	20

7. Were more bagels sold during Sunday through Wednesday or during Thursday through Saturday? How many more?

8. Extend Your Thinking Mr. Barnes kept track of the number of packages he delivered each of his last 10 work days. They are listed in the stem-and-leaf plot at the right. How many more packages did he deliver on his busiest day than on his least busy day?

Packages Delivered Daily	
Stem	Leaf
2	8
3	2 6 7 9
4	0 1 3 7
5	2
KEY: 2|8 = 28	

© Pearson Education, Inc. 4

Name _____

1. Represent Use the data to complete the frequency table.

Total Snowfall (inches)

DATA

City	Amount	City	Amount
Bluffton	12	Jacksonville	9
Maxwell	9	New Town	12
Spring City	15	Connersville	12
Carmichael	12	Harris	15
Reeseville	3	Jonestown	9

Total Snowfall (inches)

Amount	Tally	Frequency

Applying Math Processes

- How does this problem connect to previous ones?
- What is my plan?
- How can I use tools?
- How can I use number sense?
- How can I communicate and represent my thinking?
- How can I organize and record information?
- How can I explain my work?
- How can I justify my answer?

---

2. Connect Use the frequency table in Exercise 1 to complete the dot plot.

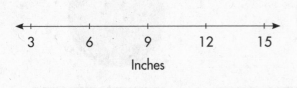

3   6   9   12   15

Inches

3. Extend Your Thinking Pia can get fencing for her dog for $6 a meter. She has $120 to spend. What is the greatest area she can fence in for her dog? Explain.

---

4. Represent Jackson listed the age of everyone who attended his family picnic. Use the data to complete the stem-and-leaf plot.

16   8   43   9   12   30   28   33   43

17   13   21   7   41   36   41   25   28

Ages of Family Members (years)

Stem	Leaf
0	
1	
2	
3	
4	

Key: 0 | 7 = 7

Error Search

Find each problem that is not correct. Circle what is wrong and rewrite the problem so it is correct.

1.
```
      468 R2
   7)3,284
    −28
      48
    −42
      64
    −56
       2
```

2.
```
      1,803 R1
   3)5,410
    −3
     24
    −24
     010
     −9
       1
```

3.
```
      1,005
   5)7,005
    −5
     25
    −25
      0
```

4.
```
       900
   9)8,100
    −81
      0
```

Target Number

Mental Math Using the single-digit numbers from the box as divisors and the remaining numbers as dividends, list as many quotients with a remainder equivalent to the target number as you can. Numbers in the box may be used more than once.

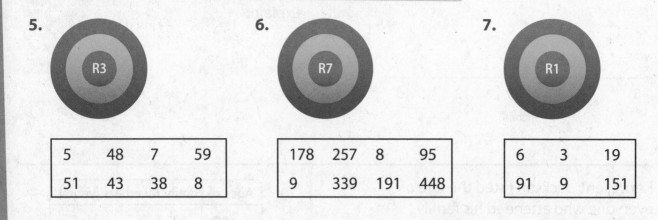

5.

R3

5	48	7	59
51	43	38	8

6.

R7

178	257	8	95
9	339	191	448

7.

R1

6	3	19
91	9	151

© Pearson Education, Inc. 4

Set A pages 835–840

Make a frequency table for the data.

Favorite Seasons				
Summer	Spring	Fall	Summer	Summer
Spring	Summer	Winter	Fall	Summer

Choose a title and label the columns.

Make a tally mark for each answer. Count the tally marks.

Record the number.

Favorite Seasons		
Season	Tally	Frequency
Fall	//	2
Spring	//	2
Summer	⊬⊬⊬	5
Winter	/	1

Remember to make sure your tally marks and numbers match the data.

In **1** and **2**, use the data below.

Votes for Team Name					
Aces	Fire	Aces	Fire	Aces	Aces
Fire	Fire	Aces	Stars	Fire	Stars
Fire	Fire	Fire	Aces	Aces	Aces
Fire	Stars	Fire	Fire	Fire	Aces
Fire	Stars	Fire	Stars	Fire	Aces

1. Make a frequency table for the data.

2. How many more people voted for Fire than for Stars?

Set B pages 841–852

Make a dot plot for the data.

Each dot represents 1 ribbon.

Lengths of Lilly's Ribbons	
Ribbon Colors	**Length**
Red	$5\frac{1}{2}$ in.
Blue	4 in.
White	$5\frac{1}{2}$ in.
Yellow	$4\frac{1}{4}$ in.
Pink	$4\frac{3}{4}$ in.

Lengths of Lilly's Ribbons

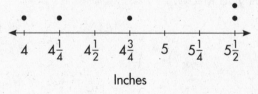

Inches

Remember that an outlier is a value that is very different from the rest of the values in a data set.

1. How many ribbons does Lilly have in all?

2. What is the length of the longest ribbon?

3. What is the length of the shortest ribbon?

4. Which length of ribbon is the most common?

5. If the two longest ribbons are combined, how much longer are these two ribbons than the shortest ribbon?

Set C pages 853–864

The waist sizes of jeans in inches that one store has in stock are listed below.

31, 32, 41, 44, 33, 21, 22, 32, 36, 37, 42, 29

A stem-and-leaf plot can display the data.

1. List the numbers in order from least to greatest.
   21, 22, 29, 31, 32, 32, 33, 36, 37, 41, 42, 44

Jean Sizes (inches)	
Stem	Leaf
2	1 2 9
3	1 2 2 3 6 7
4	1 2 4
KEY: 2|1 = 21	

2. List the tens digits in order (2, 3, and 4) to the left of the vertical line.

3. For each tens digit, record the ones digits, in order, to the right of the vertical line.

Remember to write the data in order before making your stem-and-leaf plot.

1. Use the stem-and-leaf plot at the left. How many pairs of jeans in stock had waist sizes greater than 30 inches? How did the stem-and-leaf plot help you find your answer?

2. Make a stem-and-leaf plot showing these scores: 7.5, 8.6, 9.2, 9.0, 8.8, 7.9, 9.5, 9.8, 8.5. **a.** How much greater is the highest score than the lowest score? **b.** Which is greater, the total of the 4 highest scores or the total of the 5 lowest scores?

Set D pages 865–870

Organizing data in tables or graphs can help you solve problems about the data.

How many total laps were completed by all of the students?

Laps Run by Students

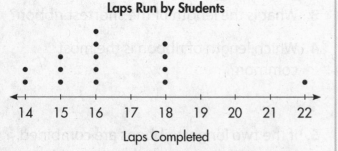

Laps Completed

Find and solve the hidden questions. Find the total laps completed for all students.

14 × 2 = 28 laps	18 × 4 = 72 laps
15 × 3 = 45 laps	22 × 1 = 22 laps
16 × 5 = 80 laps	

Add to find the total laps.

28 + 45 + 80 + 72 + 22 = 247 laps

Remember that there may be hidden questions that you need to answer before you can solve the problem.

In **1** and **2**, use the dot plot at the left.

1. How does the number of students who ran less than 16 laps compare with the students who ran more than 16 laps?

2. If 5 more students ran laps, how many laps would they most likely run? Explain how you know.

© Pearson Education, Inc. 4

1. Which is the most common height of the students in Ms. Garcia's class?

Heights of Students in Ms. Garcia's Class (feet)				
4	$3\frac{3}{4}$	$4\frac{1}{4}$	$4\frac{1}{2}$	4
$3\frac{3}{4}$	$3\frac{1}{2}$	$4\frac{1}{2}$	4	$3\frac{3}{4}$
4	$4\frac{1}{4}$	$4\frac{1}{4}$	4	$4\frac{1}{2}$

A $3\frac{3}{4}$ feet

C $4\frac{1}{4}$ feet

B 4 feet

D $4\frac{1}{2}$ feet

2. What number of siblings is most common in this class?

Siblings of Mr. Belgrave's Students

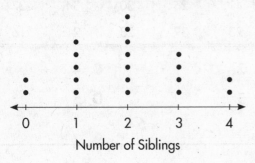

Number of Siblings

3. If a dot plot were used to represent this data, how many dots would be placed above $1\frac{3}{4}$?

Glasses of Water				
$1\frac{1}{2}$	$2\frac{1}{2}$	$1\frac{3}{4}$	2	$1\frac{3}{4}$
$2\frac{1}{4}$	3	$1\frac{1}{2}$	$2\frac{1}{2}$	$3\frac{1}{2}$
$1\frac{3}{4}$	2	$3\frac{1}{2}$	$1\frac{1}{4}$	$2\frac{1}{4}$

A 3 dots

C 1 dot

B 2 dots

D 0 dots

4. If a frequency table were used to represent the data, how many tally marks would there be for football?

Favorite Sports			
baseball	football	basketball	hockey
soccer	lacrosse	soccer	football
baseball	football	basketball	football

A 1 tally mark

C 4 tally marks

B 3 tally marks

D 5 tally marks

5. Which is the most common length of nail that Ed has in his toolbox?

Lengths of Nail

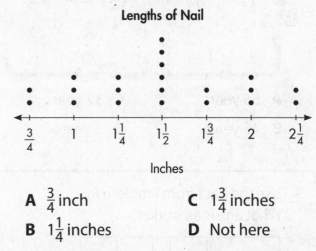

Inches

A $\frac{3}{4}$ inch

C $1\frac{3}{4}$ inches

B $1\frac{1}{4}$ inches

D Not here

6. How many hours did the greatest number of people sleep in one night?

Hours of Sleep in One Night				
9	6	7	$6\frac{1}{2}$	$5\frac{1}{2}$
8	$7\frac{1}{2}$	8	$7\frac{1}{2}$	7
6	$5\frac{1}{2}$	$7\frac{1}{2}$	$8\frac{1}{2}$	$6\frac{1}{2}$

A 6 hours

C $6\frac{1}{2}$ hours

B $7\frac{1}{2}$ hours

D 8 hours

7. The members of a soccer club represent a wide range of ages. Using the stem-and-leaf plot, how many members are in the soccer club?

A 4 members

B 5 members

C 8 members

D 12 members

Ages (years)	
Stem	Leaf
2	5 7
3	2 3 8 9
4	1 5 6
5	3 4
6	1

KEY: 2|5 = 25

10. What is the difference between the highest and lowest temperatures?

Temperatures (°F)	
Stem	Leaf
3	5 7
4	2 6 9
5	3 7 8
6	4 5
7	3 6 7

KEY: 3|5 = 35

8. The ages of houses on Clark Street are shown below. Which age is most common?

Age of Houses (years)

55	45	34	47	52
32	3	49	50	33
41	53	45	54	45

A 55 years

B 45 years

C 32 years

D 3 years

11. If this data set were placed in a stem-and-leaf plot, which stem would **NOT** appear in the plot?

Gas Mileage (miles per gallon)

25	18	38	40	32
41	26	30	34	37
23	39	28	21	16

A 2

B 3

C 4

D 5

9. Use the data from Problem 8. What age is an outlier?

			.		
⓪	⓪	⓪		⓪	⓪
①	①	①		①	①
②	②	②		②	②
③	③	③		③	③
④	④	④		④	④
⑤	⑤	⑤		⑤	⑤
⑥	⑥	⑥		⑥	⑥
⑦	⑦	⑦		⑦	⑦
⑧	⑧	⑧		⑧	⑧
⑨	⑨	⑨		⑨	⑨

12. Use the data from Problem 11. If this data set were placed in a stem-and-leaf plot, how many leaves would the stem of 3 have?

			.		
⓪	⓪	⓪		⓪	⓪
①	①	①		①	①
②	②	②		②	②
③	③	③		③	③
④	④	④		④	④
⑤	⑤	⑤		⑤	⑤
⑥	⑥	⑥		⑥	⑥
⑦	⑦	⑦		⑦	⑦
⑧	⑧	⑧		⑧	⑧
⑨	⑨	⑨		⑨	⑨

© Pearson Education, Inc. 4

Personal Financial Literacy

Essential Question: How can understanding saving options, types of expenses, and purposes of financial institutions help you make decisions about saving and spending?

Problem-solving skills are used to make informed decisions.

People make decisions when they buy food.

There are so many brands of popcorn! Here's a project on decisions.

Math and Science Project: Decisions

Do Research Use the Internet or other sources to find information about two different brands of a food item, such as popcorn.

Look on the box for claims.

Journal: Write a Report Include what you found. Also in your report:

- Compare the claims you found.

- Pick one of those claims. How could you test whether the claim is accurate? Test the claim, and report the resuts of your test.

- Compare the costs of the brands.

Name _____

Review What You Know

Vocabulary

Choose the best term from the box.
Write it on the blank.

> - cost
> - interest
> - saving
> - spending

1. Exchanging money for goods or

   services is _____.

2. Money you receive for lending

   money is _____.

3. The amount you must spend to

   purchase something is the _____.

Money

In **4** through **7**, find the sum or difference.

4. $50 − $27.92   5. $26.30 − $12.49

6. $40 + $18.06   7. $32.87 + $45.56

In **8** and **9**, list the least number of coins
and bills needed to equal the amount.
Do **NOT** include half dollars.

8. $27.53   9. $0.71

Problem Solving

10. Tia earns $7 an hour and works
    25 hours each week. How much
    money will Tia earn in 4 weeks?

11. Frank had $425 in his savings
    account. Frank spent $219 of his
    savings. Then his uncle put $62
    in Frank's savings account. How
    much money does Frank have in his
    savings account now?

Multiplication Properties

12. **Connect** For her graduation, Kayla
    received $35 from each of her three
    uncles. She also received $5 from
    each of her three cousins. Then her
    grandparents gave her $50. Show
    two ways Kayla could solve the
    equation below to find how much
    money she received.

    $3 \times (\$35 + \$5) + \$50 = t$

© Pearson Education, Inc. 4

My Word Cards

Use the examples for each word on the front of the card to help complete the definitions on the back.

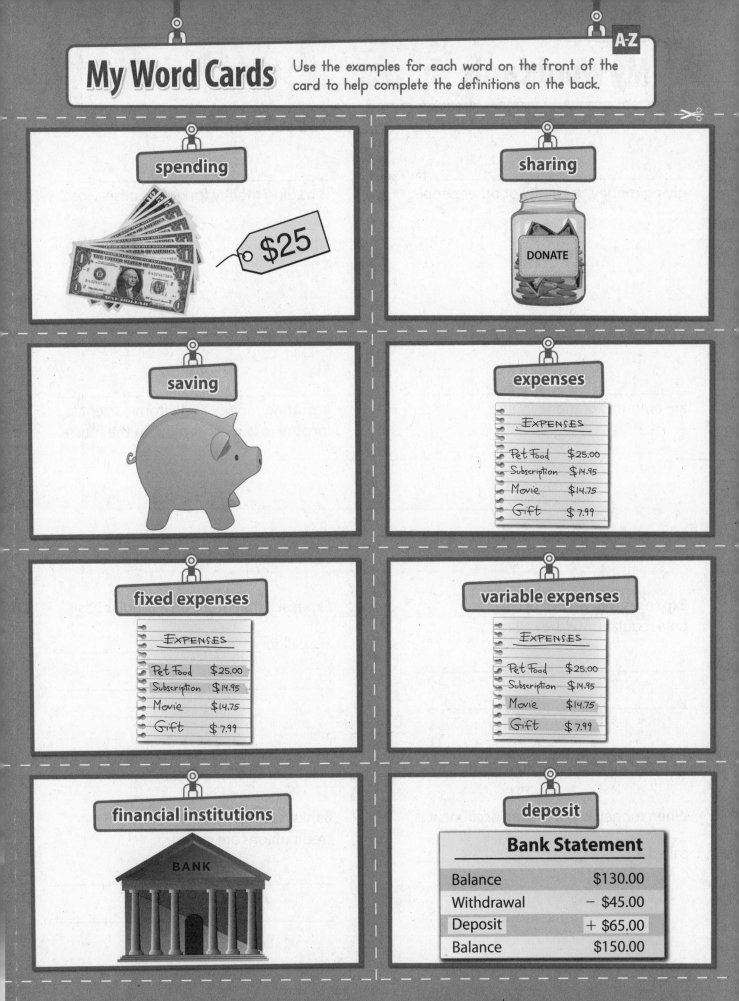

spending

$25

sharing

DONATE

saving

expenses

EXPENSES

Pet Food $25.00
Subscription $14.95
Movie $14.75
Gift $7.99

fixed expenses

EXPENSES

Pet Food $25.00
Subscription $14.95
Movie $14.75
Gift $7.99

variable expenses

EXPENSES

Pet Food $25.00
Subscription $14.95
Movie $14.75
Gift $7.99

financial institutions

BANK

deposit

Bank Statement	
Balance	$130.00
Withdrawal	− $45.00
Deposit	+ $65.00
Balance	$150.00

Complete each definition. Extend learning by writing your own definitions.

_____ is giving money to charity or other people.

_____ is trading money for goods or services.

_____ are amounts of money spent.

_____ is putting money aside from current income to buy something in the future.

Expenses that do not occur on a regular basis are called

_____.

Expenses that occur on a regular basis are called _____

_____.

When money is put into an account, it is called a _____.

Banks, savings and loans, and credit unions are called

_____

_____.

© Pearson Education, Inc. 4

My Word Cards

Use the examples for each word on the front of the card to help complete the definitions on the back.

A-Z

withdrawal

Bank Statement	
Balance	$130.00
Withdrawal	− $45.00
Deposit	+ $65.00
Balance	$150.00

balance

Bank Statement	
Balance	$130.00
Withdrawal	− $45.00
Deposit	+ $65.00
Balance	$150.00

receipts

$27.45
19.95
12.50
+ 4.25
$64.15

profit

Receipts	$35.00
Expenses	− 12.95
	$22.05

My Word Cards

Complete each definition. Extend learning by writing your own definitions.

✂

The amount of money you have in your bank account is the _____.

When money is taken out of an account, it is called a _____.

_____ is the difference between expenses and receipts.

_____ are the total money taken in.

© Pearson Education, Inc. 4

Name _____

☆ ☆
Solve & Share

Marcus gets $15 allowance. What could he do with the money? Explain.

You can **connect** to the real world by thinking about the things you would buy and how much they cost. *Show your work in the space below!*

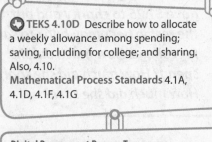

TEKS 4.10D Describe how to allocate a weekly allowance among spending; saving, including for college; and sharing. Also, 4.10.
Mathematical Process Standards 4.1A, 4.1D, 4.1F, 4.1G

Digital Resources at PearsonTexas.com

Solve Learn Glossary Check Tools Games

Look Back!

Reason Describe another way Marcus could use his allowance.

What Can You Do with Your Allowance?

A

Tikie's weekly allowance is shown. This week, she spent $4.50 on snacks and $1.75 on pencils. She gave $1.25 to charity and put the rest in her piggy bank to save for college. How much did she spend? How much did she share? How much did she save?

Spending, saving, and sharing are 3 things you can do with your allowance.

Tikie's allowance

B **Spending** is trading money for goods (like food and clothes) or services (like a haircut).

How much did Tikie spend?

$$\begin{array}{r} \overset{1}{}\$4.50 \\ +\ \$1.75 \\ \hline \$6.25 \end{array}$$

Tikie spent $6.25 on snacks and pencils.

C **Sharing** is giving money to other people.

How much did Tikie share?

Tikie shared $1.25 by giving it to charity.

D **Saving** is putting money aside from current income to buy something in the future.

How much did Tikie save?

$$\begin{array}{r} \overset{1}{}\$6.25 \\ +\ \$1.25 \\ \hline \$7.50 \end{array} \qquad \begin{array}{r} \overset{9\ \ 10}{\$10.00} \\ -\ \ \$7.50 \\ \hline \$2.50 \end{array}$$

Tiki saved $2.50, her allowance minus the total amount she spent and shared.

Do You Understand?

Convince Me! Suppose Tikie only spent $3.25 on snacks. What could she have done with the additional money that she didn't spend on snacks? How much money would that be?

© Pearson Education, Inc. 4

☆ Guided Practice*

In **1** and **2**, find how much each person spent, saved, or shared, whichever is not given. Show your work.

1. Kara spent $6.74, shared $2, and saved the rest of her $10 allowance.

2. Dwayne saved $2.50, shared $1.75 and spent the rest of his $12 allowance.

3. **Justify** In the problem on the previous page, how could Tikie have saved $2.75? Justify your answer.

4. **Connect** What are different ways to share money?

Independent Practice*

In **5** through **8**, find how much each person spent, saved, or shared, whichever is **NOT** given. Show your work.

5. Candice spent $8.28, shared $1.40, and saved the rest of her $15 allowance.

6. George saved $7.50, shared $1.70, and spent the rest of the $20 he made mowing grass.

7. Wyatt spent $7.16, saved $2.50, and shared the rest of his $11 allowance.

8. Carly spent $8 of her $12 allowance. She split the rest equally between saving and sharing.

Problem Solving

9. Brian kept track of his money for two weeks using the list on the right. Use the list to solve each of the following problems. Show your work.

   a. What is the total amount he saved?

   b. What is the total amount he spent?

   c. What is the total amount he shared?

May 2–8	
Allowance	$15
Save	$4
Skating	$3.50
Frozen Yogurt	$3.75
Paper	$1.89
Rest to charity	

May 9–15	
Allowance	$15
Save	$4
Movie	$3.25
Frozen Yogurt	$3.75
Soccer cards	$2.99
Rest to charity	

10. Martina earned $25 babysitting. She spent $15.48. How much does she have left? What could she do with the rest of her money?

11. **Extend Your Thinking** Raoul can save $6 a week. He wants to buy a baseball glove which costs $57, including tax. How many weeks does he need to save in order to buy the glove? Explain.

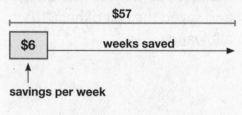

12. **Represent** The dot plot shows the number of students who shared different amounts of money for the class party. Which amount did the most students share?

   A $2

   B $3

   C $4

   D $5

Class Party Fund

Dollars Shared

© Pearson Education, Inc. 4

Name _____

Another Look!

Remember that three things you can do with your money are spend it, save it, or share it.

This week, Tom earned $18 mowing lawns. He saves $5.75 every week. How much money does he have left for spending or sharing?

$$\begin{array}{r} {\scriptstyle 7\;\overset{9}{\cancel{10}}\,10\,10} \\ \$1\cancel{8}.\cancel{0}\;\cancel{0} \\ -\;\;\;5.7\,5 \\ \hline \$12.2\,5 \end{array}$$

Tom has $12.25 left for spending or sharing.

1. Louis earned $16 tutoring. He spent $9.43, shared $2.75 with his brother, and saved the rest. How much did he save?

2. Amanda saves $3.50 and shares $1.75 every week. This week she earned $12 raking leaves. How much does she have to spend this week?

3. How much money does Miguel have left that he could share?

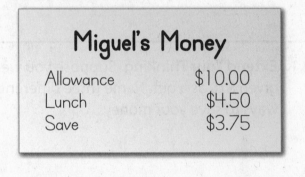

Miguel's Money

Allowance	$10.00
Lunch	$4.50
Save	$3.75

4. Ursula earns $27 allowance each week for doing chores. This week she spent $13 of her allowance on a gift for her father. She wants to share her remaining allowance equally between two charities. How much will she share with each charity? Explain.

5. Each week, Nursen saves $5 and shares $3.75. She also spends $4.95 on bus fare to get home from music lessons. This week she earned $24 babysitting. How much money does Nursen have left that she can spend?

6. Justin's allowance is $16 per week. He shares $4.25 with his little sister and spends $5.60 on lunches. How much money does Justin have left? What could he do with the rest of his money?

7. Math and Science Zoe's video game controller needs a pack of batteries. Zoe tests two brands of batteries. Brand X runs for 20 hours, and Brand Y runs for 12 hours. If Zoe plays video games for 120 hours this year, how many fewer packs of Brand X would she need than Brand Y?

8. Kevin saved $18 per month for one year in his college fund. How much money did he save? Explain.

Remember, there are 12 months in 1 year.

9. Kendra kept track of her money last week. Answer the following questions. Show your work.

   a. How much did Kendra spend?

   b. How much did Kendra save?

Allowance	$20.00
Share	$3.00
Movie	$7.50
Snack	$4.28
Pencils	$0.99
Save the rest	

10. Connect Joyce shares $2 of her $12 allowance every week. What fraction of her allowance does she share?

   A $\frac{1}{2}$

   B $\frac{1}{3}$

   C $\frac{1}{6}$

   D $\frac{1}{12}$

11. Extend Your Thinking Suppose you were given $10 as a gift. Name three different ways to save your money.

12. Ernest wrote the note shown. How much money does he have left? What could he do with that money?

I earned $18 mowing the grass.

I've spent $12.26.

© Pearson Education, Inc. 4

Name _____

Solve & Share
Juan saves his money in a piggy bank. José saves his money in a bank. Which method do you think is better? Explain.

✪ **TEKS 4.10C** Compare the advantages and disadvantages of various savings options. Also, 4.10D, 4.10E. Mathematical Process Standards 4.1A, 4.1C, 4.1D, 4.1E, 4.1G

Digital Resources at PearsonTexas.com

Solve   Learn   Glossary   Check   Tools   Games

You can **connect** math to the real world by thinking about what you and your family save for. *Show your work in the space above!*

Look Back!

Justify Suppose you got $40 for your birthday and wanted to save it. How would you save the money? Explain why.

What Are Different Ways to Save?

A

Tony saves $20 per month. How much would Tony have in 3 months with each savings option? What are the advantages and disadvantages of each option?

BANK

Option 1: Save in a piggy bank at home.

Option 2: Save at a bank that pays $0.45 total interest in 3 months.

When you save money at a bank, you receive interest from the bank.

B After 3 months, Tony would have $60 in his piggy bank.

$3 \times \$20 = \$60$

Advantages of the Piggy Bank

It is easier to put money in the piggy bank than in the bank.

Disadvantages of the Piggy Bank

Tony's money does not earn interest.

It is easier to spend money that you have at home.

Tony's money can be lost or stolen.

C After 3 months, Tony would have $60.45 in the bank.

$(3 \times \$20) + 0.45 = \$60 + 0.45 = \$60.45$

Disadvantages of the Bank

It is more difficult to take money to the bank.

Advantages of the Bank

Tony's money earns interest.

It is more difficult to spend money that you have in the bank.

Tony's money is safer in the bank.

Do You Understand?

Convince Me! Which savings option should Tony use? Explain your answer.

© Pearson Education, Inc. 4

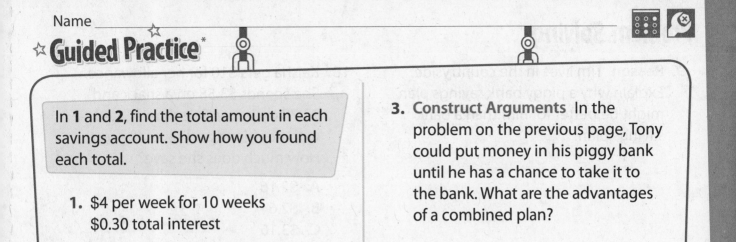

☆ **Guided Practice**☆

In **1** and **2**, find the total amount in each savings account. Show how you found each total.

1. $4 per week for 10 weeks
   $0.30 total interest

2. $18 per month for 5 months
   $1.35 total interest

3. **Construct Arguments** In the problem on the previous page, Tony could put money in his piggy bank until he has a chance to take it to the bank. What are the advantages of a combined plan?

Independent Practice☆

In **4** through **8**, find the total amount in each savings account. Show how you found each total.

4. $6 per week for 19 weeks
   $1.71 total interest

5. $20.75 per month for 2 months
   $0.21 total interest

6. $28 per month for 10 months
   $6.97 total interest

7. $5 per week for 52 weeks
   $7.80 total interest

8. The total amount at the end of 3 months, as shown in the table

Month	Amount Saved	Interest
1	$16.75	$0.04
2	$17.90	$0.09
3	$15.75	$0.13

Problem Solving

9. Reason Tim lives in the countryside. Explain why a piggy bank savings plan might be better for him than a bank savings plan.

10. Keisha gets $10 for her allowance. She spends $3.58 on a snack and $2.78 on paper. She shares $1.48 with her friend and saves the rest. How much does she save?

    A $2.16

    B $2.64

    C $3.16

    D $3.64

---

11. a. Who has saved more money at the end of three weeks, Joey or Pedro? Explain your answer.

b. Name at least one advantage of each savings plan.

Week	Joey Saved	Pedro Saved
1	$3.48	$5.25
2	$6.30	$5.25
3	$5.97	$5.25

DATA

---

12. Number Sense Trisha adds $\frac{3}{8}$ gallon of strawberry juice to $\frac{7}{8}$ gallon of lemonade. How much strawberry lemonade does she make? Give your answer as a mixed number in simplest form.

13. Extend Your Thinking Mr. Grant owns the house where his family lives. He earns $1,000 each week and saves $100. How do you think Mr. Grant spends the rest of his money?

---

14. Gulsen can save $9 per week. How many weeks will it take her to save $216? Explain.

© Pearson Education, Inc. 4

Name _____

Another Look!

Roberto saves $16 each month. Gail saves $4 each week. Who saves more in 1 year? What are the advantages and disadvantages of each savings plan?

1 year = 12 months = 52 weeks

$12 \times \$16 = \$192$ Roberto saves $192 in 1 year.

$52 \times \$4 = \$208$ Gail saves $208 in 1 year.

Roberto has more time to save, but he has to come up with more money each time he saves.

Gail ends up saving more money in the same amount of time, but she has to save some money each week.

In **1** through **5**, find the total amount in each savings account. Show how you found each total.

1. $4 per week for 17 weeks
   $0.68 total interest

2. $22 per month for 2 months
   $0.21 total interest

3. $27 per month for 6 months
   $2.43 total interest

4. $7 per week for 35 weeks
   $4.92 total interest

5. The total amount at the end of 3 months, as shown in the table

DATA	Month	Amount Saved	Interest
	1	$25.38	$0.06
	2	$12.35	$0.09
	3	$14.97	$0.13

6. Justify Melody won $100 in a contest and wants to save all of it. How should she save the money? Explain why you chose the savings plan you did.

7. Tina saved $8 per week for 17 weeks. Ike saved $32 per month for 4 months. How much more money did Tina save than Ike?

A $6
B $8
C $10
D $13

8. Extend Your Thinking Jordan has $2,000 in his college savings account at the bank. He doesn't add or take any money out for 6 months. The table shows how much interest he earns each month. Estimate how much money Jordan will have in his college savings account after six months. Explain.

Month	Interest
1	$5.00
2	$5.01
3	$5.03
4	$5.04
5	$5.05

DATA

9. Connect Luc kept track of his money last week. Show how to solve each of the following.

a. How much did Luc spend?

b. How much did Luc save?

Allowance $15.00
Share $1.75
Skating $5.50
Snack $5.28
Save the rest

10. Represent How many lines of symmetry does the logo to the right have? Draw all lines of symmetry on the figure.

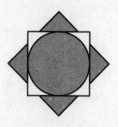

© Pearson Education, Inc. 4

Name _____

Solve & Share

Name at least 3 expenses a family must pay every month and 3 expenses a family pays once in a while.

You can **reason** to decide which expenses your family pays every month and which they don't. *Show your work in the space below!*

TEKS 4.10A Distinguish between fixed and variable expenses. Also, 4.10. Mathematical Process Standards 4.1A, 4.1D, 4.1E, 4.1F, 4.1G

Digital Resources at PearsonTexas.com

| Solve | Learn | Glossary | Check | Tools | Games |

Look Back!

Connect What is one kind of expense that is the same amount every month?

How Do You Tell Fixed Expenses From Variable Expenses?

Expenses are money spent.

Fixed expenses occur on a regular basis. Monthly bills are fixed expenses.

Variable expenses do not occur on a regular basis. Car repairs are an example of a variable expense.

Jamal's family had the expenses shown in the table. What are their total fixed expenses? What are their total variable expenses?

You can tell fixed expenses from variable expenses by deciding whether or not the expense must be paid regularly.

Expenses

Rent:	$1,138
Car repair:	$450
Car payment:	$200
Movie tickets:	$86
Shoes and clothing:	$250

B Find the family's total fixed expenses.

Rent:	$1,138
Car payment:	+ $200
Total	$1,338

Jamal's family had $1,338 in fixed expenses.

C Find the family's total variable expenses.

Car repair:	$450
Movie tickets:	$86
Shoes and clothes:	+ $250
Total	$786

Jamal's family had $786 in variable expenses.

Do You Understand?

Convince Me! Jamal's parents had $2,275 income to pay for their expenses. How much did they have left after paying all their expenses? What could they do with the rest?

© Pearson Education, Inc. 4

☆ Guided Practice *

In **1** through **3**, write whether each of the following is a fixed expense or a variable expense.

1. Restaurant bill *varible*

2. Veterinarian bill *Varible*

3. Water bill *fixed*

4. **Construct Arguments** In the problem on the previous page, if Jamal's family borrows money from the bank to buy Jamal a bike, would the monthly payments be a fixed or a variable expense? Explain.

fixed
~~*varible*~~
expence

How often will the payments be made?

Independent Practice ☆

In **5** through **12**, write whether each of the following is a fixed expense or a variable expense.

5. Rent *fixed*

6. Money to go to a movie

varible

7. Car payment

varible

8. Electricity bill

fixed

9. Money to buy tickets to a basketball game

varible

10. Car repair

varible

11. Gas to get to work

varible

12. Gas to get to grandma's house

varible

Problem Solving

13. Trevor gets $20 weekly, but each week he must buy two school lunch tickets, which are $4.50 each. How much money does he have left after his fixed expense?

- **A** $11.00
- **B** $12.00
- **C** $14.50
- **D** $15.50

14. Explain Joy shares $2.25 every week. This week she spent $4.53 and $1.48 and saved the rest of her $12 allowance. How much did she save? Show how you found the answer.

$$12.80$$
$$0.8.26$$
$$2.74$$

$$2.25$$
$$4.53$$
$$1.47$$
$$8.26$$

15. Karen's older brother, Rob, has a job and drives a car. The money he earned and spent last week is shown. Show how you found each answer.

a. What were Rob's total fixed expenses?   90.02

b. What were Rob's total variable expenses?   12.78

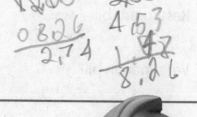

Remember, fixed expenses must be paid regularly.

$$58.74$$
$$27.50$$
$$06.08$$
$$06.50$$
$$90.22$$

c. If Rob gave Karen $6.50 so she could go to a movie with him and saved the rest of his money, how much money did he save last week?

$$12.24$$
$$-06.50$$
$$18.74$$

$$115.26$$
$$90.02$$
$$25.24$$

Earned	$115.26
Car payment	$58.74
Gas for work	$27.50
Snacks	$6.28
Movie	$6.50

16. Represent How much fence would it take to go around the playground shown in the diagram?

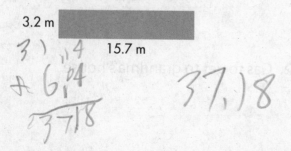

3.2 m   15.7 m

$$3) .4$$
$$+ 6.04$$
$$3.7.18$$

$$37.18$$

17. Extend Your Thinking In June, Betsy paid $68.26 for her cell phone. In July, she paid $94.10 for her cell phone. How much did Betsy pay for her cell phone over both months? Explain whether Betsy's cell phone is a fixed or variable expense.

$$68.26$$
$$94.10$$
$$162.36$$ varible

© Pearson Education, Inc. 4

Name _____

Another Look!

Trent gets $10 weekly. He has a video game subscription that costs $2 each week. This week, he also spent $2.95 at a yard sale and $3.75 for snacks. He saved the rest. What were Trent's total variable expenses? Explain.

$$\begin{array}{r} \overset{1\ 1}{\$2.95} \leftarrow \text{yard sale items} \\ +\ \$3.75 \leftarrow \text{snacks} \\ \hline \$6.70 \leftarrow \text{total variable expenses} \end{array}$$

Money that is saved is not an expense.

Yard sale items and snacks are expenses that do not occur on a regular basis.

In **1** and **2**, write whether each of the following is a fixed expense or a variable expense.

1. Money to buy a piano

2. Annual doctor checkup

3. Carter's family listed expenses for last month, as shown. What are their total fixed expenses?

Rent:	$1,960
Heating bill:	$375
Bus fare to work:	$150
Car repairs:	$280
Family fun night:	$76

4. What are their total variable expenses?

5. If Carter's parents earned $3,000 last month, how much did they have left after paying their fixed expenses?

6. Last month, the Vega family spent $548 on rent, $125 on a car loan payment, $55 on a phone bill, and $198 on doctor bills.

   a. Which of these is a variable expense?

   b. What was their total fixed expenses?

7. Connect Are groceries a fixed expense or a variable expense? Explain.

8. **Math and Science** Mr. Allen tries the detergent shown to the right. He finds that he can do 8 loads using one bottle. What fraction of the advertised number of loads was he able to do?

$10.00

10 LOADS OF LAUNDRY

9. Lexie's family lists their expenses as shown to the right. How much more did her family spend on fixed expenses than on variable expenses?

A $1,886
B $2,446
C $2,733
D $3,302

House payment: $2,843

Cooling bill: $150

Car repair: $280

Game system: $399

New suit: $428

10. **Make a Graph** Complete the stem-and-leaf plot for the following data.

Money 10 fourth graders spent on snacks: $2.75, $2.28, $4.15, $2.67, $3.49, $3.76, $2.98, $4.36, $5.19, $3.39

Money on Snacks	
Stem	Leaf
2	28 67
3	
4	
5	
Key: 2	28 = $2.28	

11. **Extend Your Thinking** Rick made $33,000 from his job last year. He also made $3,000 selling handmade vases at craft shows. Which part of Rick's total income is fixed income? Which part of Rick's total income is variable income? Explain.

© Pearson Education, Inc. 4

Name _____

Solve & Share

Financial institutions include banks, savings and loans, and credit unions.

Describe at least three things banks, savings and loans, or credit unions do.

TEKS 4.10E Describe the basic purpose of financial institutions, including keeping money safe, borrowing money, and lending. Also, 4.10.
Mathematical Process Standards 4.1A, 4.1B, 4.1D, 4.1F, 4.1G

You can **connect ideas.** Think about the different financial concepts you have already learned about. *Show your work in the space below!*

Digital Resources at PearsonTexas.com

Solve Learn Glossary Check Tools Games

Look Back!

Reason Why do you think banks, savings and loans, and credit unions are useful?

You can safely keep your money in a savings or checking account at a bank or other financial institution. Sometimes you get interest.

When you put money in the bank, you deposit it.

When you take money out of the bank, you withdraw it.

The amount of money you have in your bank account is the balance.

Debit

1234 5678 9876 5432

LIZ GARCIA

When you use a debit card, you are withdrawing money from your account.

You can't misplace money that's in a financial institution.

Bank   Bank

B Ken had $108 in his college savings account. He earned $3.24 interest and deposited $8.28 into the account. How much was in his savings account then?

$$\begin{array}{r} \overset{1}{}\overset{1}{} \\ \$108.00 \\ 3.24 \\ +8.28 \\ \hline \$119.52 \end{array}$$

Ken had $119.52 in his savings account after the interest and deposit.

C Mia's mother had $716.45 in her checking account. She wrote the check shown. What was her balance then?

$$\begin{array}{r} \overset{611}{\$716.45} \\ -20.00 \\ \hline \$696.45 \end{array}$$

Bank

Pay to the order of: _Marcie's Gymnastics_ [$20]

Twenty ————————— Dollars

Liz Garcia

Mia's mother had a balance of $696.45.

Do You Understand?

Convince Me! Why did Ken's balance go up, but Mia's mother's balance go down?

© Pearson Education, Inc. 4

Another Example

Banks, credit unions, and savings and loans allow you to borrow money. You have to pay the money back, with interest.

When you use a credit card at a store, your bank pays the store right away, and then you pay the bank back later.

Credit Card

1234 5678 9876 5432

GERALD BULLOCK

Rosemary's family borrowed $1,278 to buy a car. To pay off the bank loan, they have to make 15 payments of $97. How much interest do they have to pay?

$$
\begin{array}{r}
\overset{3}{\$97} \\
\times \quad 15 \\
\hline
485 \\
+ \quad 970 \\
\hline
\$1,455
\end{array}
\qquad
\begin{array}{r}
\overset{3\ 14\ 15}{\$1,\cancel{455}} \\
- \quad 1,278 \\
\hline
\$177
\end{array}
$$

Rosemary's family must pay $177 interest.

The statement shows what Gerald bought with his credit card. What is the total amount he charged?

$$
\begin{array}{r}
\overset{2\ 1\ 2}{\$45.28} \\
7.56 \\
+ \quad 9.67 \\
\hline
\$62.51
\end{array}
$$

	April
4/5	Harry's Market $45.28
4/7	Beth's Burgers $7.56
4/9	Books and Stuff $9.67

Gerald needs to pay back $62.51. He might also have to pay interest.

☆ Guided Practice *

1. Jenny has $348 in her checking account. She uses her debit card to pay for $50.56 worth of groceries. How much is in her checking account then? Show how you found your answer.

2. **Reason** Martha receives a loan from her bank. Is the amount she will pay the bank less than, greater than, or equal to the amount she originally borrowed? Explain.

☆ Independent Practice ☆

In **3** and **4**, show how to find each answer.

3. Alonzo has $78.46 in his checking account and then deposits $19.98. How much is in his account?

4. Jody earns $7.71 interest on the $257 in her savings account. How much does she have in her account in all?

Problem Solving

5. Reason Which bank services let you earn interest? Which services make you pay interest?

6. Yuri's family borrowed $958 to buy a refrigerator. They have to make 12 payments of $91. How much interest do they have to pay?

- **A** $43
- **B** $91
- **C** $126
- **D** $134

7. Justify Lee put the savings shown in a piggy bank. Erin put the savings shown in a bank and earned $0.21 interest. Who has more money? Tell how you know.

DATA	Month	Lee Saved	Erin Saved
	1	$9	$10
	2	$8	$6
	3	$11	$12

8. The statement shows what Amy bought with her credit card. What did she spend on restaurants in April? Show how you found the answer.

April

4/5	Steak House	$9.28
4/9	Books and Stuff	$7.48
4/14	Tacos! Tacos!	$3.47
4/25	Sandwich Factory	$4.93
4/27	Shoe Shop	$19.36
4/30	Wildlife Charity	$25.00

9. Explain If Amy gives the same amount of money to charity every month, how many months will it take her to give $200?

10. Extend Your Thinking Complete the dot plot for the following data. Which amount did the most fourth graders save?

Money 10 fourth graders saved: $1, $2, $4, $2, $3, $3, $2, $1, $5, $2

Money Saved by Fourth Graders

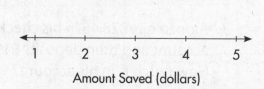

Amount Saved (dollars)

© Pearson Education, Inc. 4

Name _____

Another Look!

Which services do you have to pay a bank to do for you?
Which does a bank pay you for?

> Banks, credit unions, and savings and loans
> are financial institutions which provide money
> services. Services include loans, savings accounts,
> checking accounts, credit cards, and debit cards.

Service	Pay or Earn?
Loans	You pay interest.
Savings account	You earn interest.
Checking account and debit card	You may pay an account fee. You pay a fee if you spend more than is in the account.
Credit card	You may pay interest. You may pay a fee.

1. **Connect** Gayle had $968.43 in her college savings account at the beginning of May. She deposited $25 and earned $2.42 interest. What was the balance in her savings account then? Show how you found the answer.

2. Paul had $263.98 in his checking account at the beginning of June. He deposited $45.67, wrote a check for $36.87, and used his debit card for a $56.93 purchase. What was the balance in his savings account then? Show how you found the answer.

3. **Analyze Information** The bank statement to the right shows what Tyler bought with his credit card. What is the total amount he charged? Show how you found the answer.

March		
3/8/15	Tacos! Tacos!	$4.78
3/19/15	Craft House	$5.96
3/24/15	Everything Mart	$8.29

4. Mary's bank statement shows her beginning balance and the checks she has written. What is the balance of Mary's account now?

Mary			June
		Checking Account Information	
Check Number	**Date**	**Notes**	**+/−**
	6/20	Beginning Balance	$375.94
3146	6/29	Hair Cuts	$48.72
3147	6/29	Electric	$89.43

5. Check for Reasonableness Noah wants to save $700 in 10 months. He thinks he can earn $11 interest. Why is it reasonable that he should save $69 a month?

6. Analyze Information Hayley's family borrowed $2,045 from a bank to buy a car. To pay off the loan, they have to make 24 payments of $98. How much interest do they have to pay? Show your work.

7. Kayla's checking account statement is shown to the right. How much did Kayla spend and share through May 11? Show your work.

Kayla		May
	Checking account statement	
5/7	Y-Market	$75.96
5/9	Dance Studio	$35.00
5/10	Deposit	$575.38
5/11	City Water	$37.49
5/11	Gas and Electric	$85.42
5/11	Transfer to Savings	$200.00
5/11	Literacy Charity	$25.00
5/17	City Bank	

8. Extend Your Thinking Kala's beginning balance in May was $438.19. What was the balance in Kayla's checking account on May 12? Show your work.

9. Henry's family borrowed $486 to buy a television. They have to pay $63 interest. They need to make 9 equal monthly payments. How much do they need to pay each month?

A $65
B $61
C $54
D $7

© Pearson Education, Inc. 4

Name _____

☆ ☆
Solve & Share

Carla spent $5.40 on beads and $2.96 on cords to make necklaces. She sold 8 necklaces. How much should she sell each necklace for? Explain your answer. *Solve this problem any way you choose.*

You can **analyze relationships.** Think about what you know about financial ideas to decide how much Carla should charge. *Show your work in the space below!*

TEKS 4.1F Analyze mathematical relationships to connect and communicate mathematical ideas.
TEKS 4.10B Calculate profit in a given situation.
Mathematical Process Standards 4.1A, 4.1B, 4.1C, 4.1D, 4.1G

Digital Resources at PearsonTexas.com

Solve   Learn   Glossary   Check   Tools   Games

Look Back!

Check for Reasonableness Explain why your answer is reasonable.

How Can You Calculate Profit?

A Analyze

The fourth grade class sold 24 sandwiches at the soccer game. How much profit did they make?

Receipts are the total money taken in.

Expenses are the money spent.

Profit is the difference between expenses and receipts.

Expenses to make sandwiches

Meat	$30.50
Bread	$12.25
Cheese	$5.45
Tomatoes	$3.48
Mayonnaise	$1.50

$5 each

You can calculate profit by subtracting the total receipts minus the total expenses.

B Plan

Multiply to find the total receipts.

$$\begin{array}{r} \overset{2}{24} \\ \times\ 5 \\ \hline 120 \end{array}$$

The total receipts were $120.

C Plan

Add to find the total expenses.

$$\begin{array}{r} \overset{1\,2\,1}{\$30.50} \\ 12.25 \\ 5.45 \\ 3.48 \\ +\ 1.50 \\ \hline \$53.18 \end{array}$$

The total expenses were $53.18.

D Solve

Subtract to find the profit.

$$\begin{array}{r} \$120.00 \\ -\ 53.18 \\ \hline \$66.82 \end{array}$$

The profit was $66.82.

Do You Understand?

Convince Me! Suppose the fourth grade class also spent $3.50 on poster board and markers to make signs. What would their profit be then? Show how you found the answer.

☆ Guided Practice *

1. Stew had $46.95 in receipts and $28.37 in expenses. What was his profit?

2. Rene had $83.00 in receipts and $30.51 in profit. What were her expenses?

3. **Number Sense** In the problem on the previous page, if the fourth grade class didn't offer mayonnaise, but they still sold 24 sandwiches, would profit go up or down? Explain.

Independent Practice ☆

4. Patty had $110.28 in receipts and $75.52 in expenses. What was her profit?

5. Peter had $29.32 in receipts and $6.29 in expenses. What was his profit?

6. Fillip had $15.54 in profit and $19.46 in expenses. What were his receipts?

7. Georgia had $70.00 in receipts and $33.78 in profit. What were her expenses?

In **8** through **10**, use the table at the right.

8. What was Carson's profit?

9. What was Holly's profit?

10. **Check for Reasonableness** Why is it reasonable that Holly had more profit than Carson when both had the same amount in receipts?

DATA	Carson	Holly
Receipts	$64.00	$64.00
Expenses	$32.37	$28.37

Problem Solving

11. Analyze Information Trent kept track of his leaf-raking business as shown. What was his profit? Show how you found your answer.

Leaf Raking Business

Get $9 a yard

$5.64 for gas for leaf blower
— enough for 4 yards

Did 8 yards

---

12. Formulate a Plan Jill has a basketball game at 2:00 P.M. She is supposed to be at the gym 45 minutes before the game. It takes 20 minutes to get to the gym. She needs 10 minutes to get ready and 15 minutes to eat lunch. What is the latest time she should start eating lunch?

13. Paolo spent $3.57 on materials to make cell phone covers and $2.25 on advertising. He sold 5 covers for $3 each. What was his profit?

A $5.82
B $9.18
C $11.43
D $15.00

---

14. Communicate All triangles have 3 sides and 3 angles. How can you classify the triangles shown?

---

15. Check for Reasonableness Rachel made 6 birdhouses and sold 4 of them for $19 each. Is it reasonable that she had $57 in receipts? Explain.

16. Extend Your Thinking What are two ways to increase profit?

© Pearson Education, Inc. 4

Another Look!

The Math Club spent $3.58 on supplies to make signs for the bake sale. They didn't have any other expenses. They sold the baked goods shown. How much profit did the Math Club make?

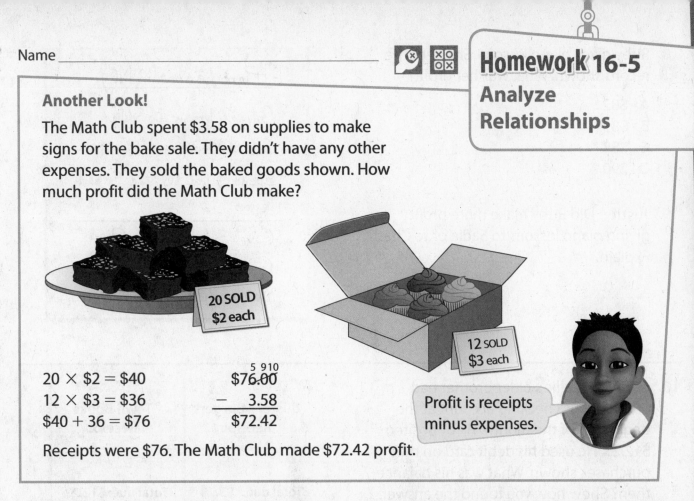

20 SOLD
$2 each

12 SOLD
$3 each

Profit is receipts minus expenses.

$20 \times \$2 = \$40$

$12 \times \$3 = \$36$

$\$40 + 36 = \$76$

$$\begin{array}{r} \overset{5\ 9\,10}{\$76.00} \\ -\quad 3.58 \\ \hline \$72.42 \end{array}$$

Receipts were $76. The Math Club made $72.42 profit.

1. Joel had $106.80 in receipts and $54.98 in expenses. What was his profit?

2. Kristy had $90.00 in receipts and $48.25 in expenses. What was her profit?

3. Brittney had $42.35 in receipts and $10.19 in expenses. What was her profit?

4. Manuel had $39.40 in receipts and $12.52 in expenses. What was his profit?

5. Cora had $50.00 in profit and $10.19 in expenses. What were her receipts?

6. Max had $75.00 in receipts and $51.54 in profit. What were his expenses?

An equation is one way you can represent a financial relationship.

7. **Connect** Valeria received $26 selling lemonade. She paid $13.50 for the supplies she needed. Find her profit by writing an equation using the variable, *p*.

8. Ruby gives piano lessons. She kept the record shown. What was her profit?

⭐

   A $82
   B $85
   C $88
   D $90

9. **Justify** Did Ruby make more profit giving piano lessons to Sadie or to Chad? Explain.

> **Piano Lessons in May**
>
> Gave 2 lessons to Sadie
> Get $20 for each lesson
> Spend $1.50 bus fare for each lesson
> ___
> Gave 3 lessons to Chad
> Get $15 each lesson
> No expenses

10. **Connect** Callie's older brother had $89.46 in his checking account at the beginning of the month. He deposited $12.25. He used his debit card on the purchases shown. What was his balance then? Show how you found the answer.

Buster's Burgers Receipt	Town Books Receipt
Total due: $3.78	Total due: $12.23
Paid by debit card	Paid by debit card

11. **Make a Graph** What is the total amount of money saved by the 6 students as shown in the stem-and-leaf plot?

Money Students Saved	
Stem	Leaf
3	50 77 85 90
4	25 50
Key: 3|50 = $3.50	

12. **Extend Your Thinking** Ryan sold 8 sock puppets for $4 each. It cost him $2 each to make 10 puppets. By how much will Ryan's profit increase when he sells the remaining puppets? Explain.

13. Ian had $567 in his savings account. He deposited $25 and earned $1.42 interest. How much was in his savings account then? Show how you found the answer.

© Pearson Education, Inc. 4

Name _____

1. **Explain** Candice earns $30 per week. She gives $6 of her earnings to charity. She puts $\frac{1}{2}$ of her earnings in savings. She spends the remainder of her earnings on things she needs. How much of her earnings does Candice spend? Explain.

Applying Math Processes
- How does this problem connect to previous ones?
- What is my plan?
- How can I use tools?
- How can I use number sense?
- How can I communicate and represent my thinking?
- How can I organize and record information?
- How can I explain my work?
- How can I justify my answer?

2. **Analyze Information** The marching band is holding a car wash to raise money for new uniforms. They spend $5 on soap, $7.50 on sponges and rags, $6.23 on car wax, and $4.75 on advertising supplies. The group charges $5 for each car wash. How many cars must the group wash to earn back the money they spent on supplies? Explain.

3. **Reason** Bernice saves her money in a jar in her room. Nigel saves his money in a savings account at a bank that pays $0.21 in interest. If they each save the same amount, who will have more money?

4. **Check for Reasonableness** Myra asked 73 people whether they have a savings account. 35 of them did. Myra estimates that about $\frac{1}{2}$ of the people she asked said they have a savings account. Is Myra's estimate reasonable? Explain.

5. **Extend Your Thinking** Howard and his family are making a plan to save money for a vacation next summer. What is something Howard and his family should consider when discussing how to save money for the trip?

6. **Connect** This week, the bank pays Val $1 in interest, she earns $40 at her job, she pays $17 in fixed expenses and $13 in variable expenses, and she donates $2 to a charity. If she puts the rest of her money in the bank, by how much does Val's savings increase this week?

Error Search

Find each problem that is not correct. Circle what is wrong and rewrite the problem so it is correct.

1. Two $1 bills + 2 quarters + 5 dimes + 2 nickels = $3.00

2. One $20 bill + two $5 bills + 7 dimes + 3 nickels + 15 pennies = $31.15

3. Two $10 bills + one $5 bill + six $1 bills + 1 quarter + 2 nickels = $31.35

4. Three $5 bills + seven $1 bills + 2 quarters + 4 dimes + 9 pennies = $23.09

Compatible Numbers

Mental Math Draw loops around two or more numbers next to each other, across or down, with a sum of 5 or 10. Look for compatible numbers (numbers that are easy to compute with mentally).

5. Find sums of 5.

1	1.82	2.08	1.1	2.5
1.25	0.45	3.29	1.71	2.50
2.75	2.0	2.3	1.70	1
4.91	2.55	0.48	3.00	1.52
0.9	3.33	0.56	1.11	3.06

6. Find sums of 10.

4.38	5.62	2.95	6.36	3.64
2.22	8.3	5.0	6.75	7.05
1.22	1.70	2.05	0.5	1.5
6.56	8.8	1.2	2.75	1.45
0.9	9.1	1.57	6.03	2.4

© Pearson Education, Inc. 4

Set A pages 883–888, 901–906

Dawn earned $42 babysitting. She gives $4 to charity. She spends $17. Then she puts the rest of the money in her savings account. How much money does Dawn put in her savings account?

Step 1 Subtract the amount given to charity.
$42 − 4 = $38

Step 2 Subtract the amount spent.
$38 − 17 = $21

Dawn deposits $21 in her savings account.

Reteaching

Remember that three things you can do with your money are share it, spend it, or save it.

1. Susan saves $4.50 and shares $2.25 every week. This week she earned $14 cleaning the garage. How much can she spend on other things this week?

2. Austin has a savings account in which he saves money for college. Last month, the balance in the account was $818.75. This month, he earned $140 picking apples and deposited all of it in his savings account. He also earned $5.16 interest. What is his new balance?

Set B pages 889–894

Carl puts $25 in his savings account each month. At the end of 3 months, the bank adds $0.70 interest to his savings account. How much money is in Carl's savings account after 3 months?

Step 1 Multiply to find the amount of money Carl saves.

$3 × $25 = 75

Step 2 Add the interest earned.

$75.00 + $0.70 = $75.70

Carl has $75.70 in his savings account.

Remember that when you save money in a bank, you usually earn interest, and your money is safer than if you keep it in a piggy bank.

1. Avery saves $22 per month. He keeps the money at home. How much will he have saved after a year?

2. Phyllis also saves $22 per month. She keeps her money in the bank. After 1 year, she earns $4.86 interest. How much will she have in her savings account after a year?

3. Describe the advantages and disadvantages of Phyllis's savings plan compared to Avery's.

pages 895–900

The Fazio family had the expenses shown.

House payment	$1,960
Birthday presents	$76
Car payment	$393
Cable TV	$85
New furnace	$1,008
County fair tickets	$32

Find the total of their fixed expenses.

$1,960 ← House payment
393 ← Car payment
+ 85 ← Cable TV
$2,438 ← Total fixed expenses

Find the total of their variable expenses.

$76 ← Birthday presents
1,008 ← New furnace
+ 32 ← County fair tickets
$1,116 ← Total variable expenses

Remember that fixed expenses are paid regularly. Variable expenses do not occur on a regular basis.

Mrs. Hill's Expenses	
New sofa	$707
Rent	$352
Sandals	$63
Ned's baseball uniform	$55
Internet provider bill	$62
Car payment	$284

1. Find the total amount of Mrs. Hill's variable expenses.

2. Find the total amount of Mrs. Hill's fixed expenses.

Set D pages 907–912

Kent spent $96 for stained glass and $28 for lumber. He made 5 stained-glass windows. He sold each window for $65. What was his profit?

Step 1 Multiply to find the receipts.

5 × $65 = $325

Step 2 Add to find the expenses.

$96 + $28 = $124

Step 3 Subtract to find the profit.

$325 − $124 = $201

Kent's profit was $201.

Remember that profit is the difference between expenses and receipts.

1. Frank bought a package of blank cards for $8.15 and a paint set for $7.51. He made 12 greeting cards which he sold for $3 each. How much profit did Frank make?

2. Dee spent $24 for fabric, $2.18 for thread, and $4.77 for a pattern. She made 4 aprons that she sold for $12 each. How much profit did Dee make?

© Pearson Education, Inc. 4

Name _____

1. Kelly wrote down the amount of her allowance and the amounts she spent. If she saved the rest of her allowance, how much did she save?

Kelly's Money

Allowance	$10.00
Share	$1.25
Skating	$4.50
Snack	$2.28

A $1.97 **C** $2.22

B $2.97 **D** $3.22

2. Which of the following is an advantage of putting your money in a bank?

A Your money earns interest.

B Your money is unsafe.

C It may be difficult to take your money to the bank.

D All of the above

3. Lindsey charged $3.45, $4.67, and $9.85 to her credit card. How much did she charge in all?

A $13.30

B $14.52

C $16.87

D $17.97

4. Tom had $103.29 in his savings account. Then he deposits $12 and earns $0.77 interest. How much is in his account now?

A $104.06

B $114.52

C $115.29

D $116.06

In **5** and **6**, use the record Dwight kept of his money.

Dwight's Money

Earn doing errands	$20.00
Share	$1.50
Golf	$8.75
Buster's Burgers	$6.28
Save rest	

5. How much did Dwight spend in all?

A $15.03 **C** $6.28

B $8.75 **D** $1.50

6. How much did Dwight save? Show how you found your answer.

7. Which of the following is **NOT** a variable expense?

  A Rent

  B Money to go bowling

  C Car repair

  D Money for shoes

---

8. Fred's checking account statement is shown. What was his ending balance? Show how you found your answer.

Checking account statement		
5/1	Beginning balance	$143.08
5/10	Paid Steak Place	$18.43
5/17	Paid Buddy's Gas	$35.00
5/28	Deposit	$39.76

---

9. Lance makes coat racks and sells them for $8 each. He spends $4 on supplies for each coat rack he makes. In the last 6 months, he has sold 47 coat racks. What is Lance's profit so far, in dollars?

---

10. Which of the following is something a bank does?

  A Loans money

  B Provides checking accounts

  C Keeps money safe

  D All of the above

---

11. The Book Club sells calendars to raise money to buy books. The club buys the calendars for $2 each. They sell the calendars for $6 each. They also spend $10.48 on advertising. If the club sells 106 calendars, what will be their profit?

  A $402.52

  B $413.52

  C $424.00

  D $625.52

---

12. Last month, the Katz family spent $782 on a house payment, $148 on clothes, $84 at a restaurant, and $45 on movie tickets. What were their total variable expenses, in dollars?

© Pearson Education, Inc. 4

Here's a preview of next year. These lessons help you step up to Grade 5.

Step Up to Grade 5

Lessons

TEKS 5.3A Estimate to determine solutions to mathematical and real-world problems involving addition, subtraction, multiplication, or division.

TEKS 5.3H Represent and solve addition and subtraction of fractions with unequal denominators referring to the same whole using objects and pictorial models and properties of operations.

TEKS 5.3I Represent and solve multiplication of a whole number and a fraction that refers to the same whole using objects and pictorial models, including area models.

TEKS 5.3J Represent division of a unit fraction by a whole number and the division of a whole number by a unit fraction such as $\frac{1}{3} \div 7$ and $7 \div \frac{1}{3}$ using objects and pictorial models, including area models.

TEKS 5.4 Develop concepts of expressions and equations.

TEKS 5.4H Represent and solve problems related to perimeter and/or area and related to volume.

TEKS 5.6A Recognize a cube with side length of one unit as a unit cube having one cubic unit of volume and the volume of a three-dimensional figure as the number of unit cubes (*n* cubic units) needed to fill it with no gaps or overlaps if possible.

TEKS 5.6B Determine the volume of a rectangular prism with whole number side lengths in problems related to the number of layers times the number of unit cubes in the area of the base.

The following Grade 5 TEKS are introduced in the Step-Up lessons.

Name _____

Renee needs 32 strands of twine for an art project. Each strand must measure 1.25 cm long. About how much twine does she need for the project? **Solve this problem any way you choose!**

Connect Ideas You know how to estimate with whole numbers. **Show your work!**

Step Up to Grade 5

Lesson 1
Estimating the Product of a Decimal and a Whole Number

⭐ **TEKS 5.3A** Estimate to determine solutions to mathematical and real-world problems involving addition, subtraction, multiplication, or division. **Mathematical Process Standards 5.1A, 5.1D, 5.1F, 5.1G**

Digital Resources at PearsonTexas.com

Solve   Learn   Glossary   Tools   Games

Look Back!

Justify Is your estimate an overestimate or an underestimate? How can you tell?

What Are Some Ways to Estimate Products with Decimals?

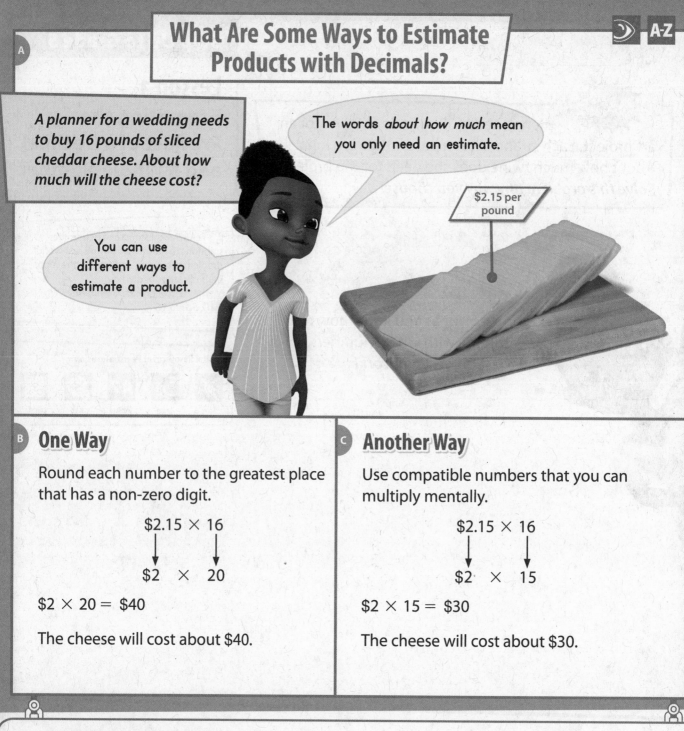

A planner for a wedding needs to buy 16 pounds of sliced cheddar cheese. About how much will the cheese cost?

The words *about how much* mean you only need an estimate.

You can use different ways to estimate a product.

$2.15 per pound

B One Way

Round each number to the greatest place that has a non-zero digit.

$2.15 × 16

$2 × 20

$2 × 20 = $40

The cheese will cost about $40.

C Another Way

Use compatible numbers that you can multiply mentally.

$2.15 × 16

$2 × 15

$2 × 15 = $30

The cheese will cost about $30.

Do You Understand?

Convince Me! About how much money would 18 pounds of cheese cost if the price is $3.95 per pound? Use two different ways to estimate the product. Are your estimates overestimates or underestimates? Explain.

© Pearson Education, Inc. 4

Name _____

Another Example

Manuel walks 0.75 mile to and from school each day. If there have been 114 school days so far this year, about how many miles has he walked altogether?

Round to the greatest place value.

114×0.75

$114 \times 1 = 114$

Use compatible numbers.

114×0.75

$110 \times 0.8 = 88.0$ Be sure to place the decimal point correctly.

Both methods provide reasonable estimates of how far Manuel has walked.

☆ Guided Practice

In **1** through **6**, estimate each product using rounding or compatible numbers.

1. 2.87×412 **2.** 943×1.98

3. 107×5.15 **4.** 4.06×73

5. 41.05×300 **6.** 8.95×21

7. Explain About how many miles does Manuel walk each month? Explain your answer.

8. Communicate Sasha estimated the product of 115×6.73 by multiplying 100×7. Is her estimate an overestimate or an underestimate? Explain.

Independent Practice ☆

In **9** through **16**, estimate each product.

9. 119×2.8 **10.** 4.7×69 **11.** 107×2.3 **12.** 35×3.5

13. 1.6×7 **14.** 9.1×53 **15.** 39×1.22 **16.** 4×7.8

Problem Solving

17. Connect Isaac is buying supplies for a birthday party. About how much money does he need to buy 3 bags of balloons and 4 packs of gift bags?

DATA	Party Supply	Cost
	Balloons	$3.95 per bag
	Gift Bags	$7.95 per pack

18. Charlie buys a cake for $23.99 and 6 bags of balloons. About how much money does he spend?

---

19. Isabel walks 0.83 mile to and from the library 3 days a week. About how many miles does she walk in 4 weeks?

   A About 3 miles
   B About 4 miles
   C About 12 miles
   D About 18 miles

20. Connect One basketball weighs 20.2 ounces. The basketball team has a total of 15 basketballs. If each basketball weighs the same, about how much do the basketballs weigh in all? Show your work.

---

21. The side lengths of a square measure 25.3 cm. Estimate the area of the square.

22. Extend Your Thinking If $n \times 4.16$ is about 200, what is a reasonable estimate for n? Explain.

Find and answer the hidden question to solve the problem.

23. Personal Financial Literacy Morgan buys 2 T-shirts that cost $14.95 each and 1 pair of shorts that costs $23.89. He gives the cashier $60.00. How much change will he receive? Show your work.

© Pearson Education, Inc. 4

Name _____

Solve & Share

Sue wants $\frac{1}{2}$ of a rectangular pan of cornbread. Dena wants $\frac{1}{3}$ of the same pan of cornbread. How should you cut the cornbread so that each of the girls gets the size portion she wants? *Solve this problem any way you choose.*

Create and Use Representations You can draw a picture to represent the pan as 1 whole. Then solve. *Show your work!*

TEKS 5.3H Represent and solve addition and subtraction of fractions with unequal denominators referring to the same whole using objects and pictorial models and properties of operations. Mathematical Process Standards 5.1C, 5.1D, 5.1E, 5.1G

Digital Resources at PearsonTexas.com

Solve   Learn   Glossary   Tools   Games

Look Back!

Justify Is there more than one way to divide the pan of cornbread into equal-sized parts? Explain how you know.

How Can You Find a Common Denominator for Fractions with Unlike Denominators?

Tyrone divided a rectangle into thirds. Sally divided a rectangle of the same size into fourths. How could you divide a rectangle of the same size so that you see both thirds and fourths?

You can divide a rectangle to show thirds and fourths.

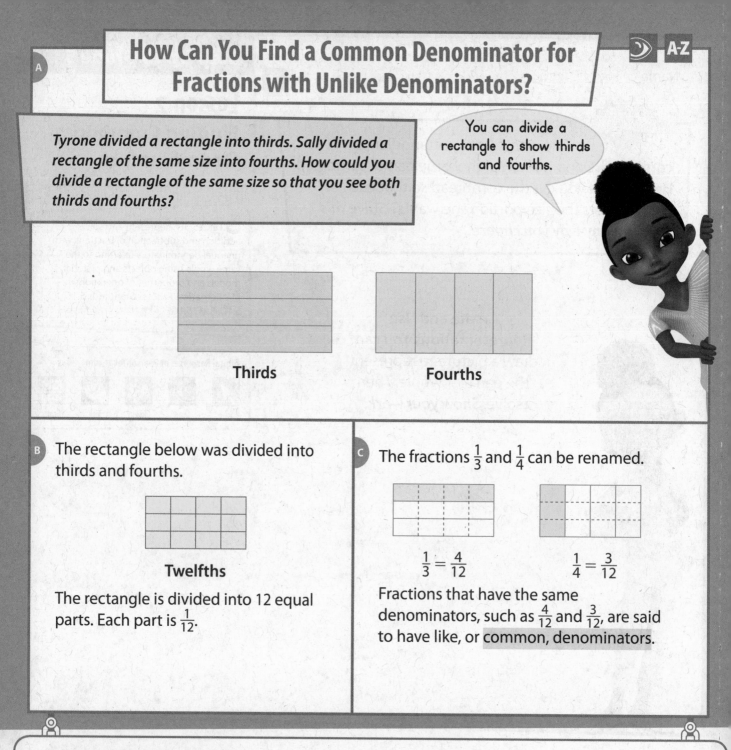

Thirds

Fourths

B

The rectangle below was divided into thirds and fourths.

Twelfths

The rectangle is divided into 12 equal parts. Each part is $\frac{1}{12}$.

C

The fractions $\frac{1}{3}$ and $\frac{1}{4}$ can be renamed.

$$\frac{1}{3} = \frac{4}{12}$$

$$\frac{1}{4} = \frac{3}{12}$$

Fractions that have the same denominators, such as $\frac{4}{12}$ and $\frac{3}{12}$, are said to have like, or **common, denominators.**

Do You Understand?

Convince Me! Draw rectangles like the ones above to find fractions equivalent to $\frac{2}{5}$ and $\frac{1}{3}$ that have the same denominator.

© Pearson Education, Inc. 4

Another Example

How can you use multiples to find a common denominator?

Find a common denominator for $\frac{7}{12}$ and $\frac{5}{6}$. Then rename each fraction.

One Way

Multiply the denominators: $12 \times 6 = 72$.

Rename both fractions so they have a common denominator of 72.

$\frac{7}{12} = \frac{7 \times 6}{12 \times 6} = \frac{42}{72}$ $\qquad$ $\frac{5}{6} = \frac{5 \times 12}{6 \times 12} = \frac{60}{72}$

So, $\frac{42}{72}$ and $\frac{60}{72}$ is one way to name $\frac{7}{12}$ and $\frac{5}{6}$ with a common denominator.

Another Way

Check to see if one denominator is a multiple of the other.

You know that 12 is a multiple of 6.

$\frac{5}{6} = \frac{5 \times 2}{6 \times 2} = \frac{10}{12}$

So, $\frac{7}{12}$ and $\frac{10}{12}$ is another way to name $\frac{7}{12}$ and $\frac{5}{6}$ with a common denominator.

☆ Guided Practice

In **1** and **2**, find a common denominator for each pair of fractions.

1. $\frac{1}{6}$ and $\frac{1}{2}$ $\qquad$ **2.** $\frac{2}{3}$ and $\frac{3}{4}$

3. On the previous page, how many twelfths are in each $\frac{1}{3}$ section of Tyrone's rectangle, and how many twelfths are in each $\frac{1}{4}$ section of Sally's rectangle?

☆ Independent Practice ☆

In **4** through **7**, find a common denominator for each pair of fractions. Then rename each fraction.

4. $\frac{3}{5}$ and $\frac{3}{8}$ $\qquad$ **5.** $\frac{2}{7}$ and $\frac{10}{21}$ $\qquad$ **6.** $\frac{4}{9}$ and $\frac{5}{6}$ $\qquad$ **7.** $\frac{1}{7}$ and $\frac{1}{9}$

Problem Solving

8. Number Sense The table shows the price for three different sandwiches sold at a local deli. Order the sandwiches from most expensive to least expensive.

Lunch Menu	
Sandwich	**Price**
Ham	$3.89
Turkey	$4.09
Chicken	$3.79

9. Draw a Picture Gemma bought two cakes that are the same size. The first one was divided into 3 equal sections. The second one was divided into 2 equal sections. Gemma wants to cut the cakes so that there are 6 pieces in each cake. Draw on the pictures to show how Gemma should cut each cake.

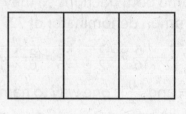

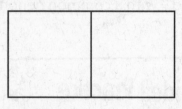

10. Justify Clara says that the only common denominator of $\frac{3}{4}$ and $\frac{3}{5}$ is 20. Do you agree? Explain.

11. Extend Your Thinking The least common denominator is the least common multiple of the two denominators. What is the least common denominator of $\frac{3}{4}$ and $\frac{5}{6}$? Show your work.

12. ★ Diego will walk the Canyon Falls Trail and the River Ridge Trail. Which of the following fraction pairs renames the length of each trail he will walk using a common denominator?

A $\frac{28}{40}$ and $\frac{30}{40}$ **C** $\frac{7}{4}$ and $\frac{3}{4}$

B $\frac{7}{40}$ and $\frac{3}{40}$ **D** $\frac{7}{10}$ and $\frac{3}{10}$

Canyon Trails	
Trail Name	**Length**
Falls Overlook	$\frac{7}{8}$ mile
Canyon Falls	$\frac{7}{10}$ mile
River Ridge	$\frac{3}{4}$ mile
Sunset Lake	$\frac{9}{10}$ mile

© Pearson Education, Inc. 4

Name _____

Solve & Share

Over the weekend, Eleni ate $\frac{1}{4}$ box of cereal, and Freddie ate $\frac{3}{8}$ of the same box. What portion of the box of cereal did they eat in all? *Use or draw fraction strips to help solve the problem.*

Lesson 3
Adding Fractions with Unlike Denominators

TEKS 5.3H Represent and solve addition and subtraction of fractions with unequal denominators referring to the same whole using objects and pictorial models and properties of operations. Mathematical Process Standards 5.1A, 5.1B, 5.1D, 5.1G

Digital Resources at PearsonTexas.com

Solve   Learn   Glossary   Tools   Games

Formulate a Plan You can use fraction strips to represent adding fractions. *Show your work!*

Look Back!

Justify What steps did you take to solve this problem?

How Can You Add Fractions with Unlike Denominators?

A

> Alex rode his scooter from his house to the park. Later, he rode from the park to baseball practice. How far did Alex ride?

You can add to find the total distance that Alex rode his scooter.

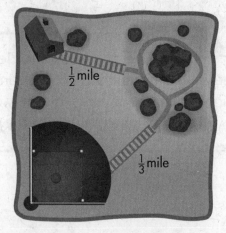

$\frac{1}{2}$ mile

$\frac{1}{3}$ mile

B ## Step 1

Change the fractions to equivalent fractions with a common, or like, denominator.

1
$\frac{1}{2}$	$\frac{1}{3}$

Multiples of 2: 2, 4, 6, 8, 10, 12, . . .

Multiples of 3: 3, 6, 9, 12, . . .

The number 6 is a common multiple of 2 and 3, so $\frac{1}{2}$ and $\frac{1}{3}$ can both be rewritten with a common denominator of 6.

C ## Step 2

Write the equivalent fractions.

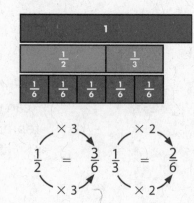

$\frac{1}{2} = \frac{3}{6}$ $\times 3$
$\frac{1}{3} = \frac{2}{6}$ $\times 2$

D ## Step 3

Add the numerators. Simplify if necessary.

$$\frac{1}{2} = \frac{3}{6}$$
$$+\frac{1}{3} = \frac{2}{6}$$
$$\frac{5}{6}$$

Alex rode his scooter $\frac{5}{6}$ mile.

Do You Understand?

Convince Me! In the example above, would you get the same sum if you used 12 as the common denominator? Explain.

930

© Pearson Education, Inc. 4

☆ Guided Practice

In **1**, find the sum. Simplify if necessary.

1. $\frac{2}{3} + \frac{1}{9}$

$$\frac{2}{3} = \frac{\square}{\square}$$

$$+ \frac{1}{9} = \frac{\square}{\square}$$

$$\overline{\quad\quad\quad}$$

$$\frac{\square}{\square}$$

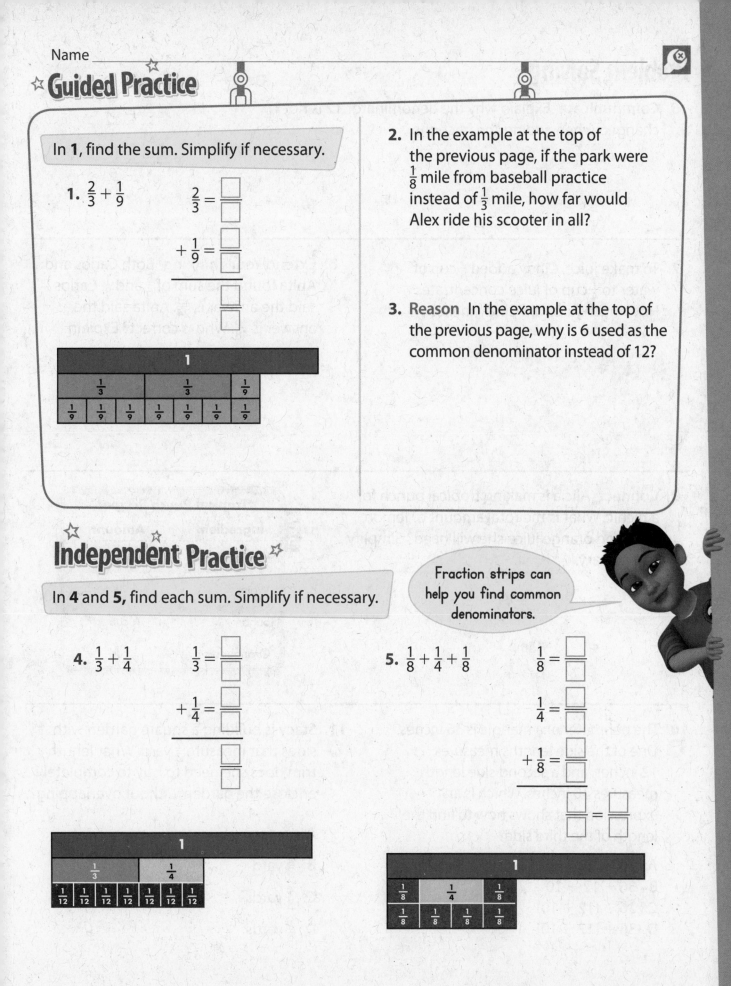

1						
$\frac{1}{3}$		$\frac{1}{3}$			$\frac{1}{9}$	
$\frac{1}{9}$	$\frac{1}{9}$	$\frac{1}{9}$	$\frac{1}{9}$	$\frac{1}{9}$	$\frac{1}{9}$	$\frac{1}{9}$

2. In the example at the top of the previous page, if the park were $\frac{1}{8}$ mile from baseball practice instead of $\frac{1}{3}$ mile, how far would Alex ride his scooter in all?

3. **Reason** In the example at the top of the previous page, why is 6 used as the common denominator instead of 12?

☆ Independent Practice ☆

In **4** and **5**, find each sum. Simplify if necessary.

4. $\frac{1}{3} + \frac{1}{4}$

$$\frac{1}{3} = \frac{\square}{\square}$$

$$+ \frac{1}{4} = \frac{\square}{\square}$$

$$\overline{\quad\quad\quad}$$

$$\frac{\square}{\square}$$

1						
$\frac{1}{3}$			$\frac{1}{4}$			
$\frac{1}{12}$	$\frac{1}{12}$	$\frac{1}{12}$	$\frac{1}{12}$	$\frac{1}{12}$	$\frac{1}{12}$	$\frac{1}{12}$

> Fraction strips can help you find common denominators.

5. $\frac{1}{8} + \frac{1}{4} + \frac{1}{8}$

$$\frac{1}{8} = \frac{\square}{\square}$$

$$\frac{1}{4} = \frac{\square}{\square}$$

$$+ \frac{1}{8} = \frac{\square}{\square}$$

$$\overline{\quad\quad\quad}$$

$$\frac{\square}{\square} = \frac{\square}{\square}$$

1			
$\frac{1}{8}$	$\frac{1}{4}$		$\frac{1}{8}$
$\frac{1}{8}$	$\frac{1}{8}$	$\frac{1}{8}$	$\frac{1}{8}$

Problem Solving

6. Communicate Explain why the denominator 12 is not changed when adding the fractions.

$$\frac{5}{12} = \frac{5}{12}$$
$$+ \frac{1}{3} = \frac{4}{12}$$
$$\overline{\quad\frac{9}{12}\quad}$$

---

7. To make juice, Cindy added $\frac{5}{8}$ cup of water to $\frac{1}{4}$ cup of juice concentrate. How much juice did Cindy make?

8. Extend Your Thinking Both Carlos and Anita found the sum of $\frac{5}{6}$ and $\frac{1}{8}$. Carlos said the answer is $\frac{23}{24}$. Anita said the answer is $\frac{46}{48}$. Who is correct? Explain.

---

9. Connect Alicia is making tropical punch for a picnic. What is the total amount of lemon juice and orange juice she will need? Simplify, if necessary.

Tropical Punch Recipe	
Ingredient	**Amount**
Lemon Juice	$\frac{1}{3}$ cup
Water	4 cups
Sugar	$\frac{2}{3}$ cup
Orange Juice	$\frac{1}{2}$ cup

DATA

---

10. The perimeter of a triangle is 36 inches. One of the side lengths measures 12 inches, and a second side length measures 10 inches. Which is an expression that shows how to find the length of the third side?

A $36 - 12 + 10$

B $36 + 12 + 10$

C $36 - (12 + 10)$

D $36 + (12 - 10)$

11. Stacy is building a square garden with sides that measure $\frac{2}{3}$ yard. What length trim does she need to buy to completely enclose the garden without overlapping?

A $\frac{8}{12}$ yard

B $\frac{2}{3}$ yard

C $\frac{4}{3}$ yards

D $\frac{8}{3}$ yards

© Pearson Education, Inc. 4

Name _____

☆ ☆
Solve & Share

Rose bought a length of copper pipe. She used $\frac{1}{2}$ yard to repair the shower. How much pipe does she have left? *Solve this problem any way you choose.*

TEKS 5.3H Represent and solve addition and subtraction of fractions with unequal denominators referring to the same whole using objects and pictorial models and properties of operations. Mathematical Process Standards 5.1C, 5.1D, 5.1F, 5.1G

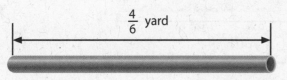

$\frac{4}{6}$ yard

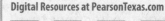

Digital Resources at PearsonTexas.com

| Solve | Learn | Glossary | Tools | Games |

You can use **mental math** to rename $\frac{1}{2}$ and $\frac{4}{6}$ as fractions with like denominators. *Show your work!*

Look Back!

Connect Ideas How is adding fractions with unlike denominators similar to subtracting fractions with unlike denominators?

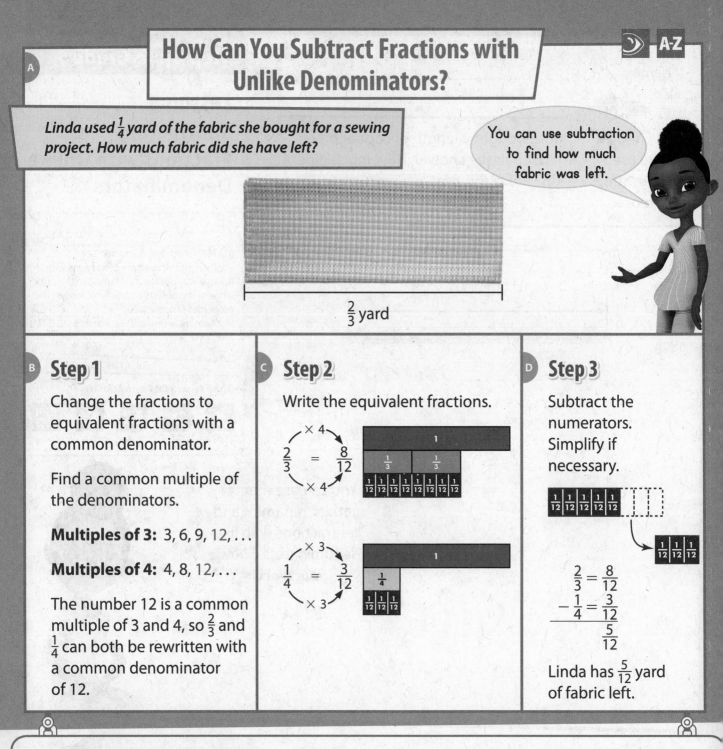

A

How Can You Subtract Fractions with Unlike Denominators?

A-Z

Linda used $\frac{1}{4}$ yard of the fabric she bought for a sewing project. How much fabric did she have left?

You can use subtraction to find how much fabric was left.

$\frac{2}{3}$ yard

B **Step 1**

Change the fractions to equivalent fractions with a common denominator.

Find a common multiple of the denominators.

Multiples of 3: 3, 6, 9, 12, . . .

Multiples of 4: 4, 8, 12, . . .

The number 12 is a common multiple of 3 and 4, so $\frac{2}{3}$ and $\frac{1}{4}$ can both be rewritten with a common denominator of 12.

C **Step 2**

Write the equivalent fractions.

$\frac{2}{3} = \frac{8}{12}$

$\frac{1}{4} = \frac{3}{12}$

D **Step 3**

Subtract the numerators. Simplify if necessary.

$$\frac{2}{3} = \frac{8}{12}$$
$$-\frac{1}{4} = \frac{3}{12}$$
$$\frac{5}{12}$$

Linda has $\frac{5}{12}$ yard of fabric left.

Do You Understand?

Convince Me! Suppose Linda had $\frac{2}{3}$ yard of fabric and told Sandra that she used $\frac{3}{4}$ of a yard. Sandra says this is not possible. Do you agree? Explain your answer.

© Pearson Education, Inc. 4

Name _____

In **1** through **4**, find each difference. Simplify, if necessary.

1.
$$\frac{3}{4} = \frac{9}{12}$$
$$-\frac{1}{3} = \frac{4}{12}$$

2.
$$\frac{5}{12} = \frac{10}{24}$$
$$-\frac{1}{8} = \frac{3}{24}$$

3.
$$\frac{2}{3}$$
$$-\frac{1}{6}$$

4.
$$\frac{7}{10}$$
$$-\frac{3}{8}$$

5. Reason In the example on the previous page, is it possible to use a common denominator greater than 12 and get the correct answer? Explain.

6. In the example on the previous page, if Linda had started with one yard of fabric and used $\frac{5}{8}$ yard, how much fabric would be left?

☆ **Independent Practice** ☆

Leveled Practice In **7** through **12**, find each difference. Simplify, if necessary.

7.
$$\frac{3}{5} = \frac{\square}{10}$$
$$-\frac{3}{10} = \frac{\square}{10}$$
$$\frac{\square}{\square}$$

8.
$$\frac{1}{2} = \frac{\square}{6}$$
$$-\frac{1}{3} = \frac{\square}{6}$$
$$\frac{\square}{\square}$$

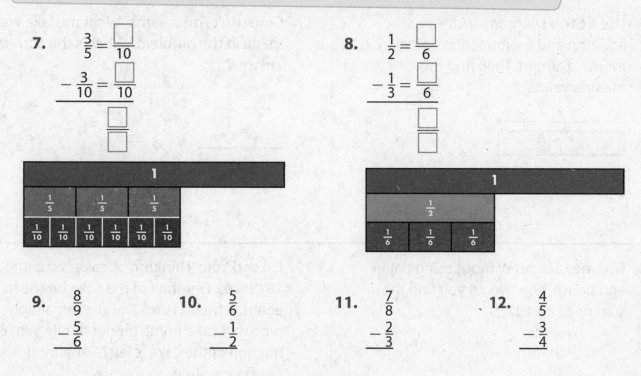

9.
$$\frac{8}{9}$$
$$-\frac{5}{6}$$

10.
$$\frac{5}{6}$$
$$-\frac{1}{2}$$

11.
$$\frac{7}{8}$$
$$-\frac{2}{3}$$

12.
$$\frac{4}{5}$$
$$-\frac{3}{4}$$

Problem Solving

13. Write a number sentence to name the difference between the locations of Point *A* and Point *B* on the ruler.

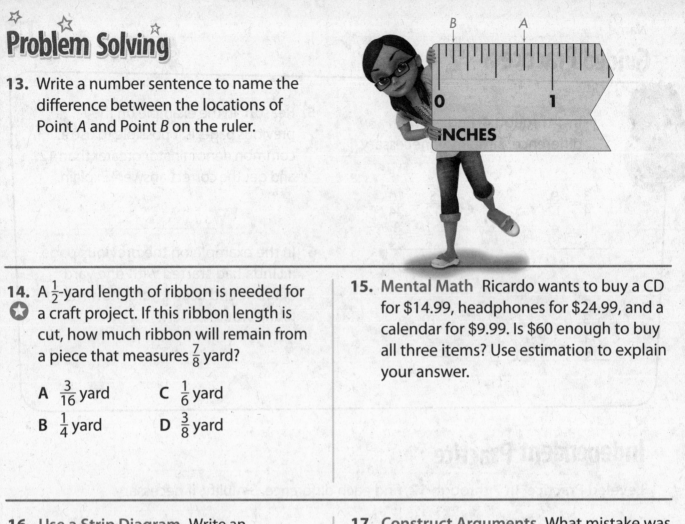

14. A $\frac{1}{2}$-yard length of ribbon is needed for a craft project. If this ribbon length is cut, how much ribbon will remain from a piece that measures $\frac{7}{8}$ yard?

   A $\frac{3}{16}$ yard   **C** $\frac{1}{6}$ yard

   B $\frac{1}{4}$ yard   **D** $\frac{3}{8}$ yard

15. Mental Math Ricardo wants to buy a CD for $14.99, headphones for $24.99, and a calendar for $9.99. Is $60 enough to buy all three items? Use estimation to explain your answer.

16. Use a Strip Diagram Write an addition and a subtraction equation for the diagram. Then find the missing value.

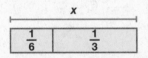

17. Construct Arguments What mistake was made in the problem? What is the correct answer?

$$\frac{7}{8} = \frac{7}{8}$$
$$-\frac{1}{4} = \frac{1}{8}$$
$$\overline{\frac{6}{8} = \frac{3}{4}}$$

18. Number Sense Without using paper and pencil, how would you find the sum of 23 and 37?

19. Extend Your Thinking A cake is cut into 18 pieces. One-half of the cake has been eaten. A friend takes 5 of the remaining pieces of cake home for her family. What fraction of the cake is left? Simplify, if necessary. Show your work.

© Pearson Education, Inc. 4

Name _____

Solve & Share

Kelly and Mara were working on their math homework. Kelly wrote $\frac{3}{4}$ as $\frac{1}{4} + \frac{1}{4} + \frac{1}{4}$. Mara looked at it and said, "I think you could use multiplication to rewrite that sum." Do you agree with Mara? **Solve this problem any way you choose.**

TEKS 5.3I Represent and solve multiplication of a whole number and a fraction that refers to the same whole using objects and pictorial models, including area models. Mathematical Process Standards 5.1A, 5.1C, 5.1D, 5.1E

Communicate You can use a drawing to explain your thinking. **Show your work!**

Digital Resources at PearsonTexas.com

| Solve | Learn | Glossary | Tools | Games |

Look Back!

Number Sense How can you write $\frac{4}{5}$ using addition? using multiplication?

How Can You Describe a Fraction Using a Unit Fraction?

A unit fraction is a fraction that describes one part of the whole.

Unit fractions always have a numerator of 1.

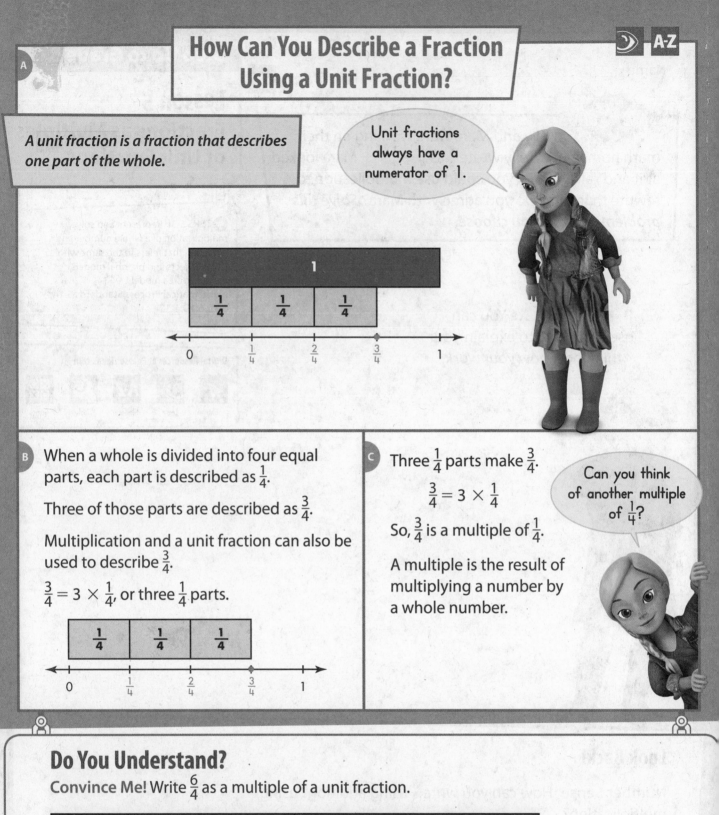

B When a whole is divided into four equal parts, each part is described as $\frac{1}{4}$.

Three of those parts are described as $\frac{3}{4}$.

Multiplication and a unit fraction can also be used to describe $\frac{3}{4}$.

$\frac{3}{4} = 3 \times \frac{1}{4}$, or three $\frac{1}{4}$ parts.

C Three $\frac{1}{4}$ parts make $\frac{3}{4}$.

$$\frac{3}{4} = 3 \times \frac{1}{4}$$

So, $\frac{3}{4}$ is a multiple of $\frac{1}{4}$.

A multiple is the result of multiplying a number by a whole number.

Can you think of another multiple of $\frac{1}{4}$?

Do You Understand?

Convince Me! Write $\frac{6}{4}$ as a multiple of a unit fraction.

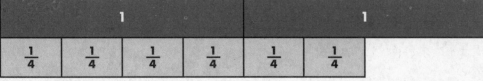

© Pearson Education, Inc. 4

☆Guided Practice

In **1** through **6**, write the fraction as a multiple of a unit fraction. Use fraction strips to help.

1. $\dfrac{4}{6} = \square \times \dfrac{1}{6}$

2. $\dfrac{7}{12} = \square \times \dfrac{1}{12}$

3. $\dfrac{8}{9} = \square \times \dfrac{1}{9}$

4. $\dfrac{9}{10} = \square \times \dfrac{1}{10}$

5. $\dfrac{6}{7} = \square \times \dfrac{1}{7}$

6. $\dfrac{3}{5} = \square \times \dfrac{1}{5}$

7. **Tools** Draw a picture to explain why $\dfrac{6}{5} = 6 \times \dfrac{1}{5}$.

8. **Represent** Susan's family ate part of a pizza for dinner. There are 3 people in her family. Each family member ate $\dfrac{1}{8}$ of the pizza. What multiplication equation represents the part of the pizza the whole family ate?

Independent Practice ☆

Leveled Practice In **9** through **24**, write the fraction as a multiple of a unit fraction. Use fraction strips to help.

9. $\dfrac{6}{8} = \square \times \dfrac{1}{8}$

10. $\dfrac{5}{9} = \square \times \dfrac{1}{\square}$

11. $\dfrac{4}{11} = \square \times \dfrac{\square}{\square}$

12. $\dfrac{4}{7} = \square \times \dfrac{\square}{\square}$

13. $\dfrac{11}{12} = \square \times \dfrac{\square}{\square}$

14. $\dfrac{5}{7} = \square \times \dfrac{\square}{\square}$

15. $\dfrac{5}{12} = \square \times \dfrac{\square}{\square}$

16. $\dfrac{8}{11} = \square \times \dfrac{\square}{\square}$

17. $\dfrac{9}{9} = \square \times \dfrac{\square}{\square}$

18. $\dfrac{11}{10} = \square \times \dfrac{\square}{\square}$

19. $\dfrac{12}{7} = \square \times \dfrac{\square}{\square}$

20. $\dfrac{9}{6} = \square \times \dfrac{\square}{\square}$

21. $\dfrac{11}{7} = \square \times \dfrac{\square}{\square}$

22. $\dfrac{7}{5} = \square \times \dfrac{\square}{\square}$

23. $\dfrac{15}{12} = \square \times \dfrac{\square}{\square}$

24. $\dfrac{11}{8} = \square \times \dfrac{\square}{\square}$

Problem Solving

25. Represent Write an equation that describes the picture. Each pear part is $\frac{1}{2}$ of a pear. Show your answer as a multiplication equation with a unit fraction as a factor.

26. Connect Look at the picture. Write and solve a problem for it. Show your answer as a multiplication equation with $\frac{1}{2}$ as a factor.

27. Extend Your Thinking A recipe calls for $\frac{2}{3}$ cup of milk. Dani needs to double the recipe. How much milk will Dani need? Explain.

28. Use a Strip Diagram The cost of a hardcover book is $13.59. This is $5.64 more than the cost of a paperback book. What is the cost of a paperback book?

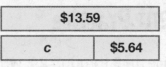

29. ⭐ Joni listed the distances from her home to different locations as shown in the table to the right. If she walks from her home to the library 4 times and from her home to the store 2 times, how far does Joni walk in all?

A 6 miles

B 2 miles

C $\frac{3}{4}$ mile

D $\frac{1}{2}$ mile

Distance From Home	
Location	**Distance (miles)**
Library	$\frac{1}{4}$
Store	$\frac{1}{2}$
Park	$\frac{1}{3}$

© Pearson Education, Inc. 4

Name _____

☆ **Solve & Share** ☆

Brandon has 6 eggs. He needs $\frac{2}{3}$ of the eggs to make an omelet. How many eggs does he need?

Lesson 6
Multiplying Fractions and Whole Numbers

TEKS 5.3I Represent and solve multiplication of a whole number and a fraction that refers to the same whole using objects and pictorial models, including area models.
Mathematical Process Standards 5.1A, 5.1C, 5.1D, 5.1G

Select and Use Tools
Would a drawing help you picture the situation?

Digital Resources at PearsonTexas.com

Solve Learn Glossary Tools Games

Look Back!

Number Sense Should your answer be less than or greater than 6? How do you know?

How Can You Multiply a Fraction and a Whole Number?

A rectangular flag has an area of 15 square feet. $\frac{4}{5}$ of the flag is red. $\frac{1}{5}$ of the flag is blue.

What is the area of the red part of the flag?

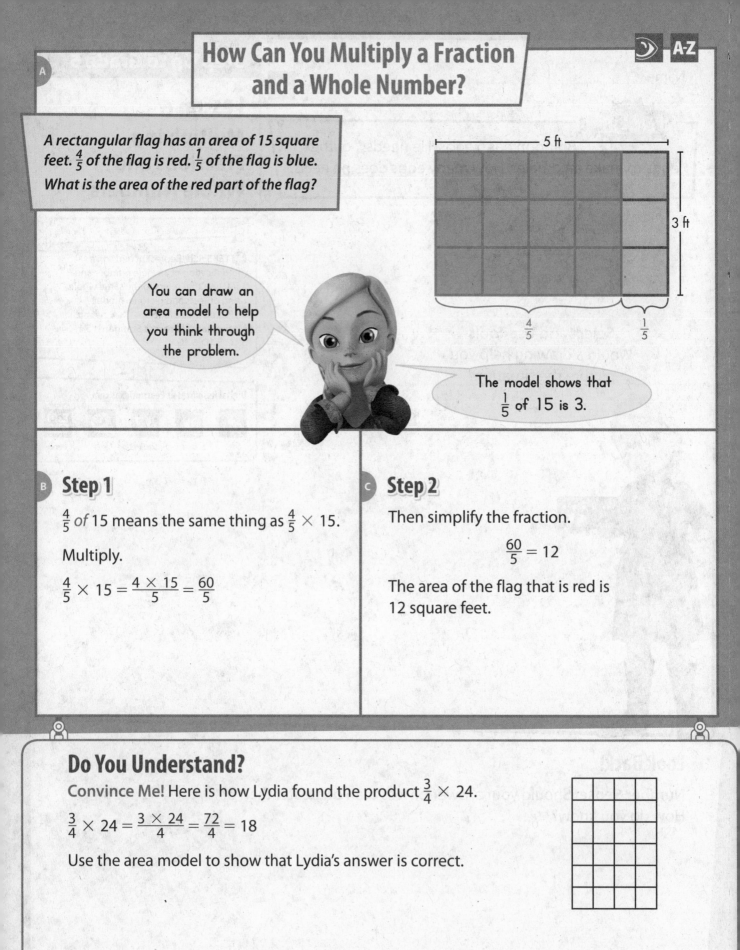

You can draw an area model to help you think through the problem.

The model shows that $\frac{1}{5}$ of 15 is 3.

B Step 1

$\frac{4}{5}$ of 15 means the same thing as $\frac{4}{5} \times 15$.

Multiply.

$$\frac{4}{5} \times 15 = \frac{4 \times 15}{5} = \frac{60}{5}$$

C Step 2

Then simplify the fraction.

$$\frac{60}{5} = 12$$

The area of the flag that is red is 12 square feet.

Do You Understand?

Convince Me! Here is how Lydia found the product $\frac{3}{4} \times 24$.

$$\frac{3}{4} \times 24 = \frac{3 \times 24}{4} = \frac{72}{4} = 18$$

Use the area model to show that Lydia's answer is correct.

Name _____

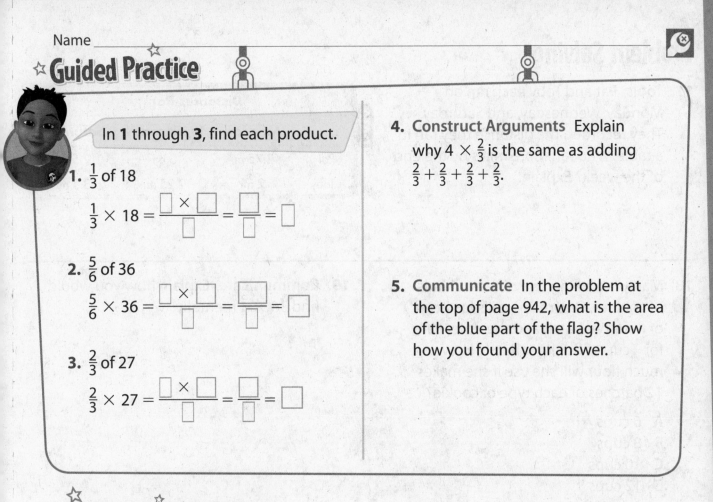

In **1** through **3**, find each product.

1. $\frac{1}{3}$ of 18

$\frac{1}{3} \times 18 = \dfrac{\Box \times \Box}{\Box} = \dfrac{\Box}{\Box} = \Box$

2. $\frac{5}{6}$ of 36

$\frac{5}{6} \times 36 = \dfrac{\Box \times \Box}{\Box} = \dfrac{\Box}{\Box} = \Box$

3. $\frac{2}{3}$ of 27

$\frac{2}{3} \times 27 = \dfrac{\Box \times \Box}{\Box} = \dfrac{\Box}{\Box} = \Box$

4. Construct Arguments Explain why $4 \times \frac{2}{3}$ is the same as adding $\frac{2}{3} + \frac{2}{3} + \frac{2}{3} + \frac{2}{3}$.

5. Communicate In the problem at the top of page 942, what is the area of the blue part of the flag? Show how you found your answer.

Independent Practice ☆

Leveled Practice In **6** through **16**, find each product.

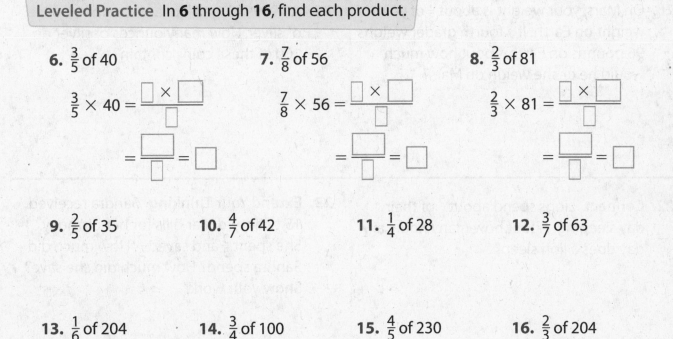

6. $\frac{3}{5}$ of 40

$\frac{3}{5} \times 40 = \dfrac{\Box \times \Box}{\Box}$

$= \dfrac{\Box}{\Box} = \Box$

7. $\frac{7}{8}$ of 56

$\frac{7}{8} \times 56 = \dfrac{\Box \times \Box}{\Box}$

$= \dfrac{\Box}{\Box} = \Box$

8. $\frac{2}{3}$ of 81

$\frac{2}{3} \times 81 = \dfrac{\Box \times \Box}{\Box}$

$= \dfrac{\Box}{\Box} = \Box$

9. $\frac{2}{5}$ of 35

10. $\frac{4}{7}$ of 42

11. $\frac{1}{4}$ of 28

12. $\frac{3}{7}$ of 63

13. $\frac{1}{6}$ of 204

14. $\frac{3}{4}$ of 100

15. $\frac{4}{5}$ of 230

16. $\frac{2}{3}$ of 204

Problem Solving

17. Tools Pat and Toby each ran on Monday, Wednesday, and Saturday. They recorded the distance they ran in a table. Who ran more miles by the end of the week? Explain.

DATA	Distances Ran		
	Monday	**Wednesday**	**Saturday**
Pat	2.75 mi	3 mi	2.5 mi
Toby	2 mi	2.25 mi	3.5 mi

---

18. ★ Marcy is making two different kinds of cookies. One recipe calls for $\frac{1}{3}$ cup of flour per batch and the other calls for $\frac{1}{2}$ cup of flour per batch. How much flour will she use if she makes 12 batches of each type of cookie?

A 6 cups

B 8 cups

C 10 cups

D 12 cups

19. Communicate Explain how you would find $36 \times \frac{3}{4}$ mentally.

---

20. On Mars, your weight is about $\frac{1}{3}$ of your weight on Earth. If a fourth grader weighs 96 pounds on Earth, about how much would he or she weigh on Mars?

21. A 1965 U.S. half-dollar contains $\frac{2}{5}$ ounce of silver. How many ounces of silver do 100 of these coins contain?

---

22. Connect Lions spend about $\frac{5}{6}$ of their day sleeping. About how many hours a day does a lion sleep?

23. Extend Your Thinking Sandra received 15 twenty-dollar bills for her birthday. She spent $\frac{3}{5}$ and saved $\frac{2}{5}$. How much did Sandra spend? How much did she save? Show your work.

© Pearson Education, Inc. 4

Name _____

☆ ☆
Solve & Share

One ball of dough can be stretched into a circle to make a pizza. After the pizza is cooked, it is cut into 8 equal slices. How many slices of pizza can you make with 3 balls of dough? *Solve this problem any way you choose.*

Lesson 7
Dividing Whole Numbers by Unit Fractions

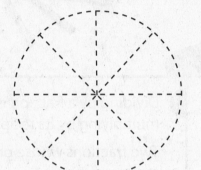

➕ TEKS 5.3J Represent division of a unit fraction by a whole number and the division of a whole number by a unit fraction such as $\frac{1}{3} \div 7$ and $7 \div \frac{1}{3}$ using objects and pictorial models, including area models.
Mathematical Process Standards 5.1A, 5.1C, 5.1D, 5.1E, 5.1F

Digital Resources at PearsonTexas.com

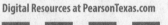

Solve   Learn   Glossary   Tools   Games

You can **create** and use a representation to help you find the answer. *Show your work!*

Look Back!

Connect Ideas Into how many slices of pizza will each ball of dough be divided? What fraction of a whole pizza does 1 slice represent?

A

Joyce is making sushi rolls. She needs $\frac{1}{4}$ cup of rice for each sushi roll. How many sushi rolls can she make if she has 3 cups of rice?

1 cup   1 cup   1 cup

You can draw a picture to find the solution.

Use models.

B

How many $\frac{1}{4}$s are in 3?

There are twelve $\frac{1}{4}$s in three whole cups. So, Joyce can make 12 sushi rolls.

You can also use a number line to find how many $\frac{1}{4}$s are in 3.

0   $\frac{1}{4}$ $\frac{2}{4}$ $\frac{3}{4}$ 1 $\frac{1}{4}$ $\frac{2}{4}$ $\frac{3}{4}$ 2 $\frac{1}{4}$ $\frac{2}{4}$ $\frac{3}{4}$ 3

$3 \div \frac{1}{4} = 12.$

C

Dividing by a fraction is the same as multiplying by its reciprocal.

Two fractions whose product is 1 are reciprocals.

For example, $\frac{1}{4} \times \frac{4}{1} = 1$, so $\frac{1}{4}$ and $\frac{4}{1}$ are reciprocals.

$$3 \div \frac{1}{4} = 12 \qquad 3 \times \frac{4}{1} = 12$$

So, Joyce can make 12 sushi rolls.

Do You Understand?

Convince Me! Use the diagram below to find $4 \div \frac{1}{3}$.

$4 \div \frac{1}{3} =$ _____

© Pearson Education, Inc. 4

Name _____

☆ Guided Practice

In **1** and **2**, use the picture below to find each quotient. Simplify, if possible.

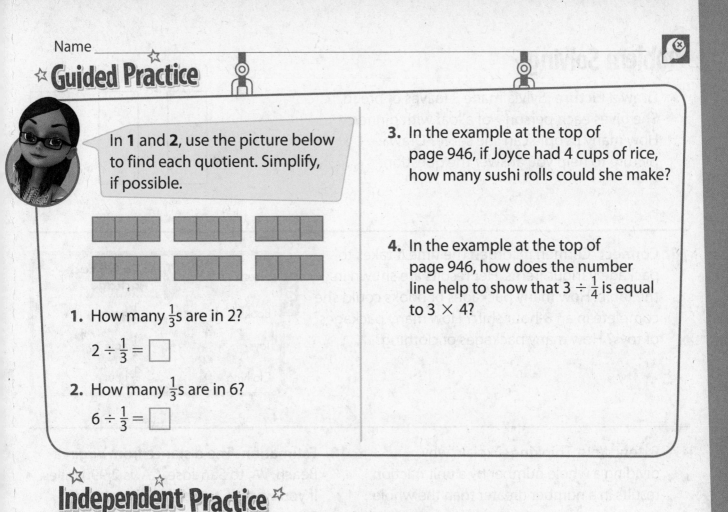

1. How many $\frac{1}{3}$s are in 2?

$2 \div \frac{1}{3} = \boxed{}$

2. How many $\frac{1}{3}$s are in 6?

$6 \div \frac{1}{3} = \boxed{}$

3. In the example at the top of page 946, if Joyce had 4 cups of rice, how many sushi rolls could she make?

4. In the example at the top of page 946, how does the number line help to show that $3 \div \frac{1}{4}$ is equal to 3×4?

Independent Practice ☆

Leveled Practice In **5** and **6**, use the picture to find each quotient.

5. How many $\frac{1}{6}$s are in 2?

$2 \div \frac{1}{6} = \boxed{}$

6. How many $\frac{1}{6}$s are in 3?

$3 \div \frac{1}{6} = \boxed{}$

In **7** through **14**, draw a picture or use multiplication to find each quotient.

7. $2 \div \frac{1}{4}$

8. $15 \div \frac{1}{5}$

9. $5 \div \frac{1}{6}$

10. $21 \div \frac{1}{7}$

11. $16 \div \frac{1}{5}$

12. $25 \div \frac{1}{2}$

13. $30 \div \frac{1}{8}$

14. $32 \div \frac{1}{5}$

Problem Solving

15. **Draw a Picture** Sylvia made 3 loaves of bread. She gives each person $\frac{1}{6}$ of a loaf with dinner. How many people can she serve? Draw a picture to help you answer the question.

16. **Connect** Carmen recorded the time it takes to package various items. Her results are shown in the table. How many packages of books could she complete in an 8-hour shift? How many packages of toys? How many packages of clothing?

DATA	Item	Time To Fill Each Package
	Books	$\frac{1}{4}$ hour
	Toys	$\frac{1}{2}$ hour
	Clothing	$\frac{1}{3}$ hour

17. **Extend Your Thinking** Explain why dividing a whole number by a unit fraction results in a number greater than the whole number. Include an example.

18. **Estimation** The distance from Virginia Beach, VA, to San Jose, CA, is 2,990 miles. If you want to travel this distance in 3 months, about how many miles need to be traveled each month?

19. Alonso is making light-switch plates cut from pieces of wood. Each piece of wood is 2 yards long. How many light-switch plates can he make if he has 2 pieces of wood?

A 12 light-switch plates
B 18 light-switch plates
C 36 light-switch plates
D 42 light-switch plates

DATA	Wood Projects	
	Item	Length Needed for Each
	Cabinet Shelf	$\frac{3}{4}$ foot
	Light Switch Plate	$\frac{1}{3}$ foot
	Shingle	$\frac{2}{3}$ foot

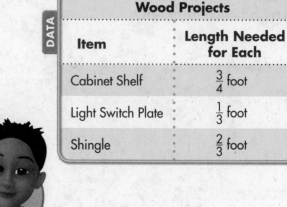

Remember that there are 3 feet in 1 yard.

© Pearson Education, Inc. 4

Name _____

Solve & Share

Every year for the past five years, the Hawks have won 2 more games than the Metros. Complete the table to show how many games the Hawks won based on the number of games the Metros won. *Solve this problem any way you choose.*

 TEKS 5.4 The student applies mathematical process standards to develop concepts of expressions and equations. Mathematical Process Standards 5.1D, 5.1E, 5.1F

Communicate You can write an algebraic expression to help you solve the given problem. *Show your work!*

Digital Resources at PearsonTexas.com

Solve   Learn   Glossary   Tools   Games

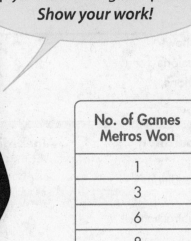

No. of Games Metros Won	No. of Games Hawks Won
1	
3	
6	
8	
10	

Look Back!

Analyze Relationships In each of the past five years, the Wildcats won 3 more games than the Hawks. How many games did the Wildcats win each year?

A

Donnie bought DVDs for $10 each. How can you represent the total cost of the DVDs?

Variables help you translate word phrases into algebraic expressions.

A variable is a quantity that can change. It is often represented with a letter.

Number of DVDs	Total Cost
1	$10 × 1
2	$10 × 2
3	$10 × 3

DATA

An algebraic expression is a mathematical phrase that has at least one variable and one operation. The total cost of *n* DVDs is represented by:

$$\$10 \times n$$

B

The table shows algebraic expressions for given situations.

Word Phrase	Operation	Algebraic Expression
three dollars more than cost *c*	addition	$c + 3$
twelve pencils decreased by a number *n*	subtraction	$12 - n$
five times a distance *d*	multiplication	$5 \times d$ or $5d$
a apples divided by four	division	$a \div 4$ or $\frac{a}{4}$
five less than three times an amount *x*	multiplication and subtraction	$3x - 5$

Do You Understand?

Convince Me! There were 5 chaperones assigned to go with students on a field trip. What algebraic expression represents the total number of students and chaperones who went on the field trip?

Use the variable *n* to represent the number of students on the field trip.

Field Trip Participants	
Number of Students (*n*)	Number of Chaperones
10	5
15	5
20	5
25	5

DATA

© Pearson Education, Inc. 4

☆ Guided Practice

In **1** through **4**, write an algebraic expression for each situation.

1. The sum of a number, *a*, and 36

2. The difference of a number, *z*, and 32

3. 19 times a number, *b*

4. 7 more than 6 times a number, *k*

5. In the example at the top of page 950, what does the variable *n* represent?

6. **Reason** Identify the variable and the operation in the algebraic expression $\frac{g}{4}$.

7. **Represent** Write an algebraic expression for this situation: 3 points less than 2 times the winning score, *s*.

Independent Practice ☆

In **8** through **13**, write algebraic expressions.

8. A number, *r*, decreased by 24

9. 25 divided by *q*

10. 18 more than a number, *t*, times 4

11. 3 less than 2 times a number, *n*

12. 10 more than the product of 3 and *p*

13. 21 less than the quotient of 145 and *b*

Problem Solving

14. Reason The perimeter of a figure can be expressed as 4 times the length of a side, *s*, or 4*s*. Draw an example of this geometric shape.

15. James sold *a* cartons of apples and *p* cartons of peaches. Write an algebraic expression to represent how many cartons of apples and peaches James sold in all.

16. Represent Juan is planning to buy a new computer monitor. He has already saved $250. Let *n* equal the amount Juan still needs to save. Write an algebraic expression that represents the cost of the monitor.

17. Extend Your Thinking How are the algebraic expressions $7 - g$ and $g - 7$ different?

18. Stephanie wants to put fencing around the perimeter of her vegetable garden. How many feet of fencing will she need?

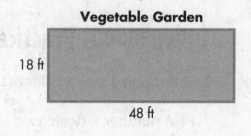

Vegetable Garden

18 ft

48 ft

19. Represent Nao has 6 fewer CDs than Emily. If *c* represents the number of CDs Emily has, write an algebraic expression to show the number of CDs Nao has.

20. A person has to be at least 48 inches tall to ride a roller coaster. Jill, who is 12 years old, is *t* inches taller than 48 inches. Which algebraic expression shows Jill's height?

   A $(12 + t) - 48$

   B $48t$

   C $(48 - 12) + t$

   D $48 + t$

© Pearson Education, Inc. 4

Name ______________________________

Solve & Share The figure shown is a design for a patio. What is the area of the patio? ***Solve this problem any way you choose.***

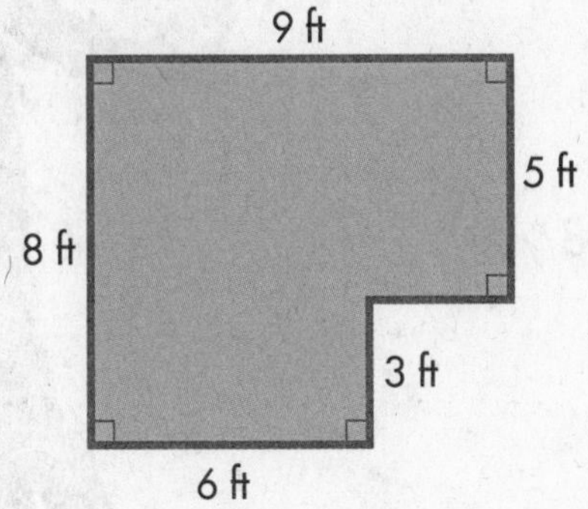

9 ft
5 ft
8 ft
3 ft
6 ft

Step Up to Grade 5

Lesson 9
Area of Composite Shapes

TEKS 5.4H Represent and solve problems related to perimeter and/or area and related to volume.
Mathematical Process Standards 5.1C, 5.1D, 5.1F

Digital Resources at PearsonTexas.com

Solve | Learn | Glossary | Tools | Games

Connect Ideas You can find the area of composite shapes by breaking them into smaller shapes. ***Show your work!***

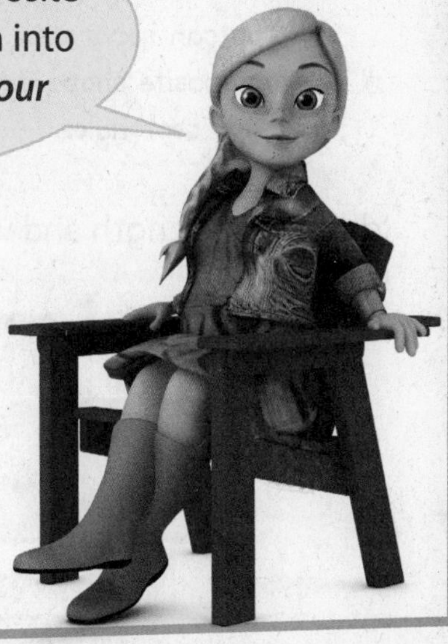

Look Back!

Communicate How does breaking up a composite figure into parts help to find the area of the whole figure?

How Can You Use Area Formulas to Solve Problems?

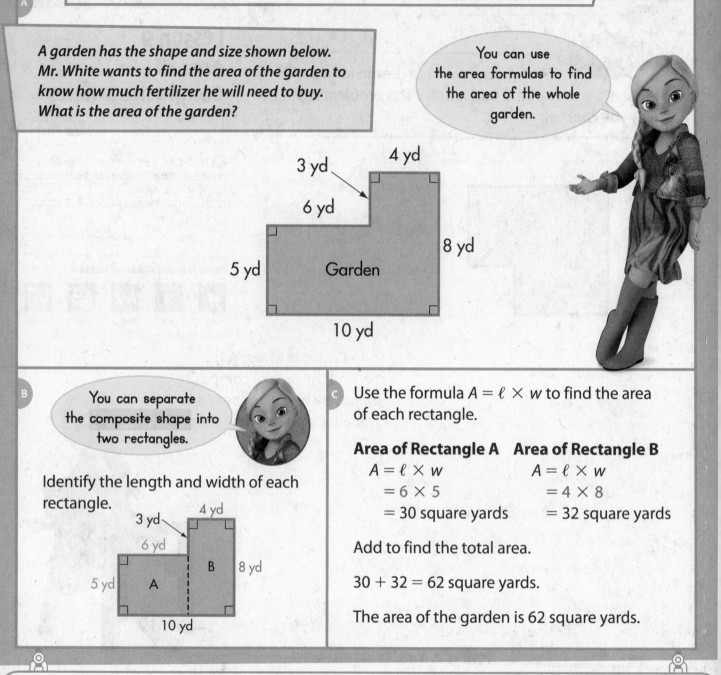

A garden has the shape and size shown below. Mr. White wants to find the area of the garden to know how much fertilizer he will need to buy. What is the area of the garden?

You can use the area formulas to find the area of the whole garden.

You can separate the composite shape into two rectangles.

Identify the length and width of each rectangle.

Use the formula $A = \ell \times w$ to find the area of each rectangle.

Area of Rectangle A
$A = \ell \times w$
$= 6 \times 5$
$= 30$ square yards

Area of Rectangle B
$A = \ell \times w$
$= 4 \times 8$
$= 32$ square yards

Add to find the total area.

$30 + 32 = 62$ square yards.

The area of the garden is 62 square yards.

Do You Understand?

Convince Me! Show a different way to break apart the garden. Is the total area the same? Explain.

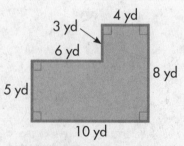

954

Name _____

In **1** and **2**, use the area formula of a rectangle to find the area of each figure.

1.

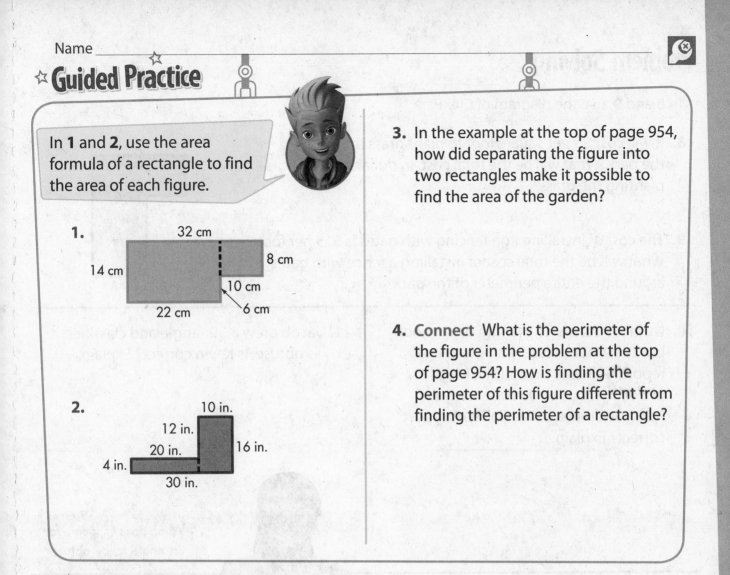

32 cm
8 cm
14 cm
10 cm
22 cm
6 cm

2.

10 in.
12 in.
20 in.
16 in.
4 in.
30 in.

3. In the example at the top of page 954, how did separating the figure into two rectangles make it possible to find the area of the garden?

4. Connect What is the perimeter of the figure in the problem at the top of page 954? How is finding the perimeter of this figure different from finding the perimeter of a rectangle?

☆ **Independent Practice** ☆

In **5** through **7**, find the area of each figure.

5.

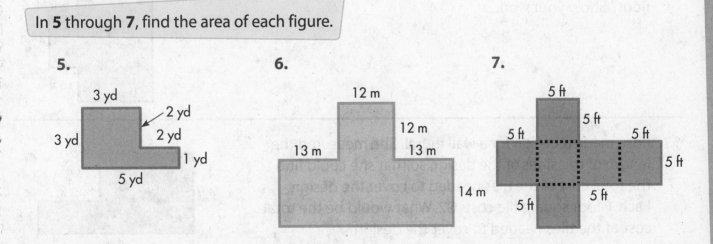

3 yd
2 yd
3 yd
2 yd
1 yd
5 yd

6.

12 m
12 m
13 m
13 m
14 m

7.

5 ft
5 ft
5 ft
5 ft
5 ft
5 ft
5 ft

Step Up | Lesson 9

955

Problem Solving

In **8** and **9**, use the diagram of City Park.

8. It will cost $3 per square foot to plant grass in the park. What will be the total cost, in dollars, of planting the grass?

9. The cost of installing iron fencing with gates is $15 per foot. What will be the total cost of installing a fence with gates around the entire perimeter of the park?

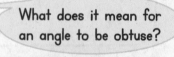

10. **Number Sense** The length of a school bus must not exceed 12 meters. In a report, Colleen said that the length of a school bus could be as long as 1,200 decimeters. Was Colleen's report correct? Explain.

11. Jacob drew a 30° angle and classified it as obtuse. Is Kevin correct? Explain.

What does it mean for an angle to be obtuse?

12. **Extend Your Thinking** How can you separate the building floor plan into 3 parts to find the total area of the building floor? Show your work.

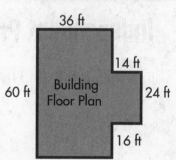

13. Rosa made a design for a wall mural. She measured the length of the sides of the design so that she could find the total cost of the tiles needed to cover the design. Each 1-foot square tile costs $2. What would be the total cost of the tiles needed to cover the design?

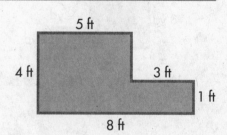

A $21
B $23
C $42
D $46

© Pearson Education, Inc. 4

Name _____

☆ *Solve & Share* ☆

Gina is building a rectangular prism out of sugar cubes for her art class project. She started by drawing a diagram of the rectangular prism that is 4 cubes high and 4 cubes wide. How many cubes does she use to make the prism? *Solve this problem any way you choose.*

Create and Use Representations You can draw a picture to find the number of cubes in a rectangular prism. *Show your work!*

🏷 TEKS 5.6A Recognize a cube with side length of one unit as a unit cube having one cubic unit of volume and the volume of a three-dimensional figure as the number of unit cubes (*n* cubic units) needed to fill it with no gaps or overlaps if possible. Also, 5.6B.
Mathematical Process Standards 5.1A, 5.1C, 5.1E, 5.1F

Digital Resources at PearsonTexas.com

| Solve | Learn | Glossary | Tools | Games |

Side View   Front View

Top View

Look Back!

Connect Ideas Gina decided to change her art project and build a rectangular prism that is 4 cubes long, 3 cubes wide, and 2 cubes high. Use the picture to determine the number of cubes she used.

A

Volume is the number of cubic units needed to fill a solid figure. A cubic unit is the volume of a cube measuring 1 unit on each edge. What is the volume of this rectangular prism?

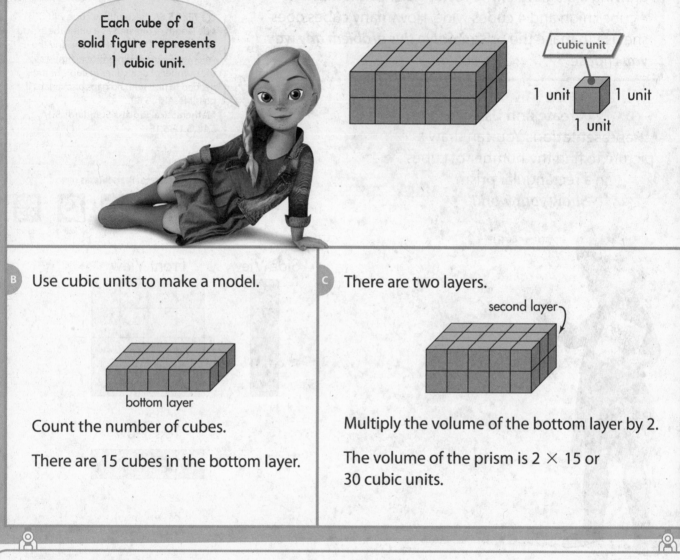

Each cube of a solid figure represents 1 cubic unit.

cubic unit

1 unit   1 unit

1 unit

B

Use cubic units to make a model.

bottom layer

Count the number of cubes.

There are 15 cubes in the bottom layer.

C

There are two layers.

second layer

Multiply the volume of the bottom layer by 2.

The volume of the prism is 2 × 15 or 30 cubic units.

Do You Understand?

Convince Me! What is the volume of the solid shown below? How did you decide?

© Pearson Education, Inc. 4

⭐ Guided Practice

In **1** and **2**, use the model or unit cubes to find the volume of each solid.

1.
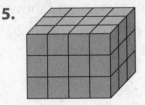

2.
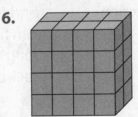

3. **Tools** Make a model of a rectangular prism with a bottom layer that is 4 cubes long by 3 cubes wide. Make a top layer that is the same as the bottom layer. Then draw a picture of your model. What is the volume?

4. If you add another layer to the top of the prism in Exercise 1, what would the new volume be in cubic units?

Independent Practice ⭐

In **5** through **10**, find the volume of each solid. Use unit cubes to help.

5.
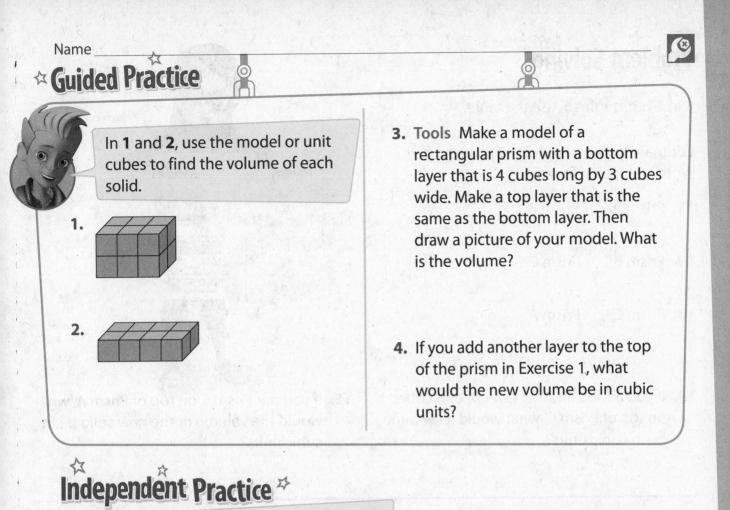

6.

7.

8.
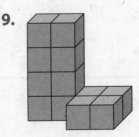

9.

10.

Problem Solving

In **11** through **15**, use the table.

Compare the volumes of the prisms.
Write >, <, or = for each ◯.

11. Prism A ◯ Prism B

12. Prism B ◯ Prism C

13. Prism C ◯ Prism A

Prism	Model
A	
B	
C	

14. If you added another layer of unit cubes on top of Prism C, what would its volume be in cubic units?

15. If you put Prism C on top of Prism A, what would the volume of the new solid be in cubic units?

16. Connect In an election, 15,392 people voted. Candidate B received 8,205 votes. Candidate A received the rest of the votes. Which candidate won the election? By how many votes?

17. Extend Your Thinking A toy company produces snow globes that come in a box that is 5 inches long, 5 inches wide, and 5 inches tall. How many snow globes can fit in a shipping case that is 20 inches long, 20 inches wide, and 20 inches tall? Explain.

18. The solid shown is made up of cubic units.
⭐ What is the volume of the solid?

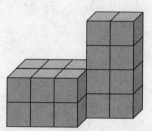

   A 8 cubic units
   B 11 cubic units
   C 20 cubic units
   D 33 cubic units

© Pearson Education, Inc. 4

Glossary

A

acute angle An angle that is less than a right angle.

acute triangle A triangle with three acute angles.

addends The numbers that are added together to find a sum.
Example: $2 + 7 = 9$
　　　　　Addends

algebraic expression An expression with variables. *Example:* $x - 3$

angle A figure formed by two rays that have the same endpoint.

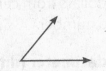

angle measure The number of degrees in an angle.

area The number of square units needed to cover a region.

array A way of displaying objects in rows and columns.

Associative Property of Addition Addends can be regrouped and the sum remains the same.

Associative Property of Multiplication Factors can be regrouped and the product remains the same.

B

balance The amount of money in a person's bank account.

bar graph A graph using bars to show data.

benchmark fractions Fractions that are commonly used for estimation.
Examples: $\frac{1}{4}, \frac{1}{3}, \frac{1}{2}, \frac{2}{3},$ and $\frac{3}{4}$.

billions A period of three places to the left of the millions period.

breaking apart Mental math method used to rewrite a number as the sum of numbers to form an easier problem.

C

capacity The amount a container can hold, measured in liquid units.

center A point within a circle that is the same distance from all points on a circle.

centimeter (cm) A metric unit of length. 100 centimeters = 1 meter

century A unit of time equal to 100 years.

circle A closed plane figure in which all the points are the same distance from a point called the center.

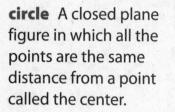

common factor A factor that two or more numbers have in common.

Commutative Property of Addition Numbers can be added in any order and the sum remains the same.

Commutative Property of Multiplication Factors can be multiplied in any order and the product remains the same.

compare Decide if one number is greater than, less than, or equal to another number.

compatible numbers Numbers that are easy to compute mentally.

compensation Choosing numbers close to the numbers in a problem to make the computation easier, and then adjusting the answer for the numbers chosen.

composite number A whole number greater than 1 that has more than two factors.

coordinate grid A grid used to show ordered pairs.

counting on Counting up from the lesser number to find the difference of two numbers.

credit **a.** Money put into a person's account. **b.** Buying something now, but paying for it later.

cup (c) A customary unit of capacity. 1 cup = 8 fluid ounces

customary units of measure Units of measure that are used in the United States.

data Pieces of collected information.

day A unit of time equal to 24 hours.

decade A unit of time equal to 10 years.

decimal A number with one or more places to the right of the decimal point.

decimal point A dot used to separate dollars from cents or ones from tenths in a number.

decimeter (dm) A metric unit of length equal to 10 centimeters.

decomposing To break into parts.

degree (°) A unit of measure for angles. $1° = \frac{1}{360}$ of a circle
Also a unit of measure for temperature.

denominator The number below the fraction bar in a fraction. The total number of equal parts in one whole.

deposit Money put into a person's account.

© Pearson Education, Inc. 4

difference The answer when subtracting two numbers.

digits The symbols used to write a number: 0, 1, 2, 3, 4, 5, 6, 7, 8, and 9.

Distributive Property Multiplying a sum (or difference) by a number is the same as multiplying each number in the sum (or difference) by that number and adding (or subtracting) the products. *Example:* $(3 \times 21) = (3 \times 20) + (3 \times 1)$

divide An operation to find the number in each group or the number of equal groups.

dividend The number to be divided.

divisibility rules The rules that state when a number is divisible by another number.

divisible Can be divided by another number without leaving a remainder. *Example:* 10 is divisible by 2

divisor The number by which another number is divided.
Example: $32 \div 4 = 8$
↑
Divisor

dot plot A display of responses along a number line with dots used to indicate the number of times a response occurred.

E

elapsed time The amount of time between the beginning of an event and the end of the event.

equation A number sentence that uses the equal sign (=) to show that two expressions have the same value. *Example:* $9 + 3 = 12$

equilateral triangle A triangle in which all sides are the same length.

equivalent Numbers that name the same amount.

equivalent fractions Fractions that name the same region, part of a set, or part of a segment.

estimate To give an approximate value rather than an exact answer.

expanded form A number written as the sum of the values of its digits. *Example:* $2,476 = 2,000 + 400 + 70 + 6$

expenses The amount of money spent.

F

fact family A group of related facts using the same set of numbers.

factors The numbers multiplied together to find a product. *Example:* $3 \times 6 = 18$
↑ ↑
Factors

financial institutions Businesses that include banks, savings and loans, and credit unions.

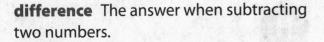

fixed expenses Expenses that occur on a regular basis. Monthly bills are fixed expenses.

fluid ounce (fl oz) A customary unit of capacity.
1 fluid ounce = 2 tablespoons

foot (ft) A customary unit of length.
1 foot = 12 inches

formula An equation that uses symbols to relate two or more quantities.
Example: $A = \ell \times w$

fraction A symbol, such as $\frac{2}{3}, \frac{5}{1},$ or $\frac{8}{5}$, used to name a part of a whole, a part of a set, or a location on a number line.

frequency The number of times that a response occurs in a set of data.

frequency table A way to display data that shows how many times a response occurs in a set of data.

gallon (gal) A customary unit of capacity. 1 gallon = 4 quarts

gram (g) A metric unit of mass.
1,000 grams = 1 kilogram

greater than symbol (>) A symbol that points away from a greater number or expression.
Example: 450 > 449

hexagon A polygon with 6 sides.

hour A unit of time equal to 60 minutes.

hundredth One part of 100 equal parts of a whole.

Identity Property of Addition The sum of any number and zero is that number.

Identity Property of Multiplication The product of any number and one is that number.

improper fraction A fraction in which the numerator is greater than or equal to the denominator.

inch (in.) A customary unit of length.
12 inches = 1 foot

income Money earned from doing work.

inequality A number sentence that uses the greater than sign (>) or the less than sign (<) to show that two expressions do not have the same value.
Example: 5 > 3

© Pearson Education, Inc. 4

input-output table A table that uses a rule to relate one set of numbers to another set of numbers.

interest Money you pay when you borrow money, or money you receive for having a savings account.

intersecting lines Lines that cross at one point.

interval A number which is the difference between two consecutive numbers on the scale of a graph.

inverse operations Operations that undo each other.
Examples: Adding 6 and subtracting 6; Multiplying by 4 and dividing by 4.

isosceles triangle A triangle that has at least two equal sides.

key Part of a graph that tells what each symbol stands for.

kilogram (kg) A metric unit of mass.
1 kilogram = 1,000 grams

kilometer (km) A metric unit of length.
1 kilometer = 1,000 meters

leaf In a stem-and-leaf plot, a number representing the least place value for the set of data.

leap year A calendar occurrence that happens every four years when an extra day is added to February. Leap years have 366 days.

less than symbol (<) A symbol that points towards a lesser number or expression.
Example: 305 < 320

line A straight path of points that goes on and on in two directions.

line of symmetry A line on which a figure can be folded so that both halves are the same.

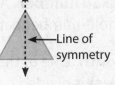

Line of symmetry

line segment A part of a line that has two endpoints.

liter (L) A metric unit of capacity.
1 liter = 1,000 milliliters

mass The amount of matter that something contains.

meter (m) A metric unit of length.
1 meter = 100 centimeters

metric units of measure Units of measure commonly used by scientists.

mile (mi) A customary unit of length. 1 mile = 5,280 feet

millennium (plural: millennia) A unit for measuring time equal to 1,000 years.

milliliter (mL) A metric unit of capacity. 1,000 milliliters = 1 liter

millimeter (mm) A metric unit of length. 1,000 millimeters = 1 meter

millions In a number, a period of three places to the left of the thousands period.

minute A unit of time equal to 60 seconds.

mixed number A number that has a whole-number part and a fraction part.

month One of the 12 parts into which a year is divided.

multiple The product of a given factor and any whole number.

numerical expression An expression that contains numbers and at least one operation.
Example: 35 + 12

numerator The number above the fraction bar in a fraction.

obtuse angle An angle whose measure is between 90° and 180°.

obtuse triangle A triangle in which there is one obtuse angle.

octagon A polygon with 8 sides.

ounce (oz) A customary unit of weight. 16 ounces = 1 pound

outlier A value that is much greater or much less than the other values in a data set.

overestimate An estimate that is greater than the exact answer.

parallel lines
In a plane, lines that never intersect.

parallelogram
A quadrilateral in which opposite sides are parallel.

partial products Products found by breaking one factor in a multiplication problem into ones, tens, hundreds, and so on and then multiplying each of these by the other factor.

© Pearson Education, Inc. 4

partial quotients A way to divide that finds quotients in parts until only a remainder, if any, is left.

pentagon A plane figure with 5 sides.

perfect square A number that is the product of a counting number multiplied by itself.

perimeter The distance around a figure.

period In a number, a group of three digits, separated by commas, starting from the right.

perpendicular lines Two intersecting lines that form right angles.

pint (pt) A customary unit of capacity. 1 pint = 2 cups

place value The position of a digit in a number that is used to determine the value of the digit.
Example: In 3,946, the 9 is in the hundreds place. So, the 9 has a value of 900.

plane An endless flat surface.

plane figure A figure that has only two dimensions.

point An exact location in space.

polygon A closed plane figure made up of line segments.

pound (lb) A customary unit of weight. 1 pound = 16 ounces

prime number A whole number greater than 1 that has exactly two factors, 1 and itself.

product The answer to a multiplication problem.

profit The difference between expenses and receipts.

proper fraction A fraction that is less than 1; its numerator is less than its denominator.

protractor A tool used to measure and draw angles.

quadrilateral A polygon with 4 sides.

quart (qt) A customary unit of capacity. 1 quart = 2 pints

quotient The answer to a division problem.

ray A part of a line that has one endpoint and continues endlessly in one direction.

receipts The total money taken in.

rectangle A quadrilateral with 4 right angles.

regroup To name a whole number in a different way.
Example: 32 = 2 tens 12 ones

remainder The amount that is left after dividing a number into equal parts.

repeated addition A way to write a multiplication expression as an addition expression.
Example: $3 \times 5 = 5 + 5 + 5$

rhombus A quadrilateral in which opposite sides are parallel and all sides are the same length.

right angle An angle that forms a square corner.

right triangle A triangle in which there is one right angle.

rounding Replacing a number with a number that tells about how many or how much.

rule A mathematical phrase that tells how numbers in a table are related.

saving Putting aside money from current income to buy something in the future.

scale Numbers that show the units used on a graph.

scalene triangle A triangle in which no sides are the same length.

second A unit of time.
60 seconds = 1 minute

sequence A set of numbers that follows a pattern.

sharing Giving money to charity or other people.

side Each of the line segments of a polygon.

simplest form A fraction in which the numerator and denominator have no common factors other than 1.

solid figure A figure with three dimensions that has length, width, and height.

solution The value of the variable that makes an equation true.

solve an equation Find a solution to an equation.

spending Trading money for goods or services.

square A quadrilateral with 4 right angles and all sides the same length.

square unit A square with sides one unit long used to measure area.

standard form A way to write a number showing only its digits. Commas separate groups of three digits starting from the right.
Example: 2,613,095

© Pearson Education, Inc. 4

stem In a stem-and-leaf plot, a number representing the greatest place value for a set of data.

stem-and-leaf plot A display that shows data in order of place value.

straight angle An angle that forms a straight line.

strip diagram A tool used to help understand and solve word problems. It is also known as a bar diagram or a tape diagram.

sum The result of adding numbers together.

survey Collecting information by asking a number of people the same question and recording their answers.

symmetric A figure is symmetric if it can be folded into two halves that fit on top of each other.

T

tablespoon (tbsp) A customary unit of capacity. 1 tablespoon = 3 teaspoons

teaspoon (tsp) A customary unit of capacity. 3 teaspoons = 1 tablespoon

tenth One of ten equal parts of a whole.

terms Numbers in a sequence or variables, such as *x* and *y*, in an algebraic expression.

ton (T) A customary unit of weight. 1 ton = 2,000 pounds

trapezoid A quadrilateral with only one pair of parallel sides.

triangle A polygon with 3 sides.

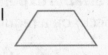

U

underestimate An estimate that is less than the exact answer.

unknown A symbol or letter, such as *x*, that represents a number in an expression or equation.

unit angle An angle that cuts off $\frac{1}{360}$ of a circle and measures 1°.

unit fraction A fraction with a numerator of 1.
Example: $\frac{1}{2}$

variable A symbol or letter that stands for a number.

variable expenses Expenses that do not occur on a regular basis.

vertex (plural: vertices) The point where two rays meet to form an angle. Also, the points where the sides of a polygon meet.

volume The number of cubic units needed to fill a solid figure.

week A unit of time equal to 7 days.

weight A measure of how heavy an object is.

whole numbers The numbers 0, 1, 2, 3, 4, and so on.

withdrawal Money taken out of a person's account.

word form A way to write a number in words.
Example: Four thousand, six hundred, thirty-two.

yard (yd) A customary unit of length. 1 yard = 3 feet

year A unit of time equal to 365 days or 52 weeks or 12 months.

Zero Property of Multiplication The product of any number and zero is zero.

© Pearson Education, Inc. 4

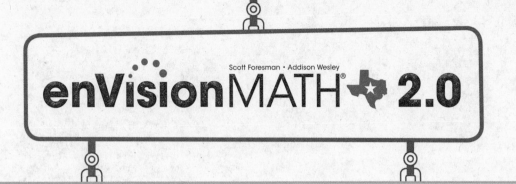

Photographs

Every effort has been made to secure permission and provide appropriate credit for photographic material. The publisher deeply regrets any omission and pledges to correct errors called to its attention in subsequent editions.

Unless otherwise acknowledged, all photographs are the property of Pearson Education, Inc.

Photo locators denoted as follows: Top (T), Center (C), Bottom (B), Left (L), Right (R), Background (Bkgd)

003 Kalafoto/Fotolia;**012T** Getty Images/Photo Disc;**043T** Mastr/Fotolia;**054** Hemera Technologies/AbleStock.com/Getty Images/Thinkstock;**068L** Hemera Technologies;**068R** Hemera Technologies;**085** Christopher Dodge/Fotolia;**102B** Alexey Usachev/Fotolia;**102T** Andy Thorington/Fotolia;**110** Digital Vision/Thinkstock;**144** Mark Sykes/Alamy;**159** Volodymyr Goinyk/Shutterstock;**221** Kichatof/Fotolia;**244CL** Corbis;**244CR** Momatiuk-Eastcott/Ramble/Corbis;**244L** Tom Brakefield/keepsake RF/Corbis;**244R** Cardinal/Corbis;**248** Bork/Shutterstock;**271** Eduard Kyslynskyy/Shutterstock;**311** Leungchopan/Shutterstock;**324** 2011/PhotostoGo;**336** Rikke/Fotolia;**338** Serp/Fotolia;**341** Barbara Helgason/Fotolia;**363** Itestro/Fotolia;**403** Margo Harrison/Shutterstock;**440B** Getty Images;**440C** Getty Images;**440T** Getty Images

461 James M Phelps, Jr/Shutterstock;**507** Barbara Helgason/Fotolia;**553** Iofoto/Shutterstock;**560** Oleksii Sagitov/Shutterstock;**562** Africa Studio/Fotolia;**615** Katrina Brown/Fotolia;**621BL** Stockdisc/Punchstock;**624BC** Jupiter Images;**628** Shutterstock;**631L** Cardinal/Corbis;**632B** Photolibrary/PhotostoGo;**634** Jenoe/Fotolia;**636BR** Getty Images;**636TC** Getty Images;**636TR** Jupiter Images;**637BL** Hemera Technologies;**637TL** PhotostoGo;**637TR** Getty Images;**638B** Royal Geographical/Getty Images;**638CT** Jupiter Images;**644B** Cardinal/Corbis;**644CL** Getty Images;**644CR** Getty Images;**644L** L. Clarke/Corbis;**644R** Jupiter Images;**654BL** Aperture51/Shutterstock;**654BR** Alekss/Fotolia;**654T** Hemera Technologies; **661TR** Photodisc/Getty Images;**667BL** Photodisc/Getty Images;**667BR** AllrightImages/Face to face Bildagentur GMBH/Alamy;**672L** Photodisc/Getty Images;**680** Jcella/Fotolia;**695** DenisNata/Fotolia;**699** Kalafoto/Fotolia;**751** Ilyas Kalimullin/Shutterstock;**752BL** Photolibrary/PhotostoGo;**752TL** Jupiter Images;**770** Cartesia/Photodisc/Getty Images;**800** Goodshoot/Thinkstock;**808** Jupiterimages/Photos.com/Getty Images/Thinkstock;**812** Gary Blakeley/Fotolia;**831** Sam D'Cruz/Fotolia;**877** Joop Hoek/Shutterstock